THE DIGITAL CHALLENGE: INFORMATION TECHNOLOGY IN THE DEVELOPMENT CONTEXT

The Digital Challenge: Information Technology in the Development Context

Edited by

S. KRISHNA
SHIRIN MADON

ASHGATE

Published by
Ashgate Publishing Limited
Gower House
Croft Road
Aldershot
Hants GU11 3HR
England

Ashgate Publishing Company
Suite 420
101 Cherry Street
Burlington, VT 05401-4405
USA

Ashgate website: http://www.ashgate.com

British Library Cataloguing in Publication Data
The digital challenge : information technology in the
development context. - (Voices in development management)
1. Information technology - Economic aspects - Developing
countries - Congresses 2. Digital divide - Developing
countries - Congresses 3. Developing countries - Economic
conditions - Congresses
I. Krishna, S. II. Madon, Shirin III. IFIP WG 9.4 (Conference
: 2002 : Indian Institute of Management)
338'.064'091724

Library of Congress Cataloging-in-Publication Data
The digital challenge : information technology in the development context / edited by S. Krishna and S. Madon.
p. cm.
Includes bibliographical references.
ISBN 0-7546-3445-0
1. Information technology--Social aspects--Developing countries. 2. Communication--Social aspects--Developing countries. 3. Information society--Developing countries. I. Krishna, S. II. Madon, Shirin.

T14.5.D56 2003
303.48'33'091724--dc21

2003045228

ISBN 0 7546 3445 0

Printed and bound in Great Britain by Athenaeum Press Ltd., Gateshead

Contents

PART II: E-GOVERNANCE AND THE DIGITAL DIVIDE

PART III: ICTs AND NEW ORGANIZATIONAL FORMS

List of Figures

List of Tables

List of Contributors

Chrisanthi Avgerou	London School of Economics, London
Abiodun O. Bada	Virginia State University School of Business, Department of Information Systems and Decision Sciences, Petersburg, Virginia
V. Balaji	International Crop Research Institute for the Semi Arid Tropics (ICRISAT), Patancheru, Andhra Pradesh, India
Grant Boyle	United Nations University, Institute of Advanced Studies, Japan
Jørn Braa	Department of Informatics, University of Oslo
Erran Carmel	Kogod School of Business, American University, Washington, DC, USA
Simone Cecchini	Poverty Reduction Group, The World Bank, Washington DC, USA
N. Dayasindhu	Indian Institute of Management, Bangalore
Nikhilesh Dholakia	E-Commerce and Information Systems Department, University of Rhode Island
Kyle Eischen	Center for Global, International and Regional Studies, Department of Sociology, University of California, Santa Cruz
Neki Frasheri	Institute of Informatics and Applied Mathematics, Academy of Sciences of Albania
Pradeep G.	Wipro Technologies, Thiruvananthapuram, Kerala, India
Robert D. Galliers	Department of Information Systems, London School of Economics, London
R.W. Harris	Independent Consultant, Hong Kong
Saheer Al Jaghoub	Manchester School of Accounting and Finance, University of Manchester, Manchester, England
Arild Jansen	Western Norway Research Institute and University of Oslo, Norway
Justine Johnstone	London School of Economics, London
Shivraj Kanungo	Department of Management Science, George Washington University, Washington DC, USA
Mikko Korpela	University of Kuopio, Computing Centre, HIS R&D Unit, Finland
S. Krishna	Indian Institute of Management, Bangalore, India
Nir Kshetri	College of Business Administration, University of Rhode Island

A. Kumar	Industries Department, Kerala State Electronics Development Corporation Ltd., Thiruvananthapuram, Kerala, India
Wei Liu	Manchester School of Accounting and Finance, University of Manchester, Manchester, England
Hugo Lotriet	Department of Informatics, University of Pretoria, Pretoria, South Africa
Shirin Madon	Department of Information Systems, London School of Economics
Anja Mursu	University of Kuopio, Department of Computer Science and Applied Mathematics, Finland
Jackie Phahlamohlaka	Department of Informatics, University of Pretoria, Pretoria, South Africa
Heba El Sayed	Manchester School of Accounting and Finance, University of Manchester, Manchester, England
Maung K. Sein	Agder University College, Norway
Vincent Shaw	University of the Western Cape, South Africa
Ingjerd Skogseid	Western Norway Research Institute, Norway
Lars T. Soeftestad	Supras Consult, Norway
H. Abimbola Soriyan	Obafemi Awolowo University, Department of Computer Science and Engineering, Nigeria
Norah Stoops	School of Public Health, University of the Western Cape, Cape Town, South Africa
Geoff Walsham	The Judge Institute of Management Studies, University of Cambridge
Chris Westrup	School of Accounting and Finance, University of Manchester, England
Louisa Williamson	School of Public Health, University of the Western Cape, Cape Town, South Africa

Preface

The contributions in this book have as their origin papers presented at the 7th working conference of the IFIP Working Group 9.4 held at the Indian Institute of Management Bangalore, India during May 29-31,2002. The Conference provided a forum for the discussion of new opportunities, perspectives and challenges of information and communication technologies in the context of developing countries.

IT-enabled changes have swept across the Globe bringing in their wake changes in economic, organizational and governance systems at diverse levels. These multi-faceted and complex changes need to be understood as they occur at local as well as global levels. The conference city of Bangalore with its cluster of software service providers and global software companies provided an 'at hand' instance of successful utilization of opportunities provided by new technologies for developing countries. However, the new economic opportunities are a limited part of the story. ICTs provide a major opportunity in terms of potential to enable and sustain communicative participatory processes at many levels. Increasing access to information and communication media has often enabled small groups and individuals to be heard on global debates and forums. They have made it possible for small cultural and ethnic groups to overcome disadvantages of physical distance. At a more local level they have enabled creation of a virtual 'public place' wherein effective democratic processes of public participation can take place. For instance, in many developing countries, local government authorities are actively considering using ICTs as a means to catalyze initiatives towards democratic decentralization and the empowerment of citizens to participate in the process of design and delivery of civic services. These attempts of using ICTs may be considered a part of a broader agenda of democratic reform in local governance, which typically include a number of other initiatives such as the formation of decentralized committees, reforms in systems of administration and privatization of civic services.

However, many of the old challenges in terms of inappropriate focus and resource allocation remain. The cost of missed opportunities is also increasing. Limitations of existing structures and decision making processes at higher levels in conjunction with greater demands placed on them increase the risk of a reverse spiral of enlarging deprivation. Addressing these challenges is an essential part of the ongoing debate. The conference aimed at addressing these issues and also the evident tension that exists for developing countries as they try to balance global and local priorities through the adoption and use of ICTs. The conference theme of considering new opportunities, perspectives and challenges provided by information and communication technologies for developing countries was further elaborated in terms of the following sub themes:

Participation in Global Economic Activity

What are the factors influencing the development of high-technology industrial activity in developing countries.

- How have companies in developing countries used ICTs to participate as vendors of goods and services in the global marketplace? What have been the constraints in realising this opportunity?
- What occupations and skills are driving the IT industry, and what skills are no longer sought?
- To what extent does participation in the new economic systems provide spin offs for the domestic user base within developing countries, for example in the public sector?
- How do we theorize about the relationship between IT-led global economic activity and socio-economic development within developing countries?

Emergence of New Organizational Types

- What have been the experiences of individuals and small groups such as NGOs that are voicing the viewpoints of the developing countries in using new infrastructures to access global platforms?
- To what extent are Internet-based organizations characterized by the specific culture and context in different settings in developing countries? To what extent have new technologies enabled individuals and non-traditional groups to participate in governance at local and national levels?
- How do we theorize about the impact of these new organizational types which rely on information technology and networks on social and political systems in developing countries?

Local Governance and Socio-economic Development

- How can we characterize new local governance structures emerging in many parts of the developing world? What is the role of the private sector in these structures?
- What has been the experience of non-governmental organizations in mediating between citizen groups and structures of governance?
- In what ways have these technologies enabled improvements in availability of health services, education and economic opportunities to economically disadvantaged areas and groups?
- In what ways are communities and social interactions changing in response to innovations in ICTs? Are there any measurable changes?
- How can we theorize about tensions facing planners in developing countries as they try to mediate between the need to participate in new economic systems and socio-economic priorities?

The issues raised above outline a vast agenda for research on ongoing engagement of IT with development. Given the limited resources and other constraints for such investigations the presentations, participation and discussions at the conference constituted a remarkably interesting and fruitful experience. The chapters in the present volume have been carefully selected from papers submitted and presentations made at the conference then further reviewed and enhanced by the authors.

We would like to thank **Ms. Sujatha Duraiswamy** for her enthusiastic and efficient support in coordinating communication with authors and reviewers as well as in preparation of the manuscript.

It is with sadness that we note a contribution missing in this volume. **Professor Kristen Nygaard**, as per our request, was to summarize the keynote address at the conference delivered by him in his inimitable style summarizing lessons from his wide experience and involvement in technical, social and political domains. His sudden demise while the manuscript was in preparation has deprived us of a valuable contribution. We briefly recount in the following the remarkable achievements of this exceptional individual.

Kristen Nygaard (1926-2002)

Professor Kristen Nygaard is widely known for developing, along with his colleague Ole-Johan Dahl, the concept of objects which appeared in the languages SIMULA and DELTA designed by them in the 60s.The object paradigm, which was slow to gain acceptance, became the dominant paradigm in the 90s in languages and systems development as computer capabilities and speed increased with corresponding increase in complexity of software systems and information system architectures. Professor Nygaard was awarded the John von Neumann Medal of the ACM and the A. M. Turing Award of the IEEE in 2001 for developing the first object-oriented programming language SIMULA.

Professor Nygaard took active interest in trade union and politics of Norway. His association with the Iron and Metal Workers' trade union led to demonstration of concepts of participatory information system development, which has been a major influence in Scandinavia and increasingly in developing country contexts. The Norwegian legislation on working environment also adopted these ideas of user involvement. Professor Nygaard's political career has also been remarkable - involving a membership of the Norwegian Parliament and a leading role in the movement against participation in the European Union. The American Association of Computer Professionals for Social Responsibility awarded him its Norbert Wiener Prize for responsibility in social and professional work in October 1990. For many who got to know him, however briefly, Kristen was not only one of the greatest computer-scientists ever, but a true humanist.

S. Krishna
Shirin Madon

Introduction: Challenges of IT in the Development Context

S. Krishna and Shirin Madon

The initiation of information technology was through mathematical and scientific applications in the late 1940s. Business data processing applications, which came in later, extended the domain of applicability, brought in processes and gave rise to the discipline of information systems. In the 1990s, the reach of the technologies was furthered considerably through home and personal computer access. Issues concerning human interfaces, psychology and related topics became subjects of interest. The integration of communication technologies and networking combined with continuously decreasing cost of hardware and improved software development methodologies have enabled creation of global, national and local communication networks that provide the infrastructure for social and economic systems. Information and communication technologies now partner with social sciences, economics and political sciences in attempting to understand the multiple strands of the emerging information society.

The possibilities for systemic change at multiple levels have encouraged hope of new opportunities for developing countries to improve their situation through economic development, improvements in governance and efficiencies in the delivery of public services. The diffusion of information technology, the construction of modern telecommunications infrastructure and the concomitant increase of communication and access to information resources are increasingly designated as top development priorities in order to achieve this. Against this background of interest in ICTs for Development, the information society discourse that emerged in industrialized countries in the 1990s was quickly transferred into the political circles of regional and international agencies such as the African Development forum in Addis Adaba in 1999, the World Bank InfoDev programme, IDRC and the UNDP as well as in academic writing (such as the three volumes of Castells, 1996; Mansell and Wehn, 1998). For example, the World Bank World Development Report entitled 'Knowledge for Development' published in 1999 clearly sees ICTs as a powerful new tool for fighting poverty and underdevelopment (World Bank, 1999). The UNDP's Human Development Reports now routinely include indices such as the Technology Development Index which measures the extent to which a country has global technology hubs, and the Internet Host Index which measures the penetration of internet connections in individual countries and regions of the world.

Much of this activity supports the developmental promise of ICTs for development through two dimensions. First, in its capacity to provide access to information sources and communications media to citizens at large in order to foster awareness and participation in development programmes. For example, the distribution of ICTs to as wide an audience as possible is at the heart of discussions about inclusion and exclusion in the information society. Second, in its aspirations to encourage public and private organizations to work more efficiently and effectively by rationalizing their work procedures, creating transparency and promoting accountability, often through the involvement of international management consultants. These two dimensions have led to a series of macro socio-economic and political interventions that are put in place by policy-makers including liberalisation of the telecommunications sector and decentralization of political control. Acknowledging the importance of parallel organizational reform and social development policies when introducing information technology intervention, recent literature in the field has been concerned with whether the developmental promise of ICTs actually translates into reality for the beneficiaries concerned (Avgerou and Walsham, 2000). These beneficiaries include government, politicians and their networks, a range of civil society organizations such as entrepreneurs, academic institutions, and non-governmental organizations. So far, the majority of studies have tended to be focused on describing pilot projects with minimal reflection on the conditions which made the pilot a success in the first place, or on the issues which need to be faced when 'scaling up', or on the long-term social costs and benefits of these initiatives. In addition, there is insufficient understanding of the demand side of these kinds of initiatives apart from the abstract assumption of the benefits of ICTs for development.

Increasingly, the potential benefits and drawbacks of the information revolution are at the centre of debates over the development of nations all around the world. Such debate in relation to the developing world has been ongoing in the IFIP WG9.4 community for several years as reflected in the papers presented at the Group's international meetings over the past decade. The contributions contained in this volume add to existing knowledge in this area. The papers have been carefully selected from presentations made at the conference and include perspectives as well as case studies and analysis of ICTs in the development scenario through the work of several researchers from developing and developed countries. They provide detailed as well as rich material and specific insights on attempts and endeavours of organizations, groups and governments as they strive to make best use of the opportunities they see in the new tools and techniques provided by technological advancement. At the risk of oversimplifying the rich material in this volume, we overview here some of the principle learning, inviting the reader to peruse the papers for a more complete discussion.

Successful applications of ICTs in developing country contexts are admittedly still rare. The challenges are perceived in terms of the simultaneously global and local reach of ICTs, the situatedness of information systems implementation, the need for localizing techniques and work practices developed from afar with specific cultural and social inscriptions, and so on. The research reported in this volume discusses many of these issues, which often tend to receive a 'broad brush' treatment. The difficulties which vary in intensity and character across individual countries have, however, a very similar pattern and significant commonalities. These include the following:

- Cultural inscriptions in ICTs and associated work practices, as these are in essence, handed down from advanced countries.
- Lack of effective participation in international bodies and organizations, which set standards and technical protocols which impact economic and technical feasibility of technologies.
- Lack of appropriate national policies on ICTs and often, inability to formulate such policies.
- Difficulties in changing pre-existing organizational structures and processes, particularly in government.
- Lack of general awareness and motivation, coupled with inadequate user skill levels for widespread use of ICTs.
- Bureaucratic appropriation of decision-making since resources and status are implicated in the implementation of ICT projects.
- Low levels of academic and research activity, which could help localization and the development of local expertise.
- Limitations of fragile civil society structures which often operate as informal networks for the communities they serve.
- Not enough attention paid to identifying local strength and capabilities when introducing ICT intervention leading to a continued imposition of values from outside.

The papers also discuss theoretically well-informed fieldwork and implementation of systems, which will hopefully provide approaches to address many of the challenges identified above. Some of the features which are reported positively through recent empirical work are as follows:

- Greater awareness of the linkages between international and national policies and standards, which impact the feasibility of systems in developing countries.
- Participatory systems, which may provide a counter-balance to influence existing power structures.
- Discursive rationality as a guiding approach to the development of systems, which have emancipatory objectives.
- Increasing levels of software and technical skills, which, though initially oriented towards export earnings, increasingly contribute towards domestic development.
- Possibility of south-south learning since developing countries themselves possess an increasing spectrum of competence.
- Increasing reflexivity in systems planning, implementation processes and usage contributing to an accelerated learning curve in the application of ICTs for development.

The papers in this volume are grouped according to themes and summarised in the rest of this chapter thus providing an overview of contributions in this volume.

Theoretical and Methodological Perspectives for the Study of ICTs and Development

We consider the development of theoretical and methodological perspectives an important way to guide further study in the field of ICTs and Development and have included six papers in this volume with different perspectives to assist testing out of concepts and development of analytical frameworks.

Relationship of culture to information systems is widely acknowledged but inadequately explored. The paper by Westrup *et al.* makes an important contribution in this direction by viewing culture as something that is temporal, contested and emergent introducing an analysis of power and negotiation amongst key stakeholders involved with ICT innovation. Rather than using culture as context or an explanation, this chapter argues that culture should be seen as an ongoing accomplishment that is often partial, disputed and changeable. ICTs can be incorporated into cultural networks to enhance, stabilize or consciously change accepted cultural characteristics. Thus we have a dynamic and complicated relationship between ICTs and differing cultures. The chapter explores this theme by discussing how culture has been expressed firstly in the anthropological literature and then in wider organizational and IS literature. Three short examples in China, Jordan and Egypt are used to illustrate the argument. An important challenge for the study of ICT and development then becomes the need to study invention and reinvention of traditional culture in different contexts through the use of ICTs.

One implication of a careful contextual study of an ICT innovation is the need to accommodate existing domain knowledge and institutional background of specific innovations. Such knowledge exists in all situations of innovation whether documented by specific disciplines – for example in the case of public administration, education and health, and the financial services industry in almost every country, or is scattered in a more diverse social, political and economic literature. The theme of knowledge, ICTs and development is fundamental in the policy manifestos and theoretical discussions in the field at global, regional, country and organizational levels. Johnstone in this volume argues that much of the focus on knowledge remains at the level of creating information resources for specific functions rather than conceptualizing knowledge as a state of mind. Johnstone explores the close coupling between the concepts of knowledge and culture arguing that culture affects the kind of knowledge we have.

The analysis of context in the information systems field has to a large extent been limited to considering immediate organizational environment. However, in examining information systems involving application of ICTs in complex developing country environments, Avgerou calls for a broadening in the focus of study beyond immediate events and actions that comprise the development, implementation or use of ICT artefacts and tracing the roots of the encountered behaviours in the economic, cultural, and political domains of the broader institutional context. In her paper, Avgerou suggests that a careful consideration of the taken for granted assumptions concerning basic concepts like Development, Management and IT reveal the influence of institutional actors whose dominance is implicit and therefore prevails more effectively. The subsequent paper by Soeftestad and Sein makes a contribution to this theme by making specific suggestions for alternative conceptualizations. These authors argue that investments in information and communication technologies (ICTs) in developing countries, have not contributed significantly to national development due to flawed conceptualization of concepts of ICT, development, and the interrelationship between the two. They suggest alternative conceptualizations of these concepts and examine the evolution of ICT policy in a specific donor agency to illustrate their contentions.

As research in the field of ICTs and Development matures, there has been increasing attention paid to methodological concerns. Walsham's paper addresses the issue of selecting appropriate research style and methodology for study in this area. Walsham addresses the question of how valid knowledge can be constructed and evaluated in the field with particular reference to interpretive/critical stance and action research designed to produce research outputs and specific intervention in a real situation. The role of theory in IS research studies; issues of validity, the importance of writing and the goal of relevance are also discussed.

Global organizations in their efforts to balance local and global priorities have to handle a variety of issues similar to those involved in contextualizing ICTs in developing countries. Galliers in this volume provides a synthesis of the different levels at which culture may be analysed in information technology interventions. Three cases are presented which discuss the interplay between culture and information technology implementation at the global, organizational and sub-organizational levels.

E-Governance and the Digital Divide

Digital divide and E-governance have become something of buzzwords amongst international and national policy circles, academics and practitioners, quite often being viewed in terms of problem and solution perspectives. For example, in 2001, both DFID and the G-8 groups launched their policy briefs concerning E-governance for development. With such international backing, country and within-country initiatives are proliferating with the promise of 'reaching out to the masses' within developing countries. E-Governance is usually taken to represent a continuum of initiatives ranging from IT automation within individual government departments to the development of government websites for improving transparency, accountability and integration in government, to the electronic delivery of government services, to the development of information centres or 'telecentres' for community development in rural areas.

Despite many initiatives undertaken under the banner of E-governance, there remains lack of clarity about how the concept as conceived by policy-makers in diverse ways, relates to the situation on the ground. While top down, large scale and budget approaches receive newspaper attention, there is need to study the reality of such projects on the ground. Five cases and two overviews presented in the section document significant contributions in this regard.

Kanungo reports on the Information village initiative undertaken by an NGO near Chennai in South India. This case is of particular interest since it has reached a stage of maturity, which permits a degree of evaluation and formalization of the implementation processes. The paper presents the challenges to and responses associated with replicating and sustaining IT-interventions in resource challenged rural contexts and is a contribution towards strengthening the empirical base in reporting IS implementations that are emancipatory in character. Data presented shows how resource-challenged information systems necessarily have to incorporate multiple paradigms in their development, use and sustenance. Kanungo also presents implications for practice based on the importance of collaboration at multiple levels for bridging the digital divide.

Though much interest has been focused on the capacity of telecentre applications to foster awareness, participation and inclusion of poor communities in development programme such initiatives are still experimental and supported by external agencies. An important question therefore is the sustainability of telecentres, especially those in rural areas where telecommunications and electricity are problematic and expensive. Harris, Kumar and Balaji point out that much of the literature related to ICTs and the digital divide in developing countries assesses impact purely in terms of connectivity to ICT infrastructure rather than in terms of how this access is able to sustain and ameliorate broader developmental concerns of poor communities. In particular they discuss one particular type of sustainability – that of financial sustainability of telecentre projects based on recent empirical work. Conclusions indicate that financial sustainability for development-oriented telecentres appears possible under specified conditions. The subsequent paper by Phahlamohlaka and Lotriet describes preliminary research concerning a community education centre project directed at providing Internet access in rural South Africa. The authors examine the challenges, opportunities and processes involved in introduction of new technologies in a relatively 'green field' environment.

Several papers in the conference were dedicated to describing health information systems as key applications of E-governance in terms of providing critical health-related information for planning and monitoring programmes. The Health Information Systems Project (HISP) is an initiative that has been under implementation in South Africa since 1999,and currently being extended to other developing countries. In this volume, Stoops, Williamson and Braa draw on their research to evaluate the extent to which information system in South Africa has been able to improve the monitoring of health care at primary health centres in the country. The authors point out that the social processes of human resource development, changing organizational infrastructure and the use of ongoing evaluation rather than those of technical infrastructure are key mechanisms to facilitate improvements. The paper by Shaw describes the development of a hospital information system in South Africa through a participatory approach. The process of software development is shown to be constantly influenced by evolving political, cultural and social factors internal to the organization as well as its dynamic external environment.

Cecchini provides an overview of E-Governance projects for development and poverty eradication. The realization of ICT potential in this regard, however, is not guaranteed. Low-cost access to information infrastructure is a necessary prerequisite for the successful use of ICT by the poor, but it is not sufficient. The role of appropriate human intermediaries is crucial to interface between the government and end-users. These intermediaries typically include the private sector, NGOs and community-based organizations, and other public institutions. These intermediaries will have to work within existing bureaucratic and political structures with a view to changing work practices and priorities.

Frasheri's paper provides a useful complement to Cecchini by emphasising that despite the drive to roll back the state, public administration remains a critical player in E-Governance processes. Discussing E-Governance initiatives in Albania, Frasheri argues that the openness of public administration information systems and decentralization processes in developing countries are a component of essential institution-building required for effective deployment of ICTs.

ICTs and New Organizational Forms

ICTs have enabled new ways of interaction and exchange of information between individuals, intra-organizational units and across organizations. In business systems and markets, these have resulted in large-scale changes. In organizational and public systems in developing countries ICT enabled changes are still at a nascent stage. Four studies reported here discuss cases and relevant issues in diverse contexts.

Jansen and Skogseid describe a project, which, though situated in a developed country context, involves small rural towns with wide geographic separation. The Book Town network involved an Internet based infrastructure to support a network organisation. The authors report that the use of the Internet both locally and between the book towns strengthened communication and collaboration, creating a better basis for the small bookshops to be competitive in the information society. However, although the infrastructure and support systems have been important for the bookshops' ability to implement and use the new technical solutions, the characteristics of the regional and local innovation systems have been the most important factor in stimulating organizational innovations.

Dholakia and Kshetri discuss the considerable potential of mobile technologies to provide novel ways of interaction to people who have been disadvantaged in their access to communication facilities. In particular, they point to the implicit assumption many policy makers in developing countries seem to harbour that the most recent technologies are meant for the more prosperous. The regulations and tax regimes derived from such assumptions in fact render the resulting situation to correspond to the presumption.

Boyle presents the case of an Internet-based research network in a university capacity-building programme in Vietnam. He points out the tendency to envision such work within the scope of the selected means like technical connectivity, computer skill and information exchange. However it is only through a discussion over the projected ends of such a deployment, like enhanced research and increased co-operation, that the full complexity of social innovation implicit in such a deployment may be envisaged. The nature and relevance of these ends in specific social contexts, in contrast to issues like providing access to technology found in popular discourses over information society, should be made more explicit in design and deployment.

Bada considers the role of institutional and strategic perspectives in influencing organizational change in banking system in Nigeria. The author argues that institutional influences of conformity and legitimacy are supported by strategic and efficiency considerations where the strategic needs of the local context and the economic realities of the Nigerian context determine the willingness to conform to, and the ability to resist, institutional influences.

ICT Development and Global Software Outsourcing

The development processes of ICT related technologies, in particular those of software, are at the core of the new developments. These processes being primarily knowledge-oriented cerebral activities have provided an unforeseen new economic opportunity to people-rich but capital-poor countries. However whether the new opportunity can be exploited by all such countries is an open question. The contributions in this section provide a close analysis of underlying processes as well as overviews of this domain.

Eischen points out that without opening the 'black box' of software production processes the nature of information industries and questions as to which countries and regions acquire proficiency in the same is difficult to address. Further, such an analysis is essential for considering social and economic impact and locating evolution paths within broader global economic patterns. The author discusses a typology of informational production and considers two apparently dissimilar regions- Iceland and Andhra Pradesh in India, to illustrate his formulation.

Mursu, Soriyan and Korpela discuss issues of developing local competence and skills in Information system development. Such abilities are particularly needed if larger component of localization and sensitivity to issues of local context are to be incorporated. Very little empirical research has been conducted on the work practice of software engineering and information systems development in most developing countries. The authors have studied the practice of information systems development in Nigerian software companies in two parts- a survey supplemented with case studies in specific companies. They focus on the issue of risk and compare perceived risk factors in software development projects in the Nigerian context in comparison to similar factors in industrialized countries.

Dayasindhu and Pradeep discuss the case of the state of Kerala in India which, while possessing all required resources for development of a software outsourcing industry, lags much behind certain other regions in India which have been far more successful in this regard. The usefulness of this and similar studies are particularly relevant in the situation described by Carmel in the subsequent contribution. A large number of countries, most of which could be grouped under the 'developing' category have aspirations of promoting software services and product export industries. The archetype in this regard is the Silicon Valley. Many states, regions and nations have ambitions of replicating its success. However, such success occurs in an economic social and historical context, which is unique. As Dayasindhu and Pradeep point out regions should discover their own unique strengths by taking the challenges head on, and developing a model that is rooted in their own economic, social, and cultural contexts.

References

Avgerou, C. and Walsham, G. (2000) *Information Technology in Context: Studies from the perspective of developing countries,* edited by C. Avgerou and G. Walsham, Ashgate Publishing Limited, Aldershot.

Castells, M (1996), The Information Age, Economy, Society and Culture, Volumes 1-3: Blackwell Publishers, Oxford 1996-2001.

Mansell, R. and Wehn, U. (1998) Knowledge societies: Information technology for sustainable development, Oxford University Press.

The World Bank (1999) Knowledge for development, World Development Report 1998/99.

PART I
ICTs AND DEVELOPMENT: THEORETICAL AND METHODOLOGICAL PERSPECTIVES

Chapter 1

Taking Culture Seriously: ICTs Culture and Development

Chris Westrup, Saheer Al Jaghoub, Heba El Sayed, Wei Liu

1. Introduction

The first part of the title of this chapter is taken from the recent book by Geoff Walsham, which engages in an extensive exploration of the theory and practice of information and communication technologies (ICTs) in both the North and South.[1] Walsham, in a discussion with Simon Bell about the use of Western methodologies such as Logframe in Third World countries, makes the comment 'My argument in a nutshell is the need to take culture *seriously*' (Walsham, 2000: 227).[2] This remark is a useful starting point: what does taking culture seriously imply? And it is an exploration (albeit preliminary at this stage) of some of the issues arising from this statement that forms the substance of this chapter. As an issue, it is interesting because it draws things together (Latour, 1990) and this chapter seeks to show that this exploration opens issues that are central to development and to the use of ICTs in general.

First, the question of culture is raised: what is it; how is it to be recognised and is culture a useful demarcation between North and South? For a word that was coined only some two hundred and fifty years ago, the term is often seen as referring to aspects that are extremely significant for different societies (Williams, 1981). Second, culture is increasingly recognised as important in the introduction and use of ICTs. Within organizations in the North aspects of organizational culture have been identified over the last twenty years and very often attempts are made to manage organizational culture to create desired outcomes (Peters and Waterman, 1982). Culture is both an explanation and a sensitizing factor in the use of ICTs in other countries and other parts of the world. Most of this analysis has been phrased in terms of Western cultures and non-Western ones, but, equally and importantly, other aspects are being identified: for example the work of Indian IS professionals in Jamaica (Barrett and Walsham, 1995). The terrain of the discussion on culture is, of course, much wider. A recent debate, that of Japanisation, the conscious following of Japanese production techniques by US and European countries, is interesting because, apparently, it is about the inculcation of non Western cultures into Western organizations. Third, if culture is to be used as a means to show the nuances of specific contexts for ICT implementation and use, then it is important to turn the relationship around and consider what does the notion of culture do in investigating the nature of ICT technologies? Are they culturally neutral, carriers of Western domination, or resources to be appropriated by the South as is suitable? Finally, as is evident from the discussion above, the notion of culture is of great practical importance and any consideration of culture and ICTs should raise the issues of how ICT introduction and use is to be researched, advised upon or implemented if the notion of culture is to be taken seriously.

The core argument of this chapter is simply that, to take culture seriously means investigating cultures, analysing how cultures are expressed, and describing cultures. In contrast, this chapter avoids using culture as an explanation in itself. The notion of culture is becoming and should become an important part of the stock in trade of those researching the development and use of ICTs and of those engaged in the processes of embedding ICTs in differing situations. However, using the notion of culture is but one resource amongst other and equally important and plausible lines of explanation (see Kuper, 1999; Ingold, 1996). Politics and power relations, social networks and ties, economics and economic interactions all need investigation, discussion, and articulation to avoid our debates becoming centred on issues of knowledge and ideas. These arenas, given the rise of knowledge management, are perhaps those that people interested in IS could easily focus on and thus we should be all the more wary of culture as an entity or stock of knowledge.

This chapter is divided in four parts. The first section seeks to explore the notion of culture drawing primarily from an anthropological literature, perhaps the academic discipline, which would lay claim to a specialist concern with culture. A second section discusses some ways in which notions of culture have been applied in the IS literatures. This discussion paves the way to a consideration of ICTs in relation to culture using examples from both North and South and an investigation of the ways in which notions of culture can assist in the research of ICTs and in the implementation and use of ICTs in a variety of settings.

2. On Culture

'*Everybody* is into culture now' (Kuper, 1999: 2 (original emphasis))

Culture is a term that everyone thinks they understand and it has become a potent aspect of identity. Anthropologists have discovered that the natives they study have found that they have cultures, which they seek to express, conserve and develop to show their distinctiveness. Recently, culture has been used as a strong expression of difference between Islamic cultures and those of the West. Within western societies cultures are widely talked about: youth cultures, organizational cultures, organizational subcultures and so on. As can be seen already the notion of culture and the ways in which it is expressed are diverse and are not confined to academia.

However the investigation of culture has given rise to a new form of academic discourse-cultural studies, which has become institutionalized as a popular academic discipline.

When it comes to the exploration of *cultures* in different parts of the world, anthropologists have been at the forefront in identifying and representing cultural diversity. Carrithers (1992) characterizes an early phase that he calls a seashell theory. The analogy is that of a vast variety of different cultures, each self-contained, like different seashells on a beach. Each shell has its own characteristics, which are to be explored, described, and classified. Similarly, each culture is to be respected, examined, and described as part of a diversity, which humans have developed as ways of living. As a consequence, anthropology as a discipline shared a scientific concern with the identification and classification of different cultures as scientific phenomena. However, while emphasizing diversity, this approach tends to neglect history, the sense of cultures as cultural wholes is supported by ignoring issues of how they might change and thus admitting that cultural boundaries may shift. One reason why the seashell theory caught hold was, as mentioned above, its aptness in providing common ground with other scientific projects. However, another reason is based on how anthropology was practiced. The standard approach was that of intensive fieldwork over several years within a particular culture followed by the writing up of these experiences in a monograph. Clifford and Marcus (1986) and others have made much of the practices of writing up, of representation, in anthropology, but it is apparent that this form of research leads to a certain timelessness when describing the culture that was visited. Carrithers gives an example of how subsequent fieldwork can change this perception. Turnbull wrote a celebrated book *The Forest People* on the Mbuti pygmies, which evoked a happy society living at peace with the world. He wrote:

> I was first among the Mbuti pygmies of the Ituri Forest, in what was the Belgian Congo, in 1951. I went back for something over a year in 1954. Even in that short space of time things had changed and initial impressions had to be corrected. When I returned again in 1957-9 I had quite a hard time reconciling some of my earlier findings with what I found then. And on returning to the same part of the same forest yet again in 1970-2, it seemed as through I had to contradict myself all over again (Turnbull, 1983 quoted in Carrithers, 1992: 22).

This recognition of change is important for three reasons. First, as discussed above, it shows that different patterns of research open up different and important issues. In this case, longitudinal intensive ethnography reveals the importance of change in the exploration of culture. Second, it is a step towards identifying the importance of history and a historical perspective. At one level, the recognition of change shows that other cultures have histories and so one element of difference, that of history, between North and South begins to be dismantled. However perhaps the most interesting reason is that, investigation begins to be directed into how cultures change and we move from a seashell view of cultures to one of cultures as products *and* processes of change. This is an important issue for those who research ICTs.

Taking change seriously can lead to a different purchase on the notion of culture itself. Kuper's (1999) discussion of the work of Clifford Geertz is a useful entry point. Geertz is one of the best-known anthropologists and his ideas have been very influential in discussions of culture and the value of ethnography in a variety of disciplines. Geertz's description of culture that is often quoted is as follows:

> Believing, with Max Weber, that man is an animal suspended in webs of significance he himself has spun, I take culture to be those webs, and the analysis of it to be therefore not an experimental science in search of law but an interpretative one in search of meaning. It is explication I am after, construing social expressions on their surface enigmatical. (Geertz quoted in Kuper, 1999: 98)

This definition focuses on how culture guides social life and how the act of interpreting culture is to be done by 'thick description'; a detailed observation followed by a necessary interpretation by the author of the material that has been observed. Geertz suggests that this process is similar to that of someone engaged in deciphering literary texts; cultures are to be read and interpreted. The literary analogy has proved to be influential in a range of other disciplines, but what Geertz's view portrays is that it is culture which matters and which acts as the main explanation of human action. As Kuper notes what he doesn't engage in is that cultural models can be used for other such as political ends and that arising from this point, it is clear that culture can be contested. While taking on board that point, there is also a difficulty in identifying culture and we are left with the notion that cultures may well be inconsistent and changing rather than texts for explication. To conclude this section, we can briefly consider a recent exchange amongst anthropologists on the notion that human worlds are culturally constructed (see Ingold, 1996).[3]

Amongst the anthropologists there was dislike of the term 'construction' and the implication that people stood outside and then engaged in the conscious construction of things. Equally there was concern about the idea of people free floating in 'webs of significance' à la Geertz as it assumes that people place significance on things out there and that meaning is disembodied. Instead, where there was agreement, it was around the notion of exploring processes by which individuals interact with their environment and how both, people and their environment constitute each other in a dialectical way. Individuals are immersed in the world and experiences become enfolded into that person, but, similarly, the environment, as well as shaping individuals, is also shaped by them. Thus we end up with a notion of culture that is not a thing, not a discrete entity, but an ongoing process that is inherently changeable and often malleable. Equally, culture becomes an ongoing accomplishment and though we do not have a privileged access to something termed culture, we can seek to identify *processes* by which meanings can be maintained, contested, shared or changed. Finally, we can become aware that when people start to talk about culture, that act, in itself, can be part of a process of redefining or maintaining relationships in order to accomplish other things.

3. Culture and ICTs

> Although the concept of culture has often been used rather narrowly in the IS literature, we have suggested that IS research in this area would benefit if more attention was paid to the contemporary anthropological view of culture which – as something which is contested, temporal and emergent – has the potential to offer information systems researchers rich insights into how new information technologies affect or mediate organizational and national cultures, vice versa, i.e. how cultures affect the adoption and use of IT. (Avison and Myers, 1995)

This quotation is a part of the conclusion of an interesting paper exploring an anthropological perspective on IT and organizational culture. As has been discussed above, there is much to agree with in this statement especially the point on the contested, temporal and emergent attributes of culture. Where there is room for development is on the question of how IS affects or mediates organizational and national cultures and *vice versa*. This is not a straightforward extrapolation because an important (and unanswered) question is how can the attributes of culture expressed above be squared with notions of national or organizational culture? Stated more precisely, does the paper retain the concept of culture when referring to national and organizational cultures? To investigate this issue, we turn to an exploration of culture in the wider setting of organizations and nation states and how culture can be related to ICTs.

About twenty years ago there was great attention on the issue of organizational culture, an interest that has remained despite the vicissitudes of other approaches such as Business Process Reengineering. Certain books are linked to the rise in interest in this phenomenon – Peters and Waterman's *In Search of Excellence,* Deal and Kennedy's *Corporate Cultures: The Rites and Rituals of Corporate Life* are perhaps the best known. One of the reasons advanced for this interest in culture was the rapid expansion of Japanese competition in manufacturing particularly in the US. Much of the success of Japanese manufacturing was placed on cultural issues such as group loyalties, the Keiretsu interlinking of companies, the flexibility of the labour force and management, and the use of approaches, which then became known as Just in Time (JIT) and Total Quality Management (TQM) (Elger and Smith, 1994). And it raises an interesting question – is it possible for seemingly Japanese cultural characteristics to be transferred to Western countries? Based on the experience of the last ten to fifteen years, the answer in short is yes. What seems to have happened is that cultural processes have either been exported to the West through Japanese management of subsidiaries or these processes have been reformulated as techniques such as JIT, TQM, and World Class Manufacturing (WCM) which are reinterpreted in Western companies mainly through the use of management consultants (Hopper *et al.*, 2000). Though it cannot be argued that western manufacturing processes mirror

Japanese processes, it appears that similar characteristics in terms of customer focus, attention to quality, and an attempt to continually improve business processes, have been embedded in many Western companies (Hendry, 1998). These findings bring us to a second issue: whether culture, and in particular, organizational culture, can be managed.

One of the main proposals of the books mentioned above, was precisely that culture is a new arena in management and that corporate culture was of importance to company performance. The aim according to one of the leading proponents was

> … to win the "hearts and minds" of employees: to define their purposes by managing what they think and feel, and not just how they behave. (Peters and Waterman, 1982: xvii)

The identification and use of corporate culture has been widespread and aspects are to be found in managerial practices in a large number of organizations (du Gay, 1997). It appears that the management of organizational culture does have consequences though it is far from clear whether employees accept at face value the corporate cultures that are promoted to them. Instead, moves to develop corporate cultures lead to countermoves by employees, though the general direction is towards a further managing of aspects of people's working lives with a consequent loss of individual autonomy (Kunda, 1991; Willmott, 1993). So though cultures can be managed, the corporate culture that is installed becomes an official culture while other modes of engagement, often cynical, are to be found but less openly. Thus, to take organizational cultures seriously we have to take on board that these are arenas of dispute, of often proactive management, and of change. To embed ICTs in organizations, requires a very careful exploration of the dynamics of the particular organizational cultures in an organization. Equally, exploring organizational cultures raises the issue of the milieu in which organizations are found.

As has been discussed above, notions of culture are often linked with locations or space. The linking of nations to cultural identities has led to the identification and measurement of national cultures. Hofstede's work has been influential in this respect. He used data on IBM executives to construct different measurable attributes to express national cultural variation (power distance – whether individuals will accept differentiation in power; uncertainty avoidance – whether individuals are prepared to accept uncertainties; individualism – whether people expect to act as individuals or in groups; and masculinity – whether there is a clear separation of roles based on gender) (Hofstede, 1980). The results indicated that national variation could be identified and that certain countries could be seen to combine into different groupings. These were interesting findings, but they can be used unreflectively. Shortcomings need to be recognized – take for example, national identity. National identity is not timeless. The example of the creation of French cultural identity through standardization and centralization shows that the linking of the nation state to cultural values is itself an achievement through the invention of national celebrations (Bastille Day in 1880) to process 'akin to colonisation' through roads, railways and national newspapers (McCrone, 1998 quoted in Urry, 2000: p.148). Indeed, the quest for regional identities and decentralization show that national cultural identities can be challenged and usurped (McCrone, 1998). Certain processes are often used in the creation of cultural identities – schooling is a good example of how a standardized curriculum can be used to create a sense of shared cultural experience. At the moment in the UK, this recognition has regenerated arguments as to whether single faith schools should receive State funding if they are seen not to follow standard approaches to schooling that are to be found in State funded schools. In short, a major problem in using Hofstede's work is that it seeks to use national culture as an *explanation* for say, variation in attitudes to ICTs, rather than seek mechanisms by which these attitudes are expressed and reformulated. With Hofstede's findings, a cultural context can be generated which appears to be static and unconditioned (cf. Myers and Tan, 2001).

However, the linking of culture to national identity is seen by some commentators as part of a phase in which national sovereignty was paramount, and they argue that globalization – economic, political and cultural, will lead to a dramatic curtailment of the functions and capabilities of the state and equally, that the equating of culture with nationalism is under pressure (see Castells, 1996, 1997, 2000, Featherstone, 1990, Waters, 2001). This is an argument that will not be developed here, but it does show tensions inherent in discussions of national identity and culture. What we wish to turn to is the involvement of ICTs in the production of culture.

The advent of ICTs has often been linked with an expansion of rationalism and a colonization of a life world of the everyday relations of kinship, sociality, religious association and community (see Barglow, 1994, Habermas, 1987). ICTs are seen to contribute to the production of a disenchanted world with the boundaries set by new technologies. However, the use of technologies can show more creative responses and appropriations by people. For example, in the UK text messaging using mobile phones, amongst teenagers in particular, has become extremely widespread. This is creating new forms of sociality with specific codes of communication based on the possession of mobile phones and it is providing new capabilities to communicate and coordinate amongst people widely dispersed in space. For some, what we are witnessing is the creation of new cultures based around ICTs, which infuse new meanings, and create different capabilities and boundaries (Bell and Kennedy, 2000). Lash has discussed the emergence (in the North) of technological forms of life: a way of doing things in which we make sense of the world through technological systems (Lash, 2001: p.107). In contrast to the notion of a cyborg (part human part computer) Lash proposes that people use technological systems as their interface to their environment. As Lash (*ibid*) comments

> I just can't function without my WAP mobile phone. I can't live without my laptop computer, digital camcorder, fax machine, automobile. I can't function without Ryanair, Amazon.com and cable, satellite and interactive channels.

Instead people begin to interact as a technological culture which is constituted as culture at a distance and sociality is achieved through ICTs.

Castells (2000) describes what he terms a culture of real virtuality which depends on changes in information technologies, but which arises from informational capitalism that encompasses networks of production, power and experience. A culture of real virtuality is characterized by timeless time in which time is annihilated by the capabilities of technology to compress time. Real virtuality is not tied to location but is found in a space of flows in which change is rapid and social relations are disembodied. Castells argues that real virtuality is a characteristic of a network society in which networks mediated by ICT penetrate societies to a greater or lesser degree and he proposes that the dynamic expansion of the network society which '... gradually absorbs and subdues pre-existing social forms.' (Castells, 2000: p.381). Alongside the network society, Castells identifies cultural communes that are constructed around specific meanings such as cultural nationalism or religious fundamentalism and are defensive reactions against the dissolving of boundaries through globalization, the network society or other causes (Castells, 1997: p.66). Reactionary groups can embrace aspects of the network society and use ICTs to communicate their message and to construct new relationships. The creative use of ICTs can also lead to the development of new cultural codes, which reformulate the reactions of cultural communes and distribute them as networks.

In this section we began by introducing the conception of culture as a context or entity, which IT affects or is affected by. This position is an important advance in a project of taking culture seriously, though there are tensions between the notion of culture as context and conceptions of culture as emergent, contested and an ongoing accomplishment. Treating culture as context opens up questions of whether cultures are capable or should they be managed? If the position taken is that of management, then ICT introduction could be facilitated by taking culture into account as one more (rather nebulous) variable. The example of Japanisation shows that what are ascribed as cultural attributes can be translated into techniques and reconstituted in Western countries. Equally the project of managing corporate cultures shows that there are no pristine cultures awaiting explication, rather organizations are sites of differing and often disputed cultural activities. The concept of national cultures as a context for ICT usage was considered using Hofstede's classification, but it does promote a static formulation of culture and can easily lead to treating culture as a causal agent while ignoring how national cultures are constituted and *maintained*. However, in reconsidering the duality of culture and ICTs set out at the start perhaps the most compelling argument is that ICTs are those resources in the constitution of cultures that can be termed as technological forms of life, à la Lash or cultures of real virtuality as put forward by Castells. In other words a posited duality cannot hold, and the relationships of culture and ICT interweave in more interesting ways.

The move to recognize that cultures are not entities and may be viewed as accomplishments that are emergent, often contradictory, and can be mediated through technologies is mirrored by changes in the ways in which technologies can be understood. Deriving initially from empirical work in the sociologies of science and technologies, there has been a growing recognition that technologies are also accomplishments that draw on many sources and can then act in various ways (Law, 1987). Technologies can be seen as phenomena that embed the formulation of networks of relations, which encompass both aspects of the social and the technical (Latour, 1987). Consequently, rather than see the relationship between culture and technologies as a duality, both culture and technologies can be viewed as networks of relations, which through mediation, can be linked. However, the likely outcome of such an interrelationship is a transformation of *both* the technology and the cultural network. In other words, through appropriating technologies, cultures can be redefined and strengthened and cultural identities changed and made more robust. Equally, the expectation should be that imported ICTs will change when they are used in any setting, let alone in the South. Such an argument leads to a symmetry of explanation as to what may occur in both the South and the North when ICTs and cultures interrelate. The differences between North and South are to be found in the different networks of relations that are found in these two situations. The next section will use some examples to illustrate and develop these points.

4. ICTs and Culture in Practice: North and South

4.1 Chinese Culture or Local Politics?

The first example is taken from the fieldwork conducted in 2001 by one of the co-authors,[4] which explored how control and co-ordination is achieved by multinational companies with headquarters in the UK and their Chinese operations. In one particular company, research was carried out with five interviews in the UK and by four weeks of participant observation and forty-two interviews in China over a period of three months in five locations. In this example, two factories were investigated in Southern China. Both factories process food and are joint ventures between local state owned companies and a UK multinational. The UK company introduced Scala, a software package in one factory and is planning to introduce Scala into the other factory in February 2002. It appears that Scala is being used as a transaction processing system without engendering any changes in business processes or being used directly for decision-making. There seems to be considerable cultural differences between the Chinese workers and managers and the UK nationals. The UK expatriates have two roles: they either come to maintain the sugar processing plant or else they are managers sent from the regional office in Hong Kong to the local factory. These cultural differences can be ascribed to national characteristics, but they can be explained somewhat differently.

Both factories were run by the local government prior to their becoming joint ventures some five years ago, and so the relationship between the local area and the factory still remains very important – for example, in dealing with other organizations, such as banks, railway companies, and so on, which too have very close links with the local government as well, so although the British managers try to treat other agencies as different and independent agencies as is in the UK, in this part of China they are all interlinked. Mistakes made in one arena affect relationships in all other areas.

A second issue is the introduction of teamworking by British managers. This appears to be a mild form of the developing of a corporate culture, but it works differently however in this situation, as relationships are already important. The Chinese workers expect team working, but they see that the teamwork does not stop at the factory gate but it should include their extended family as well, which can mean giving family members jobs at the factory regardless of their qualifications.

In the face of many difficulties in the plants, the introduction of the Scala system is seen as treating an area that is not of most importance. For the Chinese, the political dimensions are of much greater interest as this is where both in the long term and short term, their own futures as well as plants reside. These political dimensions revolve around ways in which relationships are created, recognized, sustained and developed. In this way, what is ascribed to culture is tightly bound within economic and political dimensions, which British managers do not consider as important. However, it is possible to conceive of British managers being attentive to these areas of relationships and political networks and becoming more effective in their management.

4.2 Redefining Jordan as an ICT Regional Centre

Currently Jordan does not have a very developed ICT sector and going by various indicators, its ICT infrastructure is not strong (Al Jaghoub, 2001; see Al Jaghoub and Westrup, 2002).[5] There is no indigenous hardware manufacturing and only a limited amount of software development. As a consequence, all of the hardware and most of the software is imported and the instructions and language used in ICTs in Jordan is often English even though interfaces may be presented in Arabic. In short, Jordan appears to be an archetypical case of an underdeveloped country using imported technologies. However, the government of Jordan and particularly the new King, King Abdullah, see ICTs as a means of changing Jordan into a regional centre for the production of Arabic based software and services (REACH, 2000, 2001). For a landlocked country with relatively few natural resources and a well educated population, ICTs appear to have the capabilities of removing many of the problems of location and time differences while exploiting aspects of locatedness such as Jordan's place in a large group of Arabic speaking countries and marketplaces.

There are two complementary thrusts in the use of ICTs: one is based on attempts to provide access to ICTs for marginalized groups and so to assist in reducing disparities of access to ICTs and hence to other services. These schemes are at an early stage and tend to be linked to external sponsorship. An example of this is the provision of telecentre facilities to Bedouin, part funded by the UN Information Technology Service (UNITeS). These schemes are highly publicized and the members of the royal family have been active in opening these centres in remoter parts of the country.

A second approach is to create the technical, educational, financial and institutional infrastructure to promote Jordan as a regional IS centre and an information society (Nusseir, 2001; REACH, 2001). A new ministry is in the process of being set up and this activity too is strongly promoted by the Jordan government and monarchy.

In both cases, ICTs are being redefined as a means of developing Jordan and of creating a new sense of Jordanian identity. The active involvement of the King is an important feature of this approach. The cultural milieu of Jordanian society is being changed so that ICT usage and expertise becomes seen as an important aspect of Jordanian capabilities. This is still at an early stage, but it gives an insight into ways in which ICTs can be used to redefine national identity and create new forms of culture, which seek to integrate different aspects of Jordanian society. How successful, and by what terms success is to be measured, remains to be seen, but it is possible that there will also be unexpected consequences.

4.3 Egypt: ERPs and Networks that Create Cultural Benefits

The examples here are taken from a study of three Egyptian owned companies in Egypt conducted in 2001. Each of the companies has introduced enterprise resource planning systems in the last few years.[6] One example Tronic[7] was the first company in Egypt to introduce an ERP system (El Sayed, 2001; El Sayed and Westrup, 2002). They are a company that has diversified and grown considerably in the last ten years. When they wanted to link parts of the company more closely together they called in Arthur Anderson as consultants who recommended an ERP solution and in 1999 an Oracle system began to be installed. Senior managers see the installation of Oracle as an important means of integrating the company and they are very aware of Oracle as a mark of business sophistication. As one senior manager put it

> Having an ERP solution is more of a status symbol. When it is known that I have Oracle in my company other people are impressed.

Egypt has also developed a strong ICT policy and Information Highway, which is supported at the highest levels. For a company having a sophisticated IS system it is a positive feature that accords with Governmental strategy. Similarly, the consultants, who presented the ERP system, were very positive about the benefits of Oracle to the company. One accountant who attended one of their seminars recalled it being introduced as '… the perfect system, I was convinced it was my system. This is what I was searching for, I could not work without it.'

The ERP system is now installed and, not surprisingly, has not lived up to those expectations. However, what is important is how ERP systems are being linked with company success and prestige, national success, and more individualized success. A network of relations has been brought together that links companies, ERPs, consultants, national success, and individual workers. Political and cultural agendas interweave and the use of ICTs is seen as bringing benefits that are both cultural and political. ICTs can be seen as resources that can be used to enhance and define cultural attributes and certainly not just in terms of apparently utilitarian functional benefits. These characteristics are not unique to the South alone and indeed, in England a mix of cultural, political and economic objectives can be found in the deployment of ERPs (see Caglio *et al.*,2001).[8]

5. Conclusion

This chapter strongly supports the idea that culture should be taken seriously and we advocate that doing this requires an exploration of the notion of culture and a discussion of *how* culture should be taken seriously. Culture has been shown to be used in many different ways. However, this chapter argues that culture should not be seen as context, not as an entity, but as an accomplishment, which we need to recognize through the processes by which culture is enacted. Thus, change in culture is ongoing and the relationship with ICTs is one where ICTs can interact with and provide resources for a redefinition of culture. Equally, we should come to see ICTs as both cultural artefacts and a milieu, which enacts cultures at a distance. In other words, we should find that even apparently monolithic cultures (there are, of course, no such things) will change in relation to ICTs and that equally ICTs will change – they will be applied in a variety of differing ways. We can still talk about national cultures but we should tread carefully and look to see difference as well as homogeneity, change as well as apparent stability. This brings us to the second strand: *how* can cultures be taken seriously?

A sensitivity to cultural diversity is important, but what that means is a refinement in the researchers' observation of cause and effect. The upshot of our argument is that cultures are constantly being maintained and changing and therefore it is, in principle, possible to see effects of those processes at work. This requires careful observation as to what people say, what people do, and how technologies and people interact. But the labelling on which this observation depends arises from a process of being made to be aware of the subtleness of human interaction and the meanings that are placed on them. Therefore we need time and a willingness to understand and then *observe* so as to develop our own views as to what is culturally going on. The results of this process must be a reinterpretation of what was observed, but that aspect of investigation has to be accepted (see Latour, 1988). We must also accept that the products of our observations may themselves lead to cultural consequences. In short, any analysis of culture cannot be disentangled from issues of power relations and representation practices (see Westrup, 2002).

The modes of inquiry we adopt are likely to bring out different findings. As was mentioned earlier, a different view of culture surfaced when anthropologists started to engage in longitudinal ethnographic projects rather than single (though long) periods in a particular locality. Just as cultures are not disembodied, neither are the modes of engagement used in their exploration-changing modes of inquiry and using multiple modes are likely to be helpful. Multinational teams of researchers can be an important means of incorporating diversity of cultural outlook into observation and analysis. Nonetheless this approach has a friendly danger. It is probably too easy for us to consider ourselves experts in our own 'national' cultures when what we require is careful observation rather than culturally developed views of what is happening. Nonetheless multicultural teams offer one of the best ways to start addressing the issues: those familiar with the milieu should be able to investigate subtlety in cultural interactions while those unfamiliar with the milieu can draw attention to the aspects that are often taken for granted.

Arguably this chapter has addressed central themes in the investigation of ICTs in both North and South. We can see that theory and practice, modes of inquiry and findings, are intimately linked and that is something to be recognized and celebrated rather than viewed as a failing. As a final point, taking culture seriously should also imply that we see culture as one thread in a strand of different forms of inquiry. Culture should not be seen as an ultimate form of explanation but one that is intimately linked to what we call the social, political and economic aspects of people's lives and their relations with technologies.

Acknowledgements

We would like to thank the many people who have been helpful in giving their time and assistance in the case studies reported in this chapter. We are pleased to acknowledge the contribution of comments made by anonymous reviewers for the Bangalore 9.4 conference 2002 and the helpful points made by Shirin Madon.

Notes

1 The terms North and South are used to indicate the difference widely recognised, but difficult to formulate, between different parts of the world. Developed and developing; first and third world are possible alternatives though they are problematic in different ways: much depends on what form of analysis is used in relation to the thesis of globalisation (see Held *et al.,* 1999: 1-14).
2 A view, which Bell is said to be in complete agreement. The emphasis is in the original.
3 This book is an (edited) transcription of a series of annual debates held in Manchester by anthropologists; each debate centred on a different motion for discussion.
4 Wei Liu – as part of his PhD.
5 The details of this case come from fieldwork conducted in the summer of 2001 by Saheer Al Jaghoub as part of her PhD.
6 This fieldwork has been conducted by Heba El Sayed as part of her PhD.
7 A fictitious name.
8 Space does not permit any detail on the correspondences between North and South here. For a similar argument see Westrup (2000).

References

Al Jaghoub, S., (2001), International Organizations and ICTs for Development with Reference to Jordan, *Development Studies Annual Conference,* Manchester, September.

Al Jaghoub, S., and Westrup, C., (2002), Jordan and ICT led development: Towards a competition state? *Information Technology and People* forthcoming.

Avison, D., and Myers, M., (1995), Information systems and anthropology: an anthropological perspective on IT and organizational culture, *Information Technology and People*, 8(3): pp.43-66.

Barglow, R., (1994), *The Crisis of the Self in the Age of Information: Computers, Dolphins and Dreams,* London: Routledge.

Barrett, M., and Walsham, G., (1995), Managing IT for Business Innovation: Issues of Culture, Learning and Leadership in a Jamaican Insurance Company, *Journal of Global Information Systems*, 3 (3), pp. 25-33.

Bell, D., and Kennedy, B., (eds.), (2000), *The Cybercultures Reader*, London: Routledge.

Caglio, A., Jazayeri, M., Newman, M., Westrup, C., (2001) *ERP systems and Management Accountants* Final Report, London: CIMA.

Carrithers, M., (1992), *Why Humans have Cultures: Explaining Anthropology and Social Diversity*, Oxford: Oxford University Press.

Castells, M., (2000), *End of Millennium, Vol 3 of The Information Age: Economy, Society and Culture,* Oxford: Blackwell.

Castells, M., (1997), *The Power of Identity, Vol 2 of The Information Age: Economy, Society and Culture*, Oxford: Blackwell.

Castells, M., (1996), *The Rise of the Network Society, Vol 1 of The Information Age: Economy, Society and Culture*, Oxford: Blackwell.

Clifford, J., and Marcus, G., (eds.), (1986), *Writing Culture,* Berkeley, California: University of California Press.

Deal, T., and Kennedy, A., (1982), *Corporate Cultures: The Rites and Rituals of Corporate Life*, Reading Massachusetts: Addison-Wesley.

Du Gay, P., (ed.), (1997), *Production of Culture/Cultures of Production*, London: Sage.

Elger, T., and Smith, C., (1994), *Global Japanization? : the transnational transformation of the labour process,* Routledge: London.

El Sayed, H., (2001), Spacing, Timing and Enterprise Resource Planning Systems, *International Conference on Spacing and Timing: Rethinking Globalisation and Standardisation*, Palermo, November.

El Sayed, H., and Westrup, C., (2002), Egypt and ICTs: How ICTs bring national initiatives, global actors and local companies together, *Information Technology and People* forthcoming.

Featherstone, M., (ed.), (1990), *Global Culture: Nationalism, Globalisation and Modernity,* London: Sage.

Habermas, J., (1987), *The Theory of Communicative Action, Vol. 2, Lifeworld and Systems: A Critique of Functional Reason*, Boston, Massachusetts, Beacon Press.

Held, D., McGrew, A., Goldblatt, D., Perraton, J., (1999) *Global Transformations: Politics, Economics and Culture,* Cambridge: Polity.

Hendry, L., (1998), Applying world class manufacturing to made-to-order companies: problems and solutions, *International Journal of Operation and Production Management,* 16(11) pp. 1086- 1100.

Hofstede, G., (1980), *Culture's consequences: International Differences in Work-related Values,* Beverly Hill, California: Sage.

Hopper, T, Westrup, C, Jazayeri, M., (2000), World Class Manufacturing as Idealised Accountability: Tracing Ways Companies and the State aspire to become Competitive *Conference on Interdisciplinary Perspectives on Accounting,* Manchester, July.

Ingold, T., (ed.), (1996), *Key Debates in Anthropology*, London Routledge.

Kunda, G., (1991), Ritual and the Management of Corporate Culture: A Critical Perspective, *8th Standing Conference on Organizational Symbolism,* Copenhagen, June.

Kuper, A. (1999), *Culture: The Anthropologists' Account*, London: Harvard University Press.

Lash, S., (2001), Technological Forms of Life, *Theory, Culture and Society*, 18(1): pp. 105-120.

Latour, B., (1990), Drawing Things Together, in M. Lynch and S. Woolgar (eds.) *Representation in Scientific Practice,* Cambridge Massachusetts: MIT Press, pp. 19-68.

Latour, B., (1988), The Politics of Explanation; an Alternative in S. Woolgar (ed.), *Knowledge and Reflexivity: New Frontiers in the Sociology of Knowledge*, London: Sage, pp. 153-176.

Latour, B., (1987), *Science in Action,* Milton Keynes: Open University Press.

Law, J., (ed.), (1987), *Power, Action and Belief: A New Sociology of Knowledge?* London: Routledge and Kegan Paul.

McCrone, D., (1998) *The Sociology of Nationalism*, London: Routledge.

Myers, M., and Tan, F., (2002), Beyond models of national culture in information systems research, *Journal of Global Information Management,* 10(1): pp 24-33.

Peters, T., and Waterman, R., (1982), *In Search of Excellence: Lessons from America's best run Companies,* New York: Harper and Row.

Nusseir, Y. (2001), 'ICT Initiatives in Jordan: Needs and Aspirations', *National Information Centre*, Amman, Jordan, August.

REACH (2000), 'The Reach Initiative Launching Jordan's Software and IT Industry', A Strategy and Action Plan for H.M. King Abdullah II, Amman, Jordan, March. www.reach.jo/documents/reach.pdf (accessed January, 2002).

REACH 2.0 (2001), 'The Reach Initiative Launching Jordan's Software and IT Industry', An Updated Strategy and Action Plan for H.M. King Abdullah II, prepared by Int@j, Amman, Jordan, January, 2001. www.reach.jo/documents/final_reports/3-6-2001/a4.pdf (accessed January, 2002).

Turnbull, C., (1983), *The Mbuti Pygmies: Change and Adaptation*, New York: Holt, Rinehart and Winston.

Urry, J., (2000), *Sociology Beyond Societies: mobilities for the twenty-first century,* London: Routledge.

Walsham, G., (2000), *Making a World of Difference: IT in a Global Context*, London: Wiley.

Waters, M, (2001), *Globalization*, London: Routledge (2nd Edition).

Westrup, C., (2002), Discourse, Management Fashions, and ERP Systems, *IFIP 8.2 Conference,* Barcelona, December, forthcoming.

Westrup, C., (2000), What's in Information Technology? Issues in Deploying IS in Organizations and Developing Countries, in Avgerou, C., and Walsham, G., *Information Technology in Context: Studies form the Perspective of Developing Countries,* Aldershot: Ashgate Publishing.

Williams, R., (1981), *Culture*, Glasgow: Fontana.

Willmott, H., (1993), Strength is ignorance, slavery is freedom: managing culture in modern organizations, *Journal of Management Studies,* 30(4), pp. 515-552.

Chapter 2

Knowledge Perspectives on ICT and Development: What the Theory of Knowledge can Add

Justine Johnstone

1. Introduction

Knowledge is frequently invoked in academic and strategic literature on the relationship between information and communication technology (ICT) and development (see for instance World Bank 1998, CAS tells 2000, UNDP 2001), and international development agencies have put significant resources into knowledge initiatives with heavy emphasis on ICT. These include resources not only with a general knowledge focus, such as the Global Knowledge Partnership, the World Bank indigenous knowledge project and Global Development Gateway, and the G-8 Digital Opportunity Task Force (DOTForce), but also those aimed at knowledge in specific domains such as health, science, education, democracy and the environment. Knowledge and learning paradigms at the same time are becoming increasingly prevalent in regional, community and organisational development. Technology-based knowledge and information management practices are being adopted not just in developing-world public administration and commercial enterprises, but increasingly also in voluntary-sector aid and development organisations (Powell 1999, Madon 2000, Hunt 2000). As one researcher put it there is a '. . . powerful consensus . . . within the development communities of the South regarding the centrality of knowledge creation and diffusion, especially as mediated by ICT' (Mukherjee Reed 2001).

Despite the huge endorsement that knowledge has received and its centrality in development strategy, planning and practice, analysis and explanation have remained somewhat partial and fragmented. Compared with the creation of websites, databases, electronic lists and forums, real and virtual conferences and document archives, relatively little effort has gone into developing a theoretical understanding of knowledge and its interactions with development processes on the one hand and ICT on the other. Knowledge is not alone in this. A number of senior academics have diagnosed a general lack of theoretical development in our discipline (examples are Sahay and Walsham 1995, Avgerou and Walsham 2000). More recently, Richard Heeks has called for researchers in information systems and development to engage in theory-building and theory-based insights to guide development practice (Heeks 2001).

This paper argues that while much excellent and interesting work has been done in the area of knowledge, ICT and development, the field as a whole suffers – both theoretically and in practice – from lack of explicit engagement with the fundamental concept of knowledge. Higher-level theory to do with social, political and economic influences on the creation and exchange of knowledge, is better developed and more explicit. However, by bypassing fundamental theory, high-level approaches run the risk of assuming knowledge to be a more simple and unproblematic phenomenon than it is, and of proposing strategies that are consequently overoptimistic about what ICT on its own can accomplish.

The first section of this paper reviews a range of knowledge-based perspectives on ICT and development.[1] The second looks more closely at the concept of knowledge and delineates three key dimensions – informational, epistemic and conceptual. The latter two have received less attention but raise important issues for ICT initiatives. The final section sketches some implications for both theory and practice of taking seriously the epistemic and conceptual dimensions of knowledge.

2. Knowledge-Based Views of ICT and Development

A definite knowledge agenda is emerging in the field of ICT and development. At every level of analysis, whether global, national, regional, organisational or network, knowledge-based perspectives are being proposed as a way of better understanding and harnessing ICT in the service of development.

2.1 Macro-Level Change: Manuel Castells

Castells identifies knowledge and technology as key driving forces of economic and social change on a world-historical scale. Knowledge is central to development since knowledge gives mastery of technology, and technology 'embodies the capacity of societies to transform themselves' (Castells p7). However, the contemporary 'informational mode' of development intensifies this relationship, as knowledge becomes not only a means to mastering technology but also a product of that technology:

> In the new informational mode of development the source of productivity lies in the technology of knowledge generation, information processing and symbol communication. (Castells p17)

A virtuous circle of productivity is set up in which knowledge gives mastery of technology, which increases knowledge, which leads to better technology, which further increases knowledge, leading to yet better technology etc. Development is seen to hinge crucially on knowledge, but it is knowledge of a particular type – technological knowledge – and this knowledge inhabits a historical, networked 'space of flows' which Castells juxtaposes to the temporally and spatially rooted 'space of places' where meaning and identity reside. Developing countries are caught on the horns of a dilemma: enter the magic circle (if you are able) and face a loss of identity, or stay out and condemn yourself to a pernicious cycle of deepening exclusion.

2.2 International Development: The World Development Report

The World Bank has pushed hard to persuade governments and international agencies to adopt an economically based knowledge focus. Styling itself 'the knowledge bank' and taking on the role of 'knowledge broker', it is responsible for the most systematic and influential conceptual framework on the subject, the *World Development Report 1998-9: Knowledge for Development* (hereafter referred to as WDR). The WDR analysis is primarily a macro-economic view, less concerned with the nature of knowledge per se than its economic properties and the costs and benefits equations governing its creation, exchange and use.

WDR sees knowledge as a commodity or good, requiring effort and investment to create, but also having the two key properties of a public good, being 'nonrivalrous' (utility is not diminished by sharing) and 'nonexcludable' (people cannot be stopped from using it once it is in the public domain). These properties prevent creators from appropriating all the returns on their investment, leading to market failure and the undersupply of knowledge. ICT makes the communication of knowledge more efficient, increasing the problem, and therefore the need for intervention in the form of intellectual property rights (IPR) and public investment.

WDR does not offer a theory, definition or taxonomy of knowledge, but it identifies two kind of knowledge as specially important for development: knowledge about technology, broadly defined as practical 'know-how' (nutrition, birth control, software engineering and accountancy are the given examples) and commercially important knowledge (e.g. product quality or the creditworthiness of a firm).

For the WDR the key actors in overcoming knowledge and information problems are international development agencies and national governments, the former to provide public knowledge goods and act as intermediaries, the latter to implement knowledge promoting policies and ensure a good flow of high-quality commercially relevant information. In almost all these processes ICT is seen to play a central role.

WDR was and remains a watershed document – the first, and so far the only, attempt to articulate a detailed framework for conceptualising the relationship between knowledge, development and ICT. The WDR is not exhaustive in its treatment of knowledge, however, and some writers have suggested additional categories such as 'know-why', 'know-who' and 'knowing how to learn' (Wilson and Heeks 2000). The WDR analysis has also been criticized for paying little attention to the human activities and capacities involved in acquiring and using knowledge, both at the individual and at the social level, and for ignoring political and cultural factors and the role of civil society and the media (Panos 1998).

2.3 National, Regional and Community Development

Knowledge and learning paradigms are increasingly being applied to national, regional and community development and to efforts to increase organisational efficiency in developing countries (Mansell and Wehn 1998, Boekema 2000). These approaches focus largely on the relationship between knowledge and economic development, for instance the creation of infrastructure to enable local-level participation in the knowledge economy. Knowledge and knowledge-supporting technologies are seen to be part of this infrastructure.

O'Dubhchair, Scott and Johnson apply the learning paradigm within a broad view of community development. They propose a knowledge infrastructure consisting of 'the set of locally specific physical, informational, educational, organizational and cultural resources needed to facilitate community learning and action toward a desired collective future' (O'Dubhchair et al. 2001 p6). Three essential components are identified: public engagement, high-quality information, and ICT access and applications (including communication and collaboration support, community process and decision support, and systems to record community knowledge and memories).

Mukherjee Reed too, sees knowledge as a key factor in the relationship between ICT and community development but she argues that in marginalized communities the impact is most likely to be in terms of political empowerment (Mukherjee Reed 2001). Knowledge plays a central role but it is knowledge derived from opportunities for autonomous collective learning, from communication and collaboration, and from political action. Whether ICT becomes a liberating tool will depend on the ability of communities to use it for collective decision-making, practical action and the strengthening of collective identity.

2.4 Organisational Development

Another set of knowledge-based perspectives operates at the organisational level, explaining the connection between ICT and development through the potential of ICT to promote efficiency within organisations. Walsham in his recent book on the global context of IT (Walsham 2001) reviews four knowledge frameworks taken from organisational literature. These 'knowledge management' frameworks are concerned with issues such as harnessing and creating knowledge in organisations, promoting knowledge exchange among colleagues and cross-cultural knowledge sharing in work teams.

Although knowledge management developed in commercial enterprises, it has been imported into many development organisations (see for example Weaver Smith 1998, Denning 1998, Beguin and Estrada 1999). A recent workshop organized by Bellanet, the Benton Foundation, CIDA and IDRC identified three key knowledge management practices for development organisations: defining a knowledge strategy, developing a supporting infrastructure and building collaborative networks (Hunt 2000). The Internet and World Wide Web are seen as key technologies (Ball 1998, Saywell 1999, ECDPM 2000) and a range of tools and initiatives can be accessed online, including Global Knowledge Activity

Information Management System (GK-AIMS), community-building tools, electronic list management and the International Development Markup Language (IDML) initiative. Attempts have also been made to develop tools to analyse the impact of knowledge and information on development, notably by Menou (e.g. Menou 2000). The applicability of Northern-derived knowledge management practices to international development has, however, been questioned by van der Velden (2002) on the grounds that it treats knowledge as a 'rootless commodity', removed from the context of the knower and her social and material environment. Agrawal (1995) has similarly argued against the ex situ conservation of indigenous knowledge – ironically one of the main targets of the managerial approach.

Knowledge management typically treats knowledge as a means to an end, whether the end is competitive advantage or organisational efficiency more generally. But for development organisations knowledge is part of the task as well as the process, and a number of writers have recently started to pay attention to knowledge as a development output. Meyer argues that the economic role of development organisations is largely an informational one and analyses their activity in terms of information inputs and outputs (Meyer 1997). Powell sees development organisations as information-rich, and information activities as central to their goals (Powell 1999). He has recently proposed a more knowledge-orientated perspective (Powell 2001). A switch from project-based to information-based work has been advocated in non-governmental organisations (NGOs) (Edwards and Hughes 1992), and the information and learning roles of international NGOs have been stressed (Madon 2000). Chambers analyses some notable knowledge failures in development projects in terms of the distorting effect of power relations between 'uppers' and 'lowers', and advocates epistemic virtues such as honesty and trust as correctives (Chambers 1994).

2.5 Knowledge Networking: Vikas Nath

Nath (2000) adopts an Internet-inspired networking view that cuts other levels of analysis. He sees knowledge as a weapon against poverty and social disadvantage, and the falling cost of ICT holding out the promise of vastly increased knowledge resources to be harnessed for development purposes.

For Nath knowledge empowers individuals cognitively: ' . . . to think, to analyse and to understand the existing situation, and the inter-linkages and externalities of each action.' From cognition comes action, including political and economic action: 'Knowledge empowers an individual to form his or her own opinion, to act and transform conditions to lead to a better quality of life' (Nath 2000). All forms of knowledge are important, including traditional knowledge and, particularly, knowledge to help the poor improve their lot. Although knowledge exists in the minds of individuals, processes of knowledge sharing are crucial, defined as ' . . . the interactive process of making the right information available to people at the right time in a comprehensible manner to enable them to act judiciously' (Nath 2000).

In this view ICT is a driver of knowledge, breaking down barriers, promoting information and communication, enabling new economic forms, and empowering individuals and communities. Participatory and inclusive networks such as many found on the Internet allow people to 'harvest', customize and add value to data from many sources. Creating a knowledge society, however, requires a conducive environment that nurtures individual cognitive capacity and that recognizes the value of its outputs. Developing countries are rich in intellectual diversity but less good at providing a knowledge-conducive environment. Barriers of access, content, skills and language must be overcome; governments must deregulate, provide vision, strategy and infrastructure, and promote information-sharing; state and private sectors must collaborate on education and development; and developing countries must participate in international initiatives such as those of the World Bank, Global Knowledge Project and remote volunteering schemes.

3. Three Dimensions of Knowledge

As we have seen, knowledge-based approaches to ICT and development operate at different levels, employ different forms of social theory, address different audiences and actors, and prescribe different forms of intervention. All discuss aspects of knowledge relevant to their particular concerns, but none attempts to define knowledge itself or makes explicit reference to a theory of knowledge.[2] This makes it hard to identify common ground among the various approaches, evaluate them in knowledge terms, or build up an overall appreciation of how useful – or not – knowledge is as a perspective. In this section I now attempt to show how engaging directly with the theory of knowledge can contribute useful insights. The following section sketches some practical and theoretical implications.

Knowledge is contested territory and there are several theories on offer. The one that I present here is widely – but by no means exclusively – held within contemporary epistemology and cognitive science. It also resonates closely with commonsense and intuitive notions of knowledge such as those expressed by several authors referred to in section one (Panos and Nath are two cases in point). This is an essentially cognitive view, conceiving of knowledge as a state of mind.[3] Any theoretical discussion of knowledge, it must be pointed out, leads rapidly to complex and technical debates and a great deal of controversy. I believe, however, that it is possible to sidestep most of these while still benefiting from the insights on offer. The discussion below is intended simply to do this; it is in no sense a summary even of the cognitive view of knowledge and represents only a particular set of ideas in the field, albeit fairly mainstream ones.

Both analytic philosophy and cognitive psychology accord knowledge a central place and have studied it extensively, one at a conceptual and logical level, the other empirically. The two modes of enquiry can be seen as complementary and have a history of working together within the field broadly defined as cognitive science. For most analytic philosophers, in a tradition stretching back through Kant and Plato, knowledge involves being in a state of mind with a particular kind of representational content. Such mental states fall into the logical category of 'propositional attitudes' (Crane 1995). 'Propositional' refers to the logical status of the content that is represented in the mind (i.e. an idea that is either true or false) and 'attitude' to the type of mental state involved. Typically knowledge has been considered a special case of the attitude of belief – justified, true belief – but some recent philosophers have identified it with other propositional attitudes such as 'acceptance' ('belief aimed at truth' Lehrer 1990), or as a non-reducible factive state[4] in its own right (Williamson 2000).

Whatever the precise formulation, there is general agreement that knowledge crucially involves three things: having mental representations with propositional content; having a certain kind of attitude (belief, acceptance etc) towards the content; and the content being in some sense accurate, true, factual or right. I will call these, respectively, the conceptual dimension (because mental representations do not exist as single events but as organized conceptual structures), the epistemic dimension and the informational dimension. Any intervention aimed at producing knowledge must take account of all three dimensions. At the informational level, it must provide relevant, high-quality information whether in the form of direct experience or through communication. At the conceptual level, people must understand the information they receive, and form ideas on the basis of it. At the epistemic level, they must be able to judge correctly the degree of confidence to place in the ideas they form – treating a new idea with little evidential backing as a hypothesis, for example, but accepting a long-standing, frequently tested belief as a near certainty. The informational dimension is somewhat easier to deal with than the dimensions of understanding and epistemic judgement, which are processes internal to knowers and beyond any obvious form of measurement and control.[5] Not surprisingly, ICT interventions – even those claiming to be knowledge-based – tend to focus on information provision rather more than on conceptual and epistemic matters. Sometimes the informational dimension is confused with knowledge itself, for example when the claim is made that knowledge resides in artefacts such as databases and books.[6] This certainly makes knowledge look much easier to obtain, organize and distribute, but in terms of the three-dimensional view it is inadequate.

So how are we to develop a genuinely knowledge-based approach to ICT that does justice to all three dimensions? Philosophy and psychology not only give us a clearer concept of knowledge but provide many practical insights that can be brought to bear on how to tackle the epistemic and conceptual dimensions. A comprehensive discussion is beyond the scope of this paper but in the rest of this section I will indicate briefly some promising strands of work. The final section of the paper details some practical applications and the appendix outlines a skeleton framework based on the three-dimensional view.

3.1 The Epistemic Dimension

The epistemic dimension of knowledge is concerned with how people decide what 'credal attitude' to adopt towards a proposition – whether to accept it, reject it or believe it more or less likely. Traditional epistemology concentrates on abstract notions of justification through evidence and logical relationships between beliefs, but some recent work – particularly in the 'reliabilist' mould – has taken a naturalistic turn, focusing on actual processes of belief acquisition rather than logical relationships. For theorists such as Alvin Goldman beliefs are justified not by their relation to other beliefs (about evidence, for example) but by being formed by a particular kind of (reliable)[7] process (Goldman 1976, 1986). Goldman has recently used this to open up some new areas in epistemology, particularly in its social dimension, since social and communicative processes such as testimony and argumentation can be reliable (Goldman 1999).

Two factors make Goldman's approach attractive in the context of development. Firstly, it is a liberal position that makes no presuppositions about what kinds of processes are legitimate. Reliability is established through performance not a priori, so scientific method, for example, is not assumed superior to other types of thinking. Secondly, it incorporates a detailed descriptive element lacking in conventional epistemology, connecting it with the natural and social sciences and making it more readily applicable to practical situations than most epistemology.

For Goldman, we can acquire knowledge from other people, or from any source of information (including a computer), provided the process used is reliable. Various factors contribute to reliability, such as information about the source (e.g. the author's identity, credentials and possible motivation) and particularly its reputation and history of reliability, internal consistency, and external corroboration such as evidence, references and independent expert endorsements. Knowledge interventions, ICT-based or not, therefore have not only to provide high-quality primary information (relevant, timely, accurate etc) but to support users in obtaining secondary or meta-information to evaluate the primary information.

ICT applications have both strengths and weaknesses when it comes to reliability. The Internet supports two-way and even multiway communication, allowing users to interrogate informants directly and engage in public discussion. However factors such as anonymity, ease of publication and lack of editorial controls remove important tools familiar in conventional media. In such conditions, establishing and maintaining a reputation becomes crucial for web publishers, as do mechanisms to help users gauge reliability. The Development Gateway portal (www.developmentgateway.org), for example, identifies every contributor by name and email address, and in many cases provides biographical information.

A similar situation arises where ICT is used for drawing inferences rather than supporting communication. Decision support and expert systems do not straightforwardly yield beliefs and, like communication applications, still require users to decide what credal attitude to adopt towards the results they produce: how much confidence to place, say, in a computer-generated diagnosis. Since the logic of the software is not transparent to the user it can no more be directly evaluated than can the content of a website. Instead, as in the case of a website, other methods are needed to establish reliability, such as demonstrations, evidence and trust intermediaries in the form of experts prepared to endorse the system.

Whether ICT is used for communication or for inference, reliability is a crucial aspect of knowledge-functionality. While those who design and use ICT applications can never completely control the belief-forming process of users they can go a long way towards supporting it and ensuring that their products are as reliable as possible.

3.2 The Conceptual Dimension

Some new information fits comfortably into existing conceptual structures, yielding knowledge without much mental effort. Survey results, for instance, can tell us about AIDS awareness and sexual behaviour in a given population – assuming we already have concepts similar to those employed by the survey compiler. Other types of knowledge are more demanding, requiring acquisition, change or reorganisation of concepts. Trying to find an explanation for the survey results will probably require other concepts – perhaps self-esteem, identity, power or culture – to be brought into new and complex relationships with those of awareness and behaviour.

The conceptual dimension poses perhaps the biggest challenge to knowledge-for-development interventions, whether ICT-based or not. Current thinking about how humans develop and change their conceptual structures stresses two sets of factors: ecological (regularities in the world, the immediate environment and the interaction of an individual with the environment) and intellectual (the organisation of cognitive constructs) (McCauley 1987, Neisser 1987). Although debate continues about the relative importance of external and internal factors, it is widely accepted that concepts exist as linkages of explanatory or broadly theoretical knowledge structures (Murphy and Medin 1985, Keil 1989, Murphy 1993).

It is clear that important consequences follow for interventions aimed at increasing knowledge. If concepts and categories, the building blocks of thought (Van Mechelen et al. 1993), are a type of theory, then acquiring new knowledge may mean acquiring new theories, new ways of thinking about and understanding the world. To cope with this people need not just information but understanding of basic principles and relationships (Chi, Feltovich and Glaser 1981, Murphy and Wright 1984, Keil 1989).

In my work with AIDS groups in South Africa it was frequently this kind of implicit theoretical knowledge that was most sought after: knowledge of 'what works' and 'what to do'. Most often such ideas were acquired through face-to-face contact, seldom from written sources (except after personal contact had already been established) and never from electronic sources.

Ecological views perhaps provide a partial explanation. If concepts derive partly from interactions with a particular social and material environment, they may not be readily transferable to other environments, or not without significant adaptation. The understanding necessary for knowledge may need to be to some extent homegrown, not imported. Face to face contacts – of necessity taking place between people who share something of the same environment – may therefore have a natural advantage as a medium of conceptual change. This is not to say that

ICT does not have a central role to play. Real knowledge of this type – of what works in development and why – desperately needs to be made widely available but theory suggests that it may work better channelled through local intermediaries such as trainers and capacity-builders.

Equally important is knowledge of what does not work. Conceptual structures, as implicit theories, can be wrong and are in principle always revisable, yet careful analysis of mistakes and revisions seldom forms part of ICT knowledge initiatives. Analysis is in general much less a part of such projects than information provision but the conceptual dimension of knowledge shows how critical it is. Concepts and theories exist for the sake of cognitive economy: it is much harder work for a practitioner to draw conclusions from case studies than to read a good analysis of the evidence. If databases and archives are to become real knowledge resources they need to promote the place of analytical and conceptual work.[8]

Sensitivity to the conceptual dimension also means being aware that some types of knowledge are much harder to acquire than others. Conceptual structures can be highly resistant to change and there may be social as well as epistemological matters at stake, especially where concepts represent broad modes of understanding that are widely shared and an important part of social identity.

4. Implications for Theory and Practice

How does an understanding of knowledge derived from philosophy and psychology help us to understand and use ICT better? In several ways, I believe, including improving existing theory, developing more effective practice, generating new theory and suggesting directions for research. Some examples are briefly outlined below.

4.1 Improving Existing Theory

The theory of knowledge, in particular an appreciation of the epistemic and conceptual dimensions, provides an explanatory foundation for many insights expressed, sometimes as unsupported assertions, in the literature on ICT and development. Considering what is involved in epistemic judgement and conceptual development and change, for example, makes it clear why Panos (1998) and Nath (2000) are right in emphasising the cognitive effort involved in knowledge acquisition. Understanding that concepts embody theories provides an explanatory basis for Wilson and Heeks's assertion that know-why is as important as know-how (Wilson and Heeks 2000). Van der Velden's stress on the personal and social context of the knower (van der Velden 2002) is supported both by the complexity of epistemic judgement and the role of environmental factors in concept development. In other cases some of the things that increasingly get thrown into the bag of 'knowledge' might turn out not to belong there once we start to make more rigorous demands of theory. Skills, practices, the know how without know why advocated in WDR – all may need to fight harder for a place in a genuinely knowledge-based approach. Without a basic theory of knowledge, however, we are not in a position to say what does and does not belong.

4.2 Implications for Practice

For Castells, the WDR and many others, it is a matter of urgency that more equitable access to global knowledge be provided. The theory of knowledge tells us that this means not just access to information, publications or technologies, but also access to underlying concepts in terms of which global knowledge is represented, and access to inferential processes and trusted intermediaries. Concepts, as structures of explanation and understanding, are not necessarily easy to assimilate: they require cognitive effort, they may conflict with existing valued and useful concepts, and if they originate from a specialist or technical discipline they may bear little relation to the world as it is perceived. New concepts do not arrive into a vacuum, and research indicates that interventions need to be based on an understanding of local theories of the domain (Murphy 1993). This is not good news for high-tech, low-labour solutions since it suggests that there is an absolutely critical role to be played by (human) knowledge intermediaries in bridging divides that are not just digital but cognitive.

The typical Internet strategy of 'publish once, for everyone' followed by sites such as the Development Gateway – embodying the principles of WDR and set up in its wake – appears limited in terms of the conceptual dimension of knowledge. A sounder strategy might ally such a project with initiatives geared to specific local audiences and run by those with knowledge of both local and global conceptual realms, or alternatively aim not at everyone but at key intermediaries in different local settings. Either way, connections have to be forged between local and global knowledge structures. ICT can help, but conceptual change requires large inputs of cognitive effort and imagination that can be supplied only by humans.

Knowledge theory also provides a way of looking critically at the content of portals and websites. At present most provide more of an informational service to users than a conceptual service, focusing on archives of web links, searchable databases and so on, and often using categories reflecting institutional and informational concepts rather than user-functional ones.[9] From our theory, we can see that a knowledge-portal model would need critically to include audience research (to determine existing conceptual structures) and also to provide analytical and explanatory content as well as information services such as databases.

Another practical application is the way in which the theory of knowledge highlights the centrality of human knowers, often underplayed in ICT-based initiatives (van der Velden 2002). Knowledge management seems particularly keen to decouple knowledge from conscious knowing subjects. Blackler (1995) identifies five phenomena referred to as knowledge in this literature only one of which includes all three dimensions – informational, epistemic and conceptual. Of the five, one is purely informational and includes books and databases, a particularly dangerous trap for development practice since it suggests that knowledge can be handed out as easily as paper or software, or perhaps even medicines or machines. Knowledge interventions, theory teaches us, demand a much more complex and considered response, and have to be evaluated in terms of more demanding criteria.

4.3 Generating New Theory

Basic-level theory can also help to generate new analytical and conceptual tools in higher-level domains. The three dimensions of knowledge, for instance, provide the basis of a new way of looking at development work as knowledge work. A start has already been made by writers like Meyer who highlights the informational roles of development organisations, and Chambers whose work on error shows the importance of the epistemic dimension. The three-dimensional model indicates how these insights could be expanded to build a rigorous knowledge-based analysis of development work and a better-grounded understanding of the role of ICT in such work.

4.4 New Research Directions and Interdisciplinary Working

Research is still in its infancy in the areas of knowledge organisation and structure, human inferential processes, conceptual development, conceptual change, and the individual and social factors affecting such processes. The first section of this paper illustrated that there is a clear knowledge agenda in the field of ICT in developing countries, and suggests an opportunity to participate in this. With their emphasis on real-world research, access to many different contexts, and particular interest and involvement in knowledge work, researchers in ICT and development are well placed to contribute to interdisciplinary research on knowledge. But that will be possible only by engaging with the cognitive as well as the social sciences.

5. Conclusion

In this chapter I have tried to put the case for basic-level theory and deeper analysis of the concept of knowledge, and to show how philosophy and psychology of knowledge can be used to illuminate some aspects of thinking about ICT and development. In doing so it has been impossible to do justice to the depth and complexity of either contemporary epistemology or cognitive psychology. The three-dimensional view of knowledge must be seen as an outline only of some fundamental factors and in no way a full description. Equally, it has been impossible to draw out the implications of this view of knowledge at all the different levels of analysis outlined in section one. I hope, however, that the examples given will indicate the benefits of a more analytical approach to knowledge, and how it might be applied.

ICT interventions clearly face a greater challenge in dealing with the epistemic and conceptual dimensions of knowledge than with the informational dimension. Communication applications have a critical role to play, but good reasoning and conceptual development do not automatically happen as by-products of communication. New ways of understanding come about in particular types of interactions, often demanding in terms of human inputs and not easily automated or produced for mass consumption. Understanding these interactions and designing technical systems to support them pose a challenge on the one hand to engage with other disciplines and on the other to do more research and evaluation ourselves.

Some may be tempted to write knowledge off as too long a way round when confronted with urgent development problems, especially if it means going in for conceptual change as well as information provision. Everett Rogers argues along these lines, advocating social and emotional persuasion in place of explaining the germ theory of disease when it comes to getting people to boil their drinking water (Rogers 1995). I believe this is the wrong response. Knowledge, for all its difficulty, matters profoundly. Persuasion without explanation may be an effective way to change specific behaviour[10] but unless people eventually come to understand what they are doing and why, the benefits remain highly restricted and the behaviour rigid.[11] The proliferation of knowledge-based approaches to ICT and development is, I believe, something to be welcomed. It is also something to be treated with care. Theory of knowledge is both difficult and controversial but if we are to make such extensive use of the concept we do not have the option of ignoring the theory.

Appendix

Table 2.1 Three-Dimensional Framework for Knowledge-Based Interventions

Key theoretical factors	Examples in practice
INFORMATIONAL DIMENSION	
Relevance	Local content
Accuracy	Editorial controls
Timeliness	Frequent updates
Appropriate	Accessible language, formats
Comprehensive	Reviews of content
Organized	Sorting, searching, filtering functions
EPISTEMIC DIMENSION	
Source identity	Named authors, contributors, editors
Authority	Details of qualifications and experience
Evidence	Primary material, cross-references
Transparency	Explanation of aims and methods
Motives and interests	Named publishers, funders
Trust	Local authorities; expert endorsements
Knowledge of audience	Audience research

Sender-receiver interaction Public debate	Email Bulletin boards, electronic conferencing
CONCEPTUAL DIMENSION Existing theories of domain Social and material environment Cognitive economy Conceptual change User needs	 Categories users understand Local intermediaries; local content Analysis of content 'Bridging' explanations of new concepts New ways of looking at problems

Notes

1 I will be restricting the discussion to literature relating knowledge to a general conception of development, since it is impossible to do justice to the extensive literatures on knowledge in specific domains such as health, education, agriculture and commerce.

2 Some, such as WDR, do draw explicitly on theories *about* knowledge (in the case of WDR economic theory), but this is not the same as a theory *of* knowledge, which would require at the very least some kind of definition or conceptual analysis.

3 Opposition to the cognitive view comes from behavioural psychology and behaviourally based epistemologies such as those of Craig (1990).

4 A factive state is a mental state – such as seeing, knowing or remembering – that applies only to facts. One cannot, for example, remember something that did not happen (this would be *mis*remembering).

5 The theory of knowledge shows the term 'knowledge management' to be a misnomer since knowledge resides exclusively in minds. Strictly speaking, it is only some products and resources of knowledge that are amenable to management.

6 Books and databases involve external representations, whereas knowledge is an internal representation. The two constantly interact in real life but are conceptually distinct (Billman 1999).

7 A reliable process is simply one that, when working properly, consistently delivers true beliefs – such as vision or memory but not wishful thinking or consulting your horoscope.

8 One portal that does this is the Communication Initiative (www.comminit.com), which has separate sections for analytical and theoretical material.

9 The Development Gateway has tackled the problem by creating multiple systems of categorisation. It originally listed resources only by editorial category ('Statistics', 'Documents', 'Tools', 'Publications') but now also incorporates a thematic taxonomy – such as 'Treatment', 'Prevention' and 'Funding' on the HIV/AIDS page. The problem now is the need for subcategories as some of the main categories contain more than 100 resources (listed in order of submission date).

10 There is no suggestion that behaviour performed for social and emotional reasons is any less stable than that with a basis in understanding.

11 This by no means applies only in the context of development – see Deutsch (1997), for example, on the role of explanation in science, and its superiority even over predictive success.

Bibliography

Agrawal, A. (1995) Dismantling the Divide Between Indigenous and Scientific Knowledge. *Development and Change* 26 pp. 413-439.

Avgerou, C. and Walsham, G. (eds.) (2000) *Information Technology in Context*, Ashgate, Aldershot, UK.

Ball, A. (1998) A Survey of Collaborative Internet Technologies. Document produced for IDRC Unganisha Project.
http://www.idrc.ca/unganisha/document/collab

Beguin, J-P. and Estrada, J.A. (1999) IDB Knowledge Exchange Network
http://www.bellanet.org/km/main/KEN.pdf

Billman, D. (1999) Representations. Bechtel, W. and Graham, G. (eds.) *A Companion to Cognitive Science*. Oxford: Blackwell.

Blackler, F. 1995. Knowledge, Knowledge Work and Organizations: An Overview and Interpretation. *Organization Studies*, 16 (6) pp.1021-1046.

Boekema, F. (ed.) (2000) *Knowledge, innovation and economic growth: the theory and practice of learning regions*. Cheltenham: Edward Elgar.

Castells, M. (2000) *The Information Age: Economy Society and Culture. Vol. I The Rise of the Network Society*. (2nd edition.) Oxford: Blackwell.

Chambers, R. (1994) All Power Deceives. *IDS Bulletin* Vol. 25, no. 2.

Chi, M.T., Feltovich, P.J. and Glaser, R. (1981) Categorization and representation of physics problems by experts and novices. *Cognitive Science* 5, pp.121-152.

Craig, E. (1990) *Knowledge and the State of Nature: An Essay in Conceptual Synthesis*. Oxford: Clarendon Press.

Crane, T. (1995) *The Mechanical Mind: A Philosophical Introduction to Minds, Machines and Mental Representation*. London: Penguin.

Denning, S. (1998) Building Communities of Practice, Knowledge Management – Lessons from the Edge. World Bank.
http://www.store.apqc.org/other/PDFs/Denning.pdf

Deutsch, D. (1997) *The Fabric of Reality*. London: Allen Lane.

ECDPM (2000) *Investing in Knowledge: Sharing Information Resources on the Web*. Infobrief No. 3. Maastricht: ECDPM.

Edwards, M. and Hulme, D. (1992) *Making a Difference: NGOs and Development in a Changing World*. London: Earthscan.

Goldman, A. (1976) Discrimination and Perceptual Knowledge. *Journal of Philosophy* 73: pp.771-91.

Goldman, A. (1986) *Epistemology and Cognition*. Cambridge Massachusetts: Harvard University Press.

Goldman, A. (1999) *Knowledge in a Social World*. Oxford: Oxford University Press.

Heeks, R. (2001) "What Did Giddens and Latour Ever Do For Us?": Academic Writings on Information Systems and Development. IDPM, University of Manchester, UK.

Hintikka, J. (1983) *The Game of Language*. Dordrecht: Reidel.

Hintikka, J. and Hintikka, M.B. (1989) *The Logic of Epistemology and the Epistemology of Logic*. Dordrecht: Kluwer Academic.

Hunt, P. (ed.) (2000) *Knowledge Mangement: Implications and Applications for Development Organizations.* Report of a workshop co-organised by Bellanet International Secretariat, the Benton Foundation, the Canadian Development Agency (CIDA), and the International Development Research Centre (IDRC). Benton Foundation: Washington. http://www.bellanet.org/km

Keil, F.C. (1989) *Concepts, Kinds and Cognitive Development.* Cambridge MA: MIT Press.

Lehrer, K. (1990) *Theory of Knowledge.* London: Routledge.

McCauley, R. N. The Role of Theories in a Theory of Concepts. Neisser, U. (ed.) (1987) *Concepts and Conceptual Development: Ecological and Intellectual Factors in Categorization.* Cambridge: Cambridge University Press.

Madon, S. (2000) International NGOs: Networking, Information Flows and Learning. Manchester: Institute for Development Policy and Management, University of Manchester. http://www.man.ac.uk/idpm/idpm_dp.htm#devinf_wp

Mammo, T. (1999) *The Paradox of Africa's Poverty.* Lawrenceville and Asmara: Red Sea Press.

Mansell, R. and Wehn, U. (1998) *Knowledge Societies: Information Technology for Sustainable Development.* United Nations. Oxford: Oxford University Press.

Menou, M. (2000) Toward a Conceptual framework for Learning about ICTs and Knowledge in the Process of Development. Draft document prepared for GK-LEAP. http://www.bellanet.org/gkaims/documents/docs/LEAP

Meyer, C. (1997) The Political Economy of NGOs and Information Sharing. *World Development* 25 (7).

Mukherjee Reed, A. (2001) Knowledge, Work and Human Development: What Technology Can and Cannot Do. Unpublished paper.

Murphy, G.L. (1993) Theories and Concept Formation. Van Mechelen, I., Hampton, J., Michalski, R.S. and Theuns, P. (eds.) *Categories and Concepts: Theoretical Views and Inductive Data Analysis.*

Murphy, G.L. and Medin, D.L. (1985) The Role of Theories in Conceptual Coherence. *Psychological Review* 92: pp. 289-316.

Murphy, G.L. and Wright, J.C. (1984) Changes in Conceptual Structure with Expertise: Difference Between Real-World Novices and Experts. *Journal of Experimental Psychology: Language, Memory and Cognition* 10: pp. 144-55.

Nath, V. (2000) Heralding ICT Enabled Knowledge Societies. Sustainable Development Networking Programme.
http://sdnp.delhi.nic.in/resources/internetinfo/articles/heralding.htm

Neisser, U. (ed.) (1987) *Concepts and Conceptual Development: Ecological and Intellectual Factors in Categorization.* Cambridge: Cambridge University Press.

O'Dubhchair, K., Scott, J.K. and Johnson, T.G. (2001) Building a Knowledge Infrastructure for Learning Communities, *Electronic Journal of Information Systems in Developing Countries.* 4 (4) pp.1-21.

Panos (1998) *Information, Knowledge and Development.* Panos Perspective Paper.

Powell, M. (1999) *Information Management for Development Organisations.* Oxford: Oxfam.

Powell, M. (2001) Information, Knowledge and Development. Conference paper delivered at DSA Annual Conference, Manchester, September 2001.

Rogers, E.M. (1995) *Diffusion of Innovations.* (4th edition.) New York: The Free Press.

Sahay, S. and Walsham, G. (1995) Information technology in developing countries: a need for theory building, *Information Technology for Development*, 6(3/4), pp.111-124.

Saywell, D. (1999) Electronic Conferencing and On-Line Dialogue for Development Purposes. Paper delivered at Global Knowledge Network Conference, Bonn, December 1999. http://orion.forumone.com/gdnet/files.fcgi/52_Saywell.doc

UNDP (2001) *Human Development Report.* New York: Oxford University Press.

Van der Velden, M. (2002) Knowledge Facts, Knowledge Fiction: The Role of ICTs in Knowledge Management for Development. *Journal of International Development* 14, pp.25-37.

Van Mechelen, I., Hampton, J., Michalski, R.S. and Theuns, P. (eds.) (1993) *Categories and Concepts: Theoretical Views and Inductive Data Analysis.* London: Academic Press.

Walsham, G. (2001) *Making a World of Difference: IT in Global Context.* Chichester: John Wiley and Sons.

Weaver Smith, B. (1998) Knowledge Management and the Social Sector http://www.smithweaversmith.com/kmand.htm

Williamson, T. (2000) *Knowledge and its Limits.* Oxford: Oxford University Press.

Wilson, G. and Heeks, R. (2000) Technology, Poverty and Development. Allen, T. and Thomas, A. (eds.) *Poverty and Development into the 21st Century.* Oxford: Oxford University Press.

Chapter 3

IT as an Institutional Actor in Developing Countries

Chrisanthi Avgerou

1. Introduction

In a recent article in the journal of *Information Systems Research*, Orlikowski and Iacono (2001) list four different ways IT is conceptualized in the research that has been published in that journal. Namely, IT has been viewed as a computational mechanism that executes an algorithm or follows the logic of a model, IT is considered a tool that contributes to certain outcomes; IT is conceptualized by proxy, i.e. in terms of some particular aspects assumed important enough to be taken as surrogate measures, such as invested money; IT is seen as an ensemble of technical artefacts and socio-economic structures and activities.

In this chapter I discuss a particular perspective of IT as an ensemble of technical and social entities; I suggest seeing IT as an institutional actor. Specifically, I consider IT as a heterogeneous actor that involves artefacts with certain functionality 'black boxed', professional practices, as well as industries, policies and regulations. I use here the notion of institution mainly as elaborated by organizational theorists to mean historically developed patterns of social actions and relations, which have acquired a taken-for-granted meaning, value, and significance and are not subject to technical/rational considerations (Powell and DiMaggio 1991). Institutions are established, sustained, and changed through a mix of technical, symbolic, and political mechanisms. To consider something as an institution means to pay attention to such aspects as the myths and visions that have captured the imagination of its participant actors, the mechanisms that perpetuate the norms of actors behaviour, the regulatory regimes that support what is considered to be normal behaviour, the fads and fashions that circulate imaginary modes of existence as a necessity, as well as the subjugated voices either whispered or loudly shouted in opposition to the dominant legitimate structures and practices.

The study of organizations as institutions point out institutional features formed either at the macro-societal or at the organizational levels of analysis. Within an organization the circumstances of its genesis and establishment, the visions of powerful personalities of past leaders, its perceived mission, its patterned routine everyday activities, its fragmented improvisations, and its power dynamics are elements seen at least as important as its explicitly and declared rational decision making and action processes that apply formal technical expertise. Within the broader social context institutional forces include communities' cultural aspects such as the sense of collective identity, social structures such as trade union shaping and representation of collective interests, cognitive shaping mechanisms such as education, professional training, and media influences, and regulatory frameworks such as fair competition national and international legislation.

Institutional analysis points also to the interrelation among institutions. Organizations such as the competing firms of an industry, their supplier and client enterprises, and the financial and service companies that support them influence each other, forming 'organizational fields' of similar practices and structures. More generally, the historical context of a particular society comprises multiple interacting institutions, either mutually re-enforcing each other, or in a state of friction. Historically, IT has been institutionalized internationally in close alliance with management, that is with a particular rationality of organizing which emerged as an institution in its own right in the contemporary advanced economies of Western societies. Moreover, the institutionalization of IT in developing countries in particular, has been associated with the institutional forces of 'development' as a distinct ideology of desirable conditions of life worldwide, and a set of international and national organizations that put such an ideology in action.

The institutionalist theoretical perspective followed in this paper contributes to the stream of social theory informed IS studies, building upon and complementing the ongoing research based on structurational and social constructionist approaches. In relation to structurational analysis, this paper highlights the significance of and suggests a way of accounting for the structural background that is the source of the rationality of actors' behaviour in IT innovation situations (Orlikowski and Barley 2001). In relation to the social constructionist perspectives, the view of IT as an institutional actor in negotiation with the various other actors involved in particular IS innovation processes has of course resonance with Actor Network Theory (ANT). But unlike most ANT studies in information systems so far, I am interested in the hybrid nature of IT as a network of actors that includes artefacts, but also institutionalized practices and ideals. Such a shifting of emphasis onto the structural aspects of the social context within which agents enact IS innovation processes and artefacts are circulated with black-boxed inscriptions that are perceived to have particular value is intended to provide conceptual tools that sensitive research to the significance of the interaction among social contexts. This, I believe is of paramount importance for the IS innovation efforts in developing countries.

I should also add a caveat at the outset of this paper. The following analysis highlights the institutional character of IT and refers to developing countries generically. It should be noted that information technologies vary significantly in terms of flexibility and malleability. Similarly, particular country circumstances vary in terms of the extent to which they have developed indigenous IT industries that are oriented towards indigenous innovation needs and professional know-how attuned to local organizational structures and cultures.[1] The institutional analysis suggested here has a general theoretical validity because of the extent to which in the current context of globalization, new technologies, bounded with ideals of organizing, tend to originate in advanced industrialized countries and circulated worldwide – even though subsequently they are subject to local adaptations and hybridizations.

The structure of this paper is as follows. I first discuss the micro and macro-level aspects that comprise the institutional character of IT, management and development. I then examine some of the implications of the alignment of IT with management and development for the IS implementation efforts made in the setting of organizations in developing countries. I draw examples from the literature and I use a case study conducted for the purposes of a postgraduate dissertation at the London School of Economics (Toukan 2001) to demonstrate such implications.

Finally, it has often been suggested that research concerning IT in developing countries should go beyond mere theorizing. While I believe that theoretical analysis is of paramount importance in order to understand the complex issues of IT innovation in the contemporary conditions of globalization, I share the opinion that the pressures faced by developing countries in a fast changing world create an obligation for academics to reflect on the implications of theoretical analysis for practice. Thus, in the concluding section of this paper I discuss the consequences of the institutionalist analysis for the communities of IS research and practice.

2. The Institutional Character of IT, Management, and Development

2.1 IT as an Institution

From an institutional point of view, IT is not seen as a set of material products functioning according to the technical rules embedded in their physical components, but as such products being part of social networks and embedded in social institutions. From such a perspective it is significant that IT has captured the hopes and fears of people in their professional roles as well as in their personal lives. IT occupies a central position in the discourse of socio-economic change, such as on post-industrial society (Bell 1973), information society (Webster 1995) or globalization (Giddens 1990). Such discourse provides an underlying rationale about the value of IT innovation; indeed it is so powerful that it creates a sense of inevitability regarding IT innovation. Although the merits of particular information systems may be fiercely contested within organizations the generic value of continuous IT innovation has become a 'rational myth'.

In the study of information systems a stream of studies has contributed to the understanding of IT innovation as a combination of technical tasks and social negotiations. Some authors examined these as processes of institutionalization; see for example (Silva and Backhouse 1997; van der Blonk 2000). Technical tasks to a large extent, serve institutional purposes rather than constituting a formal/rational way of addressing technology innovation. Two examples suffice here to demonstrate this point, the use of methodologies in systems development practice and methodical evaluation (Avgerou 2000). There has been little research on the extent to which systems development methodologies contribute to building systems that serve better the needs of an organization. But the effort to systematize technical practice with methodologies made possible the professionalization of systems development by assigning technical roles such as the analyst, the designer, the project manager, or the programmer with predefined skills (Avgerou and Cornford 1993). They are used for training of large numbers of 'experts' required to sustain a booming industry. They established rules of 'good practice' to develop a system, without having to assess results. Indeed, it is well known that formal information systems evaluation is rarely practised, and when it is, it may only be to legitimize decisions on systems development which have already been made on the basis of intuition and often vested actor interests, rather than the technical merits of a particular IT innovation (Farbey, Land *et al.* 1993).

Following further the institutional perspective, many authors elaborated on concepts and theories for the study of IT as embedded in an organization's internal institutional setting. They pointed out that IT implementation and use is part of the situated sense making and enactment of the roles people assume in their everyday life in the organization (Walsham 1993; Ciborra and Lanzara 1994; Suchman 1994; Orlikowski 2000). This stream of research, has linked IS research with social theory and now constitutes a highly visible, and hopefully influential, direction in IS studies, see for example (Orlikowski and Barley 2001).

Less theoretical attention has been given in IS research to the way the information systems that are embedded in organizational practice are linked with macro-institutional characteristics of IT. Such macro-level institutional aspects of IT include the formation and spread of the rational myths that sustain and promote its ever more pervasive spread in all domains of human activities and all localities, the legitimate objectives and practices of organized social entities dedicated to its diffusion, the professional norms, the macro-level power dynamics among various industrial and political/administrative entities and the various coercive mechanisms deployed by them.

There is, of course, a substantial literature on the macro-level processes that are implicated in IT innovation and diffusion in other fields, mostly in economics and government policy. Drawing from such studies, King *et al* (1994) list a number of sources of institutional forces at the macro-societal innovation. They include government authorities; international agencies; professional, trade and industry associations; research centres; trend-setting powerful domestic or multinational corporations; financial institutions; labour organizations; and religious institutions. Such entities – institutions in their own right – exert influence or enact regulation that affects market supply and demand.

Of these, particular attention has been given to national government policy. In most cases such policies have a double concern to that of assisting the exploitation of industrial potential in producing technologies and services, and of promoting the use of the new technology in order to achieve beneficial economic and social effects. A mutual re-enforcement of innovation in production and use is assumed: the development of a local IT industry enables widespread and innovative usage of technologies, while the demand that is created from widespread use is also beneficial for the local industry.

Addressing the action of particular types of organizations, such as government agencies, in the macro-dynamics of innovation does not necessarily imply recognition of institutional forces. Most policy analyses guiding government action on technology innovation are exercises of technical economic theory, for example many of the chapters included in the volumes (Dosi, Freeman *et al.* 1988; Foray and Freeman 1993).

In contrast, some analyses of macro-level innovation processes elaborate on the social, cultural and political aspects of the entities involved. One such example is the literature that emphasizes the significance of cultural conditions, such as trust and socially acquired tacit knowledge, for the cumulative learning involved in successful 'national systems of innovation' (Lundvall 1988; Lundvall 1992). Another example is the study of R&D initiatives launched by national and international government agencies as networks formed by the mobilization of powerful actors (Callon, Laredo *et al.* 1997). The political dimension of the macro-level institutions of ICT innovation has been prominent in the history of innovation of most countries and regions. A good example is the friction between the two government agencies that have orchestrated ICT innovation in Japan in the last three decades of the twentieth century (King, Gurbaxani *et al.* 1994). Another case with clear political dimensions is the launching of collaborative R&D programmes in Europe, analysed by Cram (1997).

What, however, is less often attempted is to link the internal institutional processes of IT innovation in specific organizational settings with macro-level institutional analysis of ideology, normativity, coercion, and large scale power dynamics. The situated organizational analyses of IS do not usually trace the logic of actors behaviour to their lives beyond the organizational boundaries and do not consider the way the route of an innovation process is imagined, legitimated, imposed, or enforced by extra-organizational forces.

There are some notable exceptions. Swanson and Ramiller have argued that institutional forces play a significant role in shaping the perception of organizational opportunities for the exploitation of IT, what they call an 'organizing vision' (Swanson and Ramiller 1997). Information systems innovation is partly a matter of interpretation of the potential benefits and risks entailed by a technology for the organization concerned, and partly a matter of sharing a vision about such potential with a wider inter-organizational community. Various forces contribute to the formation of common visions about IT uses and associated organizational changes. Among them Swanson and Ramiller include the rhetoric and interventions of macro-level institutions, the practices and language of information systems professionals, the practice of business and management.

More systematic studies of linking organizational with broader institutional forces are found in the literature of IS in developing countries. A stream of contextualist research emerged in the 1990s, which associates lo action with broader institutional forces, see for example (Madon 1993; Walsham 1993; Walsham 2001; Bada forthcoming), and it is to this tradition that this paper is intended to contribute.

2.2 Management as an Institution

Management too has an institutional character. One of the most prevalent features of organizations in the western world at the beginning of the 21st century is that they are governed through a particular professional rationality oriented towards efficiency in a free market environment. Management is taken-for-granted as a rational way of steering action not only in business organizations, but increasingly also in any other social domain. Unlike other forms of governing, for example through the command of the proprietors of organizations, or through a system of political command, management is considered the most suitable way to promote the fundamental principles of economic growth in the capitalist system, mainly efficiency and continuous innovation.

In organizational theory and management studies, it is assumed that management emerged as the dominant feature of modern organizations because of its fitness to the capitalist economic system, and gained its prevalence because of its proven superiority in relation to alternative forms of governing (Chandler 1962; Chandler 1969). Institutionalist analyses challenge this view, and show management as a system of meanings that has been created through the course of specific historical events. Such an institutionalist view is substantiated best by Shenhav (1999). He studied the American manufacturing industry in the period between 1880 and 1932, to answer the question of how professional managerial rationality became the almost undisputed way of running business organizations and, more recently, an all pervasive rationality for reforming non-business organizations, such as state administration, or military services. The answer, his analysis suggests, lies in the efforts of mechanical engineers to enhance and safeguard the interests of their professional position situated in the American political context of the turn of the 19th century.

In effect, in the USA mechanical engineers managed to secure their expertise on machines as an appropriate basis of organizing business organizations, in particular large corporations. The principles of systematization and standardization, first established – against voices of opposition – as the 'rational' way to produce mechanical parts, gradually won legitimacy as appropriate means for organizing work efficiently. Shenhav's research of the major engineering journals of that period provides evidence that making the engineering principles the 'scientific' principles of organizing did not happen smoothly. It faced opposition within the circles of engineers, and, more importantly, by the business owners. It also took place against serious and long lasting labour unrest.

Shenhav attributes a critical significance for the establishment of engineering principles as the core logic of professional management to two political characteristics of the American social context: exceptionalism and progressivism. Exceptionalism refers to the American nationalist ideology of the

19th century, which entertained a belief of uniqueness and superiority stemming from the circumstances of the late creation of the country on principles of 'rationality', liberalism and democracy and the values of affluence and broad opportunity. Shenhav argues that the engineering professionals both reinforced and capitalized from this ideology. They sustained the view that American manufacturing was superior to that of Europe in terms of worker productivity, machinery, and organization of business.

Progressivism was a widespread ideology in the first 17 years of the twentieth century, aspiring to revitalize the democratic values and restore equality through a pragmatic culture of pursuing efficiency, expertise, and systematic organization. It was believed that America could avoid political conflict and serve the needs of all. The progressivist ideology legitimized the roles of professionals, and engineers were well positioned to present their expertise on systematization and efficiency as tools capable of taking the industry beyond chaos and to create prosperity for all. In short, progressivism allowed the engineering instrumental rationality to expand to human, social, political and economic affairs. Management systems were seen as solutions to labour unrest and political instability. Organizations could be engineered and perfected as mechanical systems. And this is what Frederic Taylor did with 'scientific management'.

Thus, what resulted from the social contest within a particular political culture was reified as a rational practice of universal validity. Concepts, such as efficiency, maximization, standardization, that were promoted by a social group trying to claim legitimacy for their expansion into organizing activities, acquired the status of objective, rational organizational norms. Since the 1980s there has been a strong tendency throughout the world to transfer managerial rationality in all kinds of organizations, including government administration, the military, and agencies such a universities which have had their own organizational logic. Public management became a platform for public sector reform in most countries (Heeks 1999; Lane 2000). The message Shenhav's institutionalist analysis puts forward is that, governing organizations on the basis of modern management was neither technically/rationally developed, nor is one that necessarily leads to better outcomes over alternative ways of governing. Non-management governed organizations are not necessarily rationally inferior, but suffer a diminishing legitimacy within the context of an international economy under the hegemony of the USA.

2.3 Development as an Institution

It is perhaps less innovative and surprising to point out the institutional character of development. Not only there has been a long lasting controversy among the radically different 'paradigms' that have been proposed for economic development (Hunt 1989), but there have been critical analyses of development from political and cultural perspectives too, see for example (Amin 1990; Escobar 1995; Gardner and Lewis 1996). Yet, development that takes as a desirable model the industrialized nations of North America and Europe and assumes that any society of the world must 'catch up' with them is undoubtedly the dominant ideology under which technologies and expertise are mobilized.

An international network of organizations, such as the World Bank and USAID, highly influential in terms of financial and technical resources, is the most visible carrier of the logic that all societies of the world should adopt the economic, political and cultural values and practices of western modernity. Direct political and economic backing by a few powerful nations makes them vulnerable to criticism, and suspicion of intention. But, there is also a great deal of generally accepted as well-meaning academic and voluntary work that accepts the premises and assists in the implementation of the development dream: development economists, development planning specialists, policy analysts, and more recently, IT theorists. Ferguson (1990), quoted in (Gardner and Lewis 1996), captures the perspective of development such people take with the following observation:

> Like 'civilisation' in the nineteenth century, 'development' is the name not only for a value, but also for a dominant problematic or interpretive grid through which the impoverished regions of the world are known to us. Within this interpretive grid, a host of everyday observations are rendered intelligible and meaningful.

In short, the institutionalisation of development amounts to taking for granted the striving to achieve certain socio-economic conditions.

3. IS Innovation through Institutional Alliances

The institutions of IT, management, and catch-up-development are closely associated. Because of this intertwining, IT is not transferred to developing countries as artefacts and abstract information processing techniques. It is inseparable from ideas of how modern organizations should be governed, what kind of organizations are suitable for the contemporary world, and towards what imaginary ideal a local society at large should change. Even in countries that have indigenous capacity to manufacture IT, to set up their telecommunication services and construct their technology applications, such as India, the global institutional links of IT to management and development are ever present.

The alliance of the IT and management institutions is clear in the co-dependence of their development. In many countries information systems training takes place predominantly in business schools, emulating the American curriculum. Ever since the early 1980s the information systems literature has adopted the discourse of management, shifting focus from engineering-oriented research agenda to addressing business-oriented concerns (Avgerou, Siemer et al. 1999). Relatively little is written about information systems in organizations that are not governed by a managerial rationality. A business management/IT discourse is ubiquitously used by IS practitioners, irrespective of the organizational setting of the IT innovation. For example, IS practitioners in the national university of Zimbabwe come to think and act 'strategically' by trying to work out a 'portfolio of computer-based applications that assist [the] organisation execute its business goals. This involves searching for applications with a higher impact on the organisation and applications that have the ability to create an advantage of the organisation over its competitors' (Dlodlo and Ndlovu 2000). Such is the influence of the modernization view of development that centres around a free market mode of organizing and the international business management/IT discourse, that it is not questioned whether it is appropriate to think of a national university in a developing country as a competitive business organization. At the same time, management has become increasingly dependent on the rational myth of IT. Widely influential new ideas in the literature of management, such as business process re-engineering and e-commerce are centred on IT. The rationalization vision that underlies management has been strengthened by accommodating the efficiency potential of the computer and telecommunications, and has been translated into a vision of perpetual innovation.

Management and IT are no longer constituted only as functions of the formal organization. They have been externalized and have developed a corporate status, and constitute a thriving consultancy services multinational industry. With continuous management innovation, linked with IT best practice in software and implementation services, such as enterprise resource planning (ERP), organizations rely increasingly on outsourcing. The interaction between and co-development of these two institutions under the influence of business studies, computer science and the multinational services industry, constitutes a geographically disembedded institutional field, the kind compromising of flow of clusters of ideas, good practice norms and skills, and supporting technologies that tend to underlie contemporary globalization.

Literature provides ample evidence of the extent to which IT innovation is taken for granted as necessary for development, see for example (Talero and Gaudette 1995). There seems to be little doubt regarding the developmental role of IT, even in the poorest countries of the world. Earlier concerns relating to unemployment, opportunity costs, and dependency have disappeared from the mainstream discourse on socio-economic development and IT. In contemporary development reports the low diffusion of computers and telecommunications in desolate regions such as Sub-Saharan Africa is used as one of the main indications of their plight. International aid institutions, through funding, educational and regulatory influence, take it as part of their mission to assist poor countries to decrease their ICT gap from the ever faster innovating industrialized countries. A few impressive examples, such as the modernization of the economy of Singapore and the innovation initiatives of Malaysia, became icons of success.

An example that shows clearly the link between the development institution, management and IT is the series of information systems projects aiming to improve the efficiency, accountability, and responsiveness of public organizations in several sub-Saharan African countries discussed by Cain (1999). Such projects took place within the overall interventions of international agencies to reform the economy and the public sector of aid recipient countries, known as 'Structural adjustment programme', SAP for short. They determined the pathology of the dysfunctional public organizations in management terms and set 'public management' targets, including downsizing, accordingly. 'Computerized personnel' information systems were launched as instruments for the implementation of such SAP targets. In other words a particular vision of development, a particular mode of efficiency-oriented organizing, and a particular way of perceiving the potential value of IT converged to determine the legitimacy of and the mobilization of resources of particular IS projects. It could, of course, be otherwise. There are alternative diagnoses of Africa's worsening socio-economic conditions in the second half of the twentieth century, and many have been sceptical and critical of SAP interventions in that continent. In particular, analyses have pointed to deep-rooted social and political problems, for which management rationalization may not be the most suitable of feasible strategies, see for example the papers collected by Lewis (1998). Theoretically it is well known that IT could be mobilized to serve objectives other than downsizing (Zuboff 1988), but in the last two decades of the twentieth century its institutional forces were well positioned to make it serve the problematization of SAP and efficiency-oriented management interventions. Indeed, there is little institutional capacity – training, professional skills, corporate knowledge – for IS to be mobilized for purposes of social and political change, if that alternative view of Africa's problems were to be adopted.

Institutional analysis of IT and the way it is intertwined with the institutions of management and development sheds light on some of the problems experienced in IS innovation projects in developing countries (Heeks, forthcoming). The point of such analysis is not to reveal conspiracies of contemporary globalization, but to understand the forces within and beyond the immediate setting of IS projects that influence their initial conception and the course of action they comprise. The argument put forward is not that the institutional alliance of IT management and development within the contemporary global context is de facto undesirable, but that this international institutional setting very often clashes with or distorts knowledges, aspirations, and behavioural norms sustained by the local institutional context within which IS innovation initiatives are attempted.

More specifically, this institutional view suggests that IS innovation is better achieved in environments that are conducive to the techno-managerial development ideology that sustains IT as a disembedded institutional force. Environments with other institutionalized rationalities are more likely to experience difficulties in sustaining the IS innovation process and achieving its declared objectives. Such environments are likely to include government administration institutions which have not institutionalized a functioning variation of 'public management', family owned business firms, organizations with complex missions, which are not necessarily in harmony with the managerial economic rationality, such as health, education, and human development. Four case studies that demonstrate the clashes of rationality that may occur in such settings are included in (Avgerou 2002). In this paper, the example of a USAID funded project in the health care sector of Jordan can illustrate more specifically influences arising from the institutional forces of development on the innovation process (Toukan 2001) in a public sector context.

Toukan's case study presents and discusses an ongoing effort to introduce a computer based Health Management Information System (HMIS) conceived in 1998 within a broader five-year project aiming at improving access to and quality of primary health care services. The HMIS component has sought to strengthen Jordan's planning capacity for primary health care services by improving the collection, analysis and use of primary health care data. In fact inadequacy of accounts data was first documented in 1994 by a World Bank study to be at the root of health sector inefficiency and unequal services distribution in the country. Toukan notices, however, that the Ministry of Health did have routine monthly data collection processes from health centres, via district health authorities, to the Ministry. These were considered unreliable, and more importantly, they had little effect in the running of the health care system. Despite long standing indications of geographic discrepancy of primary health care workload per district, resourcing decisions for health care centres remained a political matter. For instance, it is often the parliament that decides to open or close a health centre.

The HMIS project team comprised of an American technical advisor, a local technical assistant, various local system engineers, expatriate consultants on a sporadic temporary basis and administrative support staff. The USAID funded HMIS team had its counterparts at the Ministry of Health (MOH). An HMIS working group, comprising of health directors from various districts and staff of the Ministry's Information centre, was established to participate in the system's design and implementation, in identifying information requirements, management needs and reporting priorities. Two and a half years later, while reaching the end of its budgeted schedule, the HMIS project was implemented in only seven out of the total 270 health centres and on rented computers, because the system's hardware had not yet been delivered by the vendors.

Such a delay, as well as a series of departures from the initial vague plans and improvizations that the project team devised during information determination, design and training are neither surprising, nor necessarily problematic. Accounts of delayed IS development are frequent in IS literature. Moreover, the idea of IS innovation as a planned and well-controlled process has been effectively challenged as unrealistic in the IS literature (Ciborra and Associates, 2000). IS design, implementation, and use should more accurately be seen, and more effectively be pursued as a process of situated action embedded in the social setting of an organization. From such a situated perspective, the technical/rational prescriptions of business-strategy-aligned systems development and project management are contrasted with the tortuous, fragmented and often highly political dynamics of innovation action in the context of an organization. Indeed, the narrative of Toukan's case suggests that IS practitioners and health care professionals and officials were adequately flexible and resourceful to nurture and create conditions of hospitality for the new system. For example, compensating for the vagueness of initial system requirements, training sessions were taken as opportunities of contact with end users and offered insights for revising initial specifications and reworking the system prototypes. Nevertheless, this case suggests three particular complications, which are not usually addressed by situated IS analyses.

First, the project had to satisfy two lines of authority, whose fundamental value principles about development and organizing were not in agreement: the local bureaucratic structures of the health services, and the USAID mission. These clashed on several issues. Initially, the USAID mission, consistent with its general policy of promoting administrative decentralization, favoured a system to address the planning requirements of the 12 governorates of the country, excluding the central decision makers from the system's reporting flows.

Second, during the initial conception of the project the USAID mission wished to focus exclusively on improving the quality of reproductive health services, which is another area of concern and policy for this development agency. The aid recipient negotiators of the Ministry of Health shifted the emphasis of the project to primary health care instead. Nevertheless, after analysis specifications were drawn and the first prototypes were built USAID continued to raise the family planning issue and asked for the specifications to be changed, in order to better reflect family planning issues.

Third, USAID regulations require all project hardware above $5000 to be purchased by US manufacturers, and a subcontractor was appointed in the US responsible for procurement. In effect, there were three organizations involved in acquiring hardware for this system in addition to the project team: the Ministry of Health, which was unhappy with this restriction, the USAID mission with its own bureaucratic procedures to monitor implementation of its policies, and the procurement agency.

Overall, as Toukan summarizes, the HMIS improvisations were enacted at the meeting point of three organizations: 'Central to this is the organizational structure, administrative culture, and infrastructural capacity of the MOH. The process was also significantly influenced by the rationale of the USAID and the corporate culture of the firm that implemented it'. The three organizations had different governance structures and cultures, and different interests regarding the computerization project. Mutual suspicion of intention often disrupted the implementation of the project. The Ministry of Health was critical of the corporate headquarters' push for appointing short term consultants from the US, suspicious that assistance funds are wasted for expatriate salaries and often inappropriate advice rather than delivering tangible output such as hardware, software and training. The USAID mission, on the other hand, was determined to curb centralisation and was often impatient with the bureaucratic labyrinth of the Ministry of Health.

4. Conclusions: Consequences for Research and Practice

In summary, the main consequences of the institutionalist perspective of IS innovation in developing countries followed in this paper are as follows:

- IS projects cannot be adequately understood and addressed as technical/rational initiatives to derive the information requirements of efficient and effective functioning of organizations and to deliver technical artefacts to that end. Such a view of IS projects, that tends to be taken in IS training and professional discourse, is an abstraction of much more complex situations, in which the purposes to be served by the 'information requirements', and the necessity and form of the technical artefacts themselves are shaped either through long-term and subtle institutionalization processes or by explicit negotiations.

- In the contemporary setting of many IS projects in developing countries, the purposes served by IT innovation, and the organizational changes pursued are shaped by the interaction of local historically developed and deeply rooted institutions with an international, geographically disembedded alliance of international IT, management, and development institutional forces. There is, of course, a plethora of initiatives that either explicitly or implicitly are undertaken as alternatives to the institutional forces that convey the ideology of western modernization for development and organising, such as various NGO activities. These are not discussed in this paper – and indeed have not been researched extensively – but it could be argued that analyses of the institutional character of IT is equally relevant for such cases, if naïve instrumental assumptions about technology are to be avoided.
- Such a perspective suggests the need for situated analysis of IS innovation, to understand the innovation events in their setting. In the 1990s a research stream has elaborated on the theoretical and methodological aspects of situated studies of IS innovation and organizational change. However, the institutionalist analysis that sees IT, management, and development as a global disembedded alliance suggests the need to expand the situated analyses beyond the event in its immediate setting, and beyond the 'here and now' action. It suggests the need for developing contextualist research approaches to consider the broader social dynamics that sustain particular imaginaries about IT and particular courses of innovation action as legitimate interventions. Also, it suggests the need for expanding the situated analyses to consider history, the past experiences that gave rise to certain imaginaries and actions as legitimate and suppressed others.

These points suggest a direction for further research. They lead to a research agenda for contextualist studies that can produce insights on the complex processes pursued in IS innovation in developing countries. Such research will aim at explaining the difficulties faced by IS projects, the failures reported in the literature, and the successes that become exemplary cases and provide much needed basis for optimism and perseverance. It can also reveal some aspects of contemporary globalization. To the extent that IT and telecommunications are central mechanisms for globalization, the processes involved in IT innovation, and explanations for the currently grossly uneven IT spread are at the core of understanding the emerging situation of globality.

It is more difficult to derive practical lessons from this analysis without falling into the trap of naïve instrumental advice that negates the very argument about the significance of institutionalization processes. This analysis understands professional practice not as a technical/rational exercise conducted by disinterested individuals or teams, but as modes of intervention in a socio-organizational setting by technical/rational means, which are legitimated and acquire a status of obvious logic and necessity through institutional forces, such as training, the supporting industry and others.

Nevertheless, the opposite conclusion, that institutional forces determine the behaviour of passive actors is equally misguided. Institutions should not be thought of as monolithic entities with sweeping effects of streamlining agents' action. They should rather be seen as continuously reformed as a result of their members' actions and negotiations with other institutions of their environment. Institutional contexts can be changed or overcome by reflexive agents. Moreover, as the analysis above suggests, IS innovation in developing countries tends to be a case of conflicting institutions, because it involves the interaction of disembedded forces with local institutional forces. Management is not strongly institutionalized in all countries, and therefore corporate IS/management actors are confronted by alternative institutional formations in different parts of the world and different sectors.

A basic lesson for reflexive practitioners that can be derived by the institutional analysis, therefore, is to loosen reliance on a-contextual formal packages of expertise, to question the relevance and validity of the mainstream professional jargon, which, for example, converts all organizations to competing businesses, sees only CEOs and 'customers' and is myopic to other social roles such as citizens, and to attempt hermeneutic processes for situated analyses. It is also reasonable to recommend that understanding the domain within which the innovation intervention is made should be incorporated into professional practice. This requires the development of appropriate contextualist analysis tools, since according to the institutionalist view, tools and techniques are significant for professional conduct, for symbolic as well as functional purposes. This is an area, perhaps, of fruitful collaboration of practice and academia.

Moreover, it is important that professionals should develop capabilities for situated action, being aware of and prepared to address the consequences of conflicts between the disembedded with the local institutions. There is a need for inventiveness, flexibility, and patience to engage in negotiations, or wait for the negotiations of others to reach some agreement. Perhaps more controversially, a new mode of professional situated conduct requires readiness to abandon a missionary role that many professionals, sympathetic to the cause of development undertake. Faith in the intrinsic value of technology-led interventions in organizations and in the goodness of the developmental purpose they are assigned bears the risk of imposing and patronising.

Such 'lessons' amount to the suggestion of a change of role and conduct for IS professionals from putting the potential of IT into good use for an organization, to taking part as intermediaries in the shaping of organizational and social change. While 'enlightened' individuals may consciously adopt such a role through engaging in reflexive situated action, an effective shift towards such a practice requires the de-institutionalization of existing professional norms and the institutionalization of a new basis of IS professionalism. This is, hopefully, what theoretical studies such as this paper, linked with the educational activities of academia, can contribute to practice.

Note

1 I am grateful to an anonymous reviewer who brought this point to my attention.

References

Amin, S. (1990). Maldevelopment: Anatomy of a Global Failure. Tokyo, United Nations University Press.

Avgerou, C. (2000). 'IT and organizational change: an institutionalist perspective.' Information Technology and People 13(4): pp. 234-262.

Avgerou, C. (2002). Information Systems and Global Diversity. Oxford, Oxford University Press.

Avgerou, C. and T. Cornford (1993). 'A review of the methodologies movement. ' Journal of Information Technology 5: pp. 277-286.

Avgerou, C., J. Siemer, et al. (1999). 'The Academic Field of Information Systems in Europe. ' European Journal of Information Systems(8): pp. 136-153.

Bada, A. O. (forthcoming). 'Local adaptations to global trends: a study of an IT-based organizational change programme in a Nigerian bank. ' The Information Society.

Bell, D. (1973). The coming of the Post-Industrial Society. New York, Basic Books.

Cain, P. (1999). Automating personnel records for improved management of human resources: the experience of three African governments. Reinventing Government in the Information Age: International practice in IT-enabled public sector refor. R. Heeks. London, Routledge: pp. 135-155.

Callon, M., P. Laredo, et al. (1997). Technico-economic networks and the analysis of structural effects. The strategic Management of Research and Technology: Evaluation of Programmes. M. Callon, P. Laredo and P. Mustar. Paris, Economica International: pp. 385-429.

Chandler, A. D., Jr. (1962). Strategy and Structure: Chapters in the History of the Industrial Enterprise. Cambridge, Massachusetts, MIT Press.

Chandler, A. D., Jr. (1969). 'The structure of American industry in the Twentieth century: a historical overview.' Business History Review 43(255-281).

Ciborra, C. and G. F. Lanzara (1994). 'Formative Contexts and Information Technology: Understanding the Dynamics of Innovation in Organizations.' Accounting, Management and Information Technology 4(2): pp.61-86.

Ciborra, C. U. and Associates., Eds. (2000). From Control to Drift. Oxford, Oxford University Press.

Cram, L. (1997). Policy Making in the EU. London, Routledge.

Dlodlo, N. and L. Ndlovu (2000). A critical evaluation of the information technology strategy: a case study at NUST. Information Flows, Local Improvisations and work practices, Cape Town.

Dosi, G., C. Freeman, et al., Eds. (1988). Technical Change and Economic Theory. London, Pinter.

Escobar, A. (1995). Encountering Development. Princeton, Princeton University Press.

Farbey, B., F. F. Land, *et al.* (1993). IT Investment: a Study of Methods and Practice. Oxford, Butterworth-Heinemann.

Ferguson, J. (1990). The Anti-Politics Machine: 'Development', Depoliticisation, and Bureaucratic Power in Lesotho. Cambridge, Cambridge University Press.

Foray, D. and C. Freeman, Eds. (1993). Technology and the Wealth of Nations, The dynamics of constructed advantage. London, Pinter.

Gardner, K. and D. Lewis (1996). Anthropology, Development and the Post-Modern Challenge. London, Pluto Press.

Giddens, A. (1990). The Consequences of Modernity. Cambridge, Polity Press.

Heeks, R., Ed. (1999). Reinventing Government in the Information Age: International practice in IT-enabled public sector reform. London, Routlege.

Heeks, R. (forthcoming). 'Information systems and developing countries: failure, success and local imrovisations. ' The Information Society.

Hunt, D. (1989). Economic Theories of Development. London, Harvester Wheatsheaf.

King, J. L., V. Gurbaxani, et al. (1994). 'Institutional factors in information technology innovation. ' Information Systems Research 5(2): pp. 139-169.

Lane, J. E. (2000). The Public Sector: Concepts, Models and Approaches. London, Sage.

Lewis, P., Ed. (1998). Africa: Dilemmas of Development and Change. Boulder, Colorado, Westview Press.

Lundvall, B.-Å. (1988). Innovation as an interactive process: from user-producer interaction to the national system of innovation. Technical Change and Economic Theory. G. Dosi, C. Freeman, R. Nelson, G. Silverberg and L. Soete. London, Pinter: pp. 349-369.

Lundvall, B.-Å., Ed. (1992). National Systems of Innovation: Towards a Theory of Innovation and Interactive Learning. London, Pinter.

Madon, S. (1993). 'Introducing administrative reform through the application of computer-based information systems: a case study in India. ' Public Administration and Development 13: pp. 37-48.

Orlikowski, W. J. (2000). 'Using technology and constituting structures: a practice lens for studying technology in organizations. ' Organization Science 11(4): pp.404-428.

Orlikowski, W. J. and S. R. Barley (2001). 'Technology and institutions: what can research on information technology and research on organizations learn from each other? ' MIS Quarterly 25(2): pp.145-165.

Orlikowski, W. J. and C. S. Iacono (2001). 'Research commentary: desperately seeking the "IT" in IT research – a call to theorizing the IT artifact.' Information Systems Research 12(2): pp. 121-134.

Powell, W. W. and P. J. DiMaggio, Eds. (1991). The New Institutionalism in Organizational Analysis. Chicago, The University of Chicago Press.

Shenhav, Y. (1999). Manufacturing Rationality: The Engineering Foundations of the Managerial Revolution. Oxford, Oxford University Press.

Silva, L. and J. Backhouse (1997). Becoming part of the furniture. Information Systems and Qualitative Research. A. S. Lee, J. Liebenau and J. I. De Gross. London, Chapman and Hall: pp. 389-414.

Suchman, L. (1994). 'Working relations of technology production and use. ' Computer Supported Cooperative Work 2: pp. 21-39.

Swanson, E. B. and N. Ramiller (1997).'The organizing vision in information systems innovation.' Organizational Science September/October: pp. 458-474.

Talero, E. and P. Gaudette (1995). 'Harnessing Information for development: A proposal for a World Bank Group vision and strategy.' Information Technology for Development 6: pp. 145-188.

Toukan, O. (2001). The reality of expatriate information systems practice in developing countries: the case of a Health Information System in Jordan. Information Systems. London, London School of Economics.

van der Blonk, H. C. (2000). Institutionalisation and legitimation of information technologies in local contexts. Information Flows, Local Improvisations and Work Practices, Cape Town.

Walsham, G. (1993). Interpreting Information Systems in Organizations. Chichester, John Wiley.

Walsham, G. (2001). Making a World of Difference: IT in a Global Context. Chichester, John Wiley.

Webster, F. (1995). Theories of the Information Society. London, Routledge.

Zuboff, S. (1988). In the Age of the Smart Machine. New York, Basic Books.

Chapter 4

ICT and Development: East is East and West is West and the Twain may yet Meet

Lars T. Soeftestad and Maung K. Sein

1. Introduction

Developing countries are rapidly adopting information and communication technologies (ICTs) in the hope of achieving accelerated economic growth. This hope is expressed in even a relatively well-balanced document as the most recent Human Development Report (UNDP 2001). However, studies have shown only limited correlation between investment in ICT and traditional economic growth indices (Wellenius et al. 2000, Yang 2001). The findings of general failure in such studies have led others to question whether ICTs have any real effect on national development (Heeks 1999). Whether ICT is a silver bullet or an enticing siren is a key question facing us today.

We take the stance that ICT can play a key role in national development, if applied appropriately. We believe that the model of development that has been used by the key stakeholders in this area – chiefly donor agencies – is flawed and incomplete because of two main reasons. First, such agencies have a constrained and narrow conceptualization of basic concepts, mainly, ICT and how they work, development, and the interrelationship between the two. Specifically, echoing the critiques of post-development theorists, we believe that development, conceptualized mainly through the modernization perspective, and also aspects of the dependency perspective, assumes the developing countries to be homogeneous entities leading to a 'one-size-fits-all' view of development intervention. This ignores vital local and contextual factors. Second, and following from the first reason, donor agencies do not follow a well-formulated strategy to guide their development cooperation activities. This thinking is embodied in the policy documents of such agencies for example, those produced by Norwegian Agency for Development Cooperation (NORAD).

We do not subscribe to the prevalent view on what development is, nor the way ICT is conceptualized. We argue that ICT comes out of a western intellectual and scientific tradition, and cannot be applied 'as is' to non-Western settings. The assumptions underlying this thinking are in important ways incorrect.

In this paper, we analyze this 'western view' of development and the role of ICTs in it, and propose enhancements by incorporating alternative views of development and concepts from areas such as social informatics and social science.

The rest of the paper is organized as follows: In section two we discuss the prevailing conceptualizations of ICT and development and their interrelationship. In section three we present alternative conceptualizations of these factors. In section four we examine the evolution of an ICT policy in NORAD, as evident from two specific policy documents, and critique it using as lens the traditional as well as the alternative conceptualisations. We conclude the paper in section five by discussing our contentions and offering some recommendations related to the role of ICTs and development.

2. ICT and Development: Prevalent Views

2.1 Conceptualizing Development

The notion that development in some form or another leads to a better quality of life is universally accepted. The debate is on what constitutes 'better quality of life'. Much of the thinking has been linked to Westernization, that is, nations in the third world aspire to be like nations in the west including, for example, consumerism and adoption of western culture. This is in line with the modernisation perspective of development theory.[1]

According to this perspective, the root cause of underdevelopment is that developing countries are mired in traditional modes of production, and lack the know-how, skills, tradition, and impetus to break out of this cycle. Developed countries have successfully escaped this, by dint of research and exploiting technology that resulted from these research efforts. The prime example is the industrial revolution, which brought a basic discontinuity and thus propelled these countries out of the 'traditional' mode. Much of this thinking is embodied in Rostow's stage theory (Rostow 1971).

Therefore, it is argued, to become developed, poor countries need to emulate the developed countries. In turn, the developed countries have the moral duty to help poorer countries achieve this growth. This creates a trusteeship relationship between the two worlds (Nustad 2001). Many developed countries, including the OECD collectively, take this seriously and in good conscience. Norway is a prime example, spending close to 1 percent of its GNP on development assistance (UNDP 2001). The key intervention strategy under this perspective is to create capital and a capitalist class that will be the catalyst for such modernisation. Seen in this perspective, ICTs can help developing countries get to Rostow's take-off stage of development. Although Rostow is passé, such thinking still underlies much of the models and strategies adopted by western donor agencies.

2.2 Conceptualising ICT

A prime example of the traditional conceptualisation of ICTs in the context of development is:

> ICTs encompass all those technologies that enable the handling of information and facilitate different forms of communication among human actors, between human beings and electronic systems, and among electronic systems. These technologies can be sub-divided into: capturing technologies, storage technologies, processing technologies, communication technologies and display technologies. (Hamelink 2001:2)

In addition, the literature also considers networks that use these technologies to be part of ICT. Chief among the last is of course, the Internet. Currently, in the context of development, the emphasis is mainly on such communication technologies. Hamelink's conceptualisation of ICT is narrow – one that Orlikowski and Iacono (2001) term 'tool view' (see Table 4.1).

Table 4.1 Views on how to conceptualize ICTs

View	Description
Nominal view	ICT as the object of study with no specific meaning assigned to it
Tool view	ICTs as a technical entity and a means to achieve something
Computational view	ICTs as the algorithms, codes, and models that comprise the system
Proxy view	ICTs conceptualized in terms of some surrogate measure, for example the extent of diffusion in an organisation
Ensemble view	ICTs conceptualized as parts of a bigger 'package' going beyond the technology (hardware, software) to activities and interactions performed in specific social and cultural contexts

Source: Orlikowski and Iacono (2001).

Note: The 'nominal' and 'computational' views are not germane to a discussion on ICT-in-development. We will limit our classification to the other three views.

In the traditional perspective of ICT-in-development, the tool view, as defined in Table 4.1, predominates. In essence, ICT is treated as a black box, and the specific aspect of ICT that may have differential impact on development is neglected.

2.3 The Relationship between ICT and Development

The exact impact of ICTs on national development is much debated. The literature is sharply divided into two camps. One camp paints a very rosy picture and is given names such as the 'utopian view' (Hamelink 2001) and 'silver bullet' (Sein and Ahmad 2001). ICT is seen as a catalyst for national development by being the vehicle of transformation. The rationale behind this optimism is 'leapfrogging': by being late adopters of ICT, developing nations benefit from declining costs, advances in technology and bypassing the teething problems associated with new technologies. ICTs are also viewed as tools of empowerment and enabling for common citizens. Open information flow is theorized to lead to more open government, broad citizen participation, and entrepreneurship. This argument is in line with the western view of development, and is in the core of optimistic views. It is articulated in donor agency documents (e.g., OECD 1997) and is a central argument in UNDP's recent human development report (UNDP 2001).

One specific and direct impact of this optimistic view is viewing ICT as a commodity (Sein and Ahmad 2001). By successfully leveraging their low-cost producer advantage over the developed countries, developing nations can earn foreign exchange by manufacturing computer and related products, through performing high skilled jobs (e.g., offshore software development) and even low-skilled job (e.g., offshore data entry and data processing functions).

This picture needs to be examined critically. To do so, we look at the dependency perspective of development. This perspective lays the blame of underdevelopment on the very process that made developed countries developed. Richer nations developed themselves at the cost of poorer countries – through colonialism and dominance of trade and politics. The poorer countries manufacture products; even organize their economies, solely to benefit the richer countries. Offshore computing and manufacturing ICT commodities are done mainly to feed the consumerism of the richer nations, and not for the developing countries. The rise in such 'global' ICT industries hardly indicates transfer of technology and, more importantly, transfer of knowledge. In this context, ICTs result in helping richer countries advance further, while the poorer countries remain poor.

Another problem with this view is that the potential for the entire developing world, taken as a whole, is limited. As Sein and Ahmad (2001) reasoned, not all countries can become chip manufacturers or software producers. Even where it has proved to be a success, the impact on the economy is debatable. India's software industry, mainly centred on Bangalore, is held out as the model success story. We agree that it is a remarkable achievement. Its impact has been studied quite substantially (e.g., Madon 1997). UNDP's report also highlights this achievement. Yet, a telling statistic is that India is still listed as 'Dynamic Adopter', the third of four levels on UNDP's Technology Achievement Index. India ranks fairly low because in other indices, the statistics are not as impressive.

These are the very arguments made by the second camp: the pessimistic school. They are variously termed as 'dystopian' (Hamelink 2001) and 'doom and gloom' (Sein and Ahmad 2001). This camp argues that, as of today, there are few links between ICT and national development (Heeks 1999). Statistics show increased investment in ICT in developing countries and a corresponding decrease in all economic growth indicators (Yang 2001, Harindranath and Liebenau 1998). In contrast to the benefits espoused by the optimist camp, this camp argues that ICT can actually lead to more repression by authoritarian governments who now have a more powerful tool to control its citizens.

ICT also magnifies the digital divide, the difference between knowledge and technological capabilities of the developed and the developing world. Sirimanne (1996) argues that the information gap leads to a competitive gap and the result is the development gap. As Sein and Ahmad (2001) pointed out, ICTs can even push developing countries deeper into poverty by streamlining and improving design and manufacture of goods and thereby reducing the demand of raw materials, energy, and even low-skilled labour – longstanding comparative advantages of developing countries. Thus leapfrogging is seriously questioned (e.g., Davison et al. 2000).

We take the view that both camps take extreme positions and that, if appropriately deployed and used, ICTs can have an impact on development. Taken at a macro level, the fact that investments in ICTs have not shown a positive impact on national productivity is hardly surprising. This mirrors the much discussed 'IT and productivity paradox' (Brynjolfsson 1993) at the firm level.

We also argue, echoing Heeks (2001), that much of the statistics used to support various viewpoints hide key aspects. For example, donor agencies are more preoccupied with numbers and the supply side of ICT. Thus such indicators as 'number of phones' or 'percentage of population with access to Internet' are taken to indicate ICT diffusion. While these are necessary conditions to study the impact of ICTs on national development, they are far from being sufficient conditions. These statistics only represent the first and second order effects of technology diffusion in society (Malone and Rockart 1991).

The first order or primary effect is simple substitution of old technology by new (e.g., mobile phones replacing traditional communication modes such as letters and even land phones); the second order or secondary effect is an increase in the phenomenon enabled by the technology (people communicating more). We believe that impact can truly be studied through the third order or tertiary effect, which is generation of new related businesses and societal change (virtual organizations, empowerment of women, etc.).

3. ICT and Development: Alternative Views

3.1 Alternative Conceptualization of Development

Development as we understand it goes beyond mere statistical indicators or economic theory. This is a view from the top. As seen from the local level, development is about reducing poverty, increasing the standard of living, increasing educational and health levels, and building a democratic society marked by involvement, participation, and transparency. Accordingly, development involves a better management of, among others, behaviour and customs, based on a better understanding of culture (Courier 1998). Basic to our understanding of development are three key and interlinked observations:

1. There is too much of the colonial era approach of 'we' vs. 'them' built into the way we think about and address problems of development. Development co-operation needs to focus much more on local people and local development,
2. We should understand ourselves – indeed all stakeholders active in development co-operation – as positioned within, and as bearers of, unique knowledge systems (Worsley 1997), and,
3. Whatever its overt technological appearance, ICT in the context of development is a form of communication.

A more appropriate conceptualization of development accordingly is done through the perspectives of human development and alternative development paradigms. An extensive review of these perspectives is beyond the scope of this paper. Here, we merely present a brief discussion of factors relevant to our paper.

The human development perspective arose around the mid-1980s and is influenced by Amartya Sen's work on capacities and entitlements. It takes the stance that development is enabling (Nederveen Pieterse 2001). At the core is the understanding that national development is 'the enlargement of people's choices' (Nederveen Pieterse 2001:6). The choices, specifically stated and later embodied in UNDP's human development reports, are: the choice of healthy life, the choice to be educated, and the choice to decent standard of living. The key indices are: [2]

- Human Development Index (HDI): life expectancy at birth, level of education, and GNP per capita (representing the three choices mentioned above),
- Gender Development Index (GDI): uses the same factors as the HDI, but looks at the differences between men and women,
- Gender Equity Measure (GEM): looks at the possibilities for women to be part of the decision-making in economics and politics,
- Human Poverty Index (HPI): HPI-1 for developing countries, and HPI-2 for industrialized countries.

Other factors implicit in the development index are income distribution and social mobility. It is evident that the human development paradigm emphasizes non-economic factors over economic or growth factors. There is not a necessary relationship between HDI and economic indicators, but HDI is arguably a better indicator of how far a country has raised itself from the impacts of poverty. To take an example, it is interesting to note that Costa Rica has about the same level of Human Development as South Korea with far lower GDP (UNDP 2001).

HDI has been used extensively by academics, donor agencies, and development practitioners to set development aid policies and study them. However, it is not without flaws. Setting aside concerns related to data gathering –

UNDP is dependent on national and international organizations for statistical data which are often estimates and worse, flawed – HDI does not include essential but largely subjective measures such as political freedom, human rights, and citizen participation in democratic activities. Therefore, the stated objective of enabling and expanding people's choices are not fully reflected in HDI. Another weakness of HDI is that, by its very nature, it is an indicator and does not say anything about the means – or the vehicle – of development. Who should be responsible for achieving these indices?

To seek an answer, we turn to another conceptualisation of development 'Alternative Development' (Nederveen Pieterse 2001) and following it, take the stance that the means are participatory and people-centred. Accordingly, one key vehicle of development is through civil society (including non-governmental organisations, or NGOs). We stress that equally important is local participation, initiation, and leadership of development efforts.

Thus, our alternative conceptualization of development is a marriage of two paradigms: human development and alternative development. Human development provides us with important indices to measure socio-economic development and more importantly, areas to target the use of ICTs. To these, we add other essential components such as political freedom and citizen participation in democracy. From the alternative development paradigm, we borrow the concept of grassroots participation (and thus the importance of local context and culture) and the role of civil society. Table 4.2 summarizes our alternative conceptualization of development.

Table 4.2 Alternative conceptualizations of development

Paradigms	Factors
Human Development	• Choice of healthy life • Choice to be educated • Choice to decent standard of living • Political freedom and democracy • Human rights
Alternative Development	• Culture and local context • Civil society involvement • Local participation • Decentralization • Transparency

3.2 Alternative Conceptualization of ICT

The larger context for assessing and understanding ICT is culture and variations in culture. Viewed from this perspective, ICT is a means of communication. Communication is, essentially, and at its most fundamental level, a relationship *between people* (Courier 1998). The medium of communication was traditionally oral. The content was complex, rich, and many-layered. Modern communication is also complex, but in different ways. It takes place between many more stakeholders, which often are located on different levels. The medium of communication is more and more written, and increasingly in electronic form. Modern-day communication is often asymmetrical in one way or another, the content is often instrumental, and increasingly contains data without a contextual frame of reference (Courier 1998, Soeftestad 2001).

In order to maintain the content and human-created functionality of communication, the methods used to transmit knowledge, information, and data effectively must be chosen with care. This is, in particular, the case where the aim is to mobilize populations to make them aware of what is involved in promoting their well-being and to further development. The following requirements should be fulfilled: information, education, and communication (Courier 1998).

Within this context, what is 'ICT'? In a narrow sense (or tool view), it refers to the various communication technologies available, including cellular phones, email, Internet, phones, and TV. We subscribe to a broader view and understand ICT also as an issue, a process, as content and goals, and as a theory of the relationship between technology and development. This understanding follows from the larger context of communication presented earlier, and coincide with the conceptualization of ICTs as an ensemble (see Table 4.1).

3.3 Alternative Conceptualisation of the Relationship between ICT and Development

Intellectual roots for a relevant alternative conceptualization of the relationship between ICT and development can be found in the work of Appropriate Technology (AT) theorists and activists. Stretching back to Schumacher's credo 'Small is beautiful' (Schumacher 1974), AT supports the development and use of sustainable approaches to meeting human and ecological needs through the appropriate use of technology. Today's complex problems cannot be solved by using technology independent of its context. To be appropriate, technology must be connected to the place, resources, economics, culture, and impact of its use. This necessitates a strong human and culture-centred approach to applying ICT in a development context. It is fundamental to the AT movement that the impact of ICT is emergent and dependent upon its social context.

ICT impacts development, but what does this mean? To make it manageable, we can break this question down, and ask: What is the level or levels at which there is an impact? Who is being impacted? What is being impacted?

- The level of impact. The primary beneficiaries of development cooperation projects and programmes reside at the local level. Other stakeholders operate on the regional via the national to the global level. Following from a fundamental understanding of governments as key counterparts, the modernization perspective places prior emphasis on the national level, and to some extent the regional level. The alternative views on development, on the other hand, place a prior emphasis on the local level. The dissemination or diffusion of ICTs follows different rationales according to these two broad conceptualizations. In the modernization perspective, the impact of ICTs is understood to spread from the macro-levels to the micro-levels (i.e. a case of trickling down, as it were), while, according to the alternative perspective, it spread from the micro-levels to the macro-levels through accumulation, diffusion and aggregation.

- Impact on whom. Depending on the level on which we focus, different people or stakeholders will be impacted. Can or should ICTs impact everybody? Should ICTs impact the poor only, which, it is argued, is the focus for ICT-in-development? Connected with this: can ICTs impact the poor *directly*, and/or will this impact (also) occur *indirectly*? Does 'impact' imply that the affected people in question are actually using ICT? Alternatively, is this not a necessary precondition?
- Impact on what. In section two, we proposed that the impact of ICTs on development be best studied through tertiary effects as conceived by Malone and Rockart (1991). The question remains, though, about the type of tertiary effects that we should focus on to link ICTs to development. Following Sein and Ahmad (2001), we propose that our alternative conceptualization of development represent an appropriate avenue to establish this link. We take the view that if applied appropriately and focused on deploying ICT as factors influencing human development, ICTs have a vital role in being a catalyst for national development.

3.4 Summarising Alternative Conceptualisations

Taken together, these observations have the implication of a more egalitarian approach to understanding the relations between key concepts and between key stakeholders. In particular, both donors and recipients can begin to understand themselves as equal, and as bearers of cultures that both affect and are impacted along a two-way causal connection. In more practical terms, these conceptualizations would lead to a better-formulated and well thought-out strategy to guide donor agencies in planning intervention strategies. In the next section we discuss and critique ongoing work in NORAD on ICT-in-development. We demonstrate that flawed policy conceptualizations will lead to an ill-structured strategy.

4. NORAD and ICT [3]

4.1 Background

Development cooperation – very broadly understood, and whether public sector, private sector, or civil society/NGO directed – has a special and important place in Norwegian society. Likewise, Norwegian development cooperation has a similar standing within the context of international development cooperation. Norway has become recognized for promoting broad equality-for-all values and participatory approaches in its various development cooperation activities. In the changes that current development cooperation is undergoing, these are values that Norway is keen to continue supporting. This should be the context to understand and assess the growing emphasis on ICT in Norway, and, more particularly, within NORAD.

4.2 Process

NORAD's current interest in ICTs stems from a brainstorming workshop that took place in 1999 in which NORAD staff participated. As a result of this workshop, NORAD appointed an internal working group that was charged with initiating work within NORAD on ICT and development cooperation. This work-in-progress has so far led to two internal documents. These documents, which are reviewed below, are taken to represent NORAD's stance on the cultural, societal, value, and technical contexts for Norway's present application of ICT to development co-operation at the particular times in which they were prepared. The documents are part of a larger ongoing work that will culminate in an ICT strategy document. In the following description and assessment we discuss the two documents in some detail, and, in the final summary, analyse the overall process.

4.3 The Documents

The first document was produced in 2000 by a NORAD working group, which was composed of a small number of senior staff. It was titled 'Bridging the digital divide. Information and communication technologies. Challenges and opportunities to NORAD and its development partners'. (NORAD 2000). This document will in the following be referred to as 'Bridging Report'.

A subsequent internal discussion of this report took place during 2001 and led to the second document 'Information and Communication Technology (ICT) in development cooperation: Guidelines from NORAD' that was issued in early 2002 (NORAD 2002). This document will in the following be referred to as 'Guidelines Report'.

The Bridging Report was an internal document, and although it was available for a while on NORAD's web site, it was not publicized or discussed externally, and apparently also internally. The Guidelines Report, likewise an internal document, and a product of an internal review and evaluation process, is available on NORAD's web site.

4.4 Description

The Bridging Report is organized as a very brief summary (it is actually sub-titled 'Report for busy people'). The report itself is only around ten pages, with a number of arguments and conclusions presented in a type of logical framework in tabular form. Several lengthy annexes include detailed information.

The report is divided in four parts: (1) Main ICT tendencies, (2) Potential uses of ICT in development, (3) The Norwegian resource base, and (4) Institutional implications - NORAD.

The report consists of the following columns: (1) key findings and conclusions, and (2) recommendations. The recommendations are again divided in three: (1) goal, (2) approach, and (3) actions.

The Guidelines Report represent a further development, and explicitly states its two main objectives:

(1) to clarify the main principles for NORAD's use of ICT in development co-operation, and
(2) to be a 'practical toolkit' for Norwegian embassy staff and NORAD personnel on how and when to work with ICT in development programs and projects.

It is thus fitting that this brief report (a total of twelve pages, divided into five sections and one annex) is structured differently and has a different focus. It begins by setting out the purposes of the Guidelines Report. Section one asks the question 'Why use ICT?' and also provides a definition of ICT. In Section two some principles of NORAD's use of ICT are presented. This is followed by Section three, which briefly addresses the possible use of ICT within different areas, including institutional development, private-sector development, basic social services, ICT infrastructure, the environment and natural resources, cooperation with civil society, women and gender equality, knowledge and human resource development, and contact with external institutions. Section four discusses the rationale and approach of doing ICT assessments in the course of planning projects and programmes, listing 12 specific areas of assessment. Section five contains an outline of working procedures. An Annex lists a number of NORAD's ICT-relevant projects.

4.5 Assessment

The following framework will be used for assessing the documents: (1) rationale, (2) target groups, (3) conceptualization of issues, and (4) general.

Rationale The first main finding and conclusion in the Bridging Report states that: 'The rapid, pervasive ICT development creates digital divides'. In detailing this statement, apparently neutral statements, like 'The ICT revolution penetrates and transforms almost all areas of society, and consequently most areas of development co-operation', positive effects, like 'Costs of ICT are falling rapidly', as well as negative effects, like 'This, largely market-driven transition to a knowledge based and ICT driven economy in the developed world causes a rapidly growing 'digital divide' between the developed and developing and within developing countries between rich and poor individuals and regions, particularly in Africa' all appear.

Based on this, it is tempting to conclude that the buzz around the growing so-called digital divide is a main point of departure for NORAD's ICT process. Such an argument would present some problems. For one thing, this amounts to addressing the problem of the digital divide – that is, a result of the West's application of ICT – through increasing the use of, and reliance on, ICT. Following from this, it amounts to a defensive and not necessarily constructive approach. As we see it, arguments about closing the digital divide by applying more ICT is based upon a misreading of the situation, and is unlikely to work. Bridging the digital divide may or may not address '... the overarching goals of poverty eradication through sustainable development,' and there are other means that (also) should be pursued. One could, for example, start with the resources available in developing countries, be they human, physical, or social, and consider how ICT could be applied to harness, better utilize, and coordinate them. Other than this mention of the digital divide, the report takes the optimistic view of ICT and national development.

The Guidelines Report takes a significant departure from the rationale of the Bridging Report by explicitly stating the context and resource status of the donee countries (referred to as 'partner countries'). The ICT assessment guide lists several factors that highlight the local context in terms of social, human, cultural, economic, legal, and regulatory issues. ICT is not viewed as a new sector in itself, but as an integral part of other sectors. It lists priority areas of development – social development, economic development, peace, democracy and human rights, environmental and natural resource management, and women and gender equality. ICT is to be integrated into development of these areas.

Target groups Like elsewhere in the West, ICT in Norway is within the domain of the private sector, in close proximity and relationship with academic and research communities. It should not come as a surprise that the Bridging Report, as so many others, appear to abound with references to the views and needs of the private sector. To wit, one of the main findings and conclusions deals with how ICT provides new opportunities for private sector development. At the same time, the report argues that ICT supports good governance and democracy through transparency. However, while this, in the conceptualization of the Bridging Report, would aid and benefit civil society and NGOs, they are listed as beneficiaries only of these processes that are operating on the national level. This is in keeping with the modernization perspective of development. Local people are not mentioned explicitly as an active party to the process. The trusteeship aspect of the donor-recipient relationship is evident. We would have liked to see, for example, a specific focus on how ICT can aid civil society and NGOs in developing own cultures and local communities.

The Guidelines Report redresses this inadequacy to a great extent by specifically listing areas where NORAD can – and has – aided development activities carried out by civil societies (e.g., Worldwide International Foundation), and those targeted towards disadvantaged groups (e.g., BRIDGE - database on women and equality). Once again, we see a progression in NORAD's thinking towards the alternative conceptualization of development. The need for donees to recognize the benefits and possibilities of technology as a tool for development is stressed. This indicates that the trusteeship aspect is moderated. Specific HDI factors are named as priority areas for possible use of ICT – basic social services, knowledge and human resources development, and institutional development. However, the emphasis on private sector development remains. This indicates that the modernization perspective retains its influence.

Conceptualization of issues Reading between the lines in the Bridging Report, we see that the modernization and take-off approach is present. Technology, especially of an advanced nature as here, will help developing nations 'take off'. At the same time, ICT may be understood in a too simplistic manner: in the range of ICTs available and in the application. The concept of culture is totally absent. There is no acknowledgement of the complexities emanating from the fact of ICT amounting to communication between people with different cultural and language backgrounds, as well as between people with similar or identical cultures but of very different socio-economic standing. We conclude that ICT is being viewed as a 'tool' (see Table 4.1) and not seen in context.

The Guidelines Report at first glance seems to also take a 'tool view' of ICT. In fact, it is explicitly stated as such in the first of three 'principles' for NORAD's use of ICT for development. In addition, ICT is also viewed as a commodity although in conjunction with women's participation in the production of ICT content and technology. The second principle, however, which regards ICT as an integral part of other development activities, indicates that the conceptualization of ICT is more an 'ensemble' view (see Table 4.1). An examination of areas listed in the ICT assessment guidelines in the report lend further support to this conclusion: 'appropriate technology' relates to whether ICT is appropriate for the intended use, 'capacity' and 'affordability' assessment addresses real issues of access, and 'content' assessment includes relevancy in terms of language and cultural background of intended users. Finally, assessment of legal and regulatory frameworks is aimed at identifying changes needed to create an environment to foster use of ICTs.

General Both reports presumably follow the key principles that govern NORAD's work, which include: combating poverty, all human rights are equal, emphasis on recipient responsibility, partnership involving all stakeholders, and sustainability (NORAD 1999). However, in the Bridging Report, we detect a change in emphasis when the focus is on technology and the private sector. The general theme running through the report echoes other mainstream, public, and private sector reviews of the role of ICT in development cooperation. It would seem that discussions of ICT are prone to focus squarely on the technical side of things, and to overemphasize the potential inherent in ICT. It is often forgotten that both information technology (IT) and ICT are subjective and value laden, steeped as they are in a Western ethos and discourse. The crucial appropriate technology aspect of ICT is all but absent. Also absent are specific mention of whom ICTs will impact, and what it will impact. Nor is there a discussion on how specifically ICTs will be focused. On the surface, this report purports to cover several of the factors in our alternative conceptualizations. However, the inherent contradictions in them lead us to conclude that the development goals will not be achieved.

Table 4.3 Summary of analysis and critique of the NORAD reports

Our alternative conceptualizations	Bridging Report	Guidelines Report
Development:		
1. Human development		
• Choice of healthy life	Somewhat covered	Extensively covered
• Choice to be educated	Somewhat covered	Extensively covered
• Choice to a decent standard of living	Extensively covered	Extensively covered
• Political freedom and democracy	Somewhat covered	Somewhat covered
• Human rights	Not covered	Somewhat covered
2. Alternative development		
• Culture and local context	Not covered	Extensively covered
• Civil society involvement	Somewhat covered	Extensively covered
• Local participation	Not covered	Extensively covered
• Decentralisation	Somewhat covered	Somewhat covered
• Transparency	Somewhat covered	Somewhat covered
ICT		
▪ View	Tool view	Tool/ensemble views
▪ Communication focus	Not present	Present
Relationship between ICT and development	Impact level mainly macro, impact on whom only weakly covered, primary and secondary effects only	Impact level both micro and macro, impact on whom extensively covered, while mainly primary and secondary also some tertiary effects

The Guidelines Report is a significant enhancement from the Bridging Report in terms of taking a far less constrained view of development and ICT's role in development. NORAD appears to be meaningfully addressing cornerstones of the human development perspective of development, namely, human development indices (health statistics, gender equality, education), grassroots and local initiatives, and the cultural context of the donee country. It also uses the term 'partner country' to indicate the de-emphasis of the trustee-ship position that underlies much of western approach to development assistance, and as evidenced in the Bridging Report. Table 4.3 summarizes our analyses of the two NORAD reports based on our alternative conceptualisations.

Summary of assessment Taking a bird's eyes view on NORAD's ongoing work on ICT-in-development, we try to characterize this overall process through our analyses and assessment of the two documents (see Figure 4.1).

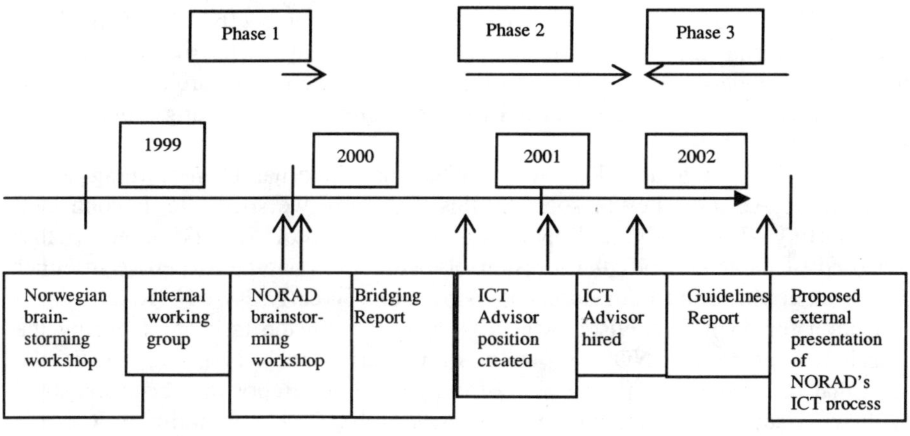

Figure 4.1 Key phases, dates, and events in NORAD's ongoing ICT-in-development process

Using the two documents to address this process admittedly represent some problems. Analysis of the overall process followed by NORAD for preparing an ICT strategy is difficult for a number of reasons:

1. There is not a lot of data available.
2. The brevity of the two documents makes it difficult to understand what lies behind many of the arguments presented, and to assess them correctly.
3. Both documents are working documents, and not strategies (although they are clearly important steps towards a strategy).
4. The overall process followed in the preparation of the documents was internal, and not open to the outside, and
5. Our assessment of this process will, of necessity, be preliminary, as the process is still ongoing and unfolding.

As viewed from the outside, it would appear that the process is not the result of a pre-determined scheme or plan. Rather, it is characterized by being a learning-as-we-go-along approach. For example, in 2001 the intention was to follow-up the Bridging Report with a full-fledged ICT strategy document. A first draft of this strategy was scheduled to be submitted to senior management by December 2001. This was, however, changed, and instead the Guidelines Report was prepared as an intermediate milestone and product.

Taken together, the two NORAD documents shed some light on how the perspective/outlook of a western donor agency can change – we dare say improve – from a traditional perspective of development to a more alternative view. We detect a clear progression and evolution in NORAD's approach to ICT-in-development. Taken separately, the two documents starkly represent the two perspectives and demonstrate the sharp contrast between the perspectives. The Bridging Report is a prime example of the traditional perspective. The Guidelines Report represents the alternative perspective containing many of the ideas we propose in this paper. While we welcome this trend, we are unsure of what led to this moderation. The process that led to a re-alignment of thinking would be an interesting area of study.

A few things are clear: it is evident that there has been learning as the work progressed. One key reason why this happened, we speculate, is connected with staffing. The Bridging Report was the product of a working group that consisted of NORAD staff that presumably had little concrete expertise in either ICT or its application to development cooperation. In early 2001 NORAD created a position for an ICT Advisor, who was charged with the task of managing the overall ICT process in NORAD, including preparing an ICT strategy. Thus, the work that resulted in the preparation of the Guidelines Report has been managed by the Advisor. To understand the progression in NORAD's thinking on ICT it is likely relevant that the Advisor has a degree in anthropology.

NORAD's ICT process is clearly driven by perceived organizational needs, goals, and priorities as defined in NORAD's overall strategy, on the one hand, and is informed by own experiences, on the other hand. There is likely some level of contact and exchange with likeminded activities in DANIDA and SIDA, NORAD's sister organizations in Denmark and Sweden, respectively.

As this ongoing work progresses, the experiences with and evaluation of the Guidelines Report will be used towards the next step, that involves selecting a sector and a country and/or region where NORAD will move in and address ICT specifically. The experiences from this work will, presumably, in turn lead to a full-fledged strategy. On a parallel track, operational work, in which support to projects and programmes with ICT is a key component, will continue.

5. Discussion

The traditional emphasis on disseminating aid, as it were, in the form of data, funding, and technology, often leads to conflicts, the causes, implications, and solutions of which are hard to grasp. As an alternative to this we posit the approach of 'studying up', that is, starting at the local level. This is the starting point for assessing needs, and for devising developmental goals and the appropriate means, including technology, to achieve them.

The extent to which an existing view of development – such as this 'western perspective' – can be reformed may be limited. As Nustad (2001) argues, the critique of post-development has a valid point when they construe, following Foucault, that the inherent assumptions and structure in any system constrain any reforming effort. Nustad, however, goes beyond this seeming impasse by suggesting that the manner in which development interventions actually play out in the field and in interaction with the context of the field may offer valuable lessons for development efforts. He discusses examples of how existing norms almost always mediate and often drastically changes the intended effects of the intervention.

This insight is particularly relevant for ICTs. If there is anything we have learnt about effects of ICT, it is that it is contextual (e.g., Avegerou and Walsham 2000, Braa et al. 1995). This viewpoint is a hallmark of social informatics, which views ICT as a socio-technical network (Kling 2000). In the specific area of ICT and development, Madon (1997) and Avegerou and Walsham (2000) have repeatedly emphasized the importance of the context. The focus should be on how a piece of technology, be it a computer or a plough, is used in a specific social, political, and cultural context. Our enhancement of development thinking also stresses this.

If we combine the two aspects – applying ICTs in context, and the mediating effect of the existing norms, structures, and beliefs – we come to a troubling issue. What will prevent the use of ICTs to perpetuate existing imbalances?

One aspect of the answer lies in the unforeseen effects of ICTs and the discontinuities they represent. The unforeseen consequences of technologies have been a hallmark of the diffusion of computers (Markus 2000). Perhaps the best example of this is electronic mail, which was an add-on to ARPANET, but became the 'killer application' of the Internet.

Another aspect of the answer can be found in the debate relating to the Appropriate Techno-logy and the Indigenous Knowledge (IK) movements. AT argues that there is a distinct divide or dichotomy between the North and the South, in terms of the culturally specific and determined view on the role of technology. Blunt and Warren (1996) articulate the IK view that IK systems constitute '... an important bridge to mutual understanding and communication ... between the local communities and the development practitioners' (Blunt and Warren 1996:xiii). Thus, while, not denying the existence of a dichotomy between IK systems in developing countries and the Western value system guiding development activities, they argue that the very same IK systems can bridge this divide. Agrawal (1995) critiques the idea of IK as currently applied to development. He argues that, initially, instead of seeking a bridging between North and South, it is necessary to go beyond the dichotomy of indigenous vs. scientific, and work towards greater autonomy for local people.

By integrating the seemingly disparate views, we postulate that ICT facilitates the development of indigenous knowledge, and thus foster autonomy for local people. This can lead to bridging the dichotomy inherent in the AT and IK thinking. In order for this to happen, these 'localized' movements and the largely macro-level oriented development activities (such as western donor agencies) need to join hands and communicate. There is an urgent need to develop such micro-macro communication links for addressing the needs for, and use of, appropriate ICT technology (Soeftestad 1998).

In summary, our conclusions are:

- ICTs should be deployed on focused and specific areas,
- The emphasis should be based on how it is used, rather than on the supply side,
- The impact should be assessed in terms of human development factors,The actual impact of ICT intervention is most likely to be different than what was intended. Local modalities will mediate its impacts, and
- ICTs have unforeseen impact and a comprehensive forecast is not possible.

The 2001 version of UNDP's human development report (UNDP 2001) concludes by emphasising that what is needed for development cooperation to work is policy and not charity.[4] We cannot agree more. We hope that by analysing a specific policy development process, and offering suggestions to create appropriate policies, we lend our voice to UNDP. In order to establish a broad, solid, and robust basis for application of ICT in development cooperation, in case of NORAD and elsewhere, it is important that:

(1) the policy development process becomes open to the outside,
(2) stakeholders outside the narrow academic and research/evaluation milieus take an active part, and,
(3) all stakeholders, in developing countries as well as in donor countries, come together to help shape the ICT-in-development agenda.

Acknowledgement

We would like to thank the valuable insights offered by an anonymous reviewer, especially related to appropriate technology, the dependency perspective and indigenous views on knowledge. These ideas helped improve our paper.

Notes

1 A critique and discussion of development theories is beyond the scope of this paper. Several excellent reviews and critiques are provided in many texts, e.g., Nederveen Pieterse (2000). For a brief discussion germane to ICT and national development, see Sein and Ahmad (2001).

2 UNDP has been producing annual reports since 1990 that calculates indices of human development achievement by various countries. We refer the readers to UNDP's human development reports (e.g., UNDP 2001) for both a comprehensive review and explanations and rationale behind the various indices.

3 This section is based partly on Soeftestad (2001) and interviews conducted with key NORAD ICT staff in 2001 and 2002.

4 The Norwegian Network on ICT and Development, established in January 2002 and funded by the Norwegian Research Council, aims to take an active part in defining this new ICT-in-development agenda. The conference "Developing countries and the network revolution: Leapfrogging or marginalization?" in (Trondheim, Norway, November 2002), organized by the Norwegian Association for Development Research and programmed by the Network, will address these issues, including a focus on NORAD's work on ICT.

References

Agrawal, A. (1995). Dismantling the divide between indigenous and scientific knowledge. *Development and Change*, 26, pp. 413-439.

Avegerou, C. and Walsham, G. W. (2000). *Information technology in context: Studies from the perspective of developing countries.* Aldershot: Ashgate.

Blunt, Peter and Warren, D. M. (1996). *Indigenous organizations and development*. London: Intermediate Technology Publications.

Braa J., Monteiro, E. and Reinert, E. S. (1995). Technology transfer vs. technological learning: IT-infrastructure and health care in developing countries. *IT for Development*, 6, pp.15-23.

Brynjolfsson, E. (1993). The productivity paradox of information technology. *Communications of the ACM,* 36, pp. 67-77.

Courier. (1998). Dossier: "Communication for development". *Courier*, no. 170.

Davison, R. M., Vogel, D. R., Harris, R. W., and Jones, N. (2000). Technology leapfrogging in developing countries: An inevitable luxury? *Electronic Journal of Information Systems in Developing Countries*, 1, pp. 1-10.

Hamelink, C. J. (1997). New information and communication technologies, social development and cultural change. Discussion paper no. 86. Geneva: UNRISD. (http://www.unrisd.org/engindex/publ/list/dp/dp86/dp86.htm)

Harindranath, G. and Liebenau, J. L. (1998). National information infrastructure policies in International Perspective. *UNIDO Emerging Technology Series*. Vienna: UNIDO.

Heeks, R. (1999). *Information and communication technologies, poverty and development.* IDPM Publications, Development Informatics: Working Papers, 5/1999.

Heeks, R. (2001). ICT and development. Presentation at Development Studies Association Conference, Manchester, UK, September 2001.

Kling, R. (2000). Learning about information technologies and social change: The contribution of social informatics. *The Information Society*, 16.

Madon, S. (1997). Information-based global economy and socio-economic development: The case of Bangalore. *The Information Society*, 13.

Malone, T. W. and Rockart, J. F. (1991). Computers, networks, and the corporation. *Scientific American*, 265, September, pp. 128-136.

Markus, M. L. (2000). Toward an integrated theory of IT-related risk control. In R. Baskerville, J. Stage, and J. I. DeGross (eds.). *Organizational and Social Perspectives on Information Technology*. Dordrecht: Kluwer/Plenum, pp. 167-178.

Nederveen Pieterse, J. (2001). *Development theory: Deconstructions/reconstructions*. London: Sage Publications.

NORAD. (1999). NORAD invests in the future. NORAD's strategy for 2000-2005. Oslo: Norwegian Agency for Development Cooperation.

NORAD. (2000). "Bridging the digital divide. Information and communication technologies. Challenges and opportunities to NORAD and its development partners". Report by the NORAD Working Group on ICT in Development Co-operation. Oslo: Norwegian Agency for Development Cooperation.

NORAD. (2002). "Information and Communication Technology (ICT) in development co-operation. Guidelines from NORAD." Oslo: Norwegian Agency for Development Cooperation. (http://www.norad.no)

Nustad, K. G. (2001). Development: The devil we know? *Third World Quarterly*, 22, pp. 479-490.

Organisation for Economic Co-operation and Development (OECD). (1997). The emerging information economy. In OECD's *Global Information Infrastructure-Global Information Society (GII-GIS): Policy Requirements*, 97, pp. 12-25.

Orlikowski, W. and Iacono, C. S. (2001). Research commentary: Desperately seeking "IT" in IT research - A call to theorizing the IT artifact. *Information Systems Research*, 12, pp. 121-134.

Rostow, W. W. (1971). *The stages of economic growth: A non-communist manifesto*, 2nd ed. Cambridge, UK: Cambridge University Press.

Schumacher, E. F. (1974). *Small is beautiful. Economics as if people mattered*. London: ABACUS.

Sein, M. K. and Ahmad, I. U. (2001). "A framework to study the impact of information and communication technologies on developing countries: The case of cellular phones in Bangladesh", *Proceedings of BITWORLD2001*, Cairo, Egypt.

Sirimanne, S. (1996). The information technology revolution: What about developing countries? *Express* No. 04 1996, IDIC, CIDA.

Soeftestad, L. T. (1998). Book review essay. *Journal of Political Ecology*, 5, pp. 23-30. (http://dizzy.library.arizona.edu/ej/jpe/jpeweb.html).

Soeftestad, L. T. (2001). Aligning needs and means: On culture, ICT and knowledge in development co-operation. *Proceedings of the 24th Information Systems Research Seminar in Scandinavia*, Ulvik, Norway, pp. 47-60. (http://www.ifi.uib.no/konf/iris24/)

United Nations Development Program (UNDP). (2001). *Human Development Report 2001: Making new technologies work for human development*. Oxford University Press, New York.

Wellenius, B., Braga, C. A. and Qiang, C. (2000). Current statistics: Investment and growth of the information infrastructure: Summary results of a global survey. *Telecommunications Policy*, 24, pp. 639-643.

Worsley, P. (1997). *Knowledges. What different people make of the world*. London: Profile Books.

Yang, S.C. (2001). *A theory of information infrastructure and information societies: New evidence on the effects of telecommunication investment*, Unpublished PhD. Dissertation. Claremont Graduate University, USA.

Chapter 5

Research Methodologies for Information Systems in the Development Context: A Tutorial

Geoff Walsham

1. Introduction

The focus of this book is the social implications of the use of computers and information systems (IS) in the context of developing countries. The purpose of this chapter is to discuss some methodological issues for empirically based researchers working in this domain. There are many different approaches to social science research in general, and IS research in particular, and it is not possible to cover this field in a comprehensive way in this short chapter. The chapter will, however, set out some broad methodological issues, and will make some observations based on my experience in the area, which I hope will be of value to other researchers working in the field.

The outline of the chapter is as follows. Firstly, I consider different styles of IS research, and I argue that an interpretive/critical stance is particularly suited to the goals of IS researchers working in developing countries. I then look briefly at some benefits and limitations of one way of operationalizing this stance, through action research designed to produce research outputs and specific intervention in a real situation. Various methods can be used in the conduct of research studies, and I next outline some of these, including the use of multi-method approaches. The penultimate section addresses the role of theory in IS research studies. Finally, I discuss issues of validity, the importance of writing, and the goal of relevance.

2. Styles of IS Research

In a widely-cited paper, Orlikowski and Baroudi (1991) split the broad styles of IS research into three categories: positivist, interpretivist, and critical. They provided definitions and examples of each type, and argued that the IS field at that time was dominated by positivist studies. There were few published interpretive studies, at least in the mainstream US-based journals cited in the paper, and almost no studies, which could be classed as critical.

Over a decade later, positivism remains a key research approach, particularly in the major US-based journals such as *MIS Quarterly* and *Information Systems Research*, but interpretivism is now 'respectable' in such outlets (see, for example, Klein and Myers 1999). In addition, the European-based journals, such as the *European Journal of Information Systems*, have always published articles with a wide range of research styles, although not always with great care in the definition of the research approach being used. Critical studies remain under-represented, although the journal *Information and Organization* (formerly *Accounting, Management and Information Technologies)* has included a higher proportion of such critical studies than other IS outlets.

I wish to argue that researchers concerned with the social implications of computer and IS in developing countries should naturally tend towards interpretive or critical studies. In such contexts, there are many different interpretations of the role and value of IS, in addition to multiple views on such fundamental questions as to the nature of 'development' itself and how to promote it. So, human interpretations are of high practical relevance and significance, and interpretive research takes these as a key focus. In addition, most developing countries display marked asymmetries in power relations, and one purpose of critical research studies is to analyse these with a view to achieving positive change in a more equitable direction.

3. Interpretive/Critical Studies

But what exactly is 'interpretive research'? A full discussion of this issue is beyond the scope of this chapter (see Mingers 1984 for a description of some alternative philosophical bases for interpretive studies). I wish instead to quote two examples of writers who have influenced my own view of this question. The first is the anthropologist Clifford Geertz who had this to say about the collection of data:

> What we call our data are really our own constructions of other people's constructions of what they and their compatriots are up to. (Geertz 1973)

The philosopher Michael Polanyi explored the nature of these 'constructions' we make of the world, using the concepts of sense-reading and sense-giving as part of a human being's individual 'tacit knowing':

> Both the way we endow our own utterances with meaning and our attribution of meaning to the utterances of others are acts of tacit knowing. They represent sense-giving and sense-reading within the structure of tacit knowing. (Polanyi 1969)

It is somewhat ironic, as noted in Walsham (2001a), that Polanyi's deeply interpretive stance, and his concept of personal tacit knowledge, has been hijacked in some of the populist knowledge management literature to justify approaches concerned with 'capturing' knowledge and storing it in 'knowledge repositories'. The whole thrust of Polanyi's work emphasizes the impossibility of such a task, noting that the very concept of 'explicit knowledge' is contradictory, since knowing is an individual human achievement.

Can interpretive research be critical? I think that Orlikowski and Baroudi's distinction here is useful but it should not be taken as a rigid dividing line, and thus that the answer to my question is yes to some extent. Saren and Brownlie (1999) defined critical perspectives as follows:

> By critical perspectives we mean modes of theorising and research practices which regard ... knowledge and its related technologies as socially constructed and enacted; which take those practices to be historically and culturally contingent; and which are understood to shape and be shaped by vested interests and power.

In a recent book (Walsham 2001b), I drew extensively on the interpretive research carried out by a range of researchers, including my own work. However, I certainly intended the work to be 'critical' in the sense of the above definition. In the book, I question the social construction of knowledge and the 'benefits' of ERP systems. For example, I argue that such issues should be viewed within a particular historical and cultural context, whereas a strong ethnocentric focus is displayed in much of the IS literature based on US and European journals. The links between knowledge and power are a central concern of the book. I believe that the interpretive/critical distinction is a rather fuzzy one, and that work on IS in developing countries, whilst interpretive in style, should also adopt a critical stance on issues such as social inequity, ethnocentricity and power relations.

4. Action Research

If one accepts, therefore, that researchers on IS in developing countries should adopt an interpretive/critical stance, there still remains the methodological issue as to whether the researcher should use a rather 'distanced' case study approach, for example, or should undertake action research. There are many different types of action research (Baskerville and Wood-Harper 1998). A well-known example is Peter Checkland's soft systems methodology (Checkland and Scholes 1991). However, despite some differences, all action research methods share the common purpose of trying to achieve positive action in a particular real world context, and to gain broader research insights of value to other contexts in the future.

It is not surprising that action research is a popular research approach for IS in developing countries, bearing in mind the many urgent problems facing those countries, and the potential benefit therefore of impacting the lives of disadvantaged people in a specific real situation. This volume contains a number of examples of work of this type. Whilst I wish to applaud such efforts, I would argue that action research is not the only vehicle for the researcher to use to change the world. Ideas, concepts and theories are powerful ways of enabling people to see things differently, and thus to take different action themselves. I see an ıportant role for research work that influences the thinking of others outside the ɔecific field research situation. This is a goal of action research, but it also can be achieved by other more 'distant' styles of research.

What are the merits and limitations of action research? The merits are the ones already outlined, namely the potential benefit of positive change in a real context, and the opportunity to learn through new conceptual or methodological ideas about how to intervene in a positive way in other contexts. In terms of limitations, one obvious issue is that it is not always possible to carry out action research, since key stakeholders in the field situation may not allow the researcher to tackle such directly active work. A second more subtle limitation is that it can be valuable to 'step back' from the real situation in order to see it more clearly, and the danger of action research is that it can become 'all action and no research' (quotation from Peter Checkland in personal conversation with the author). Researchers with limited time and other resources should choose carefully their balance of effort between 'understanding' the real situation and 'intervening' in it. Sometimes, the latter is best left to the practitioners themselves.

5. Research Methods

There are many different research methods that can be used in an interpretive/critical study of IS in developing countries, whether adopting an action research or case-based style of working. Interviews are a direct way of accessing people's interpretations, or 'collecting data' in Geertz's sense. However, it is important to note that quantitative methods, such as the use of surveys, can also be a useful tool. It is wrong to equate positivist/interpretivist with quantitative/qualitative methods respectively. A researcher's analysis of quantitative data can be a valuable input to an interpretive/critical study.

A further method of potential value in all research studies is document analysis, including computer-based methods such as the use of web sources. Participant observation is another method, offering the opportunity to observe participant action directly, rather than the more indirect approach to understanding field activity gained through interviews. In the context of an action research study, all the above methods can be valuable, in addition to specific approaches geared to direct intervention, such as the development of software solutions or training programmes.

With this wealth of methods available, the IS researcher needs to make a choice of methods, and two key criteria for this choice are relevance and feasibility. With respect to the former, a large-scale survey, for example, is unlikely to be relevant if the research is focused on perceptions of power relationships, since respondents tend to be very cautious in expressing their views on such matters in written form. Indeed, one of the main reasons why interpretive studies are often based largely on interview data, rather than surveys for example, is that it is very difficult to use surveys to access the complex socio-political perceptions of participants, whereas interviews are a better vehicle for this. Regarding the criterion of feasibility, an example is that action research methods may not always be allowed by those people providing field access to the researcher. It is certainly important, with respect to all IS research studies, to consider the use of multiple methods (Mingers 2001) in order to widen the basis of the researcher's understanding of the selected research topic.

6. Role of Theory

I have argued elsewhere (Walsham 1995) that theory can be used in a variety of ways in an IS research study: as an initial guide to study design and data collection; as part of an iterative process of data collection and analysis; or as a final product of the research. Indeed, different theories may be valuable in the different stages. For example, a theory of value in informing study design and data collection may later be discarded, like the scaffolding of a building once it is completed. Theory is a key way of 'generalising' research findings, since the interlinked concepts in the theory can then be utilised to provide insight in contexts other than that in which they were developed.

But how does the researcher arrive at 'good' theory for his or her particular research topic? This is a very difficult question to answer. A rather harsh, but relevant, comment is that collecting field data in the 'right' way does not guarantee 'success' in terms of being able to develop theory which others find insightful to them. The generation of second-order concepts (Van Maanen 1979) or theories relies on creative analysis by the researcher. Mere collection of detailed data, by any of the research methods outlined above, does not provide these concepts of itself. The use of software packages for the analysis of qualitative data, such as Nudist, is no substitute for the researcher's insight into choosing which concepts are to be used to analyse the data in the first place.

So where can researchers look for suitable theory to use and develop in their own studies? Firstly, an existing theory may be helpful. For example, one division of research topics is to consider different levels of analysis such as the individual, group, organization, or society. At each of these levels, there are a wealth of existing theories: for example, theories of identity at the individual level; of teamwork at the group level; of organizational change at the organizational level; or of globalization at the societal level. Thus, the researcher has many riches on offer, but the selection of appropriate theoretical approaches for a specific topic, and the specific field data that has been collected, relies on the researcher's judgement. As implied earlier, the choice of theory in a research study should not, however, be regarded as a one-off decision, but rather theory selection and data collection should be viewed as an intertwined process throughout the research study and its writing-up.

A second way in which relevant theory can be developed is through the use of 'grounded theory' approaches (Glaser and Strauss 1967), which aim to generate 'good' theory in a bottom-up way from the field data itself. Space restricts a substantial discussion of this theory-generation method here, but a word of warning is that grounded theory still relies on the researcher's insights to develop particular grounded concepts rather than others. There are no formulae, which guarantee success in this area of good theory generation, but a wide knowledge of existing theories and approaches does at least provide the researcher with potential tools for the job in hand.

7. Issues of Validity, Writing and Relevance

There has been considerable discussion in recent years in the IS literature on suitable criteria to 'validate' the findings of an interpretive research study. For example, Walsham and Sahay (1999) drew on work by Golden-Biddle and Locke (1993) to describe three characteristics of a 'valid' study: authenticity in that the author can present himself or herself as having an in-depth knowledge of the topic and field situations; plausibility in being able to connect to the reader's own ways of seeing the world; and criticality in terms of challenging the reader's preconceptions. Klein and Myers (1999) generate seven 'principles' that can be used to validate the merits of an interpretive IS study. Whilst commending these efforts to the reader (not least since I contributed to one of them myself), I would caution: beware of orthodoxy. There is no final set of characteristics or principles, which can determine whether a research study and its results are considered valid by a particular reader. Written work, including this chapter, is an exercise in rhetoric in trying to convince the reader, and readers will bring their own deep tacit knowledge to bear to judge whether the attempt by the author has been successful in their view.

This brings me to the art of writing, which I would like to emphasise as being an extremely important skill for any IS researcher, whether working on developing country issues or not. In an earlier book (Walsham 1993), I quoted Van Maanen (1989) on the subject of writing:

> We try to persuade others by 'presenting a coherent point of view told with grace, wit and felicity'.

More recently, I looked up these latter terms in the Concise Oxford Dictionary. Grace is 'pleasing quality … charm, especially that belonging to elegant proportions'. Wit is 'the power of giving sudden intellectual pleasure by unexpected combining … of previously unconnected ideas'. Felicity is 'happy faculty in expression … well-chosen phrase'. Now we all, including myself, fall down in trying to make our written work graceful, witty and felicitous, but at least we should know what we are trying to achieve when we write.

All of us working on IS in developing countries want our work to be relevant to the real world, and in particular to the difficult and serious problems which beset the poorer countries, regions and peoples of the world. How can we achieve this relevance? Firstly, we need to learn something ourselves about a particular topic or issue, which is not widely known or has not been looked at in this way before. Secondly, we need to try to communicate our learning to others. Thirdly, we need to use our combined learning and knowledge to engage in conversations on important topics, and to take appropriate actions. I have tried, in this short chapter, to provide some brief pointers towards how to go about each of these processes. If we can do our IS research work well, then we can make a significant contribution to our common goal of using IT to make a better world.

References

Baskerville, T. and Wood-Harper, A. (1998) 'Diversity in Information Systems Action Research Methods', *European Journal of Information Systems*, 7(2), pp. 90-107.

Checkland, P. and Scholes, J. (1990) *Soft Systems Methodology in Action*, Wiley, Chichester.

Geertz, C. (1973) *The Interpretation of Cultures*, Basic Books, New York.

Glaser, B.G. and Strauss, A.L. (1967) *The Discovery of Grounded Theory: Strategies for Qualitative Research*, Weidenfeld & Nicholson, London.

Golden-Biddle, K. and Locke, K. (1993) 'Appealing Work: An Investigation of How Ethnographic Texts Convince', *Organization Science*, 4(4), pp. 595-616.

Klein, H.K. and Myers, M.D. (1999) 'A Set of Principles for Conducting and Evaluating Interpretive Field Studies in Information Systems', *MIS Quarterly*, 23(1), pp.67-94.

Mingers, J. (1984) 'Subjectivism and Soft Systems Methodology: A Critique', *Journal of Applied Systems Analysis*, 11, pp. 85-103.

Mingers, J. (2001) 'Combining IS Research Methods: Towards a Pluralist Methodology', *Information Systems Research*, 12(3), pp. 240-259.

Orlikowski, W.J. and Baroudi, J.J. (1991) 'Studying Information Technology in Organizations: Research Approaches and Assumptions', *Information Systems Research*, 2(1), pp. 1-28.

Polanyi, M. (1969) *Knowing and Being*, Routledge & Kegan Paul, London.

Saren, M. and Brownlie, D. (1999) 'Marketing Stream' in *Proceedings of the 1st Critical Management Studies Conference* (eds H. Willmott and I. Grugulis), UMIST, Manchester.

Van Maanen, J. (1979) 'The Fact of Fiction in Organizational Ethnography', *Administrative Science Quarterly*, 24(4), pp. 539-550.

Van Maanen, J. (1989) 'Some Notes on the Importance of Writing in Organization Studies', in *The Information Systems Research Challenge: Volume 1* (eds J.I. Cash and P.R. Lawrence), Harvard Business School, Boston, pp. 27-33.

Walsham, G. (1993) *Interpreting Information Systems in Organizations*, Wiley, Chichester.

Walsham, G. (1995) 'Interpretive Case Studies in IS Research: Nature and Method', *European Journal of Information Systems*, 4(2), pp. 74-81.

Walsham, G. (2001a) 'Knowledge Management: The Benefits and Limitations of Computer Systems', *European Management Journal*, 19(6), pp. 599-608.

Walsham, G. (2001b) *Making a World of Difference: IT in a Global Context*, Wiley, Chichester.

Walsham, G. and Sahay, S. (1999) 'GIS for District-Level Administration in India: Problems and Opportunities', *MIS Quarterly*, 23(1), pp. 39-66.

Chapter 6

Information Systems in Global Organizations: Unpacking 'Culture'

Robert D. Galliers

Culture (noun)

Etymology: Middle English, from Middle French, from Latin cultura, from cultus, past participle

Date: 15th century

– the act of developing the intellectual and moral faculties especially by education expert care and training.
– enlightenment and excellence of taste acquired by intellectual and aesthetic training; acquaintance with taste in the fine arts, humanities, and broad aspects of science as distinguished from vocational and technical skills.
– the integrated pattern of human knowledge, belief, and behavior that depends upon man's (sic.) capacity for learning and transmitting knowledge to succeeding generations; the customary beliefs, social forms, and material traits of a racial, religious, or social group; the set of shared attitudes, values, goals, and practices that characterizes a company or corporation.
– cultivation of living material in prepared nutrient media; also a product of such cultivation.

Culture shock (noun)
Date: 1940

– a sense of confusion and uncertainty sometimes with feelings of anxiety that may affect people exposed to an alien culture or environment without adequate preparation.

Source: Merriam-Webster's Collegiate Dictionary

1. Introduction

As can be seen from the above set of definitions, the word 'culture' can have many meanings. Indeed, in his book *The Interpretation of Cultures*, Clifford Geertz (1973; pp. 4-5) notes:

> The conceptual morass into which the Tyrolean kind of *pot-au-feu* theorizing about culture can lead, is evident in what is still one of the better general introductions to anthropology, Clyde Kluckholn's *Mirror for Man*. In some twenty-seven pages of his chapter on the concept, Kluckholn managed to define culture in turn as: (1) 'the total way of life of a people'; (2) 'the social legacy the individual acquires from his group'; (3) 'a way of thinking, feeling and believing' (4) 'an abstraction from behavior'; (5) a theory on the part of the anthropologist about the way in which a group of people in fact behave; (6) a 'store-house of pooled learning'; (7) 'a set of standardized orientations to recurrent problems'; (8) 'learned behavior'; (9) a mechanism for the normative regulation of behavior; (10) 'a set of techniques for adjusting both to the external environment and to other men'; (11) 'a precipitate of history'; and turning, perhaps in desperation, to similes, as a map, as a sieve, and as a matrix.

This chapter aims to contribute to the discussion that is at the very heart of this book by focusing on one of the key challenges facing us as we endeavor to harness the undoubted power and potential of information and communication technology (ICT) as a force for good in the development context. It does so by attempting to unpack some of the confused and confusing thinking concerning the development and application of information systems in global organizations by highlighting the different levels at which the concept of culture may be applied. It does so since, only by understanding more fully the local context for which ICT systems are being developed and in which they are to be implemented, can we hope to fulfill their promise. And it does so by providing a complementary account of culture to that provided by Chris Westrup and colleagues elsewhere in this volume. Following Geertz,

> The concept of culture I espouse … is essentially a semiotic one. Believing, with Max Weber, that man is an animal suspended in webs of significance he himself has spun, I take culture to be those webs, and the analysis of it to be therefore not an experimental science in search of law but an interpretive one in search of meaning. (*ibid*.; 5)

In particular, an attempt is made here to unpack and interpret 'culture' at the national, organizational and sub-organizational levels.[1]

In line with the above definitions of 'culture' and 'culture shock', we aim to relieve the 'sense of confusion and uncertainty' that we feel when 'exposed to an alien culture or environment'. In doing so, the focus is on 'shared attitudes, values, goals, and practices' of and within organizations, and nations. The objective is to develop our 'intellectual and moral faculties' as regards this important topic in modern Information Systems (IS) discourse for, we believe, there is indeed a moral obligation on the part of the IS community to attempt a better understanding of the different contexts in which IS are being implemented, and for which IS are being designed.

Alternative titles for this chapter might thus reasonably have been *Taking Culture Seriously* (after Walsham, 2001a) or *Culture's Consequences* (after Hofstede, 1980). Very much in line with Walsham's (2001a) concern that in an age when globalization has become fashionable, and in which claims for the role and impact of information and communication technologies (ICT) are at times both naïve and excessive, it is important that we acknowledge and understand local contexts and sensibilities. While on the one hand, this chapter agrees with Castells' (2000) view that without ICT 'there could be no economic globalization, no network enterprise, no global media, no global communication', it questions some of the more trite interpretations concerning ICT's impacts. So, for example, while ICT 'support[s] global business strategies ... [and] ... can also be a major catalyst in the globalisation process itself' (Peppard, 1999), we would argue that global applications of ICT require very careful design and implementation, taking into account the very different contexts in which such applications are to be used. Taking a leaf from Beck's (2000a) analysis, this chapter also questions the assumption that 'we live and act in self-enclosed spaces of national states and their respective national societies', which is characteristic of what Beck terms *the first modernity*: 'a period where our stock answers ... are inapplicable and contradictory' (*ibid.*). Rather, we share Beck's view that we have been 'living for a long time in a world society ... nothing which happens on our planet is only a limited local event ... we must reorient and reorganize our lives and actions, our organizations and institutions along a "local-global" axis' (*ibid.*). We are thus, to use his term, in *the second modernity*.

This is not to say that globalization has not been the topic of many a scholarly or practitioner article, especially in the context of ICT's undoubted reach across many parts of the globe.[2] According to Beck (*ibid.*), 'Globalization has been talked to death and yet seems continually to escape our grasp. It's like trying to lasso a ghost.' Thus, Beck makes the useful distinction between *globalism* – 'the ideology of rule by the world market' – with *globality*, which is where his talk of *the second modernity* comes in. The implications of Beck's arguments are wide-ranging.[3] Thus, for example, the unsuspecting may assume that knowledge derived in one context will have general – global significance. Such an assumption or set of beliefs – culture if you will – underlies the popular, and largely unquestioned, [4] notion of 'best practice' solutions. However, taking what has been called a 'logic of opposition' (cf., Robey and Boudreau, 1999), what *may* be best practice in one context may well not be in some other. Neither do we view culture as a *barrier* to ICT adoption here. Such a view is an unfortunate, if not arrogant, overly ICT-deterministic perspective, unworthy of a 'cultured' society or profession. In the context of the export of ICT to the lesser-developed world, for example, this also smacks of colonialism, if not imperialism.

Three cases are used to illustrate the way in which cultural issues can be unpacked at the (inter-)national, organizational, and sub-organizational levels: an electronics company, and two banks. [5] Discussion of each case focuses on cultural aspects, and thereby, the significance of cultural analysis is demonstrated. The cases are meant to be interpreted as brief histories of the companies concerned. For,

> Unlike the traditional ideal of a wholly explicit, self-guaranteeing truth, from-to knowledge cannot be instantaneous; it is a stretch, not only of attention, but of effort, effort must be lived, and living takes time. Knowledge, therefore, is embedded both in living processes ... and in the uniquely human form of living processes: in history. (Grene, 1969; xi)

Following the brief case accounts, conclusions are drawn as to the manner in which further research on cultural aspects of (global) IS might be usefully extended.

A word of caution may be necessary here, however. While they may be 'brief histories', these case accounts are little more than vignettes – brief snapshots of issues confronting the companies concerned. They fail adequately to provide a sense of culture as fluid and dynamic, and in a constant state of flux and negotiation between groups, as discussed by Chris Westrup and colleagues elsewhere in this volume. As indicated in the introduction, an attempt is made here to provide a complementary account of culture. The cases, therefore, provide something of a lens on those aspects of culture that may be more static – at each of the three levels considered – than might otherwise be assumed from other accounts. This has implications when we consider the central theme of the conference from which this book emerged: 'ICTs and Development: New Opportunities, Perspectives and Challenges'. While the cases do not focus on development issues per se, they make the point that, even in the developed world, considerations of culture are crucial when we attempt to develop and implement global ICT 'solutions'.

2. Case 1: An Anglo-Japanese Electronics Company[6]

This case is illustrative of cultural analysis at the *national* level. It concerns what was meant to be a technological partnership between a Japanese company and a British company that the former had acquired. The key goal of the acquisition was to take advantage of the complementarity in each firm's knowledge and expertise, through enhanced knowledge creation and sharing. While the Japanese firm acquired a majority stake in the British firm, the latter retained a high degree of autonomy, post acquisition. Different approaches to the organization of knowledge, technical work and product development were apparent. For example, while the British relied more heavily on abstract knowledge through formal university training, the Japanese favored practical know-how and problem-solving techniques acquired in the workplace. Further, while the British approach to product development might be described as sequential and hierarchical, with self-contained stages, the Japanese adopted a more holistic approach, with multi-functional teams.

Unpacking the cultural issues at play in the two firms, we can see that the very meaning and nature of engineering was quite different in each. While the British saw engineering as embrained, embedded and potentially encodable, the Japanese viewed this knowledge more in terms of embodiment and of being enculturated.[7] This is illustrated with regard to the respective norms for group working and knowledge sharing in the two firms. Thus, while the British viewed engineering projects as a set of sequential stages enabled by document transfer between stages, the Japanese favored much more intensive interaction and iteration. Further, while the role of ICT-based knowledge systems are much more in line with the attitudes of the British engineers, the Japanese were of the view that their expertise and emergent knowledge could not be captured in or by ICT-based systems (Walsham, 2001b).

3. Case 2: The Globalizing Bank[8]

This case is illustrative of cultural analysis at the *organizational* level and concerns a major international bank, whose headquarters are located in Continental Europe. It has around 70,000 employees and operates in approximately 70 countries worldwide. The bank began to take its global strategy and operations seriously when it lost a major customer to a rival. The customer operated in many of the same countries in which the bank also operated, and had become discontented with the bank's processes, products and services because they differed quite widely from one country to the next. As a result, the bank decided to implement what it called 'Vision 2000', with a view to becoming 'the networked bank'. The idea was to integrate its processes and procedures through knowledge sharing utilizing an intranet to identify 'best practices' in the different countries. Despite its best efforts, however, the actual outcome of the 18-month project was the creation of over 150 separate intranets, with little in the way of communication between one country – or even one department – and the next. Indeed, what might be termed 'electronic fences' (cf., Newell, *et al.*, 1999) were created, reinforcing existing national and functional boundaries. In attempt to rectify the situation, a two-day strategy retreat was arranged, with senior banking and IS officials attending from each major country. The outcome of this retreat was a decision to construct a single corporate portal, to enable better communication between the numerous intranets, and to present a single face to the outside world. Within one week of the strategy retreat, seven such 'corporate' portals were being developed – quite independently.

How did this occur? Focusing on organizational culture considerations, it became clear that the vision of 'the networked bank' was in direct opposition to the structure and culture of the bank. Growth had been by acquisition, with the banks in each country being left to operate quite independently. And within each country bank, each business unit was subject to *independent* performance review. In interview, bank employees made it clear that it was believed not to be in their best interests to 'waste time' learning about what others were doing. Thus, counter to common arguments for the introduction of intranets and IT-based knowledge management systems (Alavi and Leidner, 1999), rather than preventing reinvention, the intranet project actually stimulated it.

4. Case 3: Component-Based Development[9]

This case is illustrative of cultural analysis at the *sub-organizational* level, and is based on a bank whose operations are based in many of the major financial centers of the world, including London, New York, Tokyo and Hong Kong. Its business focuses on foreign exchange, currency options and interest rate derivatives, and it posted gross profits of US $2 billion in 2000. The bank was subject to a major restructure in 1997, following which there has been a 40 percent increase in staff – mostly on a contractual basis. Indeed, currently, contract staff represent something like one-third of the total workforce. Together with central functions such as human resources, the bank is organized on the basis of its front office operations (i.e., buying and selling), the back office (i.e., settling payments) and the middle office (i.e., tracing and checking payments).

As part of a move to improve efficiency and respond quickly to changing client requirements, the bank decided to adopt component-based development (CBD) as its preferred software development approach. Unlike traditional end-to-end development, CBD reuses and assembles existing components in an attempt to speed up the development process and to avoid 're-inventing the wheel'. Thus, the desired goals included shortening development time, reducing costs and providing a flexible ICT infrastructure. Unfortunately, however, resistance to the changing nature of IS development soon became evident. This was so, particularly from end-users of the systems – primarily in view of lack of training with respect to the new systems – but also on the part of the IS staff, who saw the new approach as a potential threat – both in terms of job security, and also in terms of the manner in which 'things were done'. In addition, however, CBD requires considerable collaboration and information sharing across components, so that cross-category solutions can be devised. Such collaboration and knowledge sharing did not eventuate, however. For some, yet more investment in ICT was simply 'continuing to throw money into a black hole' (Front Office Director). For others, the requirement to share information was actually a waste of time: '... interaction between departments is minimal ... why? ... because we just don't have time ... we don't have that luxury.' (Front Office Technology Manager).

We often hear of 'the culture of an organization'. Indeed, in relation to ICT, 'organization culture' has been shown to influence the process of how technology is adopted, embedded and institutionalized within organizations. For example, Davenport (1994) and Powell and Dent-Micallef (1997) both depict the need for an information culture that is open, flexible and expansive in order to ease technology implementation. El Sawy *et al.* (2001) propose developing a culture that encourages trust and knowledge sharing for similar reasons. Sloan and Green (1995) stress the importance of a culture favorably disposed to new IT, while

Astebro (1995) explores the influence of culture from the perspective of managerial influence and resource availability.

All of these examples adopt what Martin (1992; following Meyerson and Martin, 1987) describes as an integration perspective. They depict the organization as having a single culture that is unified and consistent; or at least, one where the aim is to achieve this consistency. In this case, however, we see organizational sub-cultures at work, especially between front office personnel (whether they have banking or ICT-related roles) and their back office counterparts. The former were imbued with a sense of urgency and efficiency and were very much outward facing; the latter's focus was introspective and on accuracy and painstaking care in checking payments.

5. Towards a Synthesis

What can we learn from these three accounts? Taking each individually, we can see that in Case 2 a technological solution was applied to a business problem. One might say that the technology was 'parachuted' into the organization, without due regard to 'the way things were'. The structure and business processes remained unchanged, while role and skill changes were not considered. 'Culture' remained relatively unchanged, possibly even reinforced, by the imposition of technology. In Case 1, we saw divergent views as to the very nature of Engineering and the manner in which engineering projects might be conducted. This led to a view within the Japanese company that much of their knowledge could not be codified in ICT-based systems, for example. Again we see deep-seated 'cultures' being reinforced in a manner not foreseen prior to the amalgamation. In Case 3, we might generalize to make the point that so-called corporate-wide applications such as BPR, ERP and CBD do not automatically provide the expected business benefits in terms of efficiencies and intra-organizational communication. Further, we might conclude that there is more to sub-cultural differences than the oft-cited 'business-IT divide' (e.g., Knights and Murray, 1994). Over time, prevalent attitudes held by individuals in the IT and banking services of the organization began to coalesce as the two groups worked together for a common purpose (e.g., in the front office or the back office), thus illustrating the dynamic and changing nature of 'culture' and lending further evidence to the view that new boundaries may be formed once old boundaries are torn down (Newell, *et al.*, 2001). Overall, however, the cases seek to illustrate the power of utilizing a 'cultural' lens when considering issues associated with the development and implementation of ICT systems in (global) organizations.

Specifically, we have looked at 'culture' at three different levels here, namely at the national, organizational and sub-organizational level. When considering the literature on culture at these levels, it becomes clear that the concept is being considered, for the most part at least, at each level in isolation rather than collectively. So, for example, we see research that seeks to unveil issues associated with national (or regional) cultures in aspects of business (e.g., Schneider and DeMeyer, 1991; Shane, 1994), and more specifically in relation to

ICT (e.g., Shore and Venkatachalam, 1995). In addition, we see the early work of Hofstede (1980) being challenged (e.g., Shackleton and Ali, 1990; McSweeney, 2002). At the organizational level, the work of Schein and Smirich is well known and respected (Smirich and Calas, 1987; Schein, 1996), with the work of Orlikowski (e.g., 1992) also being predominant in relation to organizational ICT. At the sub-organizational level, we have already noted the work of Martin (1992). It is rarer, however, to see these cultural levels being discussed collectively. Exceptions include Sackman's (1992) work on organizational culture and sub-cultures, and in the field of organizational ICT, the study by Robey and Azevodo (1994).

Given the increasing global reach of ICT, and the new organizational forms that have arisen as a result, it would seem appropriate now for us who take seriously research in the field of IS to take on board such cultural issues as have been introduced in this chapter – at the national, organizational and sub-organizational levels collectively. This is particularly so when considering the strategic, managerial, organizational and development issues associated with ICT in global and virtual organizations. And it is even more important when considering ICT and development, bearing in mind the dangers of technological imperialism arising from an unthinking or ill-informed approach to technology transfer. After all, 'Technology does not make cultural and business boundaries disappear simply because it exists ... Collaborative technologies cannot single-handedly facilitate global reach.' (Newell, *et al.*, 2001). The aim here has been to introduce such considerations into our discourse, and to begin to unpack the multi-faceted nature of the concept of 'culture' in this context.

Notes

1 Alternative approaches to unveiling 'culture' are of course perfectly feasible and reasonable. See, for example, the chapter by Chris Westrup and colleagues elsewhere in this volume.

2 But note, for example, that, according to *The Guardian* newspaper in 2001, 80 percent of the world's population had never made a telephone call, let alone used the Internet, and that while the Internet connects approximately 100 million computers, it connects less than 2 percent of the world's population.

3 See also Beck (2000b).

4 The article by Swan, *et al.* (1999) being a notable exception.

5 The author owes a debt of gratitude to and draws on Geoff Walsham's (2001b) cross-cultural analysis of a number of cases, based on Giddens' (1979; 1984) Structuration Theory, particularly with regard to Case 1.

6 This account is based on Lam (1997).

7 These terms are taken from Blackler (1995). Blackler's typology categorizes knowledge into five types. Embrained knowledge refers to individual cognitive abilities; embodied knowledge relates to the ability to carry out particular actions with parts of the human body, such as a skilled craftsman might do; encultured knowledge relates to the ability to achieve and obtained shared meanings within a particular social group; embedded knowledge is a kind of subset of encultured knowledge in that knowledge is shared

through routines, and encoded knowledge refers to knowledge that is made explicit through books, databases, and other media.

8 This account is based on Galliers and Newell (2001).

9 This account is based on Huang, *et al.* (2002).

References

Alavi, M and Leidner, D E (1999). 'Knowledge management systems: issues, challenges and benefits, *Communications of the AIS*, 1(7), February, http://cais.isworld.org/articles/1-7/article.htm

Astebro, T (1995). 'The effect of management and social interaction on the intra-firm diffusion of electronic mail systems', *IEEE Transactions on Engineering Management*, 42,pp. 319-331.

Beck, U (2000a). 'The post-modern society and its enemies', *Prometheus*.

Beck, U (2000b). *What is Globalization?* Cambridge: Polity Press.

Blackler, F (1995). 'Knowledge, knowledge work and organizations: an overview and interpretation', *Organization Studies*, 16(6), pp. 1021-46.

Castells, M (2000). 'Globalization and identity in the network society', *Prometheus*.

Davenport, T (1994). 'Saving IT's soul: human-centered information management, *Harvard Business Review*, 72, pp. 119-131.

El Sawy, O, Eriksson, I, Raven, A and Carlsson, S (2001), 'Understanding shared knowledge creation spaces around business processes: precursors to process innovation implementation', *International Journal of Technology Management*, 22, pp. 149-173.

Galliers, R D and Newell, S (2001). 'Electronic commerce and strategic change within organizations: lessons from two cases', *Journal of Global Information Management*, 9(3), pp. 15-22.

Geertz, C (1973). *The Interpretation of Cultures: Selected Essays*, New York: Basic Books.

Giddens, A (1979). *Central Problems in Social Theory*, Basingstoke: Macmillan.

Giddens, A (1984). *The Constitution of Society*, Cambridge: Polity Press.

Grene, M (1969). Introduction to Michael Polanyi's *Knowing and Being*, Chicago: University of Chicago Press.

Hofstede, G (1980). *Culture's Consequences: International Differences in Work-Related Values*, London: Sage.

Huang, J C, Newell, S, Galliers, R D and Pan, S-L (2002). 'Dangerous liaisons? component-based development and organizational subcultures', *IEEE Transactions on Engineering Management* (in press).

Knights,D and Murray, F (1994). *Managers Divided: Organisational Politics and Information Technology Management*, Chichester: Wiley.

Lam, A (1997). 'Embedded firms, embedded knowledge: problems of collaboration and knowledge transfer in global cooperative ventures', *Organization Studies*, 18(6), pp. 973-996.

Martin, J (1992). *Cultures in Organizations*, Oxford: Oxford University Press.

McSweeney, B (2002). 'Hofstede's model of national cultural differences and their consequences: a triumph of faith – a failure of analysis', *Human Relations*, 55(1), pp. 89-118.

Meyerson, D and Martin, J (1987). 'Cultural change: an integration of three different views', *Journal of Management Studies*, 24, pp. 623-647.

Newell, S, Pan, S-L, Galliers, R D and Huang, J C (2001). 'The myth of the boundaryless organization', *Communications of the* ACM. 44(12), pp. 74-76.

Newell, S, Swan, J, Galliers, R D and Scarbrough, H (1999). 'The intranet as a knowledge management tool? Creating new electronic fences', in M Khosrowpour (ed.), *Managing Information Technology Resources in Organizations in the Next Millennium*, Hershey: Idea Group Publishing, pp. 612-619.

Orlikowski, W J (1992). 'The duality of technology: rethinking the concept of technology in organizations', *Organization Science*, 3(3), pp. 398-427.

Peppard, J (1999). 'Information management in the global enterprise: an organising framework', *European Journal of Information Systems*, 8(2), pp. 77-94.

Powell, T and Dent-Micallef, A (1997). 'Information technology as competitive advantage: the role of human, business, and technology resources', *Strategic Management Journal*, 18, pp. 375-404.

Robey, D and Azevedo, A (1994). 'Cultural analysis of the organizational consequences of information technology', *Accounting, Management and Information Technologies*, 4, pp. 23-37.

Robey, D and Boudreau, M-C (1999). 'Accounting for the contradictory organizational consequences of information technology: theoretical directions and methodological implications', *Information Systems Research*, 10(2), pp. 167-185.

Sackmann, S (1992). 'Culture and subcultures: an analysis of organizational knowledge, *Administrative Science Quarterly*, 37, pp. 140-161.

Schein, E (1996), 'Culture: the missing concept in organization studies', *Administrative Science Quarterly*, 41, pp. 229-240.

Schneider, S and DeMeyer, A (1991). 'Interpreting and responding to strategic issues: the impact of national culture', *Strategic Management Journal*, 12, pp. 307-320.

Shackleton, V J and Ali, A H (1990). 'Work-related values of managers: a test of the Hofstede model', *Journal of Cross-Cultural Psychology*, 21, pp. 307-320.

Shane, S (1994). 'The effect of national culture on the choice between licensing and direct foreign investment', *Strategic Management Journal*, 15, pp. 627-642.

Shore, B and Venkatachalam, A R (1995). 'The role of national culture in systems analysis and design', *Journal of Global Information Management*, 3(3), pp. 5-14.

Sloan, R and Green, H (1995). 'Manufacturing decision support architecture', *Information Systems Management*, 12, pp. 7-16.

Smirich, L and Calas, M (1987). 'Organizational culture: a critical assessment', in F M Jablin, L L Putnam and L W Porter (eds.), *Handbook of Organizational Communication*, Newbury Park: Sage, pp. 228-263.

Swan J, Newell S and Robertson M (1999). 'The illusion of 'best practice' in information systems for operations management', *European Journal of Information Systems*, 8(4), pp. 284-293.

Walsham, G (2001a). Making a World of Difference: IT in a Global Context, Chichester: Wiley.

Walsham, G (2001b). 'Globalization and ICTs: working across cultures'. Judge Institute of Management Studies Working Paper WP 8/2001, University of Cambridge.

PART II
E-GOVERNANCE AND THE DIGITAL DIVIDE

Chapter 7

Information Village: Bridging the Digital Divide in Rural India[1]

Shivraj Kanungo

1. Introduction

The genesis of the information village concept, which has operationalized into a viable experiment,[2] was a formalized set of conversations organized by the M. S. Swaminathan Research Foundation (MSSRF). According to Swaminathan (2001) the economic gap between the North and South can be accounted for, in large part, by differential in the ability of populations to absorb and use technology effectively to create value. That being the case, it is reasonable to speculate that information technology, which has the greatest potential to democratize, equalize and empower individuals, can be highly effective in improving the quality of lives of the poorest of the poor. In general economic terms, that which is profitable for the poor is also profitable for the rich. However, more often than not, the reverse does not hold. Hence, while the conceptual and ideological attraction of using information technology (IT) to improve the quality of lives of the poor is great, there are numerous infrastructural, resource-related and developmental gaps that need to be addressed concomitantly when we conceptualize, design and deploy IT in highly resource-challenged environments. The information village experiment has been detailed elsewhere (Kanungo, 2001). We address the two notions of replicability and sustainability of the information village project. While we believe that the experimental framework of the information village project, where a knowledge center (KC) is established in a village, is replicable because of the now well-developed and documented experimental protocol, the goal of sustainability is more challenging. In this paper we subject this concept to creative and constructive analytical rigor. Our results indicate that the challenge associated with the digital divide – the gap between those with access to [information and communication] technical resources and those without (O'Neil, 2001) – remains formidable. From a theoretical standpoint, viewing IT interventions in a resource-challenged environment allow us to conceptualize and view the dynamics in a manner that allows us to reframe the discourse about sustainability and replicability.

2. Background and Methodology

The information village program was initiated formally in 1998. However, the conceptual basis for such a project was laid much before that (Swaminathan, 1993). Following the initial 'success' of the information village project,[3] harder questions were raised within the MSSRF. Our objective, in this paper, is to respond to two questions as they were initially raised:

- Are overall goals of the Information Village project being met?
- Is the rural community sufficiently convinced that the KC is a valuable asset?

These two questions are directly attributable to the twin project objectives of replicability and sustainability. While section three can be seen as a response to the issue of replicability, the rest of the paper concentrates on the question of sustainability. The logic of the research questions can be justified as thus. If the project objectives, that were identified initially, can be shown to have been met, then there would be reason to believe that we can expect such projects to sustain themselves. The second question has to do with framing (and subsequent reframing) of the information village from the standpoint of village participants and users. The primary lever for sustainability lies in this dimension.

In order to respond to the questions, this research was conceptualized as an in-depth case study and is presented using frameworks based on Habermas's theory of social action (Habermas, 1971, 1979, 1984). We used this conceptual framework in order to ensure that while the case analyzed here is one of a kind, the theoretical and analytical rigor is maintained in order to allow for methodological replicability[4] (Lee, 1989). The immediate value of using the theory of social action was to be able to pose the research questions meaningfully. Our stance is to focus on the social nature of information systems. In the *theory of communicative action*, Habermas identifies four primary social action types that an agent or actor can play out as a part of organizational or social functioning. They are: *instrumental*, *strategic*, *communicative* and *discursive*. An instrumental action is taken in order to meet a specific objective. A strategic action is used to sway an opinion or influence an action of another person. A communicative action is used to gain an understanding among all parties. A discursive action is often used in order to gain agreement or restore validity. While Lytinnen and Hirschheim (1988) have been among the first to identify that the first three action types have been used in conceptualizing information systems (Huber, 1982), the discursive type has been neglected. Our approach has been to identify the relevance of the all four types of actions in the domain of information systems in rural contexts and highlight their importance. In addition the Foucauldian notion of discursive practice that is necessarily interwoven with power relations and social practices is also utilized in this study. From an operational standpoint, we have depended on Hirschheim and Klein (1989 and 1994) to provide the analytical basis for focusing on the emancipatory function of information systems. In using the conceptual framework provided by Hirschheim and Klein we are also responding to an empirical gap they identify when they state that 'virtually no published examples exist of how neohumanist values have been implemented in practice (Hirschheim and Klein, 1994).' Additionally, we undertake the task of mapping the conceptual framework onto the notions of replicability and sustainability.

Apart from a brief historical reconstruction, this study was based on a series of intensive interactions with the project staff and KC volunteers. Limited direct interaction took place with users of the KC. While in-depth interviews formed the major source of data, additional documentary evidence was based on project plans and reports, interim studies and related documents. In-depth interviews were conducted with three volunteers in different KCs. Each interview lasted roughly one hour. The interviews were conducted in the last week of August 2001 by visiting the KC sites and interacting with the volunteers who were present. Each interview was enabled by the presence of at least two project staff who not only acted as translators but also proved to be the most important source of validation (especially with reference to facts). We also benefited from numerous articles from the popular press. Our account is organized as follows. In section three we describe the KC experimental protocol and discuss it in the context of Habermas' action types in the context of replicability. Section four and five focus on sustainability issues, with section four concentrating on the governance structure of villages and section five on the timeframe during which sustainability is expected to be demonstrated. Section six presents ways to overcome barriers to sustainability by employing influence diagrams. The relevance of the discursive framework for IT use in resource-starved contexts is discussed in section seven. The concluding section summarizes the implication of this work in terms of research and practice.

3. The KC Experimental Protocol

The emergence of a stable experimental protocol[5] for the information village was the first sign that this approach is indeed replicable. The most crucial part of the entire exercise has emerged to be the process of participatory rural appraisal (PRA). This is almost always the first of the four steps in establishing a KC. The four steps are described below:

Step 1: PRA
Step 2: Signing the MoU
Step 3: Implementing the technology
Step 4: Training

One of the reasons PRA was used in these projects was because the community here can be considered semi-rural since there is a lot of interaction between villagers and the city. Hardships and repeated unfulfilled or broken promises have led villagers to harbor a negative mindset with respect to anything Government or related to NGOs. As a result, the period from February to August 1998 was spent in developing confidence and building credibility.

The PRA is iterative and the project team generally goes through four or five iterations. During the interactions in the PRA, the rights and responsibilities of the villagers and the MSSRF are clarified. In addition, the roles of both sides are clearly explicated and the team strives hard to ensure that the communication is indeed successful. It is important to ensure that the communication takes place between the community and the project team. A collective understanding is a key enabler of success in such projects. A high level of clarity and understanding resulting from these interactions lead to the support of the community. During such interactions the eligibility criteria for becoming an information village are also explicated. The project team should keep in mind the nature of the village leadership structure while designing such interactions. This issue will come up again later in this paper in the context of village governance structures. The PRA process should also be sensitive to issues like the time constraints on villagers. Most of the villagers work long hours during the day either in the fields or in cities as daily-wage workers. Women are also busy throughout the day. Hence the most appropriate time for such interactions or meetings are evenings.

Typically, the initial interactions are with the village heads. Village leadership tends to be collective. Members are either elected or nominated to this group. Interaction sessions that follow tend to engage youth and women's groups. The project team allows ample time for the villagers to meet among themselves and think through the issues for themselves. The positive outcome of such meetings is a formal application by the villagers to the MSSRF stating that they need the KC and the reasons thereof. Toward the end of these interactions, the norms for implementing a KC are also clarified. They include:

- Villagers to provide space to house the KC equipment
- Villagers to provide electricity
- Villagers to provide volunteers to run the KC

Before the MoU is signed, in parallel with the PRA process, villagers are exposed to the Villanur hub and other KCs (if possible) to demonstrate the technology and the related documentation. In addition, the crucial task of content and information item identification for that particular village is carried out in partnership with the villagers and an initial village database is created. It is also made clear to the villagers that since the MSSRF will withdraw participation after some time, it is expected that the villagers would be responsible for the future viability of the KC.

After the MoU is signed, the technology is implemented. Installing the communication system and computers takes a day. In addition, installing the solar power system takes another day.

The last step is training. Training is typically done in a train-the-trainer format with veteran volunteers from another village taking on the role of trainers. The project staff is always around to provide the necessary backup and support. Training is imparted in MS Office and in the use of Windows messaging systems (email and fax). Training and subsequent practice typically lasts a month with formal training accounting for a week of that period. By the end of one month the KC tends to achieve steady state operations.

It can be seen that the action types in these four steps are an interplay between the four paradigms of information system development namely functionalism, social relativism, radical structuralism and neohumanism. Without getting into too many details of the implementation, it is clear that system development proceeds in alternation between 'from without' and 'from within.' When project staff *expect* village residents to come *on their own volition* and *formally* request for a KC (social relativism), it is an explication of a 'from within' approach. However, the fact that these volitional acts are triggered by a larger set of actions taken by the project staff as a part of a larger social intervention points to a 'from without' dimension (radical structuralism) to systems development. Moreover, the interplay between guiding principles and operating conditions is also worth noting. The emancipatory principles on which this project is based on is clear from the objectives of the project. These objectives are premised on empowerment and enfranchisement of the dispossessed and poorest of the poor. However, the structured interactions between the project staff and the village residents, and the imposition of a high degree of formalism to clarify roles, entitlements and responsibilities, have to be well planned and executed and represents the functional paradigm. The village of Veerampattinam where the village residents understood the importance and benefits of the KC and exemplifies the neohumanist paradigm of system development. Such 'mixing of paradigms' that lead to 'interesting and creative solutions' has already been acknowledged (Hirschheim and Klein, 1994, p. 1213). We have reason to believe that such a blend of paradigms is necessary for meaningful information systems.

The notion of radical structuralism is representative of an instrumental action – which is carried out in order to obtain any specific objective. In this case the specific objective is to encourage villagers to demand their KC having convinced themselves of its benefits. In fact, in terms of action types, this kind of actions is closer to a strategic action. A strategic action is used to sway an opinion or influence an action of another person (selected villagers or villagers who influenced opinion). The actor (field staff) relates to an objective world consisting of physical facts, states of affairs and people who have been instrumentalized. The actor knows that his counterpart adjusts her actions in response to his own actions. This is important to understand because it fits into the category of the double-bind (Watzlawick, 1977). A from-without interaction is expected to result in a from-within or volitional action. Watzlawick (1977) summarizes this by stating 'it is one of the shortcomings of human communication that there is no way in which the spontaneous fulfillment of a need can be elicited from another person without creating this kind of self-defeating paradox (pp. 15-26).' In this case of the 'be spontaneous' paradox, we have the project staff working to 'ensure' or 'elicit' a volitional and spontaneous response that is imputed unto them by the project staff themselves. This is especially relevant to those villages that tend to be pioneers in establishing their KCs. After some time, other villages demand their own KCs having seen other villages deriving benefits.

It is important to note that communication takes place between the village community and the project team. This connotes openness of communication and a reduced emphasis on the importance of the individuals in that communication. Secondly, the importance given to seeing a high level of clarity and understanding due to these communications characterizes communicative action. The emphasis on collaboration and sensitivity in terms of interaction (showing sensitivity to villagers schedules) also ensure the communicative nature of the interactions. A communicative action promotes an understanding among all parties. The actors (project staff and villagers) relate to objective, social, and subjective worlds consisting of facts, states of affairs, norms and subjective feelings. Such communicative interaction is a challenge to all participants and may hold the key to evolving replicable protocols for instituting KCs of information kiosks in rural setups.

From the original four KCs the number has now grown to ten. In addition to these, there are other KCs that are in progress. They include two in Karnivadi and Oddanchatram[6] that have been funded by the Volkart Foundation. In addition, the Government of Pondicherry has sponsored four villages for housing a KC. In addition, having seen the initial success of the information village program, the Department of Agriculture of Pondicherry, which has 18 farm clinics in Pondicherry has proposed to convert them into KCs. These numbers too attest to the replicability of the KCs.

Having replicated the KC in many villages, the process of withdrawing has been initiated by the MSSRF. Withdrawals have not been easy. The two withdrawals that have taken place so far have been due to non-compliance with the terms of the MoU. Our study has shown that two issues have emerged as being critical to the notion of withdrawal of support to 'test' the sustainability of KCs. The first is the governance structure of the village and the second is the timeframe for sustainability.

4. Structure Determines Behavior

The governance structure of villages is emerging to be a critical determinant of the degree of success in the weaning process. It is becoming clear that the governance structure (typified by an elected *panchayat*[7] or the *nattanmai*[8]) influences the dynamics associated with the withdrawal of formal support for the KCs. Based on discussions with project staff directly involved in exploring strategies for seeking sustainable propositions for the KCs, it emerged that those villages which had a single social group to exert influence on subsequent decisions related to KCs, found it relatively easier to navigate through the issues and reach resolutions. However, in villages where the governance structure was an agglomeration of formal, semi-formal and informal groups (each of which had a significant enough say in the working of the KC), agreements were much harder to come by. Examples of such groups included the village leadership (either the *panchayat* or the *nattanmai*), self-help groups, village cooperatives (e.g. milk cooperative) and others.

Information system-related problems arise because information systems are technological systems embedded in human systems – for an organization is a human system. For any given system, structure determines behavior (Senge, 1990).

The term 'structure' is used in a generic sense and, in the context of this paper, can refer to the set of relationships between behavioral, technical, process-related and social variables – both at the micro and macro levels.

When viewed from the theoretical standpoint, the sustainability proposition, which we have shown to be closely linked with the structure in place, finds support in the work of Kvansy and Truex (2000). They deduce from the work of Bordieu (1980) that 'social order maybe an unseen contingency in numerous information system research areas (p. 16).' The 'broken trajectory' effect is evident in our data in two instances. In the first instance, the village *panchayat* figured that the role of women (who formed the self-help group) diverged significantly from what had been anticipated.

> It was found that situational variables account far more for the role played by women volunteers than the program design. In other words, while the overarching goals of the program did include empowering women, practical difficulties interfered to restrict the role of women. A typical woman volunteer was married and in her thirties. Adult males were conspicuous by their absence in the volunteer category. This is because men are expected to be the primary breadwinners of the family and tend to work the day. Women over 40 tended not to be literate and hence did not qualify to be volunteers in the KC. Younger women tend to either study or work full-time. As a result, in most villages, it was young males (who were either unemployed or partially employed) and young housewives who became volunteers. It is not too insignificant either to note that there is an nominal honorarium for being a volunteer. The involvement of women in the information village program was, at best, propitious, in the sense that given a choice, women would have opted for direct revenue generating activities as opposed to becoming a volunteer in a KC. Even where women self-help groups have taken on the sole responsibility for managing the KC, they have done so (at least in one village) under the assumptions made by the village *panchayat* (all males) that it would be easier to 'control' KC operations by proxy. What the *panchayat* did not anticipate was the ability of women to create 'trouble' (i.e. exercise autonomy in matters related to operations and decisions regarding the KC).

In the second instance, the discomfort of both village residents and the KC volunteers when confronted with the imminence of financial and material support was apparent.

> We devoted a part of the interview to explore the value that villagers had come to associate with the knowledge center. We started out by asking how much he would like to receive as a salary *if* his present volunteer assignment was converted into a salaried position. After significant deliberation and hesitation he weakly suggested a value of Rs 3000 per month. In coming to this figure he had raised the issue of whether the village *panchayat* would go along with this suggested change (even if it did, he mused that this possibility would hold promise only if the *panchayat* saw a sum of Rs 2000 coming its way) and whether he is indeed cut out for this role. This conversation points to two things. First, village leadership takes decisions and they hold. Secondly, villagers have not been able to formulate a basis for themselves to impute value to the information village concept. It is certainly 'useful' beyond that though the discussion meanders.

An alternative form of disruption was recounted by Dr. V. Balajee (the then project director of the Information Village project). He related an incident that captures the essence of such disruptions. When Dr. Mashelkar (Director, CSIR) and Dr. Bruce Alberts (President, US National Academy of Sciences) were visiting one of the information village KCs, an old man walked up and asked Dr. Mashelkar to read out some information from the KC notice board. Of interest here is the absence of deference that village folk tend to exhibit to strangers in western attire. While it will not be entirely wrong to conceptualize information technology as the equalizer here, a more complete picture can be provided by understanding the processes built around the technology that seeded and nurtured notions of entitlement (in terms of the right to know) and relevance of market information (need to know).

5. Stages of Growth and the Information Village

The major challenge facing the information village project at this juncture is that of ensuring sustainability for the KCs that have been established. Sustainability implies viability of the KCs fuelled by village needs and supported by local resources, manpower and expertise. While the urgency to demonstrate and experience sustainability is desirable, given that the information village project was started in 1998, it may be premature to expect true sustainability in the near-term. Such speculation is premised on the lessons learnt in realm of organizational information systems where normative estimates of the time taken by information systems to mature are well over 20 years. Nolan (1979), while proposing the stages-of-growth model for information systems, estimates that each of the six stages takes five to seven years.[9] Even if we account for time compression for this due to technological improvements, we still end up with an estimate of 10 to 15 years for organizations to reach IS maturity. In the Indian milieu this is an optimistic estimate because many organizations that initiated IT deployment in 1960s and 1970s are still struggling to reach IS maturity.

Kanungo's (1999) adaptation of multiple stage models is shown in Figure 7.1. When such models are used as frameworks for analysis, they tend to take on a normative character and can be used to predict an organization's (in our case, a village's) IT trajectory. When that happens, it is important to delineate what assumptions go into such evolutionary models. One such assumption is the implicit linear logic of Consolidation to follow stage Extension to follow stage Inception. However, organizations in India typically start from the Integration stage in terms of technology and from the Inception or Extension stage in terms of organizational preparedness. In such circumstances using the growth models in a predictive sense decreases their utility. Therefore those organizations that *attempt to have all of the cake and eat it too*, in terms of starting out late on IT investments and expecting accelerated benefits on account of those IT investments, tend to develop serious 'teething problems' by experiencing IT failures and user distress. It seems nearly impossible to avoid Senge's dictum of having 'the cake and eating it too, but slowly.'

The implications for rural information systems are quite clear. Technological maturity can be reached almost at the time of inception. Experience with the information village project has demonstrated that information technology has matured phenomenally. Since the project inception, there have been a maximum of two major technical problems. The five dimensions on which maturity is assessed include infrastructure, application portfolio, top management, IT management and end-users. The rural analogues of top management and IT management are the village governance structure and KC volunteers respectively. Most organizations have difficulty in developing top management, IT management and end-users. We can derive two major lessons from the world of formalized work and apply them to IS initiatives in rural scenarios. The first lesson is that while we can (and should) skip or leap-from the technology curve, it is almost impossible to skip the experience or learning curve.

Secondly, most organizations reach stage three with reasonable efforts; however, advancing beyond that requires them to cross the stagnation hump. This hump is the organizational equivalence for the point at which rural information systems are faced with the need for sustainability.

It is also important to realize that most IT initiatives in the corporate sector fail.[10] While the failure rate for information systems are high, we cannot take such corporate benchmarks to be our guide in the case of rural information systems because such experiments cannot afford to fail. Trusteeship is crucial. For those who believe that 'harvesting is believing,' the 'seeing is believing' framework has to be operationlized most efficiently. Novelty effects of technology erode very fast. Therefore it needs to be demonstrated that information is linked to wages, health and even survival. While it is easy to understand the importance of time in a corporate framework, time is equally crucial in a rural setting. For instance, for the rural poor a visit to a health center may result in the loss of an entire day's wages in addition to travel and medical expenses. Health centers located far from villages imply that public transportation must be used. This entails waiting periods at transport terminals and transit stops that can last from an hour to two hours. The average commute time is one hour. Depending on the availability of the doctor, the patient and those accompanying may have to extend their stay by a day or come back undiagnosed. A diagnosis on-line or online access to information becomes invaluable in such circumstances.

Consequently, such systems are indeed 'strategic' – in as much as their ability to add value goes. Figure six provides a framework for conceptualizing the rural IT journey. The first stage of dependence is characterized by external organizations and actors taking the initiative and bringing IT to the village and bootstrapping the process of informating (Zuboff,1988) the village.

The independence stage is the one that focuses on weaning the KC from its dependence on external support. However, the third stage, interdependence, is the one that enables viability of the KC and the village by developing collaborative linkages within and across villages and other organizations that are enabled by IT. How long each stage lasts depends on the local conditions and complementarities involved in the nature of investments made in economic development, infrastructure development and in social programs (including education) apart from the effort and resources put into IT.

From		Inception	Extension	Stagnation / Consolidation	Expansion / Augmentation	Integration	To
Non-existent	Infrastructure	Few PCs, may be a mini	More PCs and minis (may be workstations); modems and leased lines	LAN; leased lines; limited email facility; some client server steps	Major WAN investments; high-end computers; near total connectivity	Database integration; application level connectivity; new technology	Robust reliable and state of art
Narrow & efficiency oriented	Application Portfolio	Payroll, Inventory, Accounts	Order entry, production control, OA; Corporate applications	IS for main business processes; stable MIS; Integrated databases	Strategic applications; full fledged TPSs ; DSSs emerge	IT-based products and services; longer value chain; inter-organizational system	Pervasive & aimed at value adding and business leverage
Remote oversight	Top Management	Minimal interest; participates in budget decisions	Requires IT support; Exercise influence on IT budgets	Direct reporting from GM or VP (IT) realistic expectations; Proactive role	CEO-CIO relationship; expect hard IT benefits; think of IT in major decisions	IS/IT planning ; IS security ; information privacy; reorganizing for continued success; data quality	Enablers stewards and mentors
Technocentric	IT Management	An informal IT set up that is small; mainly programmers; not a function	Formalization of IT/ MIS/EDP manager, formal process for IT decisions	VP/GM (IT) LAN & database administrators; outsourcing; IT planning	IS/IT strategy; IT chargeback;possible profit center; IS cadre; service center		Organization or business centric
Passive recipients	Users	Partially aware of benefits; occasional IT use; mixed feelings	User base; Expectations User training becomes priority	User demands and sophistication ; satisfaction	Sophisticated and aware; IT expertise; proactive participation	Take IT support for granted; customers and vendors become users	Partners and stakeholders

Figure 7.1 Five stages of IS maturity in organizations (*Source*: Kanungo, 1999)

The foregoing discussion points to the need to concentrate on the three people-related attributes that help the move to IS maturity. They include the governance structure, IT management (or KC management) and end-user development. Based on these attributes and a few others (size of the village, state of the village economy, opportunities in surrounding villages, etc.) some KCs may stagnate in their present mode of work while others may see their KCs becoming increasingly important and sophisticated by leveraging the complementarities presented by good village governance and improved KC management practices – and thus crossing the IS maturity hump.

Information behaviors and values (IBV)	KC volunteers work under the guidance and supervision of project staff and face a steep learning curve. Villagers find the KC useful but tend to be passive information recipients	KC volunteers develop a relationship with villagers leading to high value accorded to KC information and demand for individualized and customized information services	Linkages formed between villages and other organizations that include government, industry, research institutions that enable and promote economic opportunities
Information management practice (IMP)	Most of the decisions regarding the nature and type of information to be stored is made by the project staff. KC volunteers are concerned about database creation and maintenance	Project staff's role starts diminishing in day-to-day KC management. KC volunteers take on innovative tasks such as creating Yellow pages and customized content for a village	KC managers seek out and identify value-creating opportunities on their own and inter-twine the KC closely with village activities and social and governance structures
Information technology practice (ITP)	The KC is totally dependent on the expertise provided by the project staff for infrastructure as well as for IT component like software and hardware. Project staff take on prime	The KC does not need any external supervision to operate. KC volunteers start teaching basic IT skills to villagers and act as mentors to other volunteers with start-up KCs	Sharing of insights with respect to managing the KC takes place Neighboring villages collaborate to share computing resources based on specialized needs and the availability of skills
	Dependence	**Independence**	**Interdependence**

Figure 7.2 Stages for IT maturity in a village[11]

In Figure 7.2, this hump is characterized by the 'Independence' stage – that is preoccupied with demonstrating viability of the KC as an entity that can exist on its own.

The major implication for practice in the rural context is to stick to normative guidelines for IT diffusion but to retain a flexible schedule when it comes to working toward IT infusion, that is sustainability. The concepts of IT diffusion and infusion were introduced by Sullivan (1985). We use the term 'diffusion' to denote the extent of IT deployment in villages and support agencies (e.g. the hub at Villanur) and the term 'infusion' to denote the impact of IT on village life.

6. Articulating Ways Forward

When looking for ways to overcome the barriers to sustainability that information villages face, the ability of villagers to relate the impact of IT to their way of life, value addition and perceived value acquire importance. The ability of villagers to relate the impact of IT to their way of life has to do with internalizing value. Coupled with this, frameworks need to be in place to demonstrate value as well as to quantify value (continuous metrication that is practitioner-led and customized to each village). Using the ideas of vicious and virtuous cycles (Appendix A) we use Figure 7.3 to identify regulating loops. Figure 7.3 shows the dynamics associated with various interactions, as derived from our interviews. Ways out of vicious cycles often require the situation to be reframed so that the loop depicting the runaway process can be re-conceptualized as coexisting with other regulating (or sustaining) loops.

In Figure 7.3, the main loop of concern is 1-11-4-5-1. This loop relates operations, value-addition, benefits and resources. However, this loop is not sustainable. Therefore, we identify (or add) additional variable and relations that will allow us to stabilize this system. Two loops that can be identified include 1-6-8-9-11-4-5-1 and 1-2-3-11-4-5-1. The critical variables in these two loops are conversion gaps and quality of KC activities respectively. Essentially, the conversion gap has to be narrowed and quality of KC activities has to be improved continuously.

From a practical standpoint, this implies improving the efficiency of converting opportunities into viable benefits. Allowing village residents to influence and experience the process of value-creation through IT and explicating the value chain and the role of IT in that process best accomplish this. In that sense, this becomes a process of collective learning. This requirement also calls for a renewed emphasis on the quality of leadership of the Information Village project and the project team. This is especially important when we understood in terms of the influencers of conversion gaps. Project leadership and participation is crucial in ensuring different and innovative ideas with respect to narrowing the conversion gaps. For instance, one of the project staff members has taken on the additional role of identifying possible linkages with local cable TV providers. One possible implication of such a linkage could be the establishment of processes that ensure

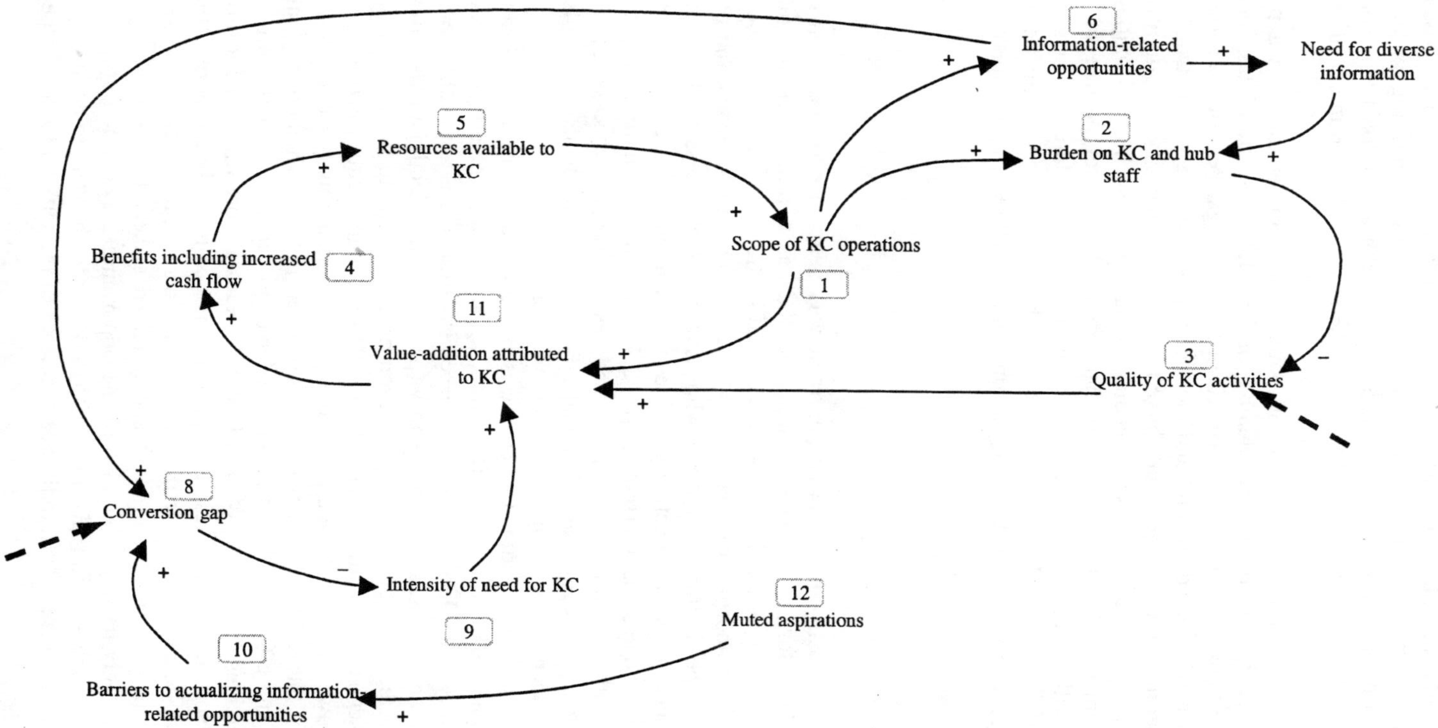

Figure 7.3 Sustainability dynamics associated with KCs in information villages[12]

that information content, created locally, is also consumed locally. This possibility directly address the conversion gap issue by not only identifying or creating information related opportunities but also by providing a solution framework for actualizing such opportunities. In the process the need for diverse information will also be met.

The second variable, or action point, is also important from a project leadership standpoint. In a way, quality of KC activities, translates into the proposition of ensuring high quality of KC operations, regardless of the short- and medium-term KC related societal and individual payoffs. This means that the KC volunteer group and the project staff have to continually identify opportunities for improvement as well as new uses. Needless to say, many such opportunities will emanate from outside the village. To that extent, the role of project staff and leadership will require new forms of networking that are addressed to not only linking the established IT infrastructure to other agencies that can be viable partners, but also to ensure that the existing infrastructure remains operationally healthy.

7. Discussion

The idea behind using the Habermasian framework is to work toward a conceptual model of the information system (here, the KC) as a framework for rational discourse (which is an ideal). As has been stated in the main text of the report that not only objects and phenomena are produced in and via discourses, the process also involves the definition of those who have rights of access to the discourse. This is because a discourse actively defines what can be said and who among the totality of individuals has the right to speak. The notion of disruptiveness (however limited or localized and personal) is more addressed to social processes than to the nature of technology in use. This (set of disruptive mechanisms enabled by technology), then, forms the basis for empowerment.

The notion of rational discourse is based on ideas offered by Habermas (1984). His notion of communicative action, when related to the utility of technical skills of basic media, leads to an ideal speech situation and is applicable here. The fact that the entire process is participatory (premised on collectivism and volitional responses – that may be induced) is reason enough for us to believe that IS can deed be practically operationalized as a vehicle for communicative action.

However, since there are multiple participants in this process and that the outcomes of the KC deployment may be separated in time (when conceptualizing the causes and effects), there is no reason for us to expect agreement in terms of the contributions of the KC. We are leaning toward a more diffused form of IT–enabled payoff in rural settings. This payoff is not so much in terms of economic benefits that donor agencies or development partners typically expect to see, but more in terms of a better informed and liberated society that is not only more aware of not only its rights but also of the opportunities available *but also* of the facilitating frameworks in place that exist to overcome barriers to achieving those opportunities. In this context, individuals' images of the self and those of others are best understood using discursive approaches. Discourse in Foucauldian terms is a group of statements, which constructs a topic in a certain way. This means that discourses are more than just words and their signifying elements, as known from Structuralism. A discourse is a practice that influences the subject and speaks through it. Here one might say that a discourse is a kind of language, which forms our knowledge and shapes our understanding. Understood in this way, knowledge specifies what can be said about objects and phenomena in a domain of knowledge (Foucault, 1972, pp. 48-49, pp. 182-183).

If one examines the fact that knowledge specifies what can be enunciated, one will see that not only objects and phenomena are produced in and via discourses, the process also involves the definition of those who have rights of access to the discourse. This is because a discourse actively defines what can be said and who among the totality of individuals has the right to speak. This is exemplified by (1) the old man who felt that it was OK to initiate a conversation with a stranger in a suit and tie, (2) women volunteers of the KC who were selected by default (as much as by decree) and went on to become participants in mainstream discussion regarding day-to-day village life and decisions. In this way experts, their interests and domain of expertise will disappear, because the specific character of a given discourse, is a product of its discourse, not its foundation. To put it differently, in the same way as objects and phenomena are produced in a discourse, users of a specific discourse are also defined by the discourse (Foucault, 1978, pp. 50-55, p. 68).

A specific instance of such a negotiation in the context of shifting of power can be seen in the case of RLWs. Regional level workers (RLWs) are government functionaries who are charged with ensuring Government programs get implemented at the village level. They form the Governmental interface to the village. Typically, the RLW has to set aside two days a week for each village. Every Friday, the RLW is provided with a manifest of activities for the next week for each of the villages he is responsible for. When the village KCs, through the hub at Villanur requested that this manifest of activities and the RLWs' schedules be made available, so that it could be made available to all villagers, the RLWs did not cooperate. The lack of cooperation was traced to an activity that had been established over a long time. By not disclosing their schedule, the RLWs made unscheduled village rounds. Such unscheduled visits result in minimal interaction with villagers. For the record, the RLWs check off their tasks in the manifest and invariably, take the remaining day, assigned to the same village, off. The fact that the villagers will be able to track and, possibly question; the schedule allows the villagers to become *active* participants in village and local governance. In this way inefficiencies that exist because of asymmetries associated with information availability will reduce. Many such possibilities exist depending on the nature of information use and actions subsequent to accessing the content. While, established practices will be hard to reform completely, the redefined role of the villagers, in terms of suggesting flexible alternatives, is expected to lead to a new consensus on how the RLWs *ought* to interact. Such issues, and others, that were beyond the scope of the information village project, are now emerging to assume importance in determining the success of such programs.

8. Conclusion

The major implication for researchers is to continuously look to adopt non-traditional and application-oriented perspectives when studying rural information systems. The now documented protocol for establishing KCs is indicative and not normative and is consisted with the federated framework (Hirschheim et al., 1996) in the domain of information systems. From the research standpoint, we have been able to reveal different assumptions relating to different actors using different techniques. These techniques (that have included discourse analysis and systems dynamics modeling) have been of great help in examining the overlapping ideological frames through which facts emerged. We plan to pursue this approach in much greater depth and intensity in the future. While sustainability is a desirable goal, rural information systems initiatives should neither pressure themselves nor should they be pressured into unreasonable timeframes to demonstrate sustainability. This is because sustainability hinges on collaborative and discursive frameworks. KCs need to partner with existing brick and mortar establishments (Krishi Vigyan Kendras, farm clinics, district headquarters, etc.) so as to morph into sustainable propositions while, at the same time, injecting viability into partnering organizations or frameworks. Collaboration can take many forms. Training the trainers among KC volunteers has proved to be successful. Such peer-level collaborative arrangements between individuals can be extended to villages. Sustainability issues that relate to village governance may be best handled by emergent collaborative influences. Nurturing collaborative relationships takes time. Using IT as an intervention in response to developmental issues needs to be studied further in terms of Weick and Roberts' (1993) work on heedful interrelation. Heedfulness may prove to be the key to elicit the collective will within and among villages to make KCs sustainable. Our understanding of the dynamics associated with generating a 'collective mind' among and across individuals and groups remains low. While seeking to understand such dynamics, we also need to avoid a techno-centric stance because the economic impact of modern information technology (centered around the Internet) is questionable. According to Drucker (Schonfeld, 2001) it is doubtful whether the Internet will be profitable as a business or as an industry. While its impact is unbelievably great and that it eliminates distance, 'the main impact of the Internet is not economic; it is psychological.' Since the Internet greatly extends the old economy, the key to sustainability may lie in using KCs to support more basic efforts like livelihood, farm productivity and social change. In doing so, some villages will be able to sustain their KCs far more effectively than others. In the meantime, we will have to live with a fragmented adhocracy of IS research (Hirschheim *et al.*, 1996).

Appendix A

We can start reading a causal influence diagram at any point. Where we start is not important. What is important though is the identification of cycles or loops. Loops can be characterized as positive feedback or negative feedback. Positive feedback loops are called reinforcing loops. Negative feedback does not imply undesirable. On the other hand, negative feedback loops regulate or control behaviors that tend to get out of control (e.g. cost escalation, manpower attrition, runaway projects etc.). In the same way, positive feedback loops can manifest themselves as either virtuous or vicious cycles. Take the loop shown in Figure 7.4 (a). It can be a virtuous or vicious cycle depending on the state of variables. Starting anywhere, we could read the loop as follows: As A increases (or decreases), B increases (or decreases); As B increases (or decreases), C increases (or decreases); As C increases (or decreases), D increases (or decreases); As D increases (or decreases), A increases (or decreases) …

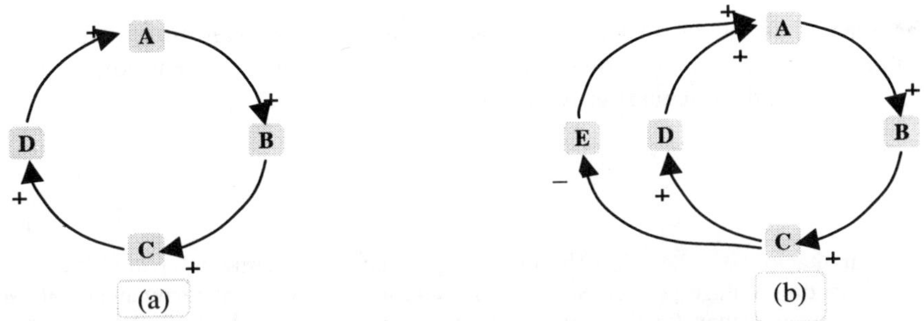

Figure 7.4 Sustaining collapsing loops or reigning in runaway loops

Over time, the behavior of any one of the variables shown in Figure 7.4 (a) can be either

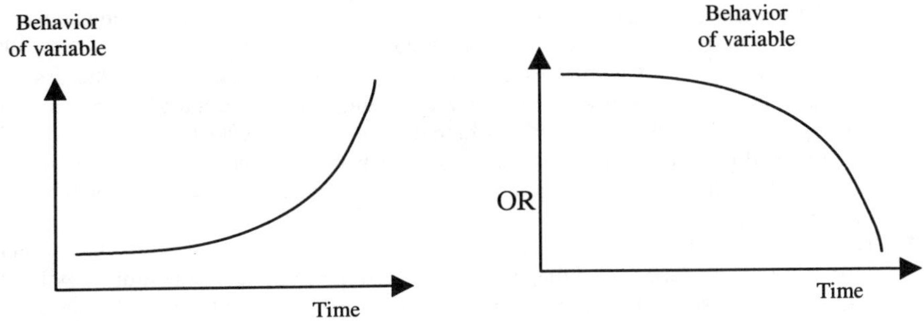

It is clear that the reinforcing loop either manifests itself as a runaway growth or and uncontrollable downward spiral – both of which are unsustainable propositions. The presence of a regulating loop as shown in Figure 7.4 (b), by the presence of element E,[13] leads to steady-state behavior as shown by

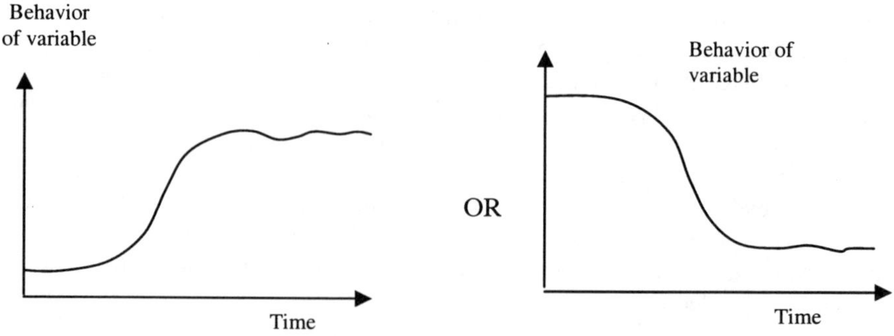

The idea, then, is to sustain the steady-state behavior over time and seek to continuously seek out opportunities and practices that help prevent nosedives and unsustainable and unnatural growth spikes.

Notes

1 I am thankful to the MSSRF for the opportunity to learn and participate in the Information Village project. Special thanks go to Prof. M. S. Swamninathan and Mrs. Mina Swaminathan for their time and interest in my work. Mr. Senthil Kumaran, Mr Rajmohan and Mr. Rajshekhar have been extremely kind with their time, ideas and insights. The paper is based on my primary experiences and I have taken the liberty to represent the ideas and values of the members of MSSRF. In doing so, I assume sole responsibility for any factual errors or differing interpretations in this paper.

2 The experiment that is being conducted by the MSSRF is being presented as a case study. The author has conducted direct field observations and has also relied on secondary sources of information.

3 While 'success' is a relative term, various reports made by peers and serious observers (Dugger, 2000; Balasubramanium, 2000; Dinakar, 2000; Venugopal, 2000; Reich, 1999; UNDP, 1999; Kumar, 1999; Ramamoorthy, 1999) allow us to use the term success.

4 Since this experiment is novel, the observations and results would almost necessarily be non-replicable. However, explication of the theory use and the analysis of findings could be compared to other attempts at similar studies using the *same* theoretical framework. Additional studies along the same lines would also augment the generalizability of similar findings.

5 The phrase experimental protocol has been used to convey the essence of the entire approach to the information village program. IS researchers and practitioners will, after reading the section on the 'experimental protocol' wonder why the term 'methodology' has not been used. We have not used the term 'methodology' because we believe that the steps mentioned are broad and indicative and far more relaxed and flexible and open to interpretation when compared to a formal methodology. Maybe herein lies the key to whatever success has been achieved in this program.

6 The case of Oddanchatram is interesting. OddanchatramMarket.com from India links the rural market with the outside world. It is an effort by Reddiarchatram Seed Growers Association (RSGA), Kannivadi and Kulumai, a Federation of Self-Help Groups (SHGs) located at Kannivadi. M.S.Swaminathan Research Foundation, Chennai,

provides the technical support to maintain the site. Oddanchatram is a big daily vegetable market. More than 150 traders operate in this market. The daily turnover was over Rs two crores. Following the establishment of a KC, inquiries for produce prices started coming in from places as far as Nagpur also. This encouraged the villagers to establish oddancahtram.com. The establishment of this site saw the turnover increase by Rs 1.5 crores (I crore = 10 million). From next year, the traders' association has decided to take care of web hosting themselves by investing Rs 25,000.

7 Collective leadership based on elected individuals.

8 Collective leadership that is based on nominated individuals as opposed to they being elected to office.

9 The idea behind Nolan's (1979) model is conceptually attractive. It is no wonder that other researchers were driven to refine and develop that idea further. For example Bhabuta (1988) developed a model that maps IT development as a progress toward formal strategic planning of information systems. Similarly, Hirschheim *et al.* (1988) present three stages of IT development in organizations namely, delivery, re-orienting and re-organization. These later models incorporated organizational change more explicitly than Nolan had. For example, Galliers and Sutherland (1991) have presented a 'revised' stages-of-growth model that has six stages (named differently from stages in Nolan's model) and is based on seven organizational variables (Pascale and Athos, 1981). Like most other post-Nolan models, this model also is suggested as a framework for planning as it helps mangers 'predict' organizational trajectories in the light of IT infusion.

10 31% software projects never reach completion (Standish, 1994). A subsequent study (Standish, 1995) reported that 73% of projects are canceled or fail to meet expectations due to poor requirements definition and analysis.

11 ITP: A village's capability to manage IT applications and infrastructure to support village life, social and institutional processes and decision-making. IMP: A village's capability to manage information effectively over the lifecycle of information use including sensing, collecting, organizing, processing and maintaining information IBV: A village's capability to instill and promote behaviors and values in its people for effective use of information. This terminology has been borrowed from Marchand et al. (2000). The terminology for Stages of Maturity has been borrowed from Enwright (2000) and Stuart (1989) and the basis for the temporal sequence is derived from Covey (1989).

12 While most variables are self-explanatory, two need to be elaborated. 'Conversion gap' refers to the mismatch between the potential of IT-related benefits (which is fairly high) and the realization of such benefits (which tends to be low). 'Need for diverse information' refers to the need for new, fresh, dynamic, customized and locally relevant information.

13 As C increases, E decreases or vice versa.

References

Balasubramanium, T. R. (2000). India at grassroot level.com: The tip of a revolution, The Economic Times, Sunday, April 9, p. 7.

Barret, R. and Maglio, P. P. (1999). Intermediaries: An approach to manipulating information streams, IBM Systems Journal, 38(4),pp. 629-641.

Bhabuta, L. (1988). 'Sustaining productivity and competitiveness by marshalling IT,' In: Proceeding, Information Technology management for productivity and strategic advantage, IFIP TC-8 Open Conference, Singapore, March.

Covey, S. R. (1989). The seven habits of highly effective people: Restoring the character ethic, Thorndike, Me.: G.K. Hall.

Dinakar, A. (2000). Now online access for poor farmers, The New Indian Express, Tuesday, March 27, p. 4.

Dugger, C. W. (2000). In India, Computers Become a Tool in Village Life, International Herald Tribune, Monday, May 29, p. 6.

Enright, M. J. (2000). Regional clusters and multinational enterprises: Independence, dependence, or interdependence? International Studies of Management & Organization, 30(2), pp. 114-138.

Foucault, M. (1972). The archaeology of knowledge, New York: Pantheon.

Foucault, M. (1978). The history or sexuality, Translated by Robert Hurley, New York: Pantheon.

Galliers, R. D. and Sutherland, A. R. (1991) 'Information system management and strategy formulation: The stages of growth model revised,' Journal of Information Systems, 1(2).

Habermas, J. (1971). Knowledge and human interest, Boston: Beacon Press.

Habermas, J. (1979). Communication and the evolution of society, London: Heinemann.

Habermas, J. (1984). The theory of communicative action: Reason and the rationalization of society, Volume 1, Boston: Beacon Press.

Hirschheim, R.; Earl, M.; Feeny, D.; and Lockett, M. (1988) 'An exploration into the management of information systems function: Key issues and an evolutionary model,' In: Proceedings, Information Technology management for productivity and strategic advantage, IFIP TC-8 Open Conference, Singapore, March.

Hirschheim, R. and Klein, H. K. (1989). Four paradigms of information systems development, Communications of the ACM, 32(10),pp. 1199-1217.

Hirschheim, R. and Klein, H. K. (1994). Realizing emancipatory principles in information systems development: The case for ETHICS, MIS Quarterly, 18(1),pp. 83-109.

Hirschheim, R.; Klein, H. K.; and Lyytinen, K. (1996). Exploring the intellectual structures of information systems development: A social action theoretic analysis, Accounting, Management and Information Technology, 6(1/2), pp. 1-64.

Huber, G. (1982). Organizational information systems: Determinants of their performance and behavior, Management Science, 28(2), pp.138-155.

Kanungo, S. (2001). On the sustainability of rural information systems: Analysis of preliminary experimental evidence, International Conference on Information Systems, December 16-19, New Orleans, LA, USA.

Kumar, G. P. (1999). Snatches of a wired rural society, The HINDU, Tuesday, September 7, p. 5.

Kvasny, L. and Truex, D. (2000). Information technology and the cultural reproduction of social order, Aalborg, Denmark (2000).

Lee, A. S. (1989). A scientific methodology for MIS case studies, MIS Quarterly, 13(1), pp. 33-50.

Lyytinen, K. and Hirschheim, R. (1988). Information systems as rational discourse: An application of Habermas's theory of communicative action, Scandinavian Journal of Management, 4(1,2), pp. 19-30.

Marchand, D. A.; Kettinger, W. J. and Rollins, J. D. (2000). Information orientation: People, technology and the bottom line, Sloan Management Review, 41(4), pp.69-80.

Nolan, R. L. (1979) 'Managing the crises in data processing,' Harvard Business Review, 57(2), March-April, pp.115-126.

O'Neil, D. (2001). Digital divide policy in the U.S.: Framing federal policies and programs to bridge the technology gap, Proceedings of the Digital Divide Doctoral Student Workshop, Alliance for Community Technology, University of Michigan, August 1-5, 2001.

Pascale, R. T. and Athos, A. G. (1981) The Japanese art of management, Harmondsworth, UK: Penguin.

Quibria, M. G. and Tschang, T. (2000). Information and communications technology and poverty: An Asian perspective, High-Level Symposium on Alternative Development Paradigms and Poverty Reduction, ADB Institute, Tokyo, December 8, 2000.

Ramamoorthy, G. (1999). Reaping Rich harvest with Information Technology, The Times of India, Mumbai, Monday January 18, p. 16.

Reich, R. B. (1999). Help the World Connect, The Wall Street Journal, Monday, October 4, p. A42.

Schonfeld, E. (2001). The guru's guru (Interview with Peter Drucker), Business 2.0, 2(8), pp.66-72.

Senge, P. M. (1990). The fifth discipline: The art and practice of the learning organization, New York: Doubleday.

Standish. (1994) The Standish Group, Chaos Report.

Standish. (1995) The Standish Group, Chaos Report.

Stuart, R (1989). Using Others to Learn: Some Everyday Practice, Management Decision, 27(4), pp. 98-105.

Sullivan, C. H. (1985) Systems planning in the information age, *Sloan Management Review*, 26(2), pp.3-12.

Swaminathan, M.S. (Ed.). (1993). Information Technology: a Dialogue, Madras: Macmillan India.

Swaminathan, M. S. (2001). Private conversation.

UNDP. (1999). Innovating with the Internet by UNDP, UNDP – Human Development Report, p. 64.

Venugopal, K. (2000). Infotech on India's farm lands, The Business Line, Friday, February 25.

Von Simson, E. M. (1990). The centrally decentralized IS organization, Harvard Business Review, 68(4), pp.158-162.

Watzlawick, P. (1977). How Real Is Real: Confusion, Disinformation, Communication. New York: Vintage-Random.

Weick, K. E. and Roberts, K. H. (1993). Collective mind in organization: Heedful interrelating on flight decks, Administrative Science Quarterly, 8, pp. 357-381.

Zuboff, S. (1988). In the age of the smart machine: the future of work and power, New York: Basic Books.

Chapter 8

Sustainable Telecentres? Two Cases from India

R.W. Harris, A. Kumar, V. Balaji

1. Introduction

Telecentres provide public access to Information and Communication Technologies (ICTs) for educational, personal, social and economic development. There are numerous examples of telecentres throughout the developing world. For example, the Canadian government's International Development Research Center (IDRC) supports many typical telecentre projects in Africa (the ACACIA Project) and in Asia (the Pan Asia Network, IDRC). Individual telecentres have been shown to foster profound developmental outcomes within the communities they serve. Despite promising indicators from a number of pilot telecentre projects, the question of sustaining any successes that emerge always arises.

Discussions of telecentre activities frequently make reference to sustainability (Whyte, 1999). Development discourse in general is laden with the need for sustainability, yet the concept of sustainability is rarely examined closely nor is it related to the specific development activity that is being discussed. There seems to be a requirement that development telecentres must be financially self-sustaining in order to remain in existence, a condition that appeals to common sense. Yet despite the encouraging examples of beneficial outcomes from some telecentres, the development community is still unclear with regard to the conditions that are required for telecentre success as well as to the wider relationship between ICTs and rural development (Harris, 2001). In this paper we describe two telecentre implementations that have targeted sustainability from the outset by providing information that customers will pay for.

2. Sustainability

The concept of sustainability in development can be traced back to a 1987 report by the World Commission on Environment and Development (WCED, 1987), known as the Brundtland Report:

> Sustainable development is development that meets the needs of the present without compromising the ability of future generations to meet their own needs. Sustainable development focuses on improving the quality of life for all of the Earth's citizens without increasing the use of natural resources beyond the capacity of the environment to supply them indefinitely.

Sustainability discourse has since extended beyond issues relating to the irreversible depletion of the environment and the inevitable exhaustion of finite natural resources. Sustainability in development is now more widely regarded as the ability of a project or intervention to continue in existence after the implementing agency has departed, a condition that often has little to do with environmental protection or with the preservation of natural resources. Nevertheless, in view of the seemingly common occurrence of project breakdowns after the departure of the implementing agent, sustainability in terms of continuity has become a key indicator of success with development activities as well as an important criterion in pre-implementation planning for obtaining funds. In many cases, the sustainability of development projects focuses on the single question, 'who will pay for the project after the implementing agent departs?' A popular response is for project implementers to design interventions that will generate sufficient income so that they will pay for themselves, where the role of the implementing agent is to provide seed inputs, including, but not limited to capital, that will get the project started and enable it to continue under its own impetus after the implementer departs.

Yet sustainability is not limited to the need of development to pay for itself. The International Institute for Sustainable Development lists three underlying common characteristics of sustainable development:

- Concern for equity and fairness
- Long-term view
- Systems thinking

These dimensions of sustainability reach outside the initial issues relating to the protection of the environment and to the replenishment of natural resources. Concerns for fairness and equity reflect the need for the benefits of development to reach those who are the least privileged, the least endowed with resources and the most vulnerable, something that development efforts often fail to achieve. The long-term view encompasses the apprehension that planners often hold for the unexpected and undesirable outcomes of development efforts, as well as the tension that emerges between implementers with short-term project orientations and beneficiaries with long-term process considerations. For example, building a bridge is a short-term project, whereas crossing the river is a long-term process. Systems thinking in sustainability engenders multi-dimensional perspectives, the identification of feedback loops and the consideration of the consequences of actions, acknowledging the complexity of social life everywhere and the inter-relatedness of everything.

The sustainability of telecentres has emerged as a key issue in the debate surrounding the use of ICTs for development. In most cases, the discussion refers to financial self-sustainability, which is often regarded as a condition for continued existence of the centre. However, experience from telecentre experiments suggests that four types of sustainability exists for telecentres:

- Sustaining financial viability (Hudson, 1999).
- Sustaining staff capability (Baark and Heeks, 1998).
- Sustaining community acceptance (Whyte, 1999).
- Sustaining service delivery (Colle and Roman).

Financial viability refers to the capacity that a telecentre has for generating sufficient income to cover its costs of operation, and/or the cost of initially establishing it. While this ability to pay for itself generally requires the derivation of revenue directly from those who use the services of the telecentre, it does not preclude the possibility of other continuing sources of revenue, for instance, from government (Hudson, 1999). Projects that introduce new skills also need to maintain the sustainability of the capabilities that are created. This will be ensured only to the extent that trained people, or their trained replacements, continue to work in the same area and that their capabilities are maintained and utilized. Sometimes, trained staff discover a better market for their skills and are lured away from the project (Baark and Heeks, 1998).

It is well to note that a telecentre's sustainability will be determined by the degree of acceptance by the community that it is able to generate. The introduction of a community telecentre, if it is successful, is going to have a major impact on the community; its culture, communication patterns, economy, social structure and future development. If telecentres are seen as technological providers rather than social and cultural community centres, experience suggests they will be less sustainable. The degree of community involvement in, and commitment to, a telecentre, is often assumed to be a success factor and measures of user behaviour and perceptions are at the heart of any evaluation of telecentres (Whyte, 1999).

Sustaining service delivery relates to the continuation of flows of information that communities find useful and useable. But it also relates to sustaining the overall services of a telecentre in terms of adapting to evolving community needs, proactively seeking new sources of useful information and alerting the community to the value of information. Colle and Roman suggest strategies for telecentre implementations that foster sustainability of telecentre service delivery, including; having local champions or innovators to mobilise others to accept the vision of a telecentre, raising awareness about information and ICTs as a valuable resource for individuals, families, organisations and communities and focusing on information services rather than on technology to build a local institution that is fully woven into the fabric of the community.

Telecentre sustainability shines a spotlight on the issue of sustainability in development as it embodies many of the dimensions of the sustainability theme as it has evolved since first coming to the attention of development practice. Of these dimensions, financial sustainability of telecentres might be argued to be the most critical or even the most difficult to achieve. Despite the plummeting cost-power ratio of computers, their price typically remains many orders of magnitude beyond the average annual incomes of telecentre users in developing countries. Therefore, the cases in this paper are described from the perspective of financial sustainability. In addition, financial sustainability warrants special attention because of the reassurance required by governments that telecentres will result in net benefits and will not become a drain on resources.

The following sections describe two case studies that were conducted by the authors in India, during December 2001 and January 2002. The authors visited each project headquarters in Hyderabad, Andrha Pradesh and in Thiruvananthapuram, Kerala. They further visited two telecentre installations in each location and interviewed both the staff and telecentre users.

3. Case One. Samaikya Agritech P. Ltd., Andhra Pradesh

Andhra Pradesh is India's fifth largest state, in both population and size. The State has a widely diversified farming base with a rich variety of cash crops. Agriculture provides for about 50 percent of the income of the State and provides the livelihood of 70 percent of the population. Most of the State suffers low and erratic rainfall, with an annual average of 125 cms. Samaikya Agritech P. Ltd was incorporated in 1999 and started operations in June 2000. *Samaikya* means 'coming together for a good cause' in Telugu, the language of Andhra Pradesh. The company operates 18 'Agritech Centres' in five districts in Andhra Pradesh. The centres provide agricultural support services to farmers, on a commercial basis.

Samaikya's Agritech Centres are permanently manned by qualified agricultural graduates called Agricultural Technical Officers (ATO) and are equipped with computers linked to the head office in Hyderabad, through a modem-to-modem telephone connection. Through these centres Samaikya provides:

- technical assistance to member farmers
- inputs such as seeds, fertilisers and pesticides
- machinery hire
- tools and spares for sale soil and monitoring
- water analyses
- field mapping
- weekly field inspections
- field visits by weather specialists

Samaikya Agritech Centre, Choutkur Village, Medak District, Andhra Pradesh

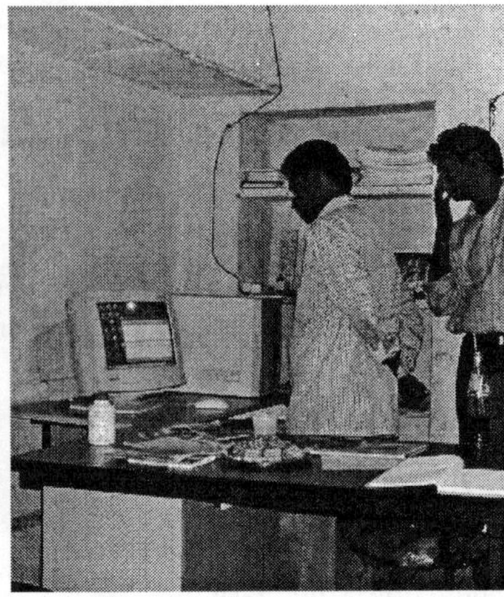

Farmers register with centres and pay a fee per growing season (two or three seasons per year) of Rs.150 (about US$3) per acre/crop. A farmer registers by the field and receives support services that are specific to the fields registered. On registration, the farmer provides detailed information concerning his farming activities, which is held on the centre's database and which provides the basis for the technical support provided. The centre in the village of Choutkur has 53 registered farmers covering 110 acres of registered land. This is out of a total of around 1,000 farmers within the centre's catchment area. Major crops include sugar cane, paddy and pulses.

Registered farmers receive technical information in support of their farming activities. Advice from the centres is based on data generated from pre-validated crop cultivation practices adopted in the State and provided by the government agricultural services and local institutions. Farming information is up-linked from headquarters to the computers at the centres. If farmers have specific needs for information that cannot be satisfied immediately by the ATO at the centre, then the ATO completes an on-line enquiry form on the computer and transmits this via modem to the headquarters. The database and information systems are operated in the English language. Information is interpreted for the farmer by the ATO. As some farmers are illiterate, the ATOs have to spend time with explanations and descriptions. There is no standard for a computerized Telegu script. Specialists with more experience and qualifications at the headquarters organize and co-ordinate replies to queries, which are typically transmitted back to the centre within 24 hours.

Prior to setting up a centre, Samaikya performs a survey of local farming and cultivation practices and to ascertain the political and cultural context of the potential centre. It conducts a pre-launch programme to familiarise farmers with the services. One centre closed down within three months of opening as no farmers registered for the service. This was due to the pressure placed on them by local marketeers, financiers and suppliers of inputs who perceived a threat to their livelihoods from the competing Samaikya services. Farmers were told that any who registered with the centre would not receive credit or essential supplies.

Samaikya Agritech P. Ltd has invested about five million rupees (US$106,000) in the agri-centre programme. At the end of 2001, the company had slightly more than 1,200 registered farmers. The company expects the programme to finance itself within in the next two years (2002/3). The programme was conceived as a self-financing, profit-making activity from the outset. Its purpose is to maintain a sustained service of agricultural assistance to farmers.

3.1 Commentary

Samaikya Agritech P. Ltd. is run for a profit, demonstrating the value of the information that farmers are ready to pay for. For Samaikya to remain in business, the farmers it serves will have to be satisfied that the value of the services they receive represents a worthwhile expense. By remaining in operation, Samaikya will demonstrate that development information can be sold and that a potential source of revenue exists for telecentres that provide information services that its customers are prepared to pay for.

As a commercial concern, Samaikya respects the demands of its customers. Transactions are conducted on a supplier to customer basis because the company knows that if its customers are not satisfied with its service then they will discontinue their patronage. The exchange sits in marked contrast to a typical exchange with a government official in India.

The directors of Samaikya recognise the potential that their network of computerized centres has for supplying additional information-based services. One opportunity is currently under development with the International Crop Research Institute for the Semi-Arid Tropics (ICRISAT), which will entail the development and implementation of an information system for mitigating the effects of drought. It will include the collection and transmission of micro-climate data at the Samaikya centres.

4. Case Two. Keltron Information Kiosks, Kerala

The State of Kerala lies along India's south-west coastline. A wet tropical climate and coastal lowlands support cultivation of rice, coconuts, tapioca and spices. The interior hills produce rubber, coffee and tea. One of India's most densely populated States; it has the highest literacy rate in India, but suffers from economic underdevelopment and unemployment. India's first communist state administration was elected in Kerala in 1957 and a communist coalition has been elected three times since.

Keltron is the Kerala State Electronics Development Corporation Ltd. It operates the Keltron Information Kiosks (KIKs), which are being implemented throughout the State. Keltron is wholly owned by the Kerala State government, but operates as separate company. The concept of the KIKs grew out of the State government's experiences with a bill-payment service called FRIENDS, (Fast, Reliable, Instant, Efficient, Network for Disbursement of Service). FRIENDS operates as a one-stop service centre equipped with computers for paying bills by the public as well as for obtaining applications and remitting registration fees. The FRIENDS kiosks:

- open from 7:00 a.m. to 7:00 p.m., seven days a week
- operate a computer-controlled orderly queuing system
- present a clean and attractive environment for the public
- do not charge for their services
- serve over one million people annually.

As yet, the FRIENDS centres are not networked. The main centre in Thiruvananthapuram, the State capital, serves 600 people and takes Rs.15 lakhs (US$32,000) a day. There is a FRIENDS centre in every district in Kerala.

Arising from the FRIENDS experience, Keltron is now developing information kiosks (telecentres) for public access to the Internet. The initial objective is to facilitate delivery of government services using ICTs. The Kiosks will experiment with various ownership models for telecentre sustainability. Ownership options vary from State Government ownership to local Government ownership and to private ownership. There are currently three kiosks in Thiruvananthapuram, and two more are being implemented in rural districts, expected to open in March 2002. The village panchyats (local councils) will operate these two new centres. In addition, five village panchyats have applied formally to operate Kiosks and all the panchayats in one district of Kottayam have expressed their interest to apply. The Kiosks will function as independent profit centres.

The Thiruvananthapuram kiosk operates a 64kbps-leased line with 20 terminals, 12 of which are connected to the internet at December 2001. The centre provides public internet access to around 50 people daily, charges Rs.25 per hour and has daily revenues around Rs. 1,400. Trained staff are on hand to provide assistance. In addition to public Internet use, the kiosk is implementing a series of government information systems for:

- agriculture support, covering crops and pests
- census data, with summaries and the official list of people below the poverty line
- the electoral role
- a grievance reporting and tracking system with facilities for email to ministers
- industry information, on a variety of licensing, regulatory and support schemes.

Keltron Information Kiosk, Thiruvananthapuram, Kerala, India

The information systems are in the English language. The centre opens from 8:00 a.m. to 12:00p.m, 7 days a week. Plans are in hand to develop further applications for:

- e-education
- income certificates
- domicile certificates
- caste certificates
- local e-mail
- employment news

The Kerala State government expects the Kiosks to provide a mix of e-government services with locally developed community-based services. Keltron will provide the hardware as well as develop the gateway to e-government services. The local partner provides accommodation and staffing. Centres are expected to be self-sustaining from their own revenue from fee-paying customers as well as from advertisements and from other services, such as computer training, for which customers will pay. By mid-2002, a kiosk in the Tirurangadi Panchayat in Mallapuram district was ready for inauguration. By giving permission to the Panchayat to participate in the project, the Local Adminstration Department of the State Government has opened the door for other Panchayats to follow. Also, Keltron were surveying the State to assess the demand for investment in kiosks by private individuals and the State Bank of Travancore along with the Small Industries Development Bank of India had shown interest in funding youths interested in taking up the kiosks as self employment ventures. It is expected that wide deployment of the kiosks will generate a new engine of growth for the State (Kumar 2001).

4.1 Commentary

Kerala has a culture of education, literacy and egalitarianism. Moreover, the government deliberately fosters local responsibility and decision-making by allocating a large proportion (one third) of its budget directly to Panchayats as opposed to the more usual process in other States of State authorities retaining spending power over services and development. These contextual factors seem to be compatible with the concept behind the Keltron kiosks; more open government through a public/private partnership. Additionally, the State enjoys a high level of connectivity and the local language newspaper has the highest circulation of any newspaper in India, indicating an interest in information.

The State government recognises the need for financial sustainability, but also acknowledges the value that the public places on e-government services from its experiences with the FRIENDS system. There is no massive plan for the entire Kerala State government administration to go on-line, but an orderly role out of the kiosks is seen as a catalyst for increasing levels of service-driven ICT-based innovation in government departments. The Kiosks are not subsidized. They are a separate strategic business unit of Keltron and are required to generate revenue of their own.

The State sees the diffusion of Kiosks as a movement that will gradually and simultaneously sensitize both government and the public to the benefits of electronic service delivery as well as fostering an environment conducive to the development of other public information services. By organising the kiosk programme through a separate, though wholly owned entity, the Government appropriates the flexibility it needs to innovate and experiment with new approaches to service delivery whilst retaining the leverage of its ownership of public information. By offering partnerships to the private sector and to Panchayats, the Government achieves several advantages. It is able to marshal external resources in support of e-government diffusion and it ensures that the need for sustainability is factored into Kiosk implementation at the early stages.

5. Discussion

The cases demonstrate two approaches to telecentre-induced development, both of which rely heavily on financial sustainability. In both cases, the need to generate income and to show a profit has been built into the centres right from the start. Samaikya Agritech is a privately owned and purely commercial organization. It provides development assistance, but it exploits the opportunity provided by alternative providers of such assistance (especially government) whose service is significantly inferior. The organization demonstrates that farmers will pay for information that helps them make more income. The technology component of the Samaikya enterprise only exists in support of its strategy to deliver useful information in a timely fashion to its clients. The strategy achieves financial sustainability by charging fees that are sufficient to cover costs and to yield a profit to the owners of the enterprise. Sustainability of staff capability is achieved through its employment practices, by engaging young graduates from agricultural colleges who need field experience. Community acceptance is sustained insofar as client farmers both continue to pay in order to register their fields and crops as well as registering more fields and crops. Service delivery is sustained though effective employment practices both at the centres and in the headquarters, where more specialized and experienced staff handle advanced queries and through the close relationships that field staff develop with their client farmers.

In the case of the Keltron centres, the entire enterprise is built around the need for Keltron to stand alone financially, despite being wholly owned by the Kerala State Government. The information services that are being developed are designed as fee-paying services from the start, where they have been piloted in order to demonstrate the viability of such an approach. The plan for proliferation of the centres is based on joint investments with the private sector and with local Panchayats in order to foster appropriate conditions for their financial viability. Sustaining staff capability remains the role of local investors, but is encouraged through the revenue generating activities that will emerge from effective and skilful marketing of information services that will be necessary in order to achieve profits. Community acceptance will also be fostered through effective outreach programmes, but as the basic government information services have been piloted, sufficient knowledge is available to point to the high likelihood of host communities accepting the services of the centres. Sustainability of service delivery is assured by the state government's commitment to the programme, its actions to computerize key aspects of government and its interface with the public and by the support it provides to Keltron as an independent and for-profit enterprise.

Arising from the discussion of the case studies, the following observations can be made:

- The delivery of development assistance using ICTs represents a business proposition. As agricultural and government information can be provided in return for fees, it seems possible that other classes of information (health, education, cultural) might similarly provide opportunities for generating revenue.
- The profit motive fosters a customer-oriented, demand-driven approach to development. The customer-orientation that is necessary for successful business enterprises fosters services that are closely aligned to client needs. Bottom up, demand driven approaches to development are commonly preferred to top-down, supply driven approaches. The profit motive contains in-built mechanisms that foster demand driven development.
- People will pay for government information services. Governments are not always aware of the customer convenience or the potential for value

addition that telecentres might offer to their citizenry. They do not always consider that such benefits represent income opportunities.

- Public/private partnerships offer potential for financially sustainable telecentres. In public/private telecentre enterprises, the public body takes responsibility for the social development role of the telecentre and the private body ensures its financial sustainability. It should be acceptable, for instance, to use the charges made for sending and receiving e-mail messages to subsidise the delivery of community health and agricultural extension programmes.
- Contextual issues have an impact on achieving sustainability with telecentres. We have seen how the implementation and the sustainability of the two cases are closely aligned with their contexts; the business opportunity represented by the latent demand for agricultural information on the part of the farmers in Andhra Pradesh, and the state government's commitment to better citizen services in Kerala. In both cases, the profit motive was at the forefront and was an integral component of the initial planning and implementation strategy.
- Government services can be a 'pump-primer' for sustainable telecentres capable of offering other information services. All governments sit on vast sources of potentially useful information, easy access to which can represent income-generating opportunities. By sharing these opportunities with telecentre operators, governments can kick-start information infrastructures that can be made capable of inducing community development in other areas such as education, health, enterprise development, cultural enrichment and so on.

6. Conclusions

Financial sustainability of telecentres is a major concern for ICTs in development. Although financial sustainability is only one of several dimensions of telecentre sustainability, it remains the most questioned and possibly the most problematic. The cases indicate that by targeting financial sustainability at the outset, telecentres stand a good chance of surviving the honeymoon start up period during which the other dimensions of sustainability often prevail, that is community and service sustainability. By achieving financial sustainability early in their lives, telecentres build a sound foundation upon which further services of unknown viability can be tested. In particular, the achievement of the State government of Kerala indicates that any developing country can begin planning for e-government services. However, evidence from the field suggests that supporting telecenters exclusively by government grants is not a good sustainability formula, financially or politically (Colle and Roman). However, telecenters need to be demand-driven, and demand should be reflected in the community's willingness to pay for some services. Public/private partnerships in telecentres for development offer the opportunity for combining innovation and responsiveness with stability and public participation and for bringing massive numbers of excluded people into the information world.

References

Baark, E. and Heeks, R., Transfer Projects in China: A Life-Cycle Approach, Development Informatics Working Paper Series, Working Paper No. 1, Institute for Development Policy and Management, University of Manchester, Manchester, UK, 1998.

Colle R.D. and Roman R., Communication Centers and Developing Nations, A State-of-the-Art Report. http://www.devmedia.org/documents/Banga..htm

Harris R.W., Telecentres in Rural Asia: Towards a Success Model, Conference on Information Technology and Communications for Development, Kathmandu, Nepal, 29-30 November 2001.

Hudson, H. 1993. 'Maximizing Benefits from New Telecommunications Technologies: Policy Challenges for Developing Countries.' in Jussawalla, Meheroo, ed. Global Telecommunications Policies: The Challenge of Change. Westport, Connecticut: Greenwood Press. IDRC. http://www.idrc.ca

International Institute for Sustainable Development. http://iisd.ca.

Kumar, A., Bridging the Digital Divide – Some Efforts from Kerala, Proceedings, International Conference on Information Technologies, Communications and Development, Kathmandu, Nepal, 29-30 November 2001.

Whyte A., Understanding the Role of Community Telecentres in Development – A Proposed Approach to Evaluation, in Gomez, R. and Hunt, P. (Eds.) Telecentre Evaluation A Global Perspective, Report of an International Meeting on Telecentre Evaluation, IDRC, 1999.

World Commission on Environment and Development (WCED). Our common future. Oxford: Oxford University Press, 1987.

Chapter 9

An Investigation into Community Development Imperatives at a Rural South African Community Education Center

Jackie Phahlamohlaka and Hugo Lotriet

1. Introduction

A worldwide race to reap maximum benefit from Information and Communications Technology (ICT) use is on, with developed countries setting the pace. According to a UNESCO (1996) position paper, the question that should be afforded high priority for developing countries is not whether they should participate in this race, but rather *how* these ICTs can effectively be applied to development. South Africa responded to this call by passing the Telecommunications Act in 1996, which established the Universal Service Agency (USA) whose purpose is to facilitate access to these technologies by all its citizens.

The passing of the Act spawned some vigorous efforts from within the country and the international community to introduce the technologies to a number of communities. These efforts have taken different forms as documented by Zongo and Benjamin (2000). The USA has been piloting these initiatives through Multi-Purpose Community Centers (MPCC). These are structures that enable a specific community to manage its own development by providing the community with access to appropriate information, facilities, resources, training and services. Although these efforts are good signs in response to the 'digital divide' race, they are all still in a piloting phase, with much more still to be learned and done. Also, with good reasons, largely associated with costs, these pilot studies are largely undertaken as close to the major cities as possible. With the largest South African population living in rural areas, this can only mean that the greatest challenge is yet to come. We have argued elsewhere (see Phahlamohlaka *et al*, 2001) that an effective way of conducting these pilot studies would be to link them to research through tertiary institutions. A recent study by the South African Information Technology Industry Strategy (SAITIS) (http://www.saitis.co.za/, 2001) found that most of these initiatives are driven by the private sector, with a disappointing involvement by tertiary institutions. Valuable lessons that could have been properly documented have already been lost.

However, not everything has been lost. There is at least one case outside the USA pilot studies where a sustained research involving a university and a community is being undertaken. This case is the cooperation between the Department of Informatics of the University of Pretoria and the Siyabuswa Educational Improvement and Development Trust (SEIDET).

The Department of Informatics has had the unique opportunity of learning through research about efficient ways of applying ICT towards locally relevant socio-economic benefits for the communities. SEIDET and the Siyabuswa community in general have also seen substantial development benefits, including the establishment of a computer laboratory in Siyabuswa and the training of tutors, learners and the general community in computer literacy. This cooperation has continued since 1994. The researchers from the Department of Informatics see themselves as part of the SEIDET project and vice-versa. A rapport of trust has been established over the years. Since 1998, the use of computers has become part of almost every component of the SEIDET project.

A local area network (LAN) and access to the Internet have recently been added to the SEIDET computer laboratory in Siyabuswa. This development brings about imperatives to respond to both opportunities and challenges related to community development through education and training using these technologies at the center. These imperatives are the focus of this research project. The management of SEIDET as a whole, through the computer committee, has the responsibility to identify, pursue and manage these opportunities on behalf of the local community and to integrate these opportunities into the functioning of SEIDET.

The LAN and Internet connection also posed new research and development opportunities that were utilized by the researchers at the University of Pretoria and the SEIDET computer committee. Due to the nature of the research, the work is expected to continue for a significant period of time. This paper is therefore a report on research in progress.

The paper contains and is organized in the following order: a description of the community development context, the research context, the research purpose and questions, the philosophical foundations, the use of theory and the research method. The research design and interpreted interim results of the early part of the study are presented.

2. Project Context

Siyabuswa is a rural town about 130 km North-East of Pretoria, in the Mpumalanga Province in South Africa. It is located within the Dr J.S Moroka municipality which has a total population of 257,771. At the time of the commencement of SEIDET, prior to the new democratic constitution in South Africa, which started in 1994, Siyabuswa was part of KwaNdebele homeland.

The total number of people from Siyabuswa who had University degrees was 0.16 percent, while 1,67 percent held college diplomas. Those who had grade 11 and 12 (matric) stood at a total of 11,73 percent (Siyabuswa structure plan, 1991).

The highest percentage of people who contribute to the total household income falls within R6000 to R10000 per annum. About 50 percent of the economically active people earn less than R6000 per annum. People commute by buses to Pretoria on a daily basis, spending nearly six hours daily on the road (Siyabuswa structure plan, op. cit).

The main impetus for the SEIDET project was the disadvantaged position of the children of Siyabuswa with regard to mathematics and science education that prevented them from entrance to tertiary institutions and education. In South Africa for every 10,000 black children who enter the first grade, there is only one matriculate with an exemption in science (SEIDET annual report, 1992/93). This is largely due to poor education standards in black schools, although many children do have the potential to pursue tertiary education in the sciences. The situation in Siyabuswa was not different from the larger educational challenges facing the rest of the country. The Siyabuswa community accepted the challenge to find an innovative way of bringing about a small but meaningful change. Their innovation took the form of a supplementary tuition project for high school learners in selected learning areas such as English, Science, Commerce and Mathematics.

This response by the local community of Siyabuswa to what essentially constituted a national problem could be described as an effective community development initiative.

There are numerous studies about how ICT could be introduced and used to support community development initiatives such as SEIDET. At the same time there is broader recognition in the ICT research fraternities that these kinds of initiatives often provide the basis for long-term sustainable development. After visiting the project, Walsham commented:

> Local initiatives such as the Siyabuswa project often receive government support, which raises the broader issue of the appropriate role of government and inter-governmental agencies in facilitating change in national contexts with respect to the introduction and use of information and communication technologies...Perhaps the most important area of all for government policy with respect to IT is education and training. The development of local people's skills and knowledge of IT, including those of the disadvantaged in society, is the only long-term sustainable way to ensure the inclusion of the excluded. (Walsham, 2001, p206).

We are of the opinion that our study, which is grounded in local need and undertaken with local consent and full participation by SEIDET, will enable us to critically assess the value of the existing theories with regard to ICT and development.

2.1 The SEIDET Project

SEIDET is a community initiated and community based educational project that started in 1991/1992, situated at Siyabuswa. It started as a supplementary tuition project for high school learners in selected learning areas such as English, Science, Commerce and Mathematics. Tuition by volunteer teachers, public servants, entrepreneurs and people working in the private sector from within the community was provided to learners on Saturdays. The response from the entire community to the project at its inception was beyond expectations, indicating that there was a need for it, and that the need was perceived as such by the community. Over the years, the project has grown from strength to strength, and there is presently the SEIDET Community Education Center, with two satellites hosted by other institutions at KwaMhlanga (Technikon Pretoria, KwaMhlanga Campus) and Vaalbank (Hlalakahle High School). The main center in Siyabuswa is a multi-purpose facility providing a variety of educational services and developmental programmes to the local community in association with several other institutions, including the Department of Education. Although the first full computer laboratory was established in 1998, the introduction of ICT at SEIDET started in 1994, after the Executive Committee of SEIDET approached the Department of Informatics at the University of Pretoria. Because of its research tradition and interest, the Department responded positively. Ever since, a mutually beneficial relationship has been in existence between the Department and SEIDET. A number of research activities have been undertaken under the leadership of Professor J.D Roode. Much of what has been achieved through these related engagements has already been reported in readily available conference proceedings and journals (see Conradie, 1998; Scheepers and De Villiers, 1999; Matthee and Roode, 1998; De Kock, 2000).

Conradie (1998) captures the context of SEIDET in the following way:

> ...if the activities mentioned in the above list of lessons learned are taken as indications of success criteria for rural telecenters, then the SEIDET center has been on target in most instances. There was, for example, a considerable level of *pre-development activity* when the center was being planned - local residents reacted to identified educational needs in their community and formed various structures such as a Board of Trustees and Executive Committee to establish and run the center. There were thus *local pioneers with vision,* and they set *clear objectives* of what had to be done. The center managed to involve a number of *other organizations/institutions in supporting roles* (e.g. the University of Pretoria, the Mpumalanga Department of Education, the Human Sciences Research Council [HSRC], and Vista University). It is clear that there has been a *significant community response* to participate and help. Especially over weekends there are many forward-thinking local teachers and residents who offer their services as *facilitators, teachers or trainers* to the center free of charge. To support and equip these individuals, there are a number of externally financed *'training-of-trainers'* types of initiatives. There is thus abundant evidence of *co-operation and collaboration* among all parties involved. SEIDET provides a prime example of how to follow a *community-centered management approach* at a center by

creating community ownership, by being accountable and transparent to community stakeholders, and by trying to be continually aware of the changing environment by initiating monitoring and *evaluation processes*. The center also managed to *avoid the pitfalls* mentioned in the list above - e.g. projects being led by technology in stead of by a previously identified local development need, using specific ICTs for inappropriate uses, or trying to do everything with technology.

The specific research being undertaken and reported about in this paper should be understood within the contexts described above. It is our belief that the valuable lessons learned from these focused and rigorous studies being undertaken at SEIDET would guide future research on how ICTs could be introduced and used in other less developed communities.

2.2 Research Methodology and Ideas

The purpose of the research is to make a contribution to the further development of the SEIDET project by assisting the computer committee to identify the opportunities and possible challenges that may be brought about by the expanded ICT facilities. In this way, the research would in a community-interactive way assist the SEIDET community in answering sets of questions reported in this paper while providing the team from the Department of Informatics with new perspectives on community development and training through the implementation of ICTs.

In the short term, the purpose is to empower the participants and tutors through skills and knowledge acquisition and to assist in structuring the integration of the LAN and Internet technologies with the activities of SEIDET in an efficient way.

In the long term, the purpose is to assist the participants in managing and sustaining LAN and Internet related activities within the context of a rural community education center.

The study seeks to respond to the following set of primary questions:

- From the perspective of the computer committee (management) what opportunities are presented by these added ICT facilities?
- What does the computer committee see as new challenges in managing the laboratory brought about by the LAN and access to the Internet?
- What would these developments mean to the local community and to the functioning of SEIDET as a whole?

In addition responses to the following secondary questions are sought:

- How are the opportunities offered by the recent installation of a network and the Internet connection recognized and utilized by the local community of Siyabuswa?
- Which challenges and issues arise from efforts to incorporate the new technology into the training and education programmes at SEIDET?

- Does the addition of these technologies change the style of instruction?
- Does the addition of these technologies change the contents of materials presented?

The community, as defined in this paper, refers to the SEIDET community, which consists of the Board of Trustees, the Executive Committee, the computer committee, tutors, learners, parents and various associated organizations.

In line with our research design and process, we are convinced that the only meaningful way to interact with the SEIDET community for the purpose of this research project would be through the computer committee. Through the consultative and participative nature of the research process, which includes the committee interacting with other players at SEIDET, we believe that the perspectives of the community would be adequately captured and encapsulated within the perspectives of the computer committee.

The research is intended to enable the researchers and the participants to have a better understanding of the implications of ICT within the community development context. This means that the underlying epistemology of the study relates to the assumption that access to reality would be through social constructions. We have already presented the context of our study. We therefore intend to contribute to the development condition of a community (SEIDET) through a *collaborative search* for effective use and better understanding of ICTs. Our basic assumption is that knowledge and action cannot be separated. Throughout the entire inquiry, we do not pretend to be neutral. We make value choices and intervene when the situation requires that we do so in the interest of an 'appropriate' action. We are able to proceed in this way because of the rapport of trust, which we have established with the community over the years. We make suggestions for action and so does the community in an emergent participatory fashion. It follows that our research is informed by both the interpretive and critical philosophies.

We believe that our contribution through this study would be to inform and critique existing theories rather than a simple application of these theories to our local situation. We prefer to align our theory development with Chamber's (1997) argument that theory grounded in local need and undertaken with local consent and participation has a greater chance of being relevant and sustainable. The issue of relevance is especially important from the perspective of developing countries. Although it would have been possible for us to postulate certain hypothetical outcomes to our study, based on these various theories, and then proceed to 'prove' or 'disprove' these theories, we have instead preferred to let the lessons emerge from our interaction with the community. Thus we seek explanations of various emergent issues from different theoretical perspectives. Sahay and Walsham (1995) and Ngwenyama (1996) have both cautioned that the researcher should not try to select a specific theory before going into the field. They argue that this biases the empirical material that is collected since the researcher 'look for specific things to collect'. However, early indications are that aspects of Critical Social Theory (Ngwenyama, 1991), Structuration Theory

(Walsham and Han, 1991) and Actor-Network Theory (Walsham, 1997) would in various ways influence our research, notably in interpreting the final results of our study.

Critical Social Theory informs our involvement and intention to influence further development of the community. In line with Ngwenyama and Lee's (1997) argument, we believe that by our presence we influence and are influenced by the social and technological systems we are studying. While some aspects of Critical Social Theory appear useful to our study, we would not go as far as its ultimate goal of emancipation as that possibly could be achieved through the empowerment of the community. In addition we have already defined our exit point while Critical Social Theory requires that we go beyond the exit point and address issues of unjust and inequitable conditions of the situation from which people require emancipation.

2.2.1 Research method The nature of the research environment imposes the following requirements:

- The nature of the project implies that the research would focus on qualitative rather than quantitative issues.
- An interactive approach would be required in which the community representatives are guided through interviews and questions towards reflection on their issues and the taking of actions to work towards achieving the requirements. At the same time, the researchers would use the interaction with the community representatives and the responses to questions posed for further reflection and the posing of further questions to guide the community, and where possible to act or suggest action.
- Research data sources are therefore mainly interviews and discussions with participants in the project and observations during field visits.

These requirements pose an argument for a research method that is collaborative, contributive to community development, yet accepted by the international scientific community as a valid method. The researchers therefore decided to adopt *action research* as the research method for this study. We are researchers who are already involved and engaged in a community development initiative. We are very aware of the severe criticisms of action research in the IS field, but for us it is the natural choice. Despite these criticisms, Baskerville and Wood-Harper (1996) argue that action research as a method could be described as a paragon of the post-positivist research methods. According to them, 'it is empirical, yet interpretive. It is experimental, yet multivariate. It is observational, yet interventionist'. In addition, the recent stated intention by Management Information Systems Quarterly to dedicate a special issue to action research suggest that there is a general recognition of the validity of this method within the IS field. The action research framework designed for this study is shown in Figure 9.1 in the appendix.

In the diagram shown in Figure 9.1, (Q1, A1), (Q2, A2) and (Qf, Af) represent question and answer sets, with (Q1, A1) representing the first set of research questions and the answers provided to these questions through interactive processes and (Qf, Af) representing a 'final' question and answer set. In between these sets there are numerous intermediate question and answer sets representing a progression of the research process through a generation of new sets of research questions in sequential project cycles. The exit point for the research depends on the extent of community development that would have taken place and the richness of perspectives related to the primary research questions.

2.2.2 Research design and process The research has been designed in accordance with action research requirements. It follows a cyclic process of interaction, reflection, action and interpretations between the researchers and the participants. The participants are seven computer committee members of SEIDET. The researchers are two faculty members of the Department of Informatics. Occasionally, when the participants need a technical training session, three Informatics honours students are requested to do the training. Liaison with the community of Siyabuswa takes place through the established channels between the Department of Informatics and SEIDET.

Sessions are held approximately once a month with the computer committee. The venue for these sessions alternate between the SEIDET center and the University of Pretoria. Sets of research questions are collaboratively developed, negotiated and agreed upon. After each session, the participants take the full set of issues raised, the research questions and their new technical skill to the rest of the SEIDET tutors. In other words, they replicate the whole session with the rest of the tutors. In this sense, the participants are also researchers.

In the process, the tutors also respond to the issues and questions raised previously while generating new ones (SEIDET has a total of forty eight tutors spread across its three centers). In one case, one researcher was invited by the participants to observe a session conducted by the participants with the rest of the tutors. After a session with the tutors, the participants bring back a new set of responses, issues and questions for negotiation and possible action by the researchers and the process is repeated. The research design and process framework diagram is shown in Figure 9.2 in the appendix.

3. Preliminary Results

3.1 Project Cycle 1:Discussion of Research Aim and the Initial Set of Research Questions

The first discussion between the researchers and the participants was focused on the research aim and the initial set of research questions. The committee members suggested initial needs and a possible process. The researchers suggested that three Informatics honours students were to be invited to participate in the discussion in order for them to perform demonstrations related to technical needs of the participants. This was because an immediate action in addressing any of the needs arising from the participants was to form part of the research. An initial set of negotiated and agreed upon research questions, together with an action plan which included the first technical training session, were completed. The date of the second session was to be 28 March 2001 at the University of Pretoria. On this day, the computer committee would respond to the initial research questions while the honours students would give a technical training session as identified by the committee. The researchers independently noted the issues raised, reflected on the research questions and prepared for all the necessary logistics of the session. They later compared their notes and jointly reflected on the action plan. A short questionnaire to determine self assessed initial technical competence of the participants was found to be necessary. The results are summarized in Table 9.1 in the appendix.

3.2 Project Cycle 2: Presentations, Training, Suggestions and Responses to the Initial Set of Research Questions

Three senior academics in Information Systems were invited to attend the session and to give some comments and possible critique. The researchers, the seven participants and the honours students attended the session. The two researchers facilitated the session. The initial technical competence self-assessment questionnaire was given to each participant to complete. The researchers collected the completed questionnaire before the presentations could start. The interpreted results showed two broad levels of understanding of the technologies involved. One level related to some participants with moderate to reasonably good understanding of the technologies involved, while the other level related to little or no understanding. After the introductions and the explanation of the aim of the session and what the expected outcomes were, two presentations were made. The first was by the computer committee, followed by a technically oriented one (on LAN, Web-server, Intranet, Internet) by two honours students. A discussion was allowed on the two presentations before the participants were taken to a computer laboratory with a LAN with the same configuration as the one at SEIDET (peer-to-peer). In the laboratory, the participants had a hands-on demonstration by the third honours student on all the aspects, which were presented earlier. They were then taken to a larger computer laboratory of the University were a different network configuration with a server was demonstrated. A final wrap-up discussion was then held in the original room. The aim here was to have a joint reflection on the proceedings as a whole; to assess the extent to which the first set of questions was responded to, to agree on the next action plan and to raise further questions.

We find it appropriate at this stage to report about an unexpected incident, which in the spirit of action research compelled us to initiate another parallel research project. We do not report on this particular research initiative in this paper as this is done elsewhere (forthcoming Phahlamohlaka, J. and Lotriet, H., 2002). On 27 March 2001, a day before the commencement of project cycle 2 of this research project, a burglary took place at the center and most of the computers as well as some of the network equipment were stolen. In the light of this event, it was decided by the research team to continue with the session of 28 March and to request the participants to continue planning and thinking about the issues as though the computers were not stolen (this with the thought in mind that the computers would be replaced in the short term and that activities would then resume as normal). The infrastructure was restored two months later, enabling this research to continue. We raise this issue here as it indeed had an impact on this research efforts. We point out this impact in our impressions, observations and interpretation later in the paper. The results of this project cycle are also summarized in Table 9.1 in the appendix.

3.2.1 Project cycle 2: General discussion points, impressions, observations and interpretation It was obvious to the researchers that the committee had taken the questions posed to them quite seriously. Some of the participants were technically more accomplished than others. For example, in informal conversations during the evening, one of the young tutors asked about the difference between a password and a username and a lady participant commented that she was slow with computers.

It was interesting to note that some of the responses were in fairly 'academic' language with a participant speaking about 'hypotheses' and 'hypotheses testing', which raises the interesting aspect that the participants may have had certain expectations about the nature and process of the research. Also the nature of research conducted by the Department of Informatics at SEIDET has never been positivist, so where do the positivist expectations arise from? The nature of the participants may have been such that the quieter members would raise no opinion or strong disagreement within a working session such as this. Alternatively, if they were less technically focused, one could expect stronger responses from them, once they were comfortable with the technology and started to think about the implications in their own fields, for instance, teaching. This would be something to lookout for during future project cycles. Also, this might be an instance where, if individual responses if required, could be elicited on a one-on-one basis during informal conversations.

The participants and the researchers both took a 'visionary' approach to the questions that were posed during the first round and also the responses to these. Interesting were the reactions of the senior academics who tended to focus in their questions and comments on 'what next'. This may have been prompted by the previous day's computer hardware theft as reported earlier. On reflection, the researchers realized the importance of the 'what next' question in two ways. Firstly, the next set of research questions were structured to elicit appropriate 'what next' responses from the participants. Secondly, a parallel research on community perceptions on the impact and perceived motivators related to computer hardware theft on ICT introduction was initiated. The overall impression was that the session was useful to the committee and that they found the experience a positive one.

3.3 Project Cycle 3: Extended Cycle - Participants Workshop with SEIDET Tutors and Subsequent Discussion Session with Researchers

A third session, which was attended by three researchers and three members of the computer committee, was only held three months later due to the theft reported earlier. The action plan from the previous project cycle was extensively scrutinized.

The report back from the computer committee was that sixteen tutors at SEIDET were called together and were given an overview of the Internet and the LAN. Afterwards the research questions were posed to the teachers and the group was divided into four focus groups, each dealing with one of the questions. The participants did not form part of the tutors' discussion groups. The group was instructed to note four points for each question and to be more practical in suggesting how the technologies could effectively be used. Demonstrations to the tutors of tools such as Encarta were well received. The teachers felt deprived for not having had the information previously. The challenge to the participants is to teach the tutors the principles of networking – this is not considered to be outside of the scope of the tutors' ability. The Impressions of the participants were that a serious and positive atmosphere was created, and that the tutors were involved and willing to contribute. The results from this session along with the participants' responses and action plan are shown in Table 9.2 in the appendix.

3.3.1 Project cycle 3:General discussion points, impressions, observations and interpretation The technically proficient participants generally find self-training to be an interesting exercise and a challenge. They saw the re-establishment of the LAN and the Internet connection after the hardware theft as a self-training opportunity. From the feedback by the participants, the researchers gathered the impression that during this cycle, the focus of the participants had shifted from visionary to the immediate actions required by the situation.

In responding to whether the research assisted them, comments from some of the computer committee members were:

'The research helped us to unpack the ideas in a systematic way.'

'The research acts as an energy provider.'

As an example, the committee identified the question 'How are you going to give feedback to the tutors?' as the most helpful question that formed part of the research. In responding to this question, the committee was able to formulate a systematic plan.

On the basis of these and similar responses it would appear that the research is contributing to further development of the SEIDET project. This is however still research in progress and due to the dynamic nature of the interaction between the researchers and the participants it would only be possible to assess the full contribution of the research at the exit point of the project.

The following aspects of the research were experienced as enriching by the researchers:

- The engagement skills on ICT related issues that were demonstrated by the participants and the questions that were thrown back at the researchers. These enabled the researchers to reflect on the project.
- The negotiation processes that were entered into each time in order to determine the next set of research questions.
- The team spirit and the level of trust that exist and are demonstrated from both sides.

These enriching aspects form part of the context of the research (see Figure 9.2).

4. Conclusions

A written response to Project cycle 3 research questions submitted by the participants indicated that the research is serving as a catalyst to action at SEIDET. This affirms the choice of action research as an appropriate research method for this project.

Through the actions generated by the research up to this point, there are specific indications that show the contribution that this research is making towards community development. For example: The workshop organized by the participants with SEIDET tutors prompted a mind-shift towards learner-centered and activity based instruction; the participants developed the necessary confidence to set up the LAN and an Internet connection on their own after the theft.

After the difficulties experienced during the early part of the research, mainly due to the computer hardware theft, the participants have demonstrated a significant capacity for action based on the research questions during project cycle 3. This means that ongoing research involvement through further project cycles should result in significant impact on further development related to the use of LAN and the Internet through the vigorous actions taken by the participants.

It is imperative that the researchers remain involved and continue to guide the process in order to ensure that the valuable lessons learnt are properly captured. In this way the weakness identified in the introduction to this article, regarding pilot studies undertaken without linkage to research, is addressed.

Appendix

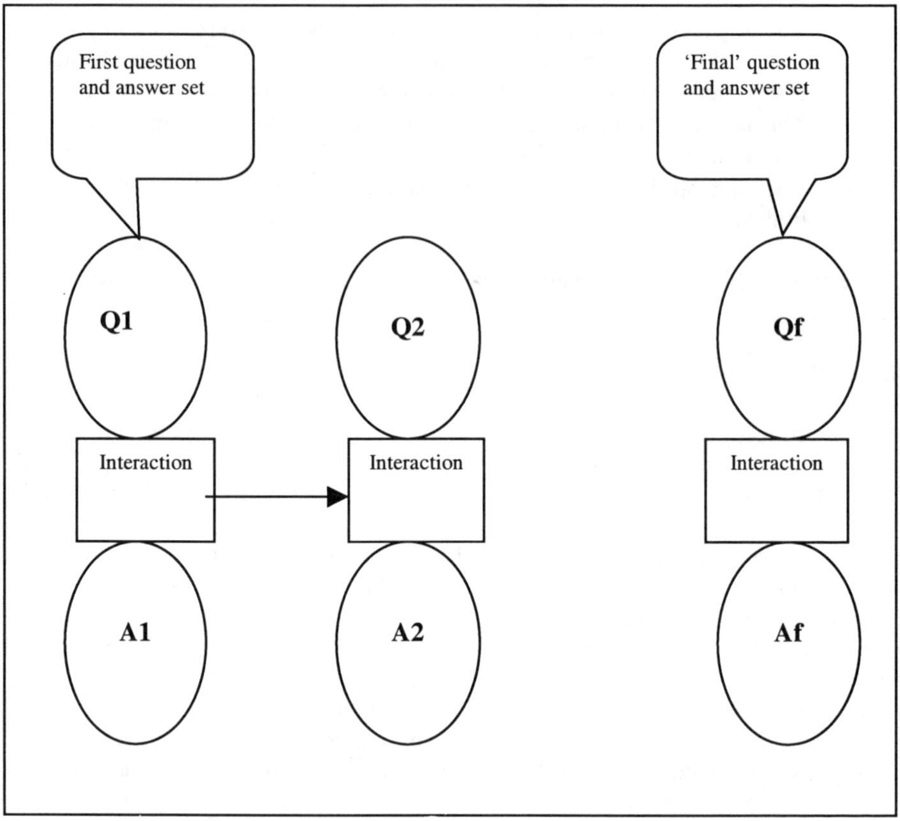

Figure 9.1 Action research framework design for this study

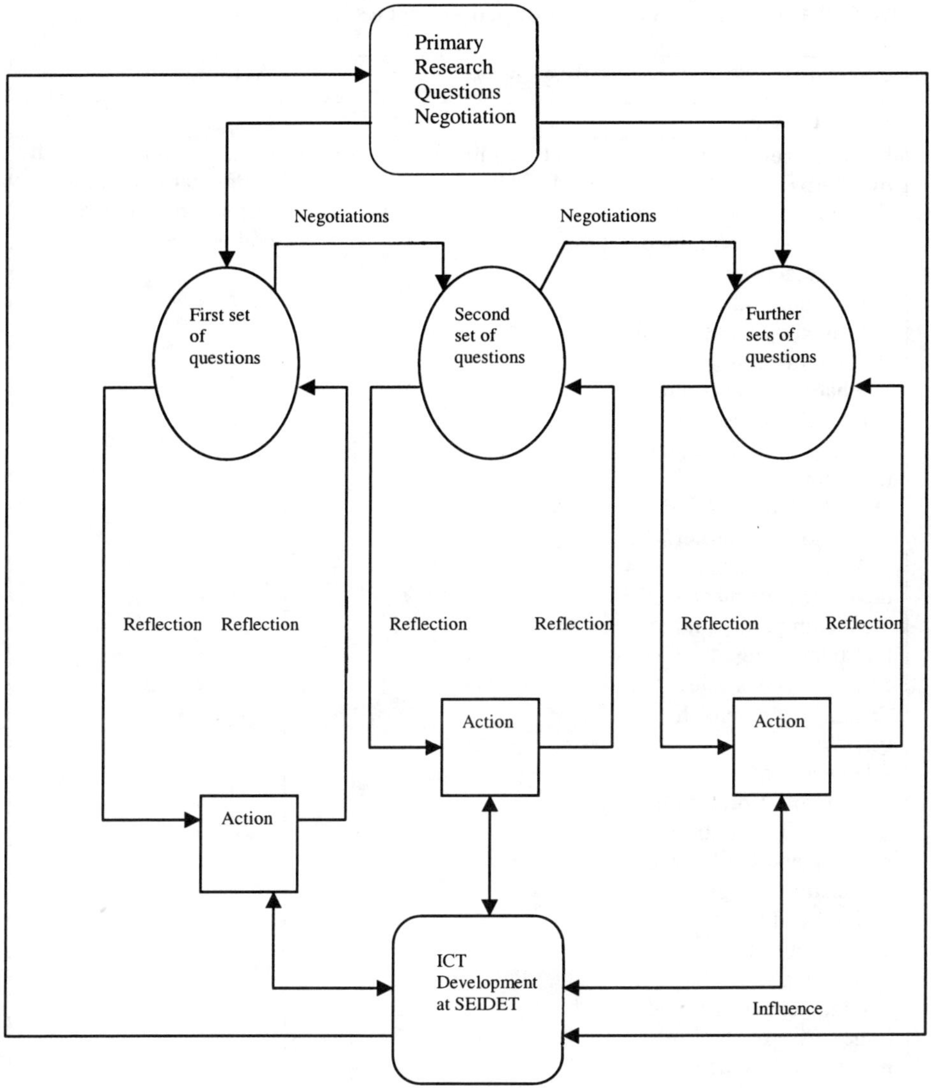

Figure 9.2 Research design and process diagram

Table 9.1 Consolidated results of project cycles

Questions	**Responses**	**Action plan**
Project cycle 1		
Primary research questions – From the perspective of the computer committee (management) what opportunities are presented by these added ICT facilities? – What does the computer committee see as new challenges in managing the laboratory brought about by the LAN and access to the Internet? – What would these developments mean to the local community and to the functioning of SEIDET as a whole? **Secondary research questions** – How are the opportunities offered by the recent installation of a network and the Internet connection recognized and utilized by the local community of Siyabuswa? – Which challenges and issues arise from efforts to incorporate the new technology into the training and education programmes at SEIDET? – Does the addition of these technologies change the style of instruction? – Does the addition of these technologies change the contents of materials	None required before project cycle 2	Considered responses by Computer Committee during project cycle 1 contact session

presented?		
	Opportunities – Sharing of resources, e.g. Printers, Files, Modem - productivity, data security, centralized storage of data – Improve communication through file distribution, e-mail, global communication, internal interaction, website development – Expose SEIDET to international community - Maintenance of SEIDET as a source of information Lab Management Challenges –Financial implications, security of files and invasion of our file systems, training of SEIDET members **Meaning of the technology to SEIDET and the surrounding community** – Will bring meaningful change to the rural community – Will be a great assistance to government as it may be very difficult for it to deal with access to information technology in rural areas – It would benefit local schools as they could use the facilities for learning	Things which the committee agreed they will do were the following: – Self-training and practice on *file sharing, resource sharing, the Internet* – Do a similar demonstration with the rest of SEIDET staff (it must be a SEIDET thing and not a committee thing they emphasized). They already have a training plan – Interact with the researchers for feedback and further reflection
Questions	**Responses**	**Action plan**
Project cycle 3		
– How does the computer committee give feedback to the tutors – – What opportunities can be identified from the	<u>Opportunities:</u> – Engage SEIDET Tutors in more IT related Workshops – Method of instruction	– Engage tutors through feedback on previous workshops and in more IT workshops

tutors' feedback? – Which of these activities are immediately actionable? – What are the priorities (first steps to be taken)? – What is the current management status of the computer laboratory at SEIDET? – (In terms of overload of issues to be addressed, more self-training of the committee, LAN related resources with NT as an example.) – Note – the feeling of the committee was that there would have to be a step backwards in terms of management in an effort to close gaps – What steps need to be taken in order to make the LAN and Internet connection meaningful and effective in the functioning of SEIDET?	will change at SEIDET to be learner-centred and activity-based because technology makes research easy – SEIDET will attract more learners – Vigorous Marketing and Developing SEIDET Web site – Entrepreneurship through the IT infrastructure that is set up at SEIDET (end-user and Internet services, amongst others) **Actionable** – Engaging SEIDET tutors in more IT related workshops – Vigorous Marketing – Entrepreneurship – Developing SEIDET Web Site <u>Priorities</u> – Give feedback of the previous workshop to the tutors coupled with e-mail address allocation and instruction on the use of the Internet – Activate the resources by making sure that the Labs are accessible to the tutors and the community at large and by working out fees. <u>Current management status of the Labs</u> – Self-training on LAN administration, network software e.g. Windows NT, soon to be installed – The committee is also facing a challenge of	– Marketing through the use of local radio stations on IT activities and SEIDET in the background, physical visits to potential clients for presentation purposes – A Close Corporation that will work on business ventures within SEIDET established and registered – Make sure that the Labs are accessible to the tutors and the community at large – Work out the affiliation fee for the use of the Lab, (i.e. establish the Lab Club)

	networking computers in other SEIDET campuses as well as networking all SEIDET campuses LAN, Intranet and Internet meaningfulness in the functioning of SEIDET – Activate the resources, viz. accessibility, Internet services, networking of all laboratories – Provide IT services, viz. IT related workshops for tutors, improved Lab Management, establishment of computer lab club	

Table 9.2 Results of workshop held by participants with SEIDET tutors

Question	Responses
What will these developments mean to the community and the functioning of SEIDET?	– Opportunities for advancing in terms of technology and information – Accessibility – SEIDET functioning: Enabled to communicate efficiently to the outside world SEIDET can compete in terms of services, resources Core value of service excellence are effected 'empowerment through enablement'
Does the addition of technology change the style of instruction and content?	– Yes – Extend technology in other learning areas – Easy for learners to do research – Learners are enabled to share and access information with learners in other countries – Expansion of knowledge of both tutors and learners in all learning areas – It makes learning and teaching interesting

Which challenges and issues arise from using these technologies to add value?	– Expensive to maintain computer laboratory in general – Expensive to keep up with standard of technology – Shortage of time to teach learners and tutors – Training of community at large to use facilities – The people who have to train the community still have to be trained

References

Baskerville, R.L. and Wood-Harper, A.T (1996). *A Critical Perspective on Action Research as a Method for Information Systems Research*, Journal of Information Technology (11)pp. 235-246.

Chambers, R. (1997). *Whose reality counts? Putting the first last.* London: Intermediate Technology publications.

Conradie, D.P. (1998). *Using information and communication technologies (ICTs) for development at centers in rural communities: lessons learned.* Communicare, 17(1), June 1998: pp. 97-116.

De Kock, D.M. (2000). *Innovative teacher education and interactive technology support.* South African Journal of Higher Education, 14(3), pp. 204-214.

Matthee, M., De Villiers, C. and Roode, J.D. (1998). *A South African Case Study: Using Computer Supported Cooperative Mathematics Learning in Teacher Training.* Working paper, Department of Informatics, University of Pretoria.

Ngwenyama, O.K. (1991). *The Critical Social Theory Approach to Information systems: Problems and Challenges* In Information Systems Research, H. E. Nissen, H. Klein, and R. Hirschheim (Eds.), Amsterdam: North Holland, pp. 267-294.

Ngwenyama, O.K. (1996). *Intensive research into organizational processes.* A research tutorial presented to the Department of Informatics seminar, University of Pretoria.

Ngwenyama, O.K. and Lee, A.S. (1997). Communication Richness in Electronic Mail: Critical Theory and The Contextuality of Meaning. *MIS Quarterly*, 21(2): pp. 145-167.

Phahlamohlaka, L.J., and Lotriet, H.H. (forthcoming, 2002). *The impact of computer hardware theft on ICT introduction to South African rural communities: an interpretive assessment through Focus Groups and Morphological Analysis.* To be presented at the United Kingdom Systems Society Conference, York, United Kingdom, 07-10 July, 2002.

Phahlamohlaka, L.J., Masilela, J and Msiza, S (2001*) Informatics and Community Development: Some strategies for an Integrated Rural Development through Education and Training at Community Centers.* Proceedings of Business Information Technology World Conference BITWorld2001, Cairo, Egypt, 04-06 June 2001.

Roode, J.D. (1997). *The development and deployment of computer supported co-operative learning at community learning centers.* Working paper, Department of Informatics, University of Pretoria.

Sahay, S and Walsham, G. (1995). *Information Technology in developing countries: A need for theory building*. Information Technology for development, 6(1995) pp. 111-124.

Scheepers, H and De Villiers, C (1999). Teaching of a Computer Literacy Course: A case study using traditional and co-operative learning, in Proceedings of the 7th European Conference on Information Systems (ECIS), Copenhagen, Denmark.

SEIDET Annual Report. (1992/93). *Annual report of the Siyabuswa Educational Improvement and Development Trust.* Siyabuswa, South Africa.

Siyabuswa Structure Plan.(1991). Planning analysis for the KwaNdebele government.South African Information Technology Industry Strategy (SAITIS) (http://www.saitis.co.za/, 2001).

UNESCO (1996). *UNESCO and the Information Society for All*, Position paper presented at the G7 ISAD Conference, Midrand, South Africa, 13-15 May.

Walsham, G. (1995). *Interpretive case studies in IS research: nature and method.* European Journal of Information Systems, Vol. 4, pp. 74-81.

Walsham, G. (1997). *Actor-Network Theory and IS Research: Current status and future prospects* in Lee, A.S, Liebenau, J and Janke, I. 1997 pp 466 - 480. Information Systems and Qualitative Research. Degross Chapman & Hall, London.

Walsham, G. (2001). *Making a world of difference: IT in a global context.* John Wiley and Sons Ltd. Chichester.

Walsham, G. and Han, C. (1991). *Structuration Theory and Information Systems Research.* Journal of Applied Systems Analysis, 17(1991) pp. 77-85.

Zongo, G. & Benjamin, P. (2000). *Telecenter models worldwide: The situation in Sub-Saharan Africa*. IDRC and LINK Center report, Johannesburg.

Chapter 10

Using Health Information for Local Action: Facilitating Organisational Change in South Africa

Norah Stoops, Louisa Williamson, Jørn Braa

1. Introduction

The optimism expressed by international funding organizations on the cost-effectiveness of information systems in primary health care settings, with debate generally exploring policy, political, fiscal and organizational factors, has been tempered by the realization that the development of technical infrastructure has often taken place at the cost of promoting internal sustainability, characterized by organizational change (Braa *et al.*, 1995, Heeks *et al.*, 1999, Opit, 1987:8, Sandiford *et al.*, 1992:34).

As early as 1981 the World Health Organization emphasized the importance of health information systems and related skills training in the implementation of an integrated primary health care approach. While the quality of primary health care services stems from an attitude that fosters service improvement, the measure of improved coverage and client satisfaction lies in the judicious use of information. Key factors that contribute to the success of services are decentralization of authority for decision making, training and strengthening of managerial support for district-based initiatives (Omaswa *et al.*, 1997:75).

1.1 South African Situation

In South Africa the historic first democratic general election held in 1994 set the stage for sweeping reform in political, social and health spheres that would redress imbalances in access to and distribution of resources. As part of this process a national restructuring of local governments was initiated in the latter half of 2000. While the demarcation of boundaries has been finalized, the allocation of governance and supporting resources is ongoing.

The restructuring of the health sector from a fragmented, centralized service to a primary health care oriented system is characterized by the development of a decentralized, district-based system that is driven by an integrated health and management information system. An outcome of discussions on the concept of a national health information system that would facilitate an equitable distribution of resources and monitoring of progress towards objectives, initiated in the early part of 1994, was a consensus to develop a national policy for health informatics in South Africa (Power, 1994). The main policy issue challenges for the development of an information system included the identification of essential information needs at national level, development of standardized routine data collection systems and the promotion of health informatics education and training.

1.2 Systems Development

Initiatives to develop a decentralized district-based health system that is driven by an integrated health and management information system, was facilitated by the Health Information Systems Programme (HISP), a collaborative project between four universities- Western Cape (Cape Town) and Cape Town, Oslo (Norway) and Eduardo Mondlane (Mozambique)), health departments at various levels and non-government organizations. It is a development project that has designed and implemented mechanisms for the collection, processing and analysis of data and use of information for decision-making at facility and district level. On completion of a three-year pilot project in the Western Cape (1996-1998), the model resulted in the development of coordinated strategy and was accepted as the national model in the latter half of 1999 (Heywood, 1998).

While the initial phase of the project focused on the development of processes that would facilitate implementation of a district based health and management information system model, the project is currently addressing issues regarding institutionalization and sustainability. The measure of organizational change is evaluated in terms of three levels of information systems development and use. The progress of implementation is monitored through an assessment of a district in terms of the extent to which the data handling processes within the information cycle are integrated into management decision-making structures. Level one reflects the use of data collection, collation, validation and feedback of raw data at a district level. Level two requires that data analysis occurs and that this information is presented in tables and or graphical format at management level on a routine basis. Level three is achieved once health indicators form the basis for decision-making and health service planning.

2. The HISP Process

The vision of HISP is to 'support the development of an excellent and sustainable health information system that enables all health care workers to use *their own information* to improve the coverage and quality of health care within our communities.'

The unique contribution of HISP was ensured by the collaborative, bottom-up nature of an action-led health and management information system (Heywood, 1998). HISP comprises a loose association of public health specialists and computer scientists who are passionate about health information systems. HISP activities include development of health information systems and structures, monitoring and evaluation methodologies, training materials and methodologies, software programmes, research and publication. The team provides a range of skills in areas that feed into the development of systems and structures that support the implementation of a District Health Information System (DHIS). These skills include software programming, management sciences, marketing and general training and facilitation skills. The establishment of a monitoring and evaluation strategy that will enable provinces to evaluate their own progress is integral to building sustainability.

2.1 National Rollout

We are currently involved in facilitating a national rollout of the District Health Information System (DHIS). The DHIS aims at developing a culture of information use amongst health care workers through the development of knowledge and skills in data handling in order to create locally relevant information for use in the management of district level health programmes. Lessons learned from the pilot project emphasized the need for management buy-in and a slower pace of implementation. Initial activities focus on provincial level marketing to ensure collaborative support for training in understanding information concepts and developing skills in the data handling processes of collection, processing and presentation. Computer training on the DHIS software focuses on data capture, data quality, validation, analysis and presentation of information.

Achievements were realised by focussing primarily on the processes involved in development of the human and organizational component rather than technical products. Successes included the creation of district-level based information systems and structures, development of practical training courses that focus on skills and understanding of information management and less tangibly, a sense of ownership and a culture of information (Braa *et al* 1998).

Identified threats to sustainability at district level and large scale application are influenced by the failure of top and middle management to support strengthening of a district based information system by allocation of human and financial resources and the slow pace of creation of decentralized district health systems with delegated authority to act on available information (Braa *et al* 1998). While the scarcity of staff trained in data analysis and interpretation has limited the effectiveness of health information systems, unless attention is focussed on constraints within the system, and they are 'designed to support the decisions and actions of health personnel', the prioritization of health information systems reform by policy makers and health managers can have limited impact (Sandiford *et al* 1992: 34).

The development of a DHIS in South Africa has taken place within the framework of an evolving technical infrastructure. However experience has demonstrated that while technical change occurs rapidly with ever increasing sophistication, the social processes within organizational structures, central to ensuring sustainability, occur slowly, with internal and external changes only apparent after many years.

2.2 Software Development

A DHIS at the primary level looks at routine aggregated anonymised patient data, which is generally collected manually. The implementation of the DHIS was kick-started by development of an open-source, user-definable, scalable and flexible computer software application system based on MS Office Professional that uses Access as a relational database for data input and pivot tables in Excel for viewing, manipulating and graphing data. The software, initially developed for monthly primary health care data, has been expanded to include quarterly Tuberculosis data, emergency medical services, environmental health and the nationally defined data set for hospitals. This HISP software has been accepted as the national standard for district-level anonymized information systems. Development of new modules, improvement to existing modules and interfacing with existing applications is ongoing.

The high profile given to the HISP software application with its associated training and support, has given rise to a situation where computers are commonly (albeit misguidedly) regarded as the central component of information management. Most managers do not appreciate that computer software is merely a tool to facilitate data processing and access to information for management decision-making (Stoops 2001). Consequently, inadequate attention is given to the process issues that facilitate sustainability.

While the importance of information technology is undisputed, the use of computers at facility level as an essential tool for processing data and interpreting information is debated. Scarce resources, lack of information technology infrastructure and skills in developing countries form significant constraints to utilization of computers as part of data handling and processing of information (Heywood *et al.*, 1997, Sabbatini, 1987:8, Southall, 1993). In South Africa a policy decision has been made that the DHIS will remain a paper-based system at facility level that becomes computerized, using the HISP software, at district level.

There has been discussion on the importance of developing a culture of information use. If front-line health workers are to use health information systems as a management tool for programme monitoring at local level, health managers and policy makers must develop a culture of information whereby information is actively used for resource allocation, planning and policy development at higher levels.

The optimistic suggestion that implementation of an action-led district information system will itself support district development and promote primary health care awareness by establishing a culture of local analysis and use of information in order to identify and follow progress towards local targets within a primary health care approach has had limited success. Reality indicates that managers seldom seek information (data, yes) and once given it, are at a loss as to how to deal with it. Thus training also needs to include supporting the managers who need to use the information.

2.3 Integration Within the Health Care System

The shift to a primary health care approach within a district health system requires a functional information system. The fragmented, overlapping health system played itself out in the information system arena with inappropriate nationally imposed data collection mechanisms, for example Epi Info for quarterly Tuberculosis data and notifiable diseases. Provinces were able to develop their own information systems for other routine data collection systems, such as routine primary health care data, anonymized HIV/AIDS data and even hospital information systems. Thus any information pertaining to a specific facility or health district could only be accessed via a multitude of different systems using the various sources functioning in each province.

DHIS training was a vehicle to facilitate a streamlined and integrated information system. This related to both the theoretical as well as the computer training required to facilitate the using of information for local action.

Strategies have been adopted to enhance the internal sustainability of the DHIS implementation process in 2001. Experience from South Africa clearly shows that a high degree of flexibility is an absolute pre-requisite for successful rollout in the current restructuring and transformation of the public sector. These strategies involve the so-called 'soft issues' that will facilitate realization of the long-term assimilation of a DHIS implementation strategy, through focussing on issues of building technical infrastructure and human resources development and support within a framework of organizational change and ongoing evaluation.

3. Human Resource Development

Programme directors, health managers, researchers and academics have identified training as a cornerstone in the successful implementation of health information systems. While training in health information systems is an essential ingredient, it in itself does not ensure successful implementation and needs to be linked to appropriate organizational change (Williamson, 2000 and Heywood, 1999).

3.1 Training Process

The HISP training course, comprised of three separate yet linked modules is designed to be presented over a period of six months in order to provide participants, working in groups, with an opportunity to consolidate both knowledge and skills gained and facilitate organizational change. The course uses health programmes (Maternal, Child and Women's Health and Communicable Diseases) as the tools to understand underlying process issues (planning and information cycles) and develop mechanisms to implement organizational change. The assignments, based on applying concepts covered in the module, completed in the inter-block period, are presented in the next module. Participants need to return to a supportive work environment in which they have the time and resources to practice new skills. The development of strategies to develop appropriate job descriptions that reflect the new skills and their use is ongoing.

Module 1, Information for Management, examines data handling within the information cycle. It focuses on the understanding of key concepts and practical skills development in data handling. Module 2, Management of Information, focuses on the specific information needs of health programmes. Module 3, Use of Information, aims at the development of skills in the interpretation and use of information.

Training contextualizes information systems within the broader health and social development perspective through incorporation of both generic and skills training components. Front-line data handlers are skilled in aspects of data handling, while service and programme managers are oriented to the rationale for health information systems as the tool needed to handle relevant data through strategies that focus on the analysis, interpretation and use of information.

Ongoing training and support of staff are crucial if their role is to be developed into its full potential. This is facilitated by 'regional health summits' in the respective provinces. District Health Management Teams are responsible for presenting district health profiles, comprised of population, health and service data. Emphasis is placed on the use of health indicators as a measurement of health status. This process provides an opportunity to facilitate ownership and a culture of information use.

Training programmes have been designed to be sensitive to service related issues that are participant and content specific, yet flexible and adapted to the local context. A localized, grassroots approach to training that is actively marketed to promote interest and involvement of health workers and their managers in health information systems, should facilitate the development of a culture of information use.

4. Organizational Change

Organizational change in job function and responsibility are needed in order to institutionalize streamlining the systems and processes created to implement, maintain and sustain a DHIS. The shifting of resources that include the appointment of appropriate levels of staff responsible for all aspects of health information issues is a first step, leading to organizational changes regarding post structures and adjustments to job descriptions. The infrastructure to support this function/ person needs to be put into place. This includes appropriate computer hardware and software, accessories (such as printers), email and ongoing technical support.

Buy-in by top management is essential for the sustainable development of the DHIS. Where the DHIS has, to date, not been seen as a strategic priority, the lack of full commitment by management at many levels has been a major obstacle to effective implementation. The low priority accorded the DHIS must be seen against the dominance accorded to hospital information systems in terms of finance, manpower and technical resources. It is estimated that district level health information systems receive less than three per cent of the budget allocation for health information systems, with the rest going to hospitals. It is proposed that a concerted effort to convince national, provincial and district management teams of the usefulness of information for management in general and the DHIS in particular be initiated (Heywood, 1999).

At each level of the system, there is a need for 'DHIS champions' – people who are committed to action-oriented information systems and are able to be drivers of the system. Initially this will usually be project-funded facilitators but through a meritocratic process of selection of local trainers and managers, this has to be handed over to local service staff. Unless the DHIS is seen to be owned by local role models, information will always be seen as a chore performed for 'other people' and not as an integral part of district development. It is this development of a locally driven information culture that is the key to sustainable development.

The goal of the HISP is to use locally generated information in order to improve the coverage and quality of health services, resulting in an improved delivery system that would impact positively on the health status of communities served and ensure accountability to local political structures.

The effectiveness of any programme can only be measured through systematic monitoring and evaluation of all phases and stages of implementation. The impact of this project is measured in terms of output and outcome indicators, rather than input and process indicators. Input and process indicators refer to budgetary allocations for capacity building. Output and outcome indicators refer to the organizational changes effected.

The progress of implementation is monitored through an assessment of a district in terms of three levels of information system establishment and use.

Level 1 Data Collected, Captured, Validated and Reported

Standardized tools and structures for collecting, collating, capturing, and disseminating data are complete. This level includes development of Essential Data Sets that is the minimum amount of data to be collected by each facility, data collection tools, data quality checks and feedback routines. This level is considered achieved when good quality data, defined as correct, complete and consistent, is submitted to higher levels within specified time periods i.e. adhering to predetermined reporting dates.

At Level 1 the HISP software is installed and used for routine primary health care data sets. Health workers have been trained to capture, validate and disseminate data in tables, graphs and reports. At the time of writing all 173 health districts in the country are using the software for data capture. Data quality and feedback of both raw and indicator data is still problematic in a number of health districts.

Level 2 Data Interpreted and Presented to Managers and Facilities

Data is converted locally into useful information (indicators, district profiles, trends) and displayed graphically in reports. Supervisors provide feedback to facilities based on analyzed information. Information is made available to managers, decision-makers and other users regularly in the form of specific and tailored monthly and/or quarterly reports. It is recommended that information be placed as a standing item on management agendas. This would provide an opportunity to discuss appropriate programme indicators. The current monitoring of the immunization status in terms of district coverage forms a valuable tool in the ongoing management of the Expanded Programme of Immunization.

Currently, all health districts have initiated mechanisms to establish a district information office to facilitate streamlined data and information flow on both vertical and horizontal levels.

Level 3 Information for Decision-making

When information is used for planning and routine management of health services, this implies the existence of a local 'information culture'. This level entails developing mechanisms for quality control, responding to local management issues, monitoring service level agreements or giving incentives for good performance and other activities. This level is considered achieved when managers at all levels are monitoring business plans using health service indicators, and these are used to ensure accountability to policy makers and local political structures.

5. Two Case Studies: Gauteng Province and Northern Cape Province

South Africa consists of nine provinces, with relative autonomy regarding health service management. Provinces are divided into regions, which are further sub-divided into districts. Each district has its own district health management team. Two provincial case studies are provided.

5.1 Gauteng Province

Gauteng province is both the industrial and economic capital of the country, with the highest population density, greatest wealth and technical and transport infrastructure. It is generally well-resourced, with the second highest per capita expenditure on health. Health service rendering at a district level is provided by local authority and provincial government structures, a legacy of the apartheid era. As part of a national restructuring of local governments, Gauteng was divided into three regions. Gauteng, with its powerful local authority structures, was the last province to accept implementation of the DHIS at the end of 2000. The lack of alignment between local government and provincial health region geographical boundaries has impacted negatively on the ability of service providers to integrate services and allocate resources effectively.

Due to the organizational and political uncertainty regarding the demarcation of local authorities that will form health districts, service functioning and roles and responsibilities, the implementation of the DHIS is centralized at provincial level. The directorate of health information systems, in an attempt to standardize processes, controls all discussion on development of the minimum dataset, data collection tools and reporting processes. Discussions regarding the implementation of an integrated health and management information system (HMIS) were initiated in 1999 with a provincial workshop at which a variety of health programme related stakeholders were invited to submit lists of desired datasets.

The resultant list, in excess of 600 data elements, was implemented as a provincially determined Essential Data Set (EDS). All health facilities at primary level are required to complete standardized data collection tools and submit routine data to regional and provincial levels. As part of this process, Gauteng has moved from a routinely collected primary health care dataset of 600 elements to one in excess of a 1000. This can be compared with the Eastern Cape Province, with 45 data elements and 11 relating to immunization and another 23 key tracer drug items for out of stock control.

In 2000, regional information officers were appointed in each of the three regions, to assume responsibility for co-ordinating the DHIS at regional level. In two regions, district information officers have been appointed to assist with the process. As part of the national rollout of the DHIS, discussions were held between HISP consultants and the provincial directorate of Health Information Systems in the early part of 2001 where a rollout strategy was explored. Due to the lack of top management buy-in, the role of HISP consultants was limited to one of providing training and follow-up support.

In an attempt to fast track the rollout, it was agreed that an initial training course would be provided to a provincial group of programme, service and information managers. The course, presented in the early part of 2001, provided both theoretical and software training. It was expected that these participants would develop the process in their respective regions. Due to the lack of management buy-in and poor technical and organizational infrastructure, this was not possible.

In the latter part of 2001, training courses were held in each of the three regions. Participants consisted largely of facility and programme managers. While participants are keen to implement the new knowledge and skills gained, they are constrained by the lack of management support and authority to do so.

A status review of the data handling processes within the information cycle found that while data collection tools and sources are formalized, to date, the provincial strategic plan does not provide operational guidance for monitoring and evaluation at local level. The provincial strategic plan has identified health priorities and set goals and objectives. The lack of understanding on the use of denominator-based catchment population figures is reflected in poorly developed targets and indicators. Notwithstanding the large dataset, the lack of consensus regarding interpretation of essential data element definitions, such as headcount, full immunization, malnutrition and sexually transmitted infections impacts negatively on the quality of data collected. While data flow is gradually being streamlined, it remains one-directional, with data being collected at facility level and sent to regional level for capture. This collated data is sent to the provincial office for 'handling'.

It found that minimal use was made of data validation and quality checks. A review of data quality highlighted the lack of understanding and consensus regarding use of data elements. The traditional approach to only using headcount as an indicator of service workload, rather than the use of population as a denominator to evaluate service impact on coverage and quality is compounded by the lack of access to accurate provincial, regional, district and facility catchment population figures. Adjusted 'rough guide' catchment and target population estimates are being developed to enable districts to look at coverage and quality of service rendering, rather than utilization.

Formalized feedback processes and mechanisms do not exist. The regional office gives feedback on data quality errors, rather than on district indicators reflecting coverage. Regional and district level health managers and workers who have undergone DHIS training are exploring the development of district information teams and grappling with attempts to adapt the national goals, targets and indicators to suit local needs. This remains a classroom exercise, as they do not have the authority to make real changes in local operational plans.

The lack of clarity regarding the functioning of different levels of health services has resulted in insecurity on processes needed to develop a functional District Health System. Although a provincial process of developing top and middle level service and programme management buy-in is demonstrated in a commitment to reduce the large dataset, Gauteng still stands on the threshold of Level 1, with the focus on standardized data collection. The poor technical infrastructure to support data capture, validation and presentation is aggravated by the lack of management support for organizational change. Regional health summits with a follow up provincial summit will explore mechanisms to address these issues and are planned for mid 2002.

5.2 Northern Cape Province

The Northern Cape is the largest province in South Africa, with the smallest population at 850,000. This sparsely populated semi-desert province with its extreme temperature ranges has a largely agricultural economic base. Kimberley, the capital city, was where diamonds were discovered in South Africa in the 1860s. Unlike in Gauteng, the restructuring of local government has had little impact on this province, as almost all health services fall within the responsibility of the Provincial Department of Health. There have been minor boundary adjustments.

This province is divided into five health districts, with District Management Teams in each. The Health Systems Trust (HST), an external funding organization, was functional in two districts prior to 1999 where they were responsible for the assisting in the development of a district health management system. In early 2000 HISP computer software training was provided in the two HST supported districts. It was soon apparent that little use was made of the available information. Data capture at local, district and provincial levels was done without validation and other data quality checks. No feedback was provided and little use of the data or information was demonstrated.

No provincial level uniform primary health care Essential Data Sets was developed until beginning 2001. Some districts were collecting new data elements some still collected old datasets. This made indicator based comparison between districts and evaluation of the province as a whole, almost impossible. The new primary health care Essential Data Set consists of 75 data elements.

The need for training in the use of information soon became apparent. The presentation of district based training courses aimed at facility and district level health workers and service managers were initiated in 2001. Provincial level health programme coordinators, responsible for policy setting, monitoring and evaluation, were specifically targeted for training. By September 2001, four training courses have been presented. Participants included management, administration clerks, pharmacists, nurses in charge and hospital matrons.

5.3 Results

- All district level managers have received training on using the reports of the HISP software. This has proved to be a valuable exercise in demonstrating the powerful use of information as a management tool.
- One district in the region has decentralized the data capturing onto sub-district level.
- The staff of four districts out of the total five have undergone the modular training course as also many of the provincial programme managers. The fifth district will be included in the plans for 2002.
- While one district has implemented a District Information Team that is responsible for guiding the district in development of an information culture, two others are in the early stages.
- One district has revised their business plan for 2002 using more output and outcome indicators.
- A review of the progress of DHIS implementation in the Northern Cape over the past 18 months has demonstrated achievement of most of the Level 1 activities. Dissemination and feedback remain problematic and data quality still needs attention. A provincial health summit is planned for mid 2002.

6. Lessons Learned

In as much as HISP facilitators responsible for the DHIS rollout have no direct influence on organizational issues, it is the resultant organizational change that is the true measure of successful implementation. The realization that organizational change is a slow process with success measured in small achievements has reinforced the relevance of evaluating the impact of HISP team intervention in terms of levels of DHIS functioning.

A gradual shift to Level 1 is achievable within a reasonably short period of time. The lack of management support for organizational change has shifted the training focus to an understanding of the data handling processes, with an emphasis on developing local goals, targets and indicators to monitor coverage and quality of health services.

Provinces retain a high degree of autonomy in determining how the DHIS will be implemented. While the development of a baseline national Essential Data Set provides a guideline, provinces are free to maintain and develop their own additional data sets, resulting in the wide disparity in the number of data items collected routinely, as demonstrated in provincial data sets that range from 45 to in excess of 1000.

The development of appropriate goals, health indicators and targets at a national level is needed in order to provide guidance for provinces and archive local level alignment. Provincial strategic plans for both Gauteng and Northern Cape provinces generally consist of input and process indicators. In order to monitor health status, output and outcome indicators must be developed.

Monitoring and evaluation of health service delivery within health programmes is only possible if the set goals, objectives and targets are known Currently programme coordinators look to the National Department of Health for guidance in setting local goals, indicators and targets (GITs) that are in line with those of the national department. At present this guidance does not adequately enable provinces to set their own GITs. A process has been initiated to facilitate this development.

The challenge for developing locally relevant GITs and ensuring good quality data for local analysis and presentation was accepted. However, local level enthusiasm and keenness does not ensure organizational change. Unless there is a demand for information from provincial health programme managers and service managers at district level and use thereof, the output remains at the level of raw data, and the process will not be sustainable. Training impact is lost if there is inadequate support from provincial and district level service managers. The buy-in and commitment of mid and top level management is an integral part of the process.

Achieving Level 2 is more complex. The lack of capacity in developing indicator based health programmes is reflected in the poor interpretation and use of information. Programme managers, who play a crucial role in the demand for information used in health service and status review, have themselves identified the need for training in setting GITs, analysis, interpretation and use of information. Service managers at all levels need substantial training and support in order to develop a culture of management use of information. Unless these cadres are appropriately targeted, institutionalization of the DHIS concept is threatened.

The development of District Information Teams plays an integral role in facilitating a streamlined, two-way flow of information and formalized feedback mechanisms. Training impact is lost if there is inadequate support from provincial and district level service managers. The buy-in and commitment of mid and top level management is integral to the institutionalization of formalized feedback mechanisms and use of information for decision-making. The ongoing power play between entrenched provincial structures and powerful local authorities creates a culture of uncertainty, resulting in an inability and unwillingness to 'rock the boat', to effect organizational changes that would result in development of a DHIS. Achieving Level 3 remains a long-term objective of a culture of information use within organizational change.

7. Conclusion

Kirkpatrick's model of training effectiveness has become the most widely used approach to the evaluation of training effectiveness (Kirkpatrick, 1996). Four levels of evaluation are proposed: perception of learning, knowledge and skills gained, behaviour change and change in organizational performance. The effectiveness of the training as regards perception, knowledge, skill and behaviour changes is well illustrated by the enthusiasm with which course participants have applied the lessons learned. Graphs on clinic walls, information as a standing item of meeting agendas and the use of facility based catchment populations to calculate facility indicators, act as confirmation of training success. District Information Teams have been initiated to coordinate the data handling processes. The challenge for these teams is to maintain the current enthusiasm by facilitating a streamlined flow of information and feedback processes.

The way forward demands the targeting of health programme, service and information managers for buy-in and support of the process. The involvement of national, provincial, regional and district managers in the coordination of goals, targets and indicators and use of information as a tool to monitor and evaluate the effectiveness of health programmes is a vital strategy in ensuring sustainable organizational change.

At the national level there is a greater awareness and understanding of the role of the DHIS in service delivery. As a result fiscal allocation to strengthen DHIS initiatives has been increased for the year 2002. A national DHIS summit was held in June 2002.

If we are serious in our commitment to the adopting of a district based primary health care approach to service delivery, we must give service providers the tools and resources to run decentralized health programmes. An action-oriented health information system is just such a tool that enables health workers at all levels to plan, implement and evaluate locally appropriate programmes. Organizational structures and training initiatives that enable the use of locally generated information as a management tool to improve coverage and quality of primary health care services are integral to the process of health service transformation.

References

Braa J, and Heywood A. (1995), South Africa, Africa and Health Information Systems – The Need for a Reciprocal Collaboration. In: M. Sosa-Iudicissa, et al. (ed.), *Health, Information Society and Developing Countries.*: IOS Press, Amsterdam, pp.173-84.

Braa J, Heywood A, and Mohamed H. Six Steps to Develop a District Health Information System. Unpublished paper presented at the ESSA Conference, 1998.

Heeks R, Mundy D, and Salazar A. Why Health Care Information Systems Succeed or Fail. Information Systems for Public Sector Management 1999 *Institute for Development Policy and Management*, Working Paper Series no. 9.

Heywood A. The Health Information Systems Pilot Project. Unpublished paper, University of the Western Cape, 1998.

Heywood A. Human Resource Development for Information Systems. Unpublished paper presented at the Helina Conference, 1999.

Heywood A, and Campbell B. Development of a primary health care information system in Ghana: Lessons learned. *Methods of Information in Medicine* 1997: 36, pp. 63-68.

Kirkpatrick D., 1996. 'Revisiting Kirkpatrick's Four-Level Model.' Journal of the American Society for Training and Development, vol. 50, no. 1, pp. 54-59.

Omaswa F, Burnham G, Baingana G, Mwebesa H, and Morrow R. Introducing Quality Management into Primary Health Care Services in Uganda. *Bulletin of the World Health Organisation* 1997: 75 (2) pp. 155-161.

Opit L. How should information on health be generated and used? *World Health Forum* 1987: 8 pp. 409-417.

Power M. Towards a South African National Policy for Health Informatics. Unpublished paper presented at the 6th ESSA Conference, 1994.

Sabbatini R. How to get the best out of automated information systems. *World Health Forum 1987:* 8 pp. 432-434.

Sandiford P, Annett H, and Cibulskis R. What can information systems do for primary health care? An international perspective. *Soc. Sci. Med.* 1992: 34 (10) pp. 1077-1087.

Southall H. Health informatics in developing countries: seven golden rules. Unpublished paper presented at the 1st Helina Conference, 1993.

Stoops N. Evaluation of the Health Information Systems Programme (HISP) computer software programme in selected health districts of the Cape Metropole Region. Masters thesis, University of the Western Cape, April 2001.

Williamson L. Evaluation of an in-house training course for district level health workers in the Cape Metropole region. Masters thesis, University of the Western Cape, September 2000.

Glossary of Terms

DHIS	District Health Information System
HISP	Health Information System Programme
HST	Health Systems Trust
GITs	Goals, Indicators, Targets

Chapter 11

Information and Communications Technology for Poverty Reduction in Rural India

Simone Cecchini

1. The Poverty-reducing Potential of ICT

The *World Development Report 2000/01: Attacking Poverty* identifies three priority areas for poverty reduction: opportunity, empowerment, and security. Opportunity makes markets work for the poor and expands poor people's assets. Empowerment makes state institutions work better for poor people and removes social barriers. Security helps poor people manage risk (World Bank 2001). In light of current experiences in rural India and elsewhere in the developing world, it is apparent that ICT – defined as the set of activities that facilitates the capturing, storage, processing, transmission and display of information by electronic means (World Bank 2002a) – can be utilized to support poverty reduction strategies. The use of ICT applications can enhance poor people's opportunities by improving their access to markets, health, and education. Furthermore, ICT can empower the poor by expanding the use of government services, and reduce risks by widening access to microfinance.

2. ICT projects for Poverty Reduction in Rural India

Although most of the rural poor in India are isolated from the information revolution, there are several examples in rural India where ICT is used to contribute to poverty reduction in the areas of opportunity, empowerment and security. The following case descriptions highlight ICT applications that are attempting to realize the potential of ICT.

2.1 Opportunity

2.1.1 Supporting pro-poor market development: Computerized milk collection centers. Small farmers and artisans living in rural areas typically lack access to information about prices, data on crops, weather conditions, credit facilities, and market opportunities. ICT can remedy such information asymmetries and stimulate poor people's entrepreneurship by better connecting them to markets (World Bank 1999).

In Gujarat, computerized milk collection centers with integrated electronic weights, electronic fat testing machines and plastic card readers are ensuring fair prices for farmers who sell milk to dairy cooperatives. Traditionally, the fat content in milk was calculated through a cumbersome measurement process hours after the milk was received. Although farmers delivered milk on a daily basis, they were only paid every ten days and had to trust the cooperative society staff's manual calculations of the quality and quantity of milk. Malfeasance and under-payment to farmers, although difficult to substantiate, were commonly alleged. Computerized milk collection centers have increased transparency, led to faster processing, shorter queues and immediate payment to farmers. Furthermore, the Dairy Information System Kiosk (DISK) software developed by the Centre for Electronic Governance at the Indian Institute of Management, Ahmedabad (CEG-IIMA) provides relevant information to farmers through a database that contains complete histories of all milch cattle owned by members of the cooperative and a dairy portal connected to the Internet. The 50,000 dairy farmers who use the computerized system feel empowered and benefit from a more transparent and efficient cooperative system (Bhatnagar 2000, Bhatnagar and Schware 2000, Cecchini 2001).

2.1.2 Improving access to basic services: India Healthcare Delivery project. The relatively low cost and wide reach of radio and television enable the delivery of education to isolated rural areas, and information technology training is beginning to be offered at rural schools and private institutes. ICT can also improve health care delivery to the poor. Telemedicine can diminish the cost and hardship of long distance travel for medical attention and diagnosis. E-mail and medical list-serves can deliver recent medical findings to health workers lacking research and technological facilities at minimal cost. Furthermore, ICT can simplify medical data collection, record management and paper filing (Cecchini and Shah 2002).

Handheld computers, or Personal Digital Assistants (PDAs), are allowing auxiliary nurse midwives (ANMs) participating in the InfoDev-sponsored India Healthcare Delivery project to reduce redundant paperwork and data entry, freeing up time for healthcare delivery to the poor. ANMs shoulder most of the responsibility for healthcare delivery in vast and densely populated rural areas. Their duty is to administer immunization, offer advice on family planning, educate people on mother-child health programs, and collect data on the rural population's growth, birth, and immunization rates. Each ANM serves 5,000 people, typically residing in different villages and hamlets, often located several kilometers apart. ANMs usually spend between 15 and 20 days per month on data collection and registration. PDAs are facilitating data collection and transmission, saving up to 40 percent of ANMs' work time. Redundant data entry prevalent in paper registers is eliminated and reports are generated automatically. These gains in efficiency multiply the impact and reach of limited resources, thus expanding access to basic services (Bhatnagar and Schware 2000, Cecchini 2001, InfoDev various years).

2.2 Empowerment

2.2.1 Improving access to government services: Gyandoot. ICT can be used by government agencies to transform relations with citizens and businesses. In India, as in much of the developing world, it is not uncommon for rural villagers to travel long distances to government district headquarters in order to submit applications, meet officials, obtain copies of public records, or seek information regarding prevailing prices in commodity markets. This involves the loss of a day's income as well as the cost of transportation. Once at the government office, the relevant official, record, or information could be unavailable, forcing repeated visits and additional expenses. In effect, government officials working with paper records enjoy a monopoly over information and records. Villagers may also face discomfort, harassment, and corruption on the part of public officials, or are often given incorrect information about government programs or market prices (Sharma and Yurcik 2000). In fact, compared to middle or upper classes, the poor end up paying a disproportionate share of their income on bribes.

With ICT, it is possible to locate service centers that provide documents, land records and other public services closer to citizens. Such centers may consist of an unattended kiosk in a government agency, or a service kiosk located close to the client. Potential benefits include increased transparency, less corruption, better delivery of government services and greater government responsiveness (World Bank 2002b). Information disclosure and the possibility of interacting with public officials also build pressure for government accountability. The poor become empowered because they feel they are getting a service rather than a favor.

Since January 2000, Gyandoot – a government-owned computer network– has been making government more accessible to villagers in the poor and drought-prone Dhar district of Madhya Pradesh. Gyandoot reduces the time and money people spend trying to communicate with public officials and provides immediate, transparent access to local government data and documentation. For minimal fees, Intranet kiosks provide caste, income, and domicile certificates, helping the villagers avoid the common practice of paying bribes. The kiosks also allow farmers to track crop prices in the region's wholesale markets-enabling them to negotiate better terms. Other services include information on school results and on the names of people included in the below poverty line list, and a public complaint line for reporting broken irrigation pumps, unfair prices, absentee teachers, and other problems. Kiosks are run by local operators along commercial lines and are placed in villages located on major roads or holding weekly markets, so that each of them can serve another 25 to 30 villages. (Bhatnagar and Vyas 2001, Cecchini 2002).

2.3 Security

2.3.1 Improving access to microfinance: Smart Cards Microfinance is an important tool for poor people to reduce, mitigate and cope with risk. Computerization, Smart Cards, and software systems providing loan tracking, financial projections and branch management information can reduce costs and help microfinance institutions reach clients more efficiently.

Smart Cards with an embedded microchip containing information on clients' credit histories are helping SKS, a microfinance institution operating in the Medak district of Andhra Pradesh to reduce transaction costs. One of the main problems faced by SKS, which follows the peer-lending model developed by the Grameen Bank, is the high cost of service delivery to the poor. All cash transactions take place at village group meetings and each transaction takes about 90 seconds per person. Much time is spent not only on paperwork but also discussing terms and conditions and counting coins. Office computerization alone would not bring much time savings because staff would have more free time during the day, but not in the mornings and evenings when people in villages are available for meetings. Smart Cards have been identified as a solution to the high cost of delivery, because they can lead to gains in efficiency, eliminating paperwork, reducing errors, fraud and meeting time. Potential savings in operations are estimated to be around 18 percent. Once all of SKS operations are conducted with handheld computers, a read-only device will be left in each village for clients to check the information stored on the Smart Cards. Microfinance projects like SKS enable poor people and their microbusinesses to gain broader access to financial services. (Akula 2000, Baramati Initiatives 2001, Cecchini 2001).

3. Realizing The Potential of ICT is not an Automatic Process

Realizing the poverty-reducing potential of ICT is not guaranteed. It requires attentive public policy formulation and careful project design. Insufficient information and communication infrastructure, high access costs, and illiteracy limit the benefits of ICT to the better off urban segments of the population to the detriment of the poor and rural areas. General theory and observation of the Indian experience illustrate these dynamics.

3.1 A Model on the Diffusion of ICT

A model developed by Chris Scott, building on earlier work by Keith Griffin (1979), shows why the poor and the rich use different communications techniques and how the nature of technical change has until now been biased towards the rich, widening the digital divide. Since the value of time is low for the poor –due to underemployment– and the cost of ICT capital is high, when ICT consists of oral and written communication on the one hand and fixed line telephony on the other, the poor tend to communicate orally. The rich, who face opposite constraints, choose to communicate via fixed line telephony, which is relatively capital-intensive. When mobile telephony and the Internet become available, both of which require more capital per unit of information communicated than any of the existing techniques, the rich switch from communicating by fixed telephony to using the Internet, while the poor continue to communicate orally. Therefore, the model has two implications for a pro-poor ICT policy. First, the relative price of capital for communications purposes needs to be reduced for the poor. Extending the electricity grid to low-income areas, selectively and temporarily subsidizing poor users, and improving access to training are essential. Second, the focus of research and development in ICT has to favor poor-user friendly hardware and software (Pigato 2001).

3.2 Access to ICT in Rural India

In India, even where telephone lines have reached rural areas through the introduction of Public Call Offices (PCOs), the poor have very limited access to ICT. As revealed by a recent survey conducted in five villages in Uttar Pradesh, West Bengal and Andhra Pradesh (Marwah, in Pigato 2001), only radios are owned by a majority of poor households. Televisions, telephones and newspapers are available to the majority of households on a shared basis. Very few families have shared access to a computer or Internet connection, and some households have never viewed television, read a newspaper or used a telephone (see Table 11.1). Surveys also suggest that the poor rely on information from informal networks of trusted family, friends and local leaders, but these networks do not adequately satisfy their information needs (Pigato 2001). This indicates that ICT could play a pivotal role in improving access to information by the poor. However, it remains very difficult for people with low levels of education to reap the full benefits of new technologies, including wide access to knowledge and information.

Table 11.1 Access to sources of information and communications for the rural poor in India

Source	Personal ownership (%)	Shared/ communal (%)	Not available (%)
Radio	77.3	22.7	-
Newspapers	11.3	80.0	8.7
Television	9.3	84.0	6.7
Telephone	-	63.3	36.7
Fax	-	0.7	99.3
Computer/ Internet	-	12.0	88.0

Source: Pigato (2001)

4. Achieving Low-cost Connectivity: A Necessary Condition for Pro-poor ICT

While many factors contribute to the success of ICT projects in rural areas of developing countries, low-cost access to information infrastructure is the basic necessary –but insufficient– condition to reach the poor. Inadequate or absent connectivity and unstable power supply clearly reduce the economic viability of ICT projects (Kirkman 1999). Gyandoot, for instance, faces problems with dial-up connections because most of the local rural telephone exchanges do not operate with optical fiber cable (Bhatnagar and Vyas 2001).

Given that it is not realistic to provide telephone lines or computers to all households in developing countries, government and regulators should be concerned with policy instruments for achieving 'universal access.' The latter is generally defined as the presence of a public telecom booth in every village, or within reasonable distance (James 2000, Kenny, Navas-Sabater and Quiang 2001). India is striving to achieve universal access through its national telecom policies focused on the provision of telecom facilities to every village at 'affordable and reasonable prices' but almost 40 percent of rural communities still lack shared access to a telephone (Telecom Regulatory Authority of India 2001).

4.1 Fostering Competition

Fostering competition in the telecom sector can significantly reduce communication costs, and thus improve physical access to ICT by the poor. In India, teledensity –the number of telephone mainlines per 1,000 people– has significantly improved between 1997 and 2000 (see Table 11.2). This has been mainly the result of market-oriented reforms in the telecom sector. Prior to 1992, the Department of Telecommunications was the sole provider of telecom services in India, and the rigid regulatory framework was a big obstacle to the development of telecom infrastructure. In 1992, the mobile market was privatized. In 1994, the fixed services market followed and finally, in 1999, national long distance operations were opened to private competition (Digital Opportunity Initiative 2001).

However, only large corporations were effectively allowed to take part in the privatization process. Privatization permitted prospective telecom operators to bid for the right to operate in a whole state. Given the size of states in India, bids of over US$1 billion were common (Jhunjhunwala 2000).

Table 11.2 Trends in Teledensity Across States in India, 1997-2000

State	Telephone Mainlines per 1,000 people		
	1997	2000	Change 1997-2000
Punjab	33.4	61.8	+85%
Maharashtra	33.8	52.8	+56%
Kerala	26.7	46.8	+75%
Tamil Nadu	21.4	37.2	+74%
Gujarat	24.4	36.4	+49%
Haryana	20.0	33.1	+66%
Karnataka	19.8	32.6	+65%
Rajasthan	13.2	25.7	+95%

Andhra Pradesh	13.5	22.0	+63%
Madhya Pradesh	10.6	18.2	+72%
West Bengal	9.6	13.9	+45%
Uttar Pradesh	6.8	12.5	+84%
Orissa	5.9	9.6	+63%
Bihar	3.6	5.9	+64%

Source: Nanthikesan (2000)

4.2 A Role for Small Entrepreneurs

Large telecom operators tend to limit their operations to higher-income urban areas because of the lower revenue potential of poor rural areas and the higher cost of servicing them. Small entrepreneurs, on the other hand, see the opportunity to make a profit even in a lower revenue environment, and thus have the proper incentive to enter rural markets. A good example of this is cable TV in India. Typically, micro entrepreneurs install dish antennas for cable TV and provide service to subscribers within a 700-meters radius. Operators sell the connection and visit homes to collect charges – between US$1.50 and US$4 per month. Customers know the operator personally, and the service operator is available to rectify problems anytime of the week. For these reasons, cable services in India are considered superior to telephone services, although cable technology is significantly more complicated than telephone technology. Consequently, it can be argued that privatization should be opened up to allow small entrepreneurs –or Local Service Providers– to supply telecom services in rural areas (Jhunjhunwala 2000).

4.3 Regulatory Mechanisms

However, the market by itself might not be able to provide a sufficient level of connectivity to the poorest and most isolated rural areas. The key to achieving connectivity for these areas is to determine how far market forces will carry the rollout of voice and data networks. The gaps left by the private sector can then be remedied by public intervention. Regulatory mechanisms that can help extend access to information infrastructure include geographic coverage requirements and universal access funds.

One alternative is to invite private operators to bid for services in areas that are not commercially viable in return for a subsidy financed from a universal access fund. A concession contract is then awarded to the company requesting the smallest subsidy. In Chile, for example, this mechanism has been used to leverage US$40 million in private investment on the basis of just over US$2 million of public subsidy. As a result 1,000 public telephones have been installed in rural towns, at around 10 percent of the costs of direct public provision. Subsidies of this kind could also be used to support the development of Internet-enabled community centers, content relevant to low-income groups and to people that speak languages not well represented on the web, and community postal and radio facilities (World Bank 2002a).

5. Project Design Lessons

Even if information infrastructure reaches rural areas, there is no guarantee that the poor will access ICT applications. Many of the projects that attempt to provide access to the Internet in rural India, for instance, end up favoring middle and upper-class men (Cecchini 2002, Cecchini and Raina 2002). Rural women tend to be excluded because of their restricted mobility, lack of education, and, in some cases, male control over information and media (Balit 1999). How can we ensure that ICT projects reach poor women and men?

5.1 Grassroots Intermediaries

In rural India, as in much of the developing world, direct ownership and use of ICT –for instance through a PC with Internet access– applies only to a very minimal fraction of the population. Although the availability of content in local languages and the use of graphic and voice interfaces can make ICT applications more accessible to poor people, illiteracy and low levels of education are powerful obstacles to the use of PCs and other ICT tools. In most cases, poor people thus have to rely on a human intermediary between them and ICT, in what is termed a 'reintermediation model' (Heeks 2001). The profile of the intermediaries who add human skills and knowledge to the presence of ICT is thus critical for projects that want to reach the poor (Heeks 1999).

Successful examples of ICT projects for poverty reduction are conducted by intermediaries that have the appropriate incentives and proven track record working with poor people. In Andhra Pradesh, ANMs have been working with poor villagers on a daily basis for years. SKS, the microfinance institution, adheres to a philosophy of reaching out to the poorest women in rural areas. In Gujarat, dairy cooperatives have been the best agent to target small farmers. If these intermediaries are grassroots-based and understand the potential of ICT for social change, they can be tremendously effective in promoting local ownership of ICT projects. In rural India, many information kiosk operators are young, educated, computer-savvy, and very attached to their communities. They are also extremely entrepreneurial. In the case of Gyandoot, successful kiosk operators –besides offering e-government services– often create and manage database and work on data entry for private clients, offer PC training, provide voice, fax, copy, Internet and many other services.

Given the right incentives and opportunities, these intermediaries are keen to make access to information easily available for everybody and are willing to train others in the villages (Cecchini 2001, Cecchini 2002, Cecchini and Raina 2002).

5.2 Community Involvement

Applications developed by or with the collaboration of local staff are more likely to be appropriate for local conditions when there is continuous involvement and feedback from the community. Local ownership fosters the success and resilience of ICT projects. Outside control and top-down approaches, on the other hand, often waste resources in the initial periods of projects endangering their future sustainability. Specifically, in the case of e-governance projects, the local administrative and political machinery needs to be involved in the implementation of the project, or otherwise the chance of failure is almost certain.

In Rajasthan, the state-sponsored RajNidhi e-governance program has failed to deliver, despite the fact that the software is easy to use and in Hindi, because of extremely centralized planning that did not take local conditions into consideration. Content, in fact, lacks regular updating because of communications problems between the state and the local government (Syngh Yadav 2001).

5.3 Information Needs, Locally-Contextualized Information and Pro-poor Services

The information needs of a community should be thoroughly assessed before launching ICT projects. Rapid, participatory rural appraisals and other survey instruments have been used for several years to ensure community ownership of development programs. These tools could be used in the context of ICT initiatives.

ICT applications should address the most pressing needs of the community. Thus, content provided through ICT should not be limited to the knowledge that can be accessed from outside sources, but rather extended to ensure that the poor have the means to speak for themselves. The poor know a great deal: they know their needs, circumstances, worries and aspirations better than anybody. In sum, the poor need access to locally contextualized information, more than access to existing information from an alien context (Heeks 1999). The InfoDev-sponsored Honey Bee Network, with its database of solutions to local development problems, is an excellent example of the creation of relevant content for the lives of poor people (Cecchini and Shah 2002).

In the case of e-governance projects, it is advisable that projects focus on a limited number of well-run pro-poor services rather than offer a great number of services that end up lying unutilized because of lack of demand. Gyandoot, for instance, offers about twenty services. However, only a handful of them are heavily requested, and of those in demand only a few –like grievances, applications for income, domicile and caste certificates or information on the below poverty line list– can benefit directly the poor (Cecchini 2002).

5.4 Awareness-Raising and Training

Raising awareness among the poor about the potential of ICT is another important aspect of successful ICT projects. In the Dhar district of Madhya Pradesh, poor people are generally not aware of the services offered by Gyandoot. Although some efforts have been undertaken to raise awareness –by designing posters with pictorial depictions of the services offered at the kiosks and by displaying prominent Gyandoot signs outside the kiosks– more could be done (Cecchini 2002). Word of mouth is often a very powerful tool for publicity. The leaders of poor communities, as well as school children, could be brought to the kiosks for a demonstration showing what ICT can do for them. Furthermore, the provision of content that is not directly related to development goals, such as news, matrimonials and entertainment information could also be a winning strategy to raise awareness about kiosks. A recent survey from rural India found that entertainment programs, together with news, are the types of information most frequently accessed by the rural poor (see Table 11.3) (Marwah, in Pigato 2001).

Table 11.3 Frequency of access to information by the rural poor in India

Information accessed	Very often (%)	Quite often (%)	Seldom (%)	Never (%)
News/ Politics	57.3	28.7	10.7	3.3
Entertainment	51.4	32.7	12.7	3.3
Health/ Education	41.3	46.7	10.7	1.3
Training Programs	17.3	42.0	28.7	12.0
Agriculture/ Markets	13.3	46.0	26.0	14.7
Welfare Programs	11.3	31.3	41.3	16.0
Employment Opportunities	10.7	25.3	38.0	26.0

Source: Pigato (2001)

Training poor women and men in information technology skills is also important. Failure to get the poor involved in the use of technology can lead to further marginalization. Participatory communications approaches require innovative and interactive training processes, since learning is more effective through practice (Balit 1999). SEWA (the Self Employed Women Association), for instance, has successfully trained poor women in the use of video cameras and audiovisual equipment. A team of eight full-time and 20 part-time members is now producing videotapes as a tool for learning, education, development, and policy action.

5.5 Financial Sustainability, Monitoring and Evaluation

Finally, a major challenge for ICT projects is reaching financial sustainability. Connectivity can be particularly expensive. In urban areas of India, each telephone connection costs more than US$650. A phone booth operator needs to earn at least US$190 per year to break even. Telephones in rural areas are even dearer – a line can cost US$1,500–1,700. To break even, the annual revenue per line would have to be around US$425 (Syngh Yadav 2001). Since most ICT projects are recent and not expected to reach self-sustainability for three or four years, experience on sustainability is limited. Gyandoot, which started operating in 2000, has seen few kiosks reach commercial viability.

How will we know whether the benefits derived from ICT projects outweigh the costs? In order to answer this and other questions, rigorous monitoring and evaluation (M&E) of the social and economic benefits of ICT projects in rural areas are needed. M&E measure performance, identify and correct potential problems early on, and improve the understanding of the relationship between different poverty outcomes and ICT policies (Kenny, Navas-Sabater and Quiang 2001). M&E are especially needed to measure the success of many pilots currently under way. In fact, in the case of pilots, successful outcomes might be implicitly biased due to the choice of favorable places and conditions. Projects might not yield the same results in more challenging and realistic situations.

6. Conclusion

Reaching the poor and realizing the potential of ICT for poverty reduction in the areas of opportunity, empowerment and security is a difficult endeavor. Nevertheless, ICT projects implemented by grassroots-based organizations and individuals who have the appropriate incentives to work with marginalized groups can achieve encouraging results. Successful ICT projects are characterized by local ownership and the participation of the community.

Acknowledgements

I am grateful to Deepa Narayan and Giovanna Prennushi for the opportunity to conduct research on ICT for poverty reduction in India, and to the World Bank's External Development Assignment Program (EDAP) for funding. I also want to thank all of those who spent time meeting with me and showing me projects in the field, including Albert M. Lobo, ADP Madhavan, Ujval Parghi, Dhara Patel, Naveen Prakash, Roy Sastry, and Rajesh Sivanesan. A special thanks goes to the staff of the Electronic Governance Centre at the Indian Institute of Management, Ahmedabad: Dhawal Bathia, Ciny Mathew, Kalpesh Mehta, Monica Raina, and Shilpa Ramadesikan. Precious comments were received by Subhash Bhatnagar, Shirin Madon, Giovanna Prennushi, Chris Scott, and Robert Schware. All findings, interpretations and conclusions in this report are entirely those of the author and do not necessarily represent the views of the World Bank, its Executive Directors or the countries they represent.

References

Akula, Vikram Byanna (2000). 'Putting Technology to Work for Poverty Alleviation: A Draft Proposal for $151,030 to Develop Smart Cards for Microfinance.' Hyderabad, Andhra Pradesh: Swayam Krishi Sangam.

Balit, Silvia (1999). 'Voices for Change: Rural Women and Communication.' FAO: Rome, Italy. www.fao.org/docrep/X2550E/X2550E00.htm.

Baramati Initiatives (2001). 'SKS-Smart Cards: Case Study.' www.baramatiinitiatives.com/cases/case10.htm.

Bhatnagar Subhash. (2000). 'Empowering Dairy Farmers through a Dairy Information and Services Kiosk.' World Bank: Washington D.C. www.worldbank.org/publicsector/egov/diskcs.htm.

Bhatnagar Subhash and Nitesh Vyas. (2001). 'Gyandoot : Community-Owned Rural Internet Kiosks.' World Bank: Washington D.C. www.worldbank.org/publicsector/egov/gyandootcs.htm.

Bhatnagar Subhash and Robert Schware, eds. (2000). *Information and Communication Technology in Rural Development. Case Studies from India.* World Bank Institute Working Papers. www.worldbank.org/wbi/pubs_case37160.html.

Cecchini Simone. (2001). 'Back to Office Report: Information and Communications Technology for Poverty Reduction in Rural India.' Mimeo, World Bank: Washington D.C.

Cecchini (2002). 'Back to Office Report: Evaluation of Gyandoot and Bhoomi and International Conferences on ICT for Development.' Mimeo, World Bank: Washington D.C.

Cecchini, Simone and Monica Raina (2002). 'Warana: The Case of an Indian Rural Community Adopting Information and Communications Technology' in Information Technology in Developing Countries, Volume 12, No. 1, April 2002. www.iimahd.ernet.in/egov/ifip/apr2002/apr2002.htm.

Cecchini, Simone and Talat Shah (2002). 'Information and Communications Technology as a Tool for Empowerment' in *Empowerment and Poverty Reduction:A Sourcebook.* World Bank: Washington D.C. www.worldbank.org/poverty/empowerment.

Digital Opportunity Initiative (2001). 'Creating a Development Dynamic: Final Report of the Digital Opportunity Initiative.' www.opt-init.org/framework.html.

Griffin, Keith (1979) *The Political Economy of Agrarian Change*, 2nd edition. London, Macmillan Press.

Heeks, Richard (1999). 'Information and Communication Technologies, Poverty and Development.' Development Informatics Working Paper Series, Paper No. 5. idpm.man.ac.uk/idpm/di_wp5.htm.

Heeks, Richard (2001). 'Understanding e-Governance for Development.' i-Government Working Paper Series, Paper No. 11. idpm.man.ac.uk/idpm/igov11abs.htm.

InfoDev (various years). InfoDev Quarterly Report. The World Bank: Washington D.C. www.infodev.org/projects/quarterly.htm.

James, Jeffrey (2000). 'Pro-Poor Modes of Technical Integration into the Global Economy' in *Development and Change*, Vol. 31 (2000), pp. 765-783.

Jhunjhunwala, Ashok (2000). 'Unleashing Telecom and Internet in India.' Paper presented at India Telecom Conference at the Asia/Pacific Research Center, Stanford University, November 2000. www.tenet.res.in/Papers/unleash.html.

Kenny C., J. Navas-Sabater and C. Quiang (2001). 'Information and Communication Technologies and Poverty' in World Bank, Poverty Reduction Strategies Sourcebook. www.worldbank.org/poverty/strategies/ict/ict.htm.

Kirkman, Geoffrey (1999). 'It's More Than Just Being Connected: A Discussion of Some Issues of Information Technology and International Development.' Working Paper presented at the Development E-Commerce Workshop, The Media Laboratory at the Massachusetts Institute of Technology, August 16-17, 1999. www.cid.harvard.edu/ciditg/resources/beingconnected.pdf.

Nanthikesan, S.(2000). 'Trends in Digital Divide.' Harvard Center for Population and Development Studies, November 2000. www.undp.org/hdro/backgroundpapers/nanthikesan.doc.

Pigato, Miria (2001). 'Information and Communication Technology, Poverty and Development in sub-Saharan Africa and South Asia.' World Bank: Washington D.C. www.worldbank.org/afr/wps/.

Sharma, Aashish and William Yurcik (2000). 'The Emergence of Rural Digital Libraries in India: The Gyandoot Digital Library Intranet.' Proceedings of the ASIS Annual Conference (ASIS 2000), Chicago: Illinois. [www.sosresearch.org/publications/asis2000.PDF]

Syngh Yadav, Kushal Pal (2001). 'Virtually There' in Centre for Science and Environment, *Down to Earth Magazine*, Vol. 9, No. 18, February 2001. www.cseindia.org/html/dte/dte20010215/dte_analy.htm.

Telecom Regulatory Authority of India (2001). Recommendations of the TRAI on 'Universal Service Obligation.' www.trai.gov.in/USOREC.htm.

World Bank (1999). *World Development Report 1998/99. Knowledge for Development.* World Bank: Washington D.C. www.worldbank.org/wdr/wdr98/index.htm.

World Bank (2001). *World Development Report 2000/01: Attacking Poverty.* World Bank: Washington D.C. www.worldbank.org/poverty/wdrpoverty.

World Bank (2002a). *Information and Communication Technologies: A World Bank Group Strategy.* World Bank: Washington D.C. info.worldbank.org/ict/ICT_ssp.html.

World Bank (2002b). 'A Definition of E-Government' in E-Government Website. World Bank: Washington D.C. www1.worldbank.org/publicsector/egov/definition.htm.

Chapter 12

Critical View of E-Governance Challenges for Developing Countries

Neki Frasheri

1. Introduction

Talking about Information and Communication Technologies (ICT) and their impact on developing countries, about the information society, electronic-governance and the development leapfrogging of these countries, is becoming commonplace for researchers, managers, journalists, and politicians. ICT are changing the world, enriching and integrating the communication means worldwide, breaking all geographical and social borders. We are at the beginning of a new technological revolution whose consequences are difficult to evaluate. It is the creation of the conditions for more economic and political freedom, which may lead to new movements and institutions for democracy. The ICT impacts get shaped as a result of the fusion of globalization, worldwide connectivity and knowledge networking. A revolution, where technology is the catalyst and makes new power structures raise over old ones.

In this paper we critique different views on the supposed role of ICT for the future of human society, with particular attention to developing countries. This criticism is seen from the point of view of a small developing post-communist country as Albania, hoping that the conclusions would throw more light for developing countries in general, especially those at a transition stage. Analyzing examples from Albania and trying to generalize emerging problems, we will focus on three important issues:

(1) What are the prospects of ICT impact in developing countries?
(2) Are we doing our best to ensure efficiency in the deployment of ICT?
(3) How do we need to collaborate with developed countries and international organizations in order to narrow down the so-called 'digital divide'?

The analysis of Albanian experience and reflections of global issues are centered around the public administration as a key sector, trying to understand the role of public administration and the structure of its interface with the public at large and NGOs in the framework of e-governance. Based on these arguments, the role of ICT best policies and practices is examined as well.

Dispersed investments and disoriented development characterize the transition period after 1990 in Albania. The telecommunications network has been rebuilt in main cities, and new optical links have been installed with neighboring countries. Beginning in 1998, several private Internet Services Providers (ISPs) have been created, together with numerous Internet Cafés, mainly in the capital city, Tirana. Now in big cities it is possible to use dial-up connections for Internet and data communication. Mobile telephony will be extended to cover the whole country, with the second operator starting its activities during the year 2001. As result of the improvement in marketing policy by introducing prepaid cards, mobile telephony is becoming quite popular. Some ICT are used in central public administration institutions, and new projects are in place for their improvement, as well as for their implementation in local administrations. Education on ICT is widespread, and even included experimentally in the high school curriculum. The country is experiencing a technological leapfrogging.

The 'leapfrog' concept is widely analyzed by some authors; considering it a direct deployment of new modern technologies, without step-by-step use of previous technologies already abandoned in developed countries (Davison, Vogel and Harris, 2000). The key question is not about the technological leapfrogging, but what impact such technological leapfrog creates for the development of society. Bangemann Report (1994) presents the actual development as 'throughout the world, ICT are generating a new industrial revolution… this revolution adds huge new capacities to human intelligence and… changes the way we work together and the way we live together.' Until the technological leapfrog 'changes the way we work together and the way we live together', there is no real leap towards developed countries of the present, and the information society of the future. It means 'digital divide', and widening the gap of digital-divide will have serious consequences for DC societies, and for regional collaborations and security.

2. 'Towards an Information Society' – Where are we going?

In order to think about ICT used in public administration and related issues concerning its interaction with local and international communities, it is necessary to evaluate the reality where public administration 'lives', and the prospects of this reality. There is already an enormous quantity of writings by many scholars about the role of ICT transforming the human society towards a future 'information society'. Opinions vary from one extreme to the other, and all this reminds you of a folk tale where the wise man of a village says 'either it is something, or it is going somewhere.'

In the context of ICT deployment, even Albania with all its problems is going somewhere. There are already signs of development and of first bricks of the e-governance being laid in Albania. A typical case is the Central Elections Commission that used the Internet to communicate with citizens regarding voters' lists. These lists were usually put up on shop windows or building walls. During the last local elections the lists were done using computers and the names were sorted alphabetically; however, there were many errors. While preparing for the new parliamentary elections, the Commission put the lists on its web page, improving the ways citizens and all interested subjects might check their names. The web site had also information on the polling rules and the procedures, the decisions of the Commission, and other such matters.

In other public administration institutions the implementation of ICT is going from top to bottom, central government institutions having higher priority compared to the local administration. The following data refer to the beginning of the year 2002: ministries representing fifty percent of domain names registered under 'gov.al', others are government agencies. Within ministries, eighty percent of them have active web sites, maintained in-house or by ISPs, the other twenty percent of them have email and non-active sites (only ping to such sites receives an echo from ISP). The only ministry, which has outsourced all its ICT development and maintenance, has only a domain name. From city halls only that of Tirana has registered a domain name, they are working on it but there is no web site yet. Government agencies such as those of Customs and Taxes registered their domain names only recently, despite the fact that they are more advanced on deploying ICT. Social Insurance is also lagging behind (the social insurance number is not introduced yet, despite several years of work on it). Agencies of Economic Development and of Privatization have domain names and web sites, publishing their activities on projects, tenders and other such matters.

In many public administration institutions ideas are emerging for the creation of 'information centers' equipped with good ICT infrastructure, where citizens may look for information related to the activities of particular institutions. The first steps for the creation of such centers are undertaken by institutions such as Open Society Institute (Soros Foundation), USAID, World Bank, Stability Pact and others in collaboration with the public administration of main cities, running parallel with actions for the computerization of local public offices. Such projects include the cities of Tirana, Durres, Fier, Berat, Gjirokaster, Kucova. These centers are expected to exchange data with different offices of local administration and provide especially marginal communities with the necessary information about their relations with the public administration. Such information would include data about real estate, police, civil status, social status, finance, taxes and others.

The future of these centers is not clear. There are two main problems identified – sustainability and legitimacy. Actually these centers are sponsored by NGOs, and their activity supported by local authorities. The sponsorship from NGOs may not last forever, and self-financing may be a problem due to the fact that these centers are dedicated mainly to poor people. The legitimacy of their activities has to do with the fact that they may remain simply centers of information where people may learn about their status and possible solutions. Also, these centers may receive a legal value so people may conclude their affairs there without being forced to run from one office to the other. Time will show how these centers will progress. Within the framework of e-governance such centers represent an ICT-based embryonic interface between public administration and citizens (Fig.1).

The question 'where are we going?' seems to have an answer – 'going toward progress', but the reality is more complex (see also Beqiraj and Frasheri, 1998; Frasheri, 1998; Frasheri, 2000). The Krantzberg First Law states: 'technology is neither good nor bad, nor is it neutral' (Brodnig and Schonberg, 2000). The real impact of ICT is not simply an issue of access – it depends on usage and its impact. Bimber (1998) suggests that ICT impact may be related with cognitive phenomena more than the increase of information flows. Following the Wriston's logic (1997) that 'despite all the advantages of science and the ways in which it is changing the world, science does not remake the human mind or alter the power of the human spirit,' what we might say about this progress is that:

1. The widespread use of ICT is radically changing our world, our work and our living in a community.
2. ICT are creating a worldwide public space (Cyberspace), breaking all borders of space and time.
3. All communication-related human activities are extended into this new public space.
4. The more important Cyberspace becomes a public space, more human problems will emerge there.

In this context, the Cyberspace phenomenon does not resolve problems, but simply shifts them to another dimension. We find in Cyberspace lots of information and misinformation. There is the dominance of big operators, the risk of being lost (not visible even when search engines are used), the risk of being 'attacked' by others, the risk of being observed and losing privacy, even the risk of being manipulated. The role of ICT seems to be dependent on politics.

Making possible a fast and free worldwide exchange of information, ICT serve as a tool of acquiring knowledge, a non-material kind of wealth. ICT increase the power of individuals rendering outmoded old hierarchies in all components of the order that emerged from the Industrial Revolution (national sovereignty, economy, and military power) (Wriston, 1997). This phenomenon theoretically implies possible democratic development of humanity in a 'knowledge society' (Nath, 2000). At the other extreme stays Guehenno (Kaase, 2000), who considered the ICT revolution as the end of democracy.

The fact that technology makes governance more transparent worldwide, breaking the borders of space and time, does not mean that the new society will be 'unified' and democratized. Many problems make the 'cyber-life' difficult in marginal developing countries, due to lack of economic means and technical knowledge. The poor would not be able to follow the development of technology day by day, and Cyberspace security issues may lead to the creation of 'cyber-quarantines'. In this context political issues gain absolute priority, compared to technological ones. We may take concrete steps on building e-governance, but that does not guarantee that our problems would be solved as we expect them to. It may become even worse if the e-governance structures are built the wrong way.

3. Challenges of E-Governance: Public Administration versus Citizens

Heeks (2001) defines e-governance as 'the use of ICT to support good governance', improving information exchanges between governments and citizens. While automation by using computers in past decades addressed the internal work of governments, e-governance implies the transformation of the external work of governments in their relations with citizens. Interaction between public administration and citizens through networking contributes to transparency and accountability, putting governance under criticism by society, improving coordinated actions between government and civil society, and decreasing possibilities for manipulation of the public. The key to such achievements lies in the Information Systems of public administration as the core element of e-government. This process is pretty contradictory, because dissemination of information is a threat to power structures. ICT changes the way wealth is created and, consequently, challenges ruling elites that control society.

3.1 Interfacing with Public Administration

The Green Paper (1999) of the European Commission considers that: 'public sector information plays a fundamental role in the proper functioning of the internal market and the free circulation of goods, services and people... Without user-friendly and readily available administrative, legislative, financial or other public information, economic actors cannot make fully informed decisions.' Following these arguments, we may theorize on functionalities of ICT within public administration in an e-governance environment as in Fig.12.1

The medium layer 'interface' in Fig. 12.1 is the sub-system that connects public administration with citizens. This layer ensures the exchange of data between the public administration and citizens. Its structure is crucial for developing e-governance. The ICT of public administration must in all its levels guarantee an effective circulation of information with the public outside, that is, both NGOs and citizens. In this design NGOs are considered as an interfacing structure itself, situated between the public administration and their communities of citizens. All this implies that work has to be based on public inter-connected databases and services implemented or mirrored at the border of the public administration layer (for example, 'interconnection of networks and interoperability of services and applications are recommended as primary Union objectives' Bangemann et al., 1994).

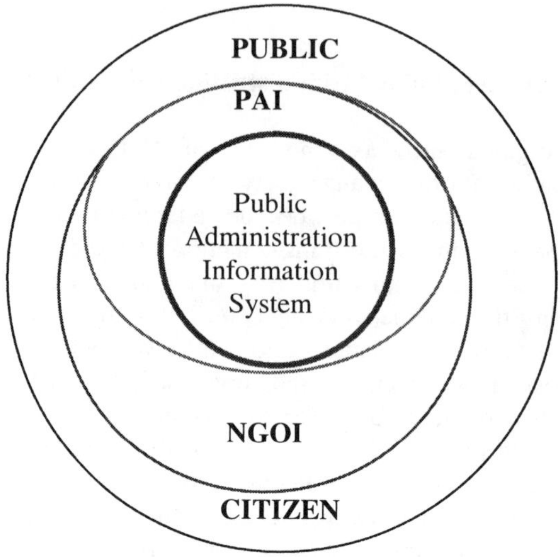

NGOI = non governmental organization Interface
PAI = public administration Interface

Figure 12.1 Interfacing Public Administration with Citizens

Actually there are many embryonic examples of how different initiatives and projects use ICT to improve the dialogue between citizens and governments (see for example http://www.digitalgovernance.org/). Evaluating these cases, we may conclude that:

1. Examples of dialogue between citizens and governments are mainly in developed countries (UK, US etc.), where the development of the society, governance and democracy have been consolidated gradually through centuries. They can also be found in 'half-developed' countries (India, Malaysia, and South Africa) where the average development of society may be low, but there are some highly developed communities.

2. In many cases ICT are used simply as an alternative media for information processing - typical cases being CDs versus printed paper, or some centers where people may go and consult a database instead of asking an official for information. This is a step forward, but it is far from the transformation and democratization of governance. By simply adding ICT, it may only increase confusion and costs.

To really improve the governance, we need to improve the decentralization and the role of the civil society.

3.2 Decentralization and Interoperability Issues

Heeks (2001) writes, 'E-governance lies at the heart of two global shifts: the information revolution and the governance revolution'. When correctly implemented, it changes the ways society works and is governed. To achieve this, the public administration must create collaboration possibilities with the surrounding environment. This cannot be done without decentralization – centralized systems in a distributed environment cannot have any future, the human society in itself being a distributed system. Decentralization and interaction with the outside makes development of Information Systems using ICT for e-governance a complex process. Interoperability is a key issue for the success of ICT deployed in the 'experiment' of e-governance, leading to what Landsbergen and Wolken (2001) define as 'a fundamentally different way of doing government'. Due to this complexity, Heeks concludes that the e-governance gap is 'increasingly separating developed and developing countries, and elite and ordinary citizens within developing countries'. In this complex transformation of society, not only governments but also citizens need to change in the right way. Garcia (2001) recommends the necessity for marginal communities to 'reengineer themselves to meet the requirements of a knowledge-based network economy ... (they) must integrate their economic activities, and thicken their institutions by reinforcing their local and regional ties.' This requires a positive partnership (or 'political interoperability') between governments and citizens, which is not always the case with developing countries.

Taylor and Williams (1991) point out that the usage of ICT in governance raises important issues about the vertical organization related to the decentralization and horizontal fragmentation of government. Hood (1990) and Willcocs (1994) suggest that fragmentation of management structures within a certain organizational and technological environment may lead to contradictions if separate processes do not converge. We may conclude that decentralization increases the need of interoperability between autonomous Information Systems implemented at different levels of government. Interoperability is a way of keeping the integrity of public administration while decentralizing it, balancing between control and monitoring. Decentralization implies monitoring while releasing direct control. It is necessary to challenge the difficulties of decentralization through interoperability, and not to solve strategic decentralization problems through operative re-centralization; the latter is a hidden trend to strengthen monopolization of decision-making in a distributed environment.

Public administration may become an unfriendly environment due to corruption and lack of capabilities to solve problems. Both decentralization and deployment of ICT may become problematic when used in a corrupted environment, and in many cases it may lead to worse public services. Bardhan and Mookherjee (2000) suggest that decentralization creates possibilities for the reduction of corruption, particularly in developing countries. It is argued that central governments do not have the adequate local information to properly monitor local officials. But, in transition countries, the tendency of corrupted local authorities is to profit from their position as much and as soon as possible. This leads to the creation of certain cupolas that take control of every significant activity within their territory. Heeks (1998) argues that ICT may create new opportunities for corruption while detecting and neutralizing the old opportunities. In this context, interoperable information services are a means of effectiveness, efficiency and responsiveness for new working ways such as:

(1) within government permitting collaborative thinking,
(2) between government and public by strengthening accountability, and
(3) within communities supporting concerted actions and building social and economic development.

By forcing the development of distributed Information Systems into the public administration and despite ICT low usage, there are created some conditions that may improve exchanges between citizens and government, increasing empowerment and democracy for citizens.

3.3 Governance and Civil Society

While Internet is becoming a political space, its use does not lead automatically to empowerment and democracy. It is up to civil society to democratize Cyberspace, in particular by serving as interface for marginalized communities. This process of democratization relies on the democratization potential of NGOs, both on the local and international scale. Madon (2000) argues that the role of NGOs is increasing within the framework of neo-liberalism and globalization, becoming an important factor in influencing the global policies addressing development and democratic issues that are important components of e-governance. The ICT revolution has cracked government monopolies, amplifying social and political fragmentation, enabling more NGO identities and interests to emerge worldwide. It may lead to new ways of policy-making and new shapes of political forces. Ironically, one is reminded of the old postulate of socialist times, that 'mass organizations are branches of the party'...

NGOs are an important component of the distributed environment making possible the redundancy of network links and of information. This redundancy has two implications. First, contribution to the neutralization of information manipulation that may happen in monopolistic environments. The Yugoslav scenario is a typical example of a civil war promoted by manipulated media (Skoric, 1996). Second, it may serve as backup when public administration Information Systems break down in times of crisis. Such a case was the scenario of Albania in 1997, when public administration services were partially interrupted during the revolt, and the lack of this redundancy of NGOs made the situation much more confused as result of the lack of information from hot regions.

The role of 'redundant' NGOs becomes also important because of the growth of the information quantity circulating in worldwide networks. In this context the role of information and documentation services changes from simply archiving towards information brokering. The role of NGOs would be to serve as 'information brokers' for their communities, strengthening the common knowledge necessary for the identity and activism of their communities. To achieve their objectives, NGOs need to exchange data between each other, as well as with the public administration. This exchange of data becomes more and more important with the deployment of ICT in developing countries. The ICT revolution perhaps will favor non-state entities, argues Mathews 1997. This is another argument for the necessity of a redundant NGO 'shell' around the public administration systems in the framework of e-governance. But it is a contradictory phenomenon – Mathews concludes that the shifting of power from governments towards other entities in the framework of globalization may also lead to new conflicts and problems. While increasing voices of individuals and groups with different interests may lead to a less common identity and interest for public good, threatening democracy itself.

In this context, to achieve the collaboration between three entities (governments – NGOs – citizens) and to keep the right balance between democracy, human rights and public security, all this is crucial for the future of e-governance. Due to different clashes of interests, citizens may become the most important but in certain ways an 'abandoned' entity, due to lack of education and access to new technologies. This means that not only must the technology match with the existing reality, but the training and education of people is critical as well. The sharing of information requires not only technology, but also institutional and human infrastructures.

The other side of the coin has to do with the over-estimation of the role of NGOs. There is a global trend of giving importance to civil society and the private sector. It may lead to a re-distribution of political power and generate new clashes, according to arguments of Huntington (Vittal, 1999), until society accommodates itself with new ways of public management. The role of NGOs and private entities is crucial for the development of society, because of:

- Increasing successful initiatives of individuals, SMEs and activist groups.
- Breaking monopolies of public administration and reducing corruption.
- Improving interaction between citizens and public administration.

At the same time, the rise of NGOs may lead to negative impacts, due to:

- Increasing the gap between public administration and citizens, monopolizing their interface.
- Overloading pluralism, increasing the confusion within communities in transition.
- Overshadowing specialized (technical) institutions, manipulating processes and opinions.

Some of those negative effects are present in the Albanian practice:

- In the late nineties a big international NGO launched an important project (already terminated) for the introduction of computers in schools. They reached formal agreements with the Ministry of Education. During the implementation of the project, several round tables were organized. Key speakers for technical pedagogical issues were invited through personal contacts from the administration, people who were not directly involved in education processes.
- A coastal lagoon near the city of Vlora was targeted for oil prospecting, which created alarm among environmentalists in the beginning of 2002 (http://www.youthparliament.org.al/narta.htm). In several round tables and interviews broadcasted by mass media, people from all kinds of NGOs were involved and their opinions only created confusion, making it difficult for specialized institutions to be heard by the public.
- International organizations launched a project for the preparation of the national strategy on ICT development. People from all sectors are involved in working groups. But during the top-level kick-off of the first ICT Conference in July 2002, the academic sector was excluded from speaking, a fact emphasized with concern even by some speakers from the private sector (http://ictd.org.al/).

Human society needs core public functions carried out either by classic public administration or new civil society, the former having a more permanent character compared with the latter. Even in a distributed and autonomous environment, these functions must follow a unique pattern despite their space and time, in order to fulfill the needs of citizens and society in a process of 'centralized management' into a 'distributed environment', as it will be discussed later in this paper. In this context, it is important to consider NGOs as a crucial but partial interface between public administration and citizens, keeping sufficient direct contacts between them and balancing the redundancy of civil society with the uniqueness of public administration and technical specialized institutions. Considering these arguments, the public administration remains the key-factor for emerging e-governance initiatives, conditioning its trends towards democracy.

4. ICT Deployment Strategies and Practices – Good or Bad?

Arguing on the importance of social factors, Davison, Vogel and Harris (2000) wrote that it is the social order, with its individuals, groups and institutions, that has the responsibility for the consequences of technological impact on society: 'the notion that technologies can preserve their own course of action is mythical.' They argue also that the necessary synergy between technology and social context is a non-determining one and it requires the adaptation of both technology and social context. On the other hand, they point out that the changes that ICT are generating in power relations within governments, between governments, citizens and institutions, impact the power of governments. To achieve national goals, it may be useful if some shift in the power occurs, or strategies of development are modified in order to match with the impact of ICT. The key to success is the anticipation of these changes, at which governments have not been so successful. Technology impact on society will depend on policies and strategies adopted to address this impact. To better address the interests of society as a whole, a well-planned and managed evolution process is necessary, taking account of resulting social consequences. Such planning is not always used in developing countries, as the case of Albania shows.

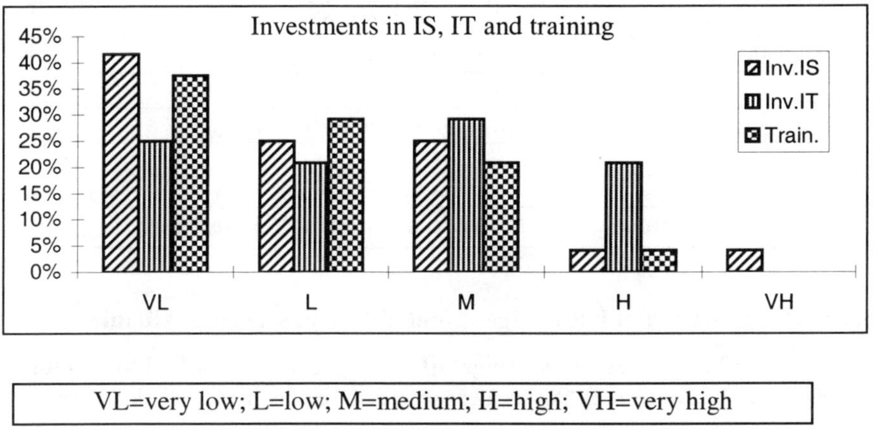

Figure 12.2 Investments on ICT in Albania

A preliminary analysis of factors, responsible for bad results in ICT deployment in Albania, has been done in previous works such as (Frasheri, 2000). In Fig 12.2 we present the current level of investments in Albanian public administration, seen from the point of view of in-house ICT staff of public administration. The bar chart represents investments in Information Systems (IS), Information Technologies (IT) and ICT training.

There is not a good balance between investments in technology (IT), usage and content (IS), and training. Technology is overestimated, but only in part of institutions (Medium and High investments); while usage and training is generally underestimated (predominance of Low and Very Low investments). All this leads to low efficiency in ICT deployment. But the problem is not merely because of unbalanced investments.

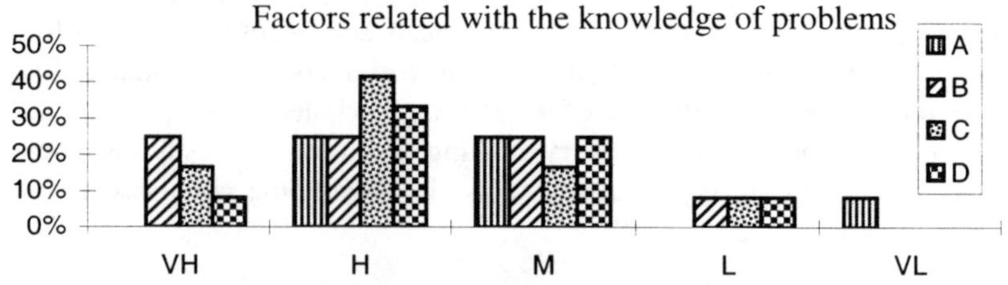

A	Solution found before understanding problem
B	Misunderstanding user requirements
C	Non-involvement of users
D	Importance of Employees (agreement, satisfaction)

VL=very low; L=low; M=medium; H=high; VH=very high

Figure 12.3 Evaluation of knowledge-oriented ICT practices in Albania

In Fig 12.3 we present the weight of several factors identified in literature (see for example Kitiyadisai, 2000) as a cause of bad results in ICT deployment:

1. Deciding solutions before understanding problems.
2. Misunderstanding the users' requirements.
3. Not involving users in the development of applications.
4. Not considering psychological factors related to employees.

ICT people in public administration consider all these negative factors as relatively important (average evaluation High). Despite this consideration, the balance of investments is not built in such way to neutralize their negative impact. This is because of the real but not considered factors that negatively impact the deployment of ICT that may be reformulated as follows:

1. Building ICT infrastructure without structured Information Systems in place.
2. Manipulating ICT implementation and deployment projects.
3. Confusing between production knowledge and conceptual knowledge.

The first factor is reflected in big projects dedicated to heavy ICT infrastructure without a clear idea of the manner in which it will be used, in environments characterized by a lack of structured Information Systems and working practices based on local improvisations. As a result, equipment may be used to improve somehow the work of individuals but it has little impact on the function of the organization as a whole.

The second factor has to do with the influence of administrative managers, their role in the definition of technical objectives of projects instead of functional objectives. As a result, projects are oriented toward the infrastructure implementations instead of institution building and human resources. Unfortunately, sometimes even foreign experts are involved in such manipulations. For example, the practice of PMUs (Project Management Units) has also had a negative effect, leading the administration to undertake technical projects without collaboration with local technical public organizations. This seems to be part of a global phenomenon of abandoning local public research and development sectors in favor of local or foreign private sectors.

The third factor leads to involvement of good computer users in the role of 'computer experts', able to design and deploy ICT applications. Good users have less conceptual knowledge, and they have the tendency to orient projects toward infrastructure, neglecting crucial usage and content issues. Moreover, when involved in management of ICT infrastructure, these good users may fail in the security issues, leaving their sites open to unauthorized access and hacking.

The presence of such factors does not fit in well with the idea of sustainable growth in the context of globalization. Not only are ICT investments low and their result ineffective, but it also implies the policy of neglecting human resources, especially the qualified ones. Public research in developing countries is not simply an 'importer' of know-how, but also a support for the national education and knowledge management. As a result of hostile environments, the majority of good ICT experts are emigrating abroad. Such negative phenomena happen even in the presence of foreign experts coming to help in the deployment of ICT in public administration.

5. Deployment of ICT and Institution Building

In a global society, 'information' means 'knowledge'. If national governments would manage to build robust knowledge-based societies, globalization may become an opportunity for progress rather than a threat for destruction. Deployment of ICT is the key for building 'knowledge society', but impact of ICT is conditioned by human behavior. To understand relations between deploying of ICT and building of knowledge, we may combine the logic of Arquette (2001) on 'institutional capitals' and of Bimber (2001) on the role of human cognitive phenomena. In this context, the process that leads to the social-economic-political impact of ICT may be represented in Figure 12.4.

The bottleneck in the case of Albania, as well as other developing countries, lies in the 'middle' of the chain, i.e. the 'usage'. Without proper usage that can develop such particular cognitive phenomena in people, and lead them to improving ways of living and working in a community, we cannot achieve impact of ICT simply by building the infrastructure. Human and organizational issues must be prioritized instead of technology. This means that:

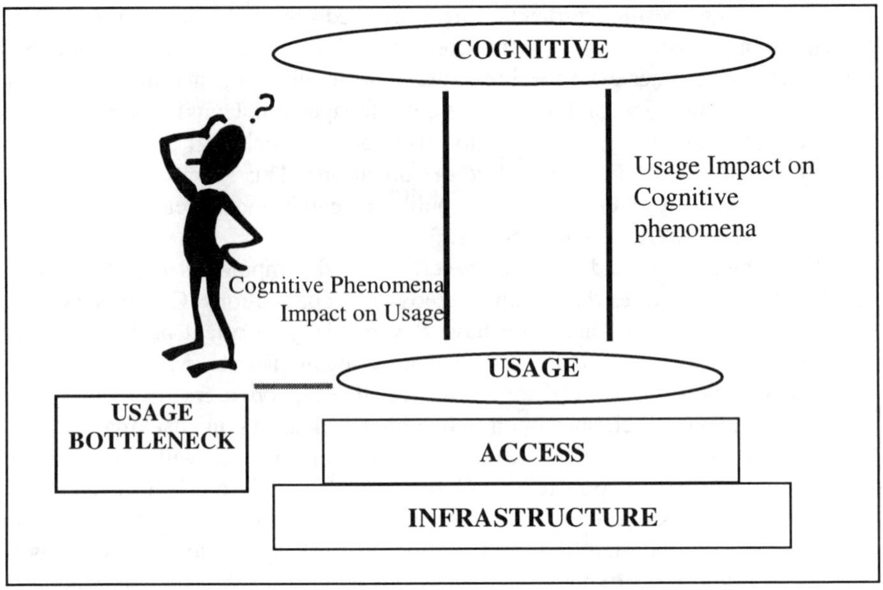

Figure 12.4 Relations between Infrastructure, Usage and Cognitive Phenomena

- The tasks must be distributed according to technical capacities of people through the management of human resources.
- To address organizational issues, it is necessary to balance internal in-house expertise, which is more user-oriented, with external expertise, technologically oriented. Moreover, external expertise must assure some longevity to ensure the continuation of support for the organization.
- Again it is necessary for organizational issues to take into account the requests of decision-makers. When they do not know what they need (case of bad institutionalization), or they charge lower ranking officials with deciding what they (decision-makers) want, the results of presumed 'computerization' will be negligible.

This logic leads to an important issue – 'institution building'. With the final objective being the development of e-governance on a local and national scale, it implies:

- Decentralization of public administration, followed by improvement of monitoring procedures.
- Development of open systems in public administration, to support monitoring and accountability.
- Ensuring of interoperability between autonomous systems in a distributed environment composed of public administration, NGOs and SMEs.

To achieve these goals it is necessary to follow certain strategies and practices. Many scholars analyze the question of development strategies (see, for example, Davison, Vogel and Harris (2000); Kitiyadisai (2000). Such strategies and practices are related to the balance between top-down and bottom-up ways of development. While the top-down approach is difficult to be designed and managed, the bottom-up approach can penalize integration and interoperability.

The attitude of in-house ICT staff in the Albanian public administration on these issues is presented in Fig 12.5. The bar chart represents the weight of some 'how to do' practices implied by the bottom-up strategy:

(J) A step-by-step approach in deployment of ICT may become problematic.
(K) A strategic approach is much more important than learning-by-doing.
(L) Improvisations leading to sub-optimal solutions may prohibit radical new ones.

The data shows that ICT people in public administration correctly consider all these factors to be more or less negative. At the same time, when asked for their opinion on top-down versus bottom-up strategies, the answer of ICT people was in contradiction with their previous opinions. These results are presented in Fig 12.6, comparing two contrasting attitudes on:

(M) Evaluative bottom-up strategies.
(N) Analytical top-down strategies.

Impact of practices for deployment of ICT

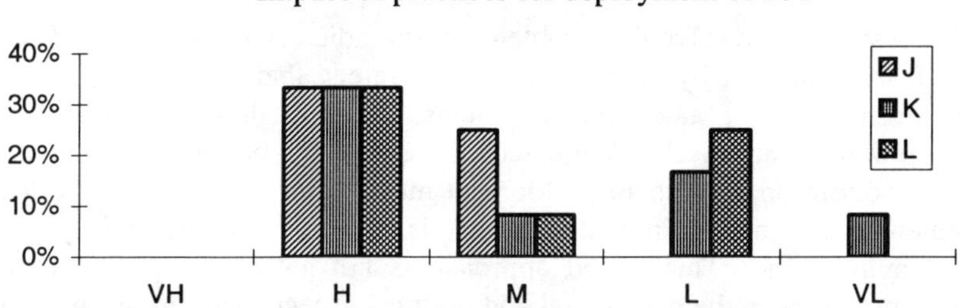

J	Drawback of step-by-step approach
K	Strategic planning compared to improvisations and 'learning by doing'
L	Improvization leads to sub-optimal solutions and may prohibit radical new ones

VL=very low; L=low; M=medium; H=high; VH=very high

Figure 12.5 Evaluation of bottom-up ICT practices in Albania

From the charts of Fig.12.5 and 12.6 it is seen that ICT people in public administration, while correctly considering the negative impact of different aspects of bottom-up practices (step-by-step, learning-by-doing and improvisation approaches), about two-thirds of them consider top-down strategies as not important. One cause of such contradictory attitude towards strategies and practices is the lack of conceptual knowledge among ICT people working in the public administration.

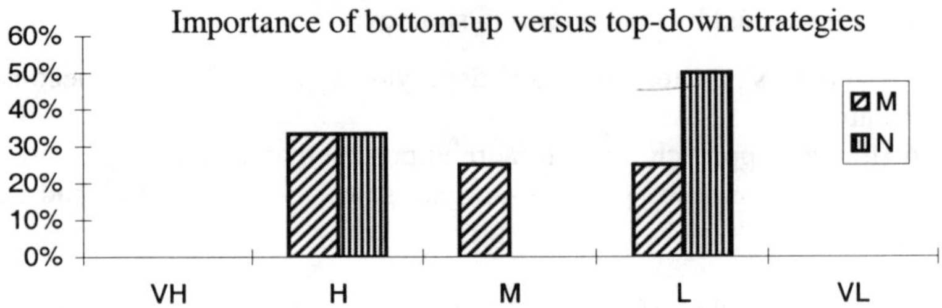

M	Evaluative bottom-up strategies
N	Analytical top-down strategies

VL=very low; L=low; M=medium; H=high; VH=very high

Figure 12.6 Evaluation of top-down and bottom-up strategies in Albania

The best way to resolve this problem of contradictory attitudes would be a blending of both strategies, by defining a mixed strategy that would promote the bottom-up development of autonomous systems, ensuring their interoperability through a top-bottom approach. While technology would be implemented and deployed in a bottom-up way, this development must be included in a single top-bottom framework of institution building, that is, a 'central coordination' in a 'distributed environment'. This mixed approach is not an easy one due to the complexity of problems in the managerial and political aspects. During recent years many institution-building projects were undertaken in Albania to improve and consolidate public institutions. Information Systems were not given the necessary attention, or considered a-priori without matching real institutional requirements. As a result, considerable ICT infrastructure was installed without being integrated with the content components of institution building.

Technically, public administration institutions need internal databases, and simple web-like interfaces for interconnection and access to non-confidential data. This kind of technology is already available, with potential capacities much higher than the needs of a small developing country. What is missing is the structured institutional content. This content, distributed in decentralized institutions of public administration and interconnected to a national information network, including networks of NGOs and SMEs, would make effective the coordinated development in a decentralized environment. In situations such as in Albania, being in a transition stage and without well-structured institutions, the effect of having merely an ICT strategy would be marginal – the real problem is not technology but the unstructured content. In cases as in Albania there is a need for the development and application of strategies for institution building, including the creation of structured institutional content over modern ICT, considering the implementation and deployment of ICT as a result of this process. Arguing on institution building, Mainwaring (1998) states that 'Institutionalization means the process by which a practice or organization becomes well established and widely known, if not universally accepted.' For such institutional reforming processes to have success, besides crisis and ideology elements for a reform, a third element is necessary - the political will to achieve the reform (Heeks, 1998). The recent Albanian experience is proof of this necessity - there are institutions in crisis, there are ideological elements, but it is the political will that is missing.

6. Conclusion

Developing countries are taking progressive steps, but the question of gaps between them and developed countries remains open. We invest in ICT infrastructure without considering how and why it will be used. We give priority to the private sector, creating problematical marginal communities; one of them being the academic community in whose hands rests the education of society at the very least. Subbaih (1999) is right in being pessimistic regarding the digital divide between developed and developing countries: 'leapfrogs' of developing countries seems to be too ineffective compared with 'kangaroo-leaps' of developed countries. Many of the problems in developing countries are 'imported' from developed countries, such as the emphasis on technology neglecting social issues, or the emphasis on the private sector neglecting the public one. There are early warnings from many researchers, and increased evidence on the necessity of keeping a careful balance on many issues such as between public and private sectors, content and infrastructure, human and technology issues. But many foreign agencies working in developing countries follow a neo-liberal agenda oriented towards a free global market, helping in one direction and creating new problems in another one. And it is not only the 'western rationality' that does not fit in well with the reality of developing countries (Avgerou, 2000). Many of the problems have already been warned of by social scientists even in developed countries (see for example Willcocs (1994).

Evaluating the comments of many social science researchers during the last ten years, and also the actions of producers (from developed countries), ICT experts and decision makers, there is evidence of a gap in particular in human society. It is a gap existing in developed countries between social sciences, developing technology and decision-making. In practice, the warnings of social sciences are ignored or misused when plans to help developing countries are prepared and executed. The gap between social sciences, technology and decision-making is reflected in the history of the technology assessment movement. The Office for Technology Assessment, created in 1974 as an advisory entity for the American Congress, was not able to resist new policy-making ways and ceased its activities in 1995, just as the Internet entered the market (Bimber, 1998). A proverb says, 'One is incorrigible if one falls twice in the same hole'...

It is not simply ICT that we need for the development of a country. First of all we need the political will to develop and integrate the country, and clear political objectives of how to do it. Secondly, we need an institution building strategy, considering ICT deployment as part of the institution building process. Thirdly, we need close collaboration with both private and public ICT specialized sectors, for the development of Information Systems over ICT and for massive training at all levels, considering 'investment in education as the fundamental source of national power' (Choucri, 2000). The sustainable implementation and deployment of ICT will come as a result of these combined activities.

But, going through the political 'black box', all this seems as difficult as 'to tie a bell to a cat's tail...'

References

Arquette T.J., (2001) 'Assessing ICT development', Work in progress, assisted by an award from the Social Science Research Council's Program on Information Technology, International Cooperation and Global Security.

Avgerou C., (2000) 'Recognizing alternative rationalities in the development of information systems'. EJISDC, vol 3, r7.

Bangemann M. et al., (1994) 'Europe and the global information society – Recommendations to the European Council'. Brussels.

Bardhan P., Mookherjee D., (2000) 'Corruption and Decentralization of Infrastructure Delivery in Developing Countries'. Institute of International Studies, UC Berkeley.

Beqiraj G., Frasheri N., (1998) 'Albania – a contradictory story of applied information systems', IFIP Work Group 9.4 Working Conference on Implementation and Evaluation of IS in Developing Countries, Bangkok.

Bimber B., (1998) ' The Internet and political transformation: populism, community, and accelerated pluralism.' Polity, vol 31, n1.

Bimber B., (2001) 'Information and political engagement in America: the search for effects of information technology at the individual level'. Political Research Quarterly, vol 54, n.1.

Brodnig G., Schonberg V.M., (2000) 'Bridging the gap: the role of spatial information technologies in the integration of traditional environment knowledge and western science'. EJISDC, vol 1, r1.

Choucri N., 2000. 'Cyber-politics in international relations.' Political Science Review, vol 21 n.3.

Davison R., Vogel D., Harris R., (2000) 'Technology leapfrogging in developing countries – an inevitable luxury?' EJSDC, vol 1, d5.

Frasheri N., (1998) 'Reflections on policies for the effectiveness of IS implementations in developing countries'. Newsletter of IFIP WG 9.4 and Commonwealth Network for IT, vol 8, n3.

Frasheri N., (2000) 'Recent IST development in Albania – new trends and new problems' IFIP WG9.4 Conference on Information Flows, Local Improvisations and Work Practices. Cape Town.

Garcia L., (2001) 'Cooperative networks and the rural – urban divide'. Paper Proposal for the Social Science Research Council Volume on Cooperation and Conflict in a Connected World.

Green Paper, (1999) 'Public sector information: a key resource for Europe'. European Council, Brussels.

Heeks R., (1998) 'Information Technology and Public Sector Corruption'. Working Paper no.4, IDPM, University of Manchester.

Heeks R., (2001) 'Understanding e– governance for development'. Working Paper no.11, IDPM, University of Manchester.

Hood C., (1990) 'Beyond the public bureaucracy state'. Extended Text of Inaugural Lecture, London School of Economics.

Kaase M., (2000) 'Political science and the Internet'. International Political Science Review, vol 21, n.3.

Kitiyadisai K., (2000) 'The implementation of information technology in reengineering the Thai revenue department' IFIP WG 9.4 Conference 'Information flows, local improvisations and work practices', Cape Town.

Landsbergen D. Jr., Wolken G. Jr., (2001) 'Realizing the Promise: Government Information Systems and the Fourth Generation of Information Technology'. Public Administration Review, vol 61, n2.

Madon S., (2000) 'International NGOs: Networking, Information Flows and Learning'. Working Paper no.8, IDPM, University of Manchester.

Mainwaring S., (1998) 'Party Systems in the third wave'. Journal of Democracy, vol .9, n.3.

Mathews J.T., (2000) 'The information revolution.' Foreign Policy, Summer (2000).

Nath V., (2000) 'Networking Networks for Empowerment and Governance'. Global Development Network (2000), World Bank, Japan, (under Publication). http://www.cddc.vt.edu/digitalgov/gov-menu.html.

Skoric I., (1995) 'ZaMir: Peace Network in the War Zone'. http://www.igc.org/balkans/MF-draft/ztn0.htm.

Subbaih A., (1999) 'Information technology: what does it means for scientists and scholars in the developing world'. Newsletter of IFIP WG 9.4 and Commonwealth Network for IT, vol 9, n2.

Taylor J., Williams H., (1991) 'Public administration and the information polity' Public Administration, vol 69, n2.

Vittal N., (1999) 'Impact of IT on international security and warfare'. http://www.rediff.com/computer/1999/jun/14vittal.htm.

Willcocs L., (1994) 'Managing information systems in UK public administration: issues and prospects'. Public Administration, vol 72, n1.

Wriston W., (1997)b 'Bits, bytes, and diplomacy.' Foreign Affairs, vol 76, n5.

Chapter 13

The Development of an Information System for District Hospitals – A Case Study from the Eastern Cape Province, South Africa

Vincent Shaw

1. Introduction

This is the story about the development of a hospital based information system. It is presented as a story because one of the conflicts that we experienced in the process of developing the hospital information system was to establish a balance between a reductionist approach where local contextual issues were ignored (as so often happens in bureaucracies), and the need to be aware of local needs and practices.

This is also a story about the difference between a system based on a positivist- empiricist paradigm and one that adopts a hermeneutic approach, having at its aim the development of capacity to understand, interpret and utilize information to improve services.

Essentially this chapter describes how a participatory approach has been used in developing a hospital information system. The chapter is divided into four sections. The first sketches the context in which the case study is described; the second describes the process followed in developing the District Hospital Information System. The third section explores two main themes arising from the participatory approach adopted and the fourth section is the conclusion.

2. The Context

The story begins in the Eastern Cape Province of South Africa (See Map of South Africa and its Provinces). This is a huge province, with many different aspects to it. The Eastern Cape Province and the Northern Province have the dubious honour of vying for the title 'Poorest Province in South Africa', having as their unemployment rates 48.5 % and 48 % respectively, compared to that of the Western Cape Province which is 20.1 % and Gauteng Province being 28.2 %.

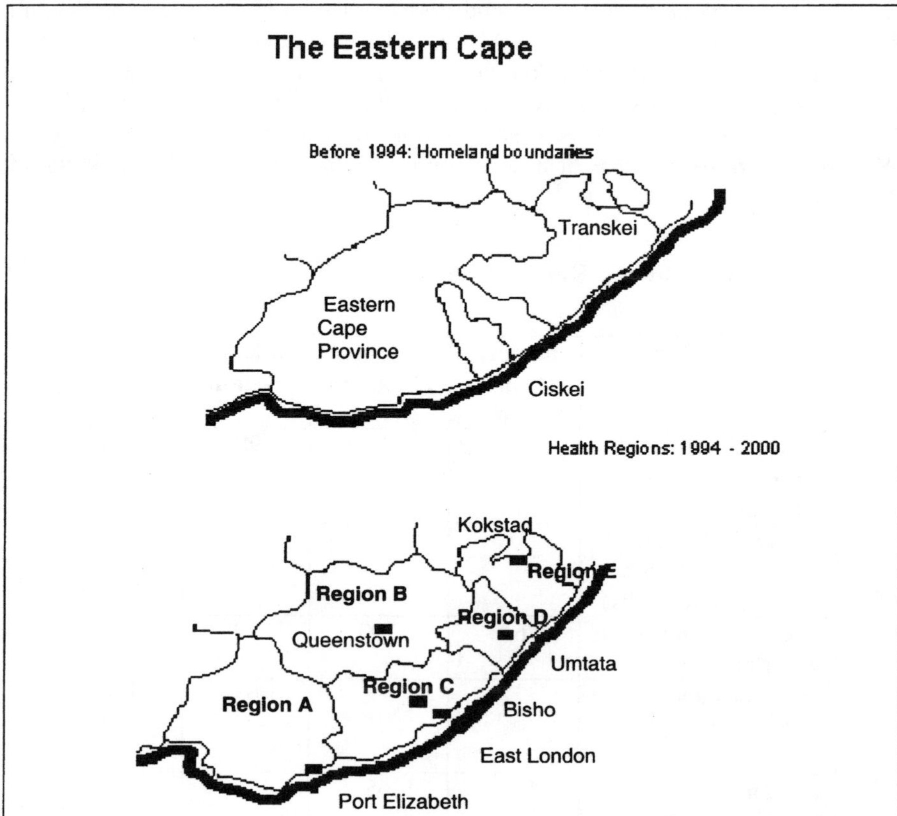
The Eastern Cape
Before 1994: Homeland boundaries
Transkei
Eastern
Cape
Province
Ciskei
Health Regions: 1994 - 2000
Kokstad
Region E
Region B
Region D
Queenstown
Umtata
Region C
Region A
Bisho
East London
Port Elizabeth

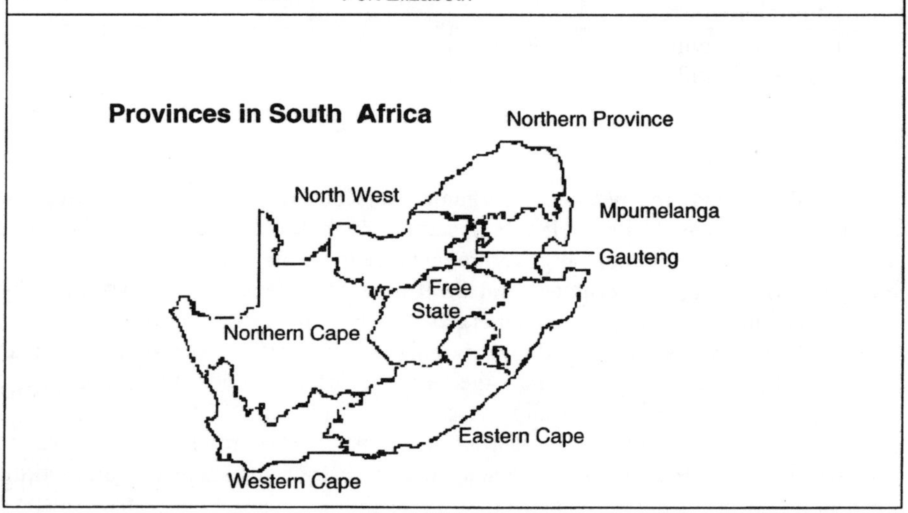
Provinces in South Africa
Northern Province
North West
Mpumelanga
Gauteng
Free
State
Northern Cape
Eastern Cape
Western Cape

The Eastern Cape can be divided into two worlds. It consists of a very well developed western section, around Port Elizabeth. This is the area that falls within the area of the former South Africa, and a more underdeveloped area in the East, which falls into the area known formerly as the Transkei. The indicators differ remarkably across these two areas, as shown in the table below, with the Eastern area tending to reflect health status of a developed country, and the Western area reflecting that of a developing country. Table 13.1 highlights this discrepancy.

Table 13.1 Comparison of Key Indicators

Indicator	Eastern Cape Province	Port Elizabeth Region	Kokstad Region	SA Average
Infant Mortality (1998) (Deaths per 1000 live births)	61.2	35	99	45.4
Under-5 Mortality rate (1998) (Deaths per 1000 live births)	80.5	35	108	59.4
% Clinics with piped water (1999)	61	100	19	-
% Clinics with water-borne toilets (1998)	72	100	65	100
Percentage children fully immunized	52.6	65	37	-
% Clinics with access to grid electricity (1998)	82.4	100	66	-

Post 1994, the need to re-organize services was highlighted during the development of the 'District Health System' which had to incorporate, within a single structure three homeland governments (see map) and numerous other service providers, both local government and the fragmented departmental systems. The District Health System that has emerged consists of clinics providing Primary Health Care services to the indigent population at various points in the health district. Clinics are grouped into geographic areas called sub-districts, and generally refer patients that require more sophisticated care to district hospitals or community health centres. The district hospitals in turn refer their patients to regional hospitals. Each district is managed by a district management team and the team is made up of supervisors who work at the sub-district, or district hospital level. District Managers report directly to the Provincial Management.

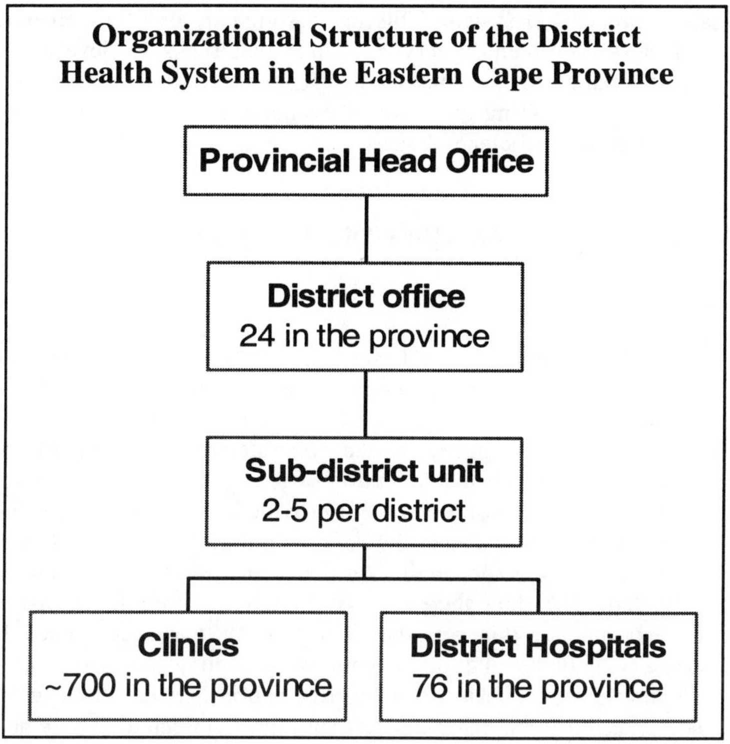

The Hospital sector in the province reflects the same diversity that is reflected in the population indicators mentioned in the table. There are huge infrastructural backlogs that need to be addressed, particularly in those hospitals in the former Transkei area. Huge discrepancies exist between staffing ratios in the Western areas, particularly in the East London area (which includes some of the former Ciskei homeland), and the Eastern half of the province. In the Ciskei area, during the apartheid era, staff went on strike, and were dismissed and new staff were employed. The Government was overthrown, and the successor found the dismissal of staff to be an unfair labour practice and had the dismissed staff reinstated. The result was that in several facilities, there were twice as many staff as are actually needed. On the other hand, in the former Transkei area, staff have not been replaced as natural attrition occurred, resulting in staff shortages in these facilities. The former Transkei area also has a very poor road infrastructure, with many roads to hospitals being impassable in the summer rainy months. Vehicles quickly rattle to pieces in the bad conditions, leaving hospitals with little or no transport to transfer critically ill patients. In the Western half of the province the road infrastructure is much better developed and although distances are large, there are more vehicles per capita population than in the Eastern half. In addition to these woes, the new regime in South Africa has emphasized the development of the

Public Health Care (PHC) system. This has resulted in a shift in finances from what used to be a hospi-centric service to one that seeks to develop the PHC services. The hospital sector has thus seen significant reduction in real terms in its per capita allocation, resulting in a critical evaluation of the services it provides and how best to improve efficiency levels.

3. The Development of a District Hospital Information System

3.1 Introduction

The data set for the Hospitals in the Eastern Cape Province had been determined shortly after the new government had been elected in 1994. It consisted of 13 data elements. Of these, five related to financial data, and were seldom completed, as many facilities did not have access to the computerized Financial Management System (FMS), and as a result the collection of these elements were meaningless. In addition, although clear definitions were provided, data was not collected in a uniform manner. The result was that the data submitted for a single data element, often meant different things, depending on the nature of the facility and how the data was collected. The data therefore, could not be used to compare across facilities. An example of this was the data element 'casualty' visits. In some facilities, casualty patients and outpatients were seen at the same place, and recorded in a single register. However, no distinction between these groups was made and as a result in some instances data submitted reflected all patients seen in that venue, while in others, it reflected only the casualty patients.

Data from hospitals was supposed to be submitted regularly to the provincial office. However, in the provincial office there was no system for collection of this data, its recording, evaluation and no feedback to facilities was ever given. A spiral developed whereby facilities lost interest in the data collected, submission became haphazard and the data was not used by anyone at the provincial level.

3.2 The Process of Developing a New Hospital Information System

During 1999, an assessment of information use in various hospitals in the province was undertaken. The resultant report indicated that:

- Data is collected 'at all levels in hospitals, but most of it is never used'
- Indicators are submitted to the district offices, but give a 'very bland picture of administrative activities, and no *feeling* of what goes on inside hospitals'
- 'Registers are non-standardized and tend to be anarchic, and hand written', and often on an assortment of different types of paper and books
- 'analysis of data is minimal at all levels'.

The author, who was at that stage working in the Provincial Office of the Department of Health as Acting Director for District Hospitals, decided to convene a workshop consisting of a select group of people who had knowledge about hospital information systems. The aim was to identify key indicators that should be measured, at hospital, district and provincial level. The group, consisting of workers at the provincial, district, and hospital level met and developed a series of indicators (see appendix 1). The next step was to assess how the data elements of the indicators could be collected.

In order to do this, we invited health care workers (doctors, nurses and administrators) from ten hospitals in the province to meet at a district hospital. They were requested to bring along copies of data collection tools that were used in their facilities. We divided into teams and visited wards in the hospital and evaluated the types of information that was collected, how it was collected and who used the information. The findings were that:

There were numerous systems in place in the province (different hospitals use different methods for collecting and aggregating data. This was a reflection of the historical background of different administrations and systems);

- duplication of data collected at various points in the hospital system occurred (in some wards, different registers were maintained. So for example, a register was kept of all hypersensitive patients, or diabetic patients, in addition to an admission register and a discharge register. Each register required the entry of the patients name and address);
- data was collected but there was very little analysis of data;
- data was often collected 'in case' it was needed at a later stage;
- data was largely collected by the nurses, with little or no involvement of the doctors.

In order to address these issues, a system was developed which:

- Could with reasonable uniformity be applied throughout the province, utilising standardized registers which had space for local needs as well;
- tried to avoid unnecessary duplication;
- allowed for ease of analysis;
- encouraged all health workers (nurses, doctors and administrators) to work together to make sense of the data and enabled management to make decisions based on the information available to them and to improve the quality of patient care through analysis of data collected;
- was a paper-based system, allowing local analysis of data as required (was not dependant on computers for analysis, but at the same time was a system which could in future be easily computerized).

The system was piloted in 13 district hospitals for a six-month period, following which a workshop was convened, where the users gave feedback for modification of the system. The adjustments have been incorporated in the final version, and this has now been printed and distributed (see extracts in Appendix 2).

The Hospital Essential Dataset (EDS) utilizes a register as a tool for collecting data at the hospital unit (these are for example, various wards – paediatrics, maternity, or theatre, out-patients or casualty department, pharmacy, stores) level and report forms for transmitting the data to managerial level. Management then uses a Monthly Hospital report to collate data from the registers and transmit the data to the district level. The flow of information through the system is indicated in Table 13.2.

Table 13.2 Information Flow for the District Hospital Essential Dataset

Level	Reporting format
Hospital unit (ward, theatre, pharmacy) (Registers are the data collection tools)	Reports collate data from registers, and are submitted to management
Hospital management	Hospital monthly report collates data from wards for the hospital as a unit. Submitted to District Office
District Information Office	Data entered into District Health Information System, and submitted to next level electronically or via reports
District Management	Electronic data submission to province
Provincial Office	Data from districts collated and submitted to National office electronically

It is envisaged that data will be entered into the District Health Information Software at the District Information Office level, following which it would be transmitted electronically through the system. In future, it is likely that as hospitals become computerized and linked to the departmental information network, data entry would take place at the hospital level. The District Hospital EDS concentrates on the collection of data elements at this stage. Once this has been implemented, the next phase will look at using this data to report on indicators, and systems to provide feedback to the various role-players.

The table below summarizes the steps taken in the development of the District Hospital Essential Dataset.

Table 13.3 Steps in the Development of the District Hospital Essential Dataset

Activity	Participants	Purpose
Workshop	Health workers at provincial, district + facility levels + National office	Determine indicators to be assessed in an IS
Visit District Hospital	Managers, clinicians from district hospitals across province	Evaluate existing data collection instruments + systems in use
Development of uniform registers	Subset of people visiting the district hospital	Establish a system that allowed data to be collected in a more standardized manner that also allowed comparison across facilities
Piloting of registers	13 District Hospitals	Test the newly developed system
Evaluate registers	13 District hospitals	Collate feedback and make final adjustments to system

4. Discussion of Themes Arising from the Case Study

As mentioned in the introduction, one of the challenges was to balance the reductionist approach adopted by the National Department of Health (NdoH) (See story in Text Box) with a more holistic approach, which took into account the local needs and context.

From the NDoH point of view, their need was for a set of data that would enable them to make certain decisions regarding hospitals. They had defined the data elements, but had little concern for how the data was collected. The assumption was that if the data elements were well defined, they could be compared across facilities and provinces. This is the typical reductionist approach that has been alluded to by many authors, and which, it has been asserted, has resulted in questionable data sets and inappropriate assumptions regarding information collected. Hirscheim and Boland mention in the Series Foreword to Walsham that *'Research into IS failure has concluded that the primary cause of failure is the lack of consideration given to the social and behavioural dimensions of IS'*.

In order to understand the context, within which the District Hospital Information System was developed, we need to evaluate a few socio-political dimensions of life in the South African health sector. These will be explored under two main themes, one looking at power issues, and the other at the process of capacity development.

A Contrasting Scenario

During the development phase of the District Hospital EDS, an interesting interaction occurred with the National Department of Health (NDoH) whereby the NDoH indicated a list of data elements that they required to be collected from district hospitals. Initially the NDoH requested that hospitals should report to them directly on these data elements. Provinces reacted strongly against this, indicating that the reporting should be through the provincial office, as provincial offices were in charge of the district hospitals and not the NDoH.

The format in which the NDoH required the reporting was fixed, and did not take into consideration the local arrangement of district hospitals. An example is where the NDoH required reporting on the number of surgical beds and surgical admissions, while in many district hospitals, surgical beds were not clearly identified, nor were surgical patients always specifically delineated. This is because in many district hospitals, the nature of the work performed is of a generalist nature, and often both medical and surgical and sometimes even paediatric patients are mixed in a single ward, with the mix of these groups varying from month to month and season to season, depending on the health problems occurring during these periods!

NDoH indicated that they required this breakdown in order to be able to say at a National planning level that the country had XX number of surgical beds and YY number of medical beds. While this may have been the need at the National level, at a local level this kind of breakdown does not make much sense! We agreed to adjust our data collection instrument in order to accommodate certain of the National requirements but indicated that we were unable to meet all the National requirements.

4.1 Exploring the Issue of Power

Within the medical hierarchy in the country, the NDoH is the ultimate authority, although the relationship between the provinces and the NDoH is sensitive of the relative independence of the Provincial management regarding health services. The

NDoH plays an important role in co-ordinating services and ensuring uniform systems are applied. Provinces are usually required to 'comply with requests from the NdoH', and it is only where strong leadership exists that Provinces will dare to deviate from National norms and standards.

Within the provinces, the Provincial Managers are more powerful than facility and district managers, and the same principles generally apply between the Provincial and District/Facility Managers as between the Provincial and NDoH.

There is another aspect to consider and that is the hierarchy that exists within facilities. In general doctors are seen to be in charge, especially when they are South African doctors. However, some provinces are particularly dependant on Foreign Qualified Doctors (i.e. those that have obtained their degree outside of South Africa), because South African doctors are unwilling to work in rural hospitals or in unpopular places. Foreign Qualified Doctors are often less willing to adopt a leadership role because they feel that '*they only work in the system*', and in some instances then, nurses will take on a leadership role.

A third aspect to consider is the historical context from which the New South Africa emerges and in particular, the Eastern Cape where, particularly in the former Transkei part of the country, the Homeland Head Office played an exceptionally strong, centralized role in the management of health services with little autonomy or decision making authority vested in the peripheral facilities. The result has been that health workers in the periphery have taken some time since the establishment of the 'New South Africa' to accept that they have some degree of decentralized authority and decision-making capacity.

Given this context, it is understandable that if a data set is thrust upon health workers by a higher authority, it may happen that the response will be an unquestioning implementation of the set, with little or no consideration to the meaning of what is being collected, its accuracy and its relevance.

Given the description of the power relationships that exist in the province, and between different levels, it becomes clear that developing an information system that is appropriate to needs, and used at various levels, will require more than a top down instruction on data elements to be collected. John Heron describes a process of co-operative enquiry in Rowan and Reason, in which he argues that it is important for a relationship to be established between researcher and those researched, whereby the researcher and the subjects interact in such a way that they both learn from the process. Of relevance to the process described above, Heron argues that this process of co-operative enquiry is required because of:

- the nature of research behaviour where, as researchers (in this case the author in the Provincial Office) we cannot expect our subjects to engage in a process which is unacceptable to ourselves, and thus we need to understand ourselves and explore our own issues before we interact with our subjects who then become our fellow researchers. Through the interaction that results, the generation of new ideas is *'not a logical product of empirical observation, but rather they arise unpredictably..'*

- language enables us to communicate. When we have a common language, we are able to symbolize our experiences. When we agree on the use of language, we agree on the set of rules that govern its use.
- science involves propositional knowledge, practical knowledge and experiential knowledge. For the researcher to be able to accurately reflect these forms of knowledge there needs to be a special relationship between the researcher and subject (or co-researcher), which allows the aspects of knowledge to be explored and understood.
- a statement of truth can only be made when it gives credit to the *'values and norms of our sub-culture'*. He argues that the first step is understanding the values of being, next the norms of language (and other practical procedures) and then the truth-value propositions. He suggests that *'our statements are true because we know how to formulate I to do justice to a valued experience.'*
- lastly, traditional research reflects the power of the researcher over his/her subjects. Those in power make the decisions for others.

It is interesting to reflect on the provincial process in the light of the ideas raised by Heron. The provincial office has attempted to involve role-players from all levels in the process of developing the DHEDS from the beginning. The purpose of the process of consultation was to:

- flatten the hierarchical relationship so as to attempt to empower all levels of health workers to determine their information requirements and to encourage them to interact on the development of the system.
- determine the data set that is needed at each level, taking into consideration the existing data that was being collected so as to ensure that those that were to collect the data would have a vested interest in the completeness and quality of the data (this resulted in some data elements being collected because *'we want to collect this data'* despite them being considered to be of less significance). This could be equated to a process of incorporating experiential and practical knowledge in the system.
- encourage an awareness of the value of information for evaluating, planning and developing health services at a local level.
- encourage the team of doctors and nurses and other health workers to meet and discuss the meaning of the information as a group and to recognize the different roles that each contributed to the process.

While the provincial approach is yet to be formally evaluated, initial responses during the pilot phase have been encouraging:

- *'this has been a challenge, but it has resulted in an increased awareness for information'.*

- *'these registers have given hospitals the power to say "No" to ridiculous requests for information by matrons, Bisho* (the Provincial Head Office) *and others'.*

4.2 Exploring the Process of Building Capacity

One of the findings into how data was used in hospitals was that a great deal of data was collected but very little analysis applied. In many cases, information was collected *'in case we need it'*. This may be a reflection of poor numeracy skills (experience with the PHC dataset has highlighted the lack of adequate numeracy skills amongst health workers), with health workers not feeling able to take the information to the next level of understanding, or it may be a reflection of the fact that nurses collect information for their reports but because of their position in the hierarchy, feel it is not their role to take the initiative of analyzing the data.

Zuboff speaks about processes that informate as well as automate. This is the process whereby technology not only automates operations but through this process also provides a deeper level of understanding. She applies this to the use of machines and technology in the industrial sector. However, the Hospital Information system uses registers to help automate and standardize the recording of information and collection of data. Through the use of this standardized data collection, the possibility exists that users at the local level can interpret and analyse the data with ease, thus, through a deeper understanding of their services, shift the traditional power and knowledge hierarchy.

The further aim of the system, despite the fact that it is a paper based system at the hospital unit level, is to allow users to determine basic indicators and targets by clearly defining numerators and denominators for each indicator. If this phase is to succeed, careful attention will need to be paid to the development of a system that allows the calculation of the indicators using basic mathematical skills.

An aspect requiring further consideration is on the nature of the organization and how it is viewed. Walsham describes a number of metaphors for organizations – from that of cultures, brains, organisms, to machines, and political systems. How one views the organization, will influence the behaviour patterns we display in dealing with it. To this end, if we believe that it is purely a machine, we will be mechanistic and cold in our approach. On the other hand, understanding the organisation as a culture or a political system, will require that we are sensitive to a different set of rules when dealing with it. Mechanistic approaches have little consideration for the human element and tend to rely more on machines, and even to see humans as machines within the system. On the other hand a culture, or political system is in a continuous state of evolution and growth and development. This is particularly the situation we experience in South Africa at present where new systems are being established, authority is being challenged and replaced, based on a new set of rules and principles. People in general are eager to learn, explore and improve their personal skills. Thus, one needs to create a space and allow people to come into that space in order to grow and develop. The hospital information system strives to do this through taking the users on a journey, raising questions and creating awareness, and encouraging them to think on their own needs and expectations. Jørn Braa suggests, '*the health system (in developing countries) must be developed in a holistic approach integrating the development of organizations, technology, and human capability. What is required is an evolutionary approach to systems development that encourages ongoing broad participation and mutual learning*'.

5. Conclusion

This paper has, through the use of a case study, explored the steps taken to design a District Hospital Information System in a participatory manner. In the ensuing discussion, two themes identified during the process have been explored. I have argued that within our current context, a system that is based on a hermeneutic process is more appropriate if reliable data is to be collected and if, as one of its aims, the information system wishes to instil a culture of information use at a local level. All too often, governmental bureaucracies tend to force systems on users in a mechanistic fashion, without adequate consultation and with little concern for the development of their workers within the system. Managers are encouraged to reconsider how they view organizations and to take cognisance of the fact that in general they are 'living', constantly changing political and cultural systems and to use this knowledge when developing information systems.

References

Braa, J. Decentralisation, primary health care and information technology in developing countries: Case studies from Mongolia and South Africa.

Primary Health care in the Eastern Cape 1997 – 2000. Equity project, Management Sciences for Health. http//www.msh.co.za/publications/Primary Health Care.

Rowan and Reason (1981) Human Inquiry: A sourcebook of new paradigm research; John Wiley and Sons, p. xiv.

Shaw, V. (1995) Decentralisation and Health Systems Change: Provincial Report on the Queenstown District (Report prepared as part of a 21 country WHO study on decentralisation and health system change), p.41.

Walsham, G (1995) Interpreting Information Systems in Organisations. John Wiley Series in Information Systems, John Wiley and Sons, pp. 29-41.

Zuboff, S. (1988) In the Age of the Smart Machine: the future of work and power. Heineman Professional Publishing, pp.9-11.

Appendix 1: Set of Indicators for the District Hospital Information System

	Proposed Provincial Indicators	Frequency	Numerator	Source	Denominator	Source
In Patient	Bed Occupancy Rate (Bed utilization rate)	M	Inpatient days	Midnight census	Active beds	Semi-permanent data
Activity	Average length of stay		In patient days	Midnight census	Discharges + Deaths + Transfers out	Ward report
	% TB patient days	M	TB patient days	Ward report	Total inpatient days	Midnight census
Deaths	Crude Death Rate	M	# deaths in hospital	Ward report	Total hospital admissions	Ward report
	Perinatal Mortality Rate	A	Still Births + deaths in first week	Labour Ward Report	Total births	Labour ward report
	Maternal Mortality Rate		Maternal deaths	Maternity ward report	Total deliveries	Labour ward report
	Death audit rate		Total deaths audited	Ward Report	Total deaths	Ward report
Nutrition	% severe childhood malnutrition	M	# children with severe malnutrition	Paediatric Ward Report	# children < 5 admitted	Paediatric Ward report

Gynaecology	# ToP performed	M	# ToP performed	Theatre register	N/A	
	Couple year protection	M	# family planning methods utilized	Ward report	Female population 15-45	
Obstetrics	Low Birth Weight rate	M	# live babies with birth weight <2,500 grams	Labour ward report	Total live births	Labour ward report
	% Deliveries with WR recorded	M	# deliveries with WR recorded	Labour ward report	Total deliveries	Labour ward report
	% assisted deliveries		% Assisted deliveries	Labour ward report	Total deliveries	Labour ward report
	Cesarean Section Rate		# cesarean sections	Theatre book	Total deliveries	Labour ward report
	Teenage delivery rate	M	Deliveries to women <18 years	Labour ward report	Total deliveries	Labour ward report

Outpatient						
O P D	% Referrals from clinics	M	Patients with clinic referral letter	OPD report	OPD + casualty headcount	OPD report
	% Trauma		MVAs + interpersonal violence	OPD report	OPD + casualty headcount	OPD report

Support						
	% stores items out of stock	A	# store items out of stock	Store report	# items should be in stock	Store report
Pharmacy	% EDL items out of stock	A	# EDL items out of stock	Pharmacy report	# items should be in stock	Pharmacy report
	Items per script		# Items prescribed		# prescriptions	
	Cost per PDE	M	Total amount spent in last calendar month	Financial Management System (FMS) Reports	Patient day equivalent	Hospital monthly report
Financial	% Budget spent to date		Expenditure to date this year	FMS Reports	Budget for the year	Semi-permanent data
	% Target Income collected	M	Total income in last calendar month	Cash Book	Target for last month	

Annual Survey indicators						
Other Systems	Notifiable Diseases Submission rate	A	# Monthly reports submitted	Reports at District Office	12 months	Reports at District Office
	Termination of Pregnancy	A	# Monthly reports submitted	Reports at District Office	12 months	Reports at District Office

	Submission rate					
	Maternal death notification	A	# Monthly reports submitted	Reports at District Office	12 months	Reports at District Office
	% Transaid reports sent	A	# Transaid reports sent	Reports at District Office	12 months	Reports at District Office
	PHC reports		# PHC reports	Reports at District Office	12 months	Reports at District Office
Finance	Budget allocation per PDE	A	Annual Budget	FMS	PDE for year	Hospital monthly report
	% Expenditure on					
	- Personnel	M	Total spent on personnel in last year	FMS	Total expenditure	FMS
	- Drugs	M	Total spent on drugs in last year	FMS	Total expenditure	FMS
Quality	% hospitals instituting					
	- PIPP program	A	Written record of meetings	Minutes	# monthly meetings scheduled	PIPP guidelines
	- Financial mgt checklist	A	Written record of supervisory visits	Minutes	# supervisory visits scheduled	

	Case fatality rate	A	# deaths	Hospital monthly report	# admissions	Hospital monthly report
Personnel	% Critical posts filled					
	- Management	A	# critical posts filled	Personnel data base (PERSAL)	# critical posts allocated	PERSAL
	- medical	A	# critical posts filled	PERSAL	# critical posts allocated	PERSAL
	% hospital managers with identified indicators	A	# hospital managers with indicators		# hospital managers	
Support	Cost per patient day for support service	A	Total money spent on service	FMS	PDE	Hospital monthly report
	% critical lab services performed (WR, Sputum, FBC;)	A		Lab register	# services should be performed (FBC, AFB sputum, U&E, CSF micro	

Appendix 2 Examples of Tools used for Data Collection at the Unit Level in the District Hospital Information System

Extract from the Pediatric Ward Register

Ward: Paediatric ward		Month:			Age					
Admission Date	Name	Address	Next of kin/head man	Folder no.	< 5 yrs	=> 5 yrs	Sex M/F	T/F in from other ward/hospital	Private patient	Admission diagnosis
a	B	c	d	e	f	g	h	I	j	k

Extract from the Paediatric Ward Report

Report from Ward: _______________					Month/Year: _______________		
All wards					Paediatric	Admissions < 5 yrs	
Admissions:	From ward register:	Male				Admissions => 5 to < 12 yrs	
Transfers in		Female				BCG at birth	

From other Hospital		(Total)				Immunized fully <1 year (new)	
From other Ward						TB New	
Separations	From separati on tally:					Severe Malnutrition < 5 yrs New	
Discharges	Total					Gastro-enteritis/deh ydration	
Transfers out	To another hospital					Acute Respiratory Infection	
	To other ward					Convulsions	
Deaths		Deaths				Cardiac	
	Under< = 7 days					Nephritis	
	8-28 days					Measles	
	29 days - under 5 yrs					Others	
	Total audits under 5 yrs						
	5 years - under 12 years						
	12 years and older						

PART III
ICTs AND NEW ORGANIZATIONAL FORMS

Chapter 14

Book Towns and the Network Society: New Perspectives on Developing Rural Enterprises

Arild Jansen, Ingjerd Skogseid

1. Introduction

The story behind this chapter dates back to the early sixties, when the young Richard Booth founded the world's first 'book town' in Hay-on-Wye, a small Welsh rural village, threatened by economic decline and migration. His idea was to turn this depression to upturn by selling second-hand and antiquarian books. Initially, there was little faith in the concept, but during the 40 years since, the idea has spread throughout Europe, and an increasing number of book towns play a significant role in their local economies.

Today, however, the new economy based on information and communication technology (ICT) and in particular the Internet represents a new challenge for the traditional bookshop. To face these challenges the representatives of five book towns took an initiative to create a project, which would strengthen the bond between the bookshops and book towns, the *Book Town network*. The aim has been to establish an ICT infrastructure that would support an organizational network between the book towns, which provides the bookshops in the book towns with a common communication channel with each other and also offers access to the wider Internet audience.

The focus in this paper is to study how such small enterprises and the corresponding local economies have risen to meet the challenge of the network society. Departing from Castells' (2000a) notion of the network enterprise, supplemented with elements from innovation theory, we are analysing the experiences of building the Book Town network. We believe that the many lessons learned from these efforts can be applied in building similar networks between small businesses in developing countries.

The structure of the chapter is as follows. Sections two and three describe the theoretical background, research issues and research method. In section four we describe and analyse the empirical case, with the conclusion in section five.

2. Theoretical background

Manuel Castells, in the first book of his trilogy, claims that the new economy that is growing out of the information technology revolution is said to be *informational, global and networked* (Castells 2000a). The new economy is informational because 'the productivity and competitiveness of units or agents in this economy ... fundamentally depend on their ability to generate, process and apply efficient knowledge-based information'. It is global because 'the core activities of production, consumption and circulation, as well as their components (...) are organized on a global scale, either directly or through a network of linkages between economic agents'. The new economy can be referred to as networked because its productivity is generated through and competition is played out in a global network of interaction between business networks (Castells 2000a, p.77).

Castells argues that we see new modes of development that relate the way we use technology to improve efficiencies in production. The informational mode of development is 'flexible, pervasive, integrated and reflexive rather then additive evolutionary' (Castells 2000b). Reflexivity refers to the speeding-up process of innovation because both raw materials and end products are information, which is easy to feedback to the production process, to improve the product in the next phase. This reflexivity is the basis for an informational and global economy. The result of this is a restructuring of all economic activities into a new mode of production. This informational mode of production is a challenge for rural regions to cope with. Important factors are access to information and processing capability. Processing capability may become a challenge if the 'brain drain' continues, this is also affected by the more immediate problem of access to an adequate infrastructure which is crucial for the enterprise's ability to participate in the network society' (Jansen 1998).

Further, Castells claims that although the economy is global it is distributed asymmetrically, and it is the 'traditional' western countries that are driving the development. Large areas and population groups are excluded, while at the same time the development of the new economical paradigm is affecting all groups directly or indirectly (Castells 2000a). This fundamental asymmetry affects the level of integration, competitiveness and the ability to benefit from economic growth. To avoid marginalization it is particularly important for rural areas to stay abreast of the development of this new type of society.

Castells claims that the rise of the informational, global economy is characterized by the development of a new organizational logic, which however manifest itself under different forms in various cultural and institutional contexts (*op cit.* p.164). The first form has been the move from mass production to flexible production. The second is the crisis of the large corporation and the resilience of small and medium firms as agents of innovation and sources of job creation. The networking structure can be a mix of vertical and horizontal; it is vertical through subcontracting relations between a central coordinating enterprise and the SME that make up the production and distribution channels. It is horizontal if there exists independent networks between the sub-contracted enterprises in a broader sense than through the sub-contracting network. In these kinds of networks the enterprises can be distributed independent of the location of the other enterprises in the network (Castells 2000b).

Another form of organizational flexibility can be seen in multidirectional network models enacted by SME and large corporations alike. In these networks, enterprises seek collaboration with similar enterprises, where no single enterprise leads the network; instead it is a flexible structure where closer alliances are made on a project basis between the enterprises. In this way they may establish themselves in a market niche and gain competitive advantage.

Castells discusses different trends that are occurring in parallel and interact and influence each other, even though they are independent of each other and along very different dimensions. However, the crucial point is that 'networks are the fundamental stuff of which new organisations are and will be made' (Castells 2000a, p180), and they have the potential to expand and integrate enterprises both locally and globally.

2.1 Research Issues

While Castells primarily discusses innovations in networks at a macro or global level, our focus is at a micro level. We are studying the development of a small-scale network between rural enterprises. This implies both technical and organizational innovations that require various type of support. In traditional regional economics and innovation theory, the term *regional innovation system* has been introduced to explain part of this complexity. The main characteristics of the regional innovation systems, as defined through evolutionary research in the fields of regional economics, are learning and innovation, which includes both individual and collective innovations (Morgan 1997). Collective innovations are seen as interactive processes where the firms' networks are an important part of their collective innovative capability. This term captures the trend to build regional organizations and networks to strengthen the innovation capability of enterprises (Cooke 1998). Results from studies show that the innovative capability of enterprises is highly dependent on their ability to come in contact and co-operate with other actors, such as customers, suppliers and R&D organisations (Asheim and Isaksen 1997; Lundvall 1992; Smith 1997). The innovative activity is seen as partly local and partly regional phenomenon. This represents a new theoretical understanding of how the innovation processes occurs, and is concretised in the interactive innovation model (Asheim and Isaksen 1997; Isaksen 2000), which defines innovations as interactive, non-linear knowledge development and transfer: technology and knowledge flows freely between R&D activities, the industry and other stakeholders.

Based on this interactive innovation model we have developed a research framework that includes the external environment, the regional innovation system and infrastructure and the individual organizations where innovations take place (Jansen 1998b, Grøtte et al. 2000). This framework has been applied in the study of some regional development initiatives; among them the Book Town network (Skogseid and Jansen 2001).

Our aim in this paper is to analyse some of the challenges in building this type of small-scale 'virtual' enterprise network, which span different regions. We combine Castells' notion of the network enterprise with elements from the innovation theories discussed above. In particular, we will address the following questions:

- Which types of support seem to have been most important in developing and implementing organizational networks between small rural businesses?
- What type of relations can be identified in such networks and what type of different interest has been voiced?
- What types of interaction patterns are going on in the network, and how do these strengthen the network organization?

3. Research Method

This research study is based on an analysis of the five book towns that were directly involved in developing the ICT network and the organizational structure: the Book Town network. This approach is situated within the interpretative strand of information systems research (Walsham 1995), aiming at doing more in depth analysis of the history of the case. It has some of the characteristics of action research, as one of the authors has had an active role as project manager in the project, and has been involved in most aspects of the project. She has been involved in problem definition and requirement specification as well as in the design and implementation work and the final evaluation, corresponding to Baskerville's diagnostic and therapeutic stages (Baskerville 1999). This work has been carried out in close co-operation with the future users; the bookshop owners, book town association representatives and other stakeholders, as the aim of the project has been to link theory and practice (Baskerville and Wood-Harper 1998).

The empirical data has been collected during a five-year period; in two of these, the activity was much higher due to the collaborative project between the five villages. Our analysis is based on the 17 units comprising the 13 bookshops and four book town associations that have been active in the collaborative project. The main methods of data collection have been project documentation along with semi-structured and free interviews and questionnaires which was conducted at regular intervals as part of the analysis of user needs and the in-project evaluation, during the design, implementation and testing of organizational and technical solutions. In total 61 interviews with 30 different persons have been carried out. Over 200 Internet users have responded to surveys administered through the Internet. These are documented in Skogseid and Seaton (1998), Alford and Seaton (1999), Seaton (1998) and Seaton and Alford (2001).

4. Case Description and Discussion

In the following section we will firstly give a description of the case and then discuss it with regard to the theoretical contributions.

4.1 BookTownNet – A Network Between Five European Book Towns

The book town phenomenon has developed from the first book town established in 1962 in Hay-on-Wye (Seaton 1996) on the border between England and Wales, and to date almost 30 book towns have been established worldwide and several are under development. Most book towns exist in villages of historic interest or of scenic beauty, allowing for the conservation of the cultural heritage coupled with retaining the unique atmosphere. As the number of book towns increased, so did the requirement for more and better communication between the villages. In 1996 five of the villages decided to establish an organizational network. In addition to Hay-on-Wye, the four other villages are Bredevoort (NL), Fjærland (NO), Montolieu (FR) and Redu (BE). The villages have a population of between 300 and 1600, including between 12 and 36 bookshops and up to 500 000 visitors in a year. In the individual villages the relationship between the bookshops is characterized both by a high degree of collaboration in developing the village and attracting visitors combined with competition in selling most books. As increasing numbers of books were being sold on the Internet, each village was facing the threat of marginalization. They saw benefits of collaborating as a 'global village', while simultaneously trying to attract most visitors to their own town. They have thus identified different communication needs, these being:

- *Communication between bookshops:* The success of a book town is first and foremost a question of successful book trade. Many bookshops recognise that the future success of their business requires international specialization and a closer communication between the individual bookshops independent of location.
- *Communication between book towns*: Book town associations and enterprises have individual strengths and weaknesses and the participants in the BookTownNet were interested in improving book town quality by effective communication of information and ideas between villages. The book towns constituted a European-wide network with great potential for cultural inter-linkages, which would promote traffic between the villages.
- *Market communication:* Though the book towns are different, they are characterized by a common atmosphere that the visitors find particular attractive. Presenting information about the book towns by way of a common IS were seen as important.

Thus, developing an efficient ICT-based information and communication system was seen as necessary. The system consists of both an intranet and Internet applications. Five application areas were defined:

- Wholesale of books between book selling enterprises within and between book towns.
- The establishment of an international network (the virtual Book Town organisation).
- Marketing the book town network as a pan-European tourist trail.
- Specialized global marketing of high value book items.
- Information about activities in the book towns to the global book-lovers community.

The application areas were divided into two distinct components:

1. an Intranet for dialogue and communication between users participant, and
2. an Internet web site for communication with external users. The Intranet application was developed to facilitate communication and collaboration between bookshops within and between the different book towns, and for maintaining the information on the Internet site.

The information presented on the Internet belongs to three general categories,

1. general information about the book town movement,
2. information about the individual book towns and
3. information about the individual bookshops. Initially other services were envisaged, but later they were prioritized away or they were developed and tested and deemed not useful.

The common ICT platform is an infrastructure that supports three types of collaboration patterns:

- Collaboration between local bookshops (within a village).
- Communication and business-related transactions (between the book towns' bookshops and associations).
- Information exchange between users/customers and the book shops.

The actors involved are both the bookshops and the book town associations; they have both taken the initiative in the project and participated in the development of the infrastructure.

5. Innovative Activity

The Book Town network appears to fit into Castells' framework. It is becoming *global*; currently the network spans many countries in Europe. It is *informational* in that the network supports various kinds of information and knowledge exchange. It is truly a *networked* organisation.

Furthermore, Castells claims that working in networks strengthens the innovative capabilities of the individual participants. In the Book Town network, we have identified different patterns of innovative activities. The project itself has clearly been an innovative activity, including both technical and organizational challenges, the project network offered substantial support in developing and implementing the technical solutions, and these have been rather successful. The in-project evaluations (Alford and Seaton 1999; Seaton and Alford 2001) show that the bookshop users have gained confidence and knowledge in using the ICT based tools, and there is also increasing usage of ICT in terms of the bookselling business. The Internet part of the system seems to have been serving its function, while the Intranet part of the service has had limited success. There are several reasons for this: firstly, the amount of communication was insufficient in volume and regularity to encourage users to access the site. This is the typical problem of gaining critical mass of users: increased usage is needed to make the Intranet interesting. Secondly, in the initial phases of the project, e-mail was provided as the main communication channel, which many of the users felt was sufficient for communication. Furthermore, the usability of the Intranet has been criticized for not being sufficiently tailored to the user requirements. Part of the problems seems to be related to organizational matters.

What has the role of the local environment been? According to regional economic theory, the local innovation system comprises the 'network' of relevant resources, in our case the bookshops, the book town associations, public administration, local computer retailers and other support organizations. We found that these were of various type and quality throughout the different book towns, related to resources, competence and attitudes. In some of the book towns the only available local support system was the book town association. These book town associations have different roles. In some villages they are a more strategic, political organization. In one village the local public administration was unsupportive towards the development of the book town, and the development efforts were left to their own initiative. In other villages, however the association carried out by a number of functions to the common good of the bookshops and have also been the driving force in introducing computers in the bookshops.

The five villages have been allowed to choose their own local diffusion strategy. In some of the book towns (Fjærland, Montolieu and Redu) all bookshops and other related organisations have been given access. In other villages (Bredevoort and Hay), only the project partners were included, and they did not want to let other bookshops become users before the project phase had concluded. Within the project it was a conscious decision to allow each village to choose how they diffused the tool to potential users. The assumption being that the local partner's best knows their colleagues, for example same culture and language.

These individual strategies have led to differing numbers of users and usage patterns across the book towns, this far it seems that the 'open and including' strategy has been more successful both in involving more users in the villages and in introducing the Internet to more bookshops. They have a larger test bed and in general increased the ICT competence in the community.

Those who chose the more exclusive strategy argued that it would be more appropriate that a selected group of more motivated and competent users tested the prototypes before they were made generally available to the bookshops. However, they have not so far succeeded in spreading the technology, which is, as least partly, an organisational challenge that therefore needs to be addressed.

Our data highlights the fact that the book town network has been able to compensate for the lack of support in the regional innovation system when it comes to resolving technical issues, which provides evidence for the importance of the book town infrastructure in supporting such activities. It appears however, that the characteristics of the local innovation system are more critical for stimulating organizational innovations, and that resources in the virtual network cannot compensate for shortcomings locally, at least in a short-term perspective.

6. Network Organizations and Interaction Patterns

The book towns and the bookshops in the villages are members of several collaborative networks; which partly overlap and have common nodes. In each village we find an *intra-town* network, which then is linked together in the *inter-town* network. These networks can also be seen as one, where parts of the actors in the network have started to change and increase in number, but that have not stabilized yet.

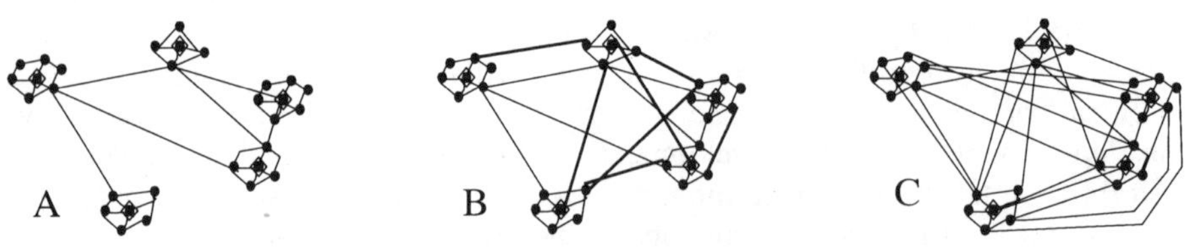

Figure 14.1 Pre and post situation for communication in and between the villages, the circles represent the intra-town networks and the lines the communication patterns. The development from situation A to C represents an increase in number and communication links and frequency

Establishing a bookshop in an existing book town automatically makes you a member of the intra-town network, and if the village also has a connection to one of the other book towns then the bookshop can more easily hook up to the global network of book towns (inter-town network). The communication channels used in this network were mainly the *traditional medium* such as face-to-face dialogs, telephone, and fax; from 1996-97 there was also some use of e-mail.

Communication between the villages was primarily between a few individuals and not very frequent and in some of the villages the contacts were more frequent than others, Figure 14.1.A is an illustration of this network. In terms of our research framework, this network is part of the local innovation system in each village. All the book towns have been developed from the same concept, Hay-on-Wye, whereby knowledge has been transferred from one village to the other and the links between the villages have been established. Some links are stronger and more frequently used, while others are not maintained and will eventually be lost.

Figure 14.1.B is an illustration of the second inter-town network that was the result of the BookTownNet project and the introduction of technology in the book town setting. In this process the network has slowly been extended and is taking over from the 'old' network. This assisted communication and allowed for more open and interactive dialogue between members in the network. This intermediate state has further developed into what is described in Figure 14.1.C. New members have joined the network, coming both from the initial five villages and extending outside this group, an additional eleven book towns have signed up to join the network, which is now managed by a new *International Organisation of Book Towns*. The primary aim is to support the technical infrastructure and stimulate the further development of the Book Town network. Only one of the book towns has decided to not join in the organization.

6.1 Different Relations and Different Interest

Important issues in the design and development of the Book Town network have been:

Different goals: to develop a bookshop or to develop a book town or develop the whole local community. There was a difference in the partners who were booksellers and those who were working actively in the book town association; the association representatives worked for the local community while the bookshop owners had the bookshop as their primary focus. Thus, the degree to which the latter acknowledged the importance of developing the community varied.

Decentralization and local autonomy. How much of the operation of the project could be decentralized? How to organize and operate the project? The project was organized in a number of activities some of which ran decentralized and some more centralized. It was important to decentralize as many activities as possible to ensure alignment of different interests. One important reason for this was the multi-lingual character of this community, as more than five different languages we represented. At the same time there were activities that needed to be run centrally, such as development and operation of the system.

E-commerce or to stay with the traditional way of selling books. At the start of the project it was decided that a 'book town bookstore' be established on Internet, but this idea was discarded.

Some of these conflicts have been resolved during the project period, but there are obviously tensions between creating a common international organization, which may impose certain uniformity versus that of maintaining local autonomy and the cultural heritage. The basic ambition is that each book town should remain local and unique and not just become one of many nodes in a global book town network.

7. Conclusion

Our findings indicate that the establishment of the Book Town network, both individually and between the book towns has strengthened the communication and collaboration between them, whereby creating a better basis for the small book towns to be competitive in the new economy was achieved.

Our data shows that the network has been critical for the bookshops ability to implement and use the new technical solutions, which highlights the importance of the Book Town infrastructure in supporting such activities. This indicates that the Book Town network has at least partly been able to compensate for the inability of the local infrastructure and support system related to solving the technical issues. On the other hand, we find that the network has been insufficient for stimulating the organizational changes in all book towns. It seems therefore that the characteristics of the local innovation system are most important for stimulating organizational innovations than relying on available support from outside.

The Book Town network resembles the structure of the horizontal, multidirectional network model of SME as described by Castells. It illustrates that it is possible to establish an international cooperation based on use of ICT that are spanning both geography and cultural differences. Castells claims, however, that the development of a network society is asymmetric, it does not benefit all. This seems to conform with our findings; in the Book Town network, we have experienced a difference between the actors that are participating in the changes, that are active and the ones that the action is carried out in relation to but do not actively participate. This is not at all surprising.

Healey et al. (1999) have examined the factors that may enable a region to make a brake from the existing, path dependent trajectory and mobilize their initiative to '*model*' the external pressure to suit their own needs. They claim that to be able to make adequate changes it is necessary to strengthen the local institutional capacities; that is both the knowledge and relational resources and their mobilization capability. Our findings clearly supports this view; in those book town where they have been able take an initiative to face external threat they have mobilized their local resources to use new technology in a way that can help them in developing the local economy.

The Book Town network has so far resisted joining a larger corporation. Instead, it has started co-operation with one of the dominating E-book businesses, though without giving away its independence. In this way, the BookTownNet may appear as a kind of 'indigenous network' linking small rural enterprises.

We believe that these findings are relevant for similar efforts in building networks between small enterprises also in developing countries. Our case shows that it is possible to stimulate local economies through collaborate efforts based on horizontal networks between small and independent enterprises across borders and cultures. However, one should give priority to strengthening the local innovation system in order to help organizational implementation of ICT-systems in the individual enterprises. A key factor is to allow for interplay between the common network infrastructure and the local innovation system (Skogseid and Jansen 2001). Stakeholders should put effort into not only strengthening the knowledge resources, but also the relational resources and the mobilization capabilities (Healey et al 1999). It is important to develop the infrastructure as an integral part of the local innovation system, including organizational and human resources that can support collaboration between various types of enterprises locally and across the network.

References

Alford, Philip and Anthony V. Seaton. 1999. *D08.2 BookTownNet verification trials evaluation report.*: Stiftinga Vestlandsforsking.

Asheim, Bjørn T. and Arne Isaksen. 1997. Regionale innovasjonssystemer – en teoretisk diskusjon. In *Innovasjoner, næringsutvikling og regionalpolitikk.*, ed. Isaksen: Høyskoleforlaget AS.

Baskerville, R. 2000 Investigation Information Systems with Action Research *Communications of The Association for Information Systems 2,* Article 19, http://cais.isworld.org, October, 1999.

Baskerville, R. and A.T. Wood-Harper, 1998 A.T. 'Diversity in Information Systems Action Research Methods,' *European Journal of Information Systems* (7:2), 1998, pp. 90-107.

Castells, M. 2000a. *The Rise of the Network Society,* Second edition. Blackwell Publishers.

Castells, M. 2000b *Materials for an exploratory theory of the network society.* British Journal of Sociology No 51 , No 1. London School of Economics.

Cooke, P. 1998. Introduction. Origins of the concept. In *Regional innovation systems*, ed. H-J Braczyk:2 - 25. London: UCL Press.

Healey, Patsy, Claudio de Magalhaes, and Ali Madanipour. 1999. Institutional capacity-building, urban planning and urban regeneration projects. *FUTURA (Journal of the Finnish Society for Futures Studies)*, no. 3.

Isaksen, Arne. 2000. Kunnskapsaktører i teorien om regionale innovasjonssystemer. In *Innovasjonspolitikk, kunnskapsflyt og regional utvikling.*, ed. Gammelsæter: Norges forskningsråd, Oslo.

Jansen, A. 1998a. *Utkanten i den globale landsbyen: Integrasjon eller identitet*, University of Oslo.Oslo, Norway.

Lundvall, B. Å. 1992. *User relationship*. In *National systems of innovation*, ed. B. Å. Lundvall. London, England: Pinter, London.

Morgan, K. 1997. The learning region: Institutions, innovations and regional renewal. *Regional Studies* 31, no. 5: 491-503.

Seaton, A. V. (1996). *Book towns and rural tourism development: Hay-on-Wye 1961-1996*: The Scottish Tourism Research Unit, The Scottish Hotel School, University of Strathclyde.

Seaton, A. V. 1998. *D8.1 Booktownnet evaluation plan.*: Stiftinga Vestlandsforsking.

Seaton, Anthony V. and Philip Alford. 2001. *D08.3 Booktownnet demonstrations evaluation report.*: Stiftinga Vestlandsforsking.

Skogseid, Ingjerd, and Jansen, Arild. (2001). *Booktowns on Internet - Rural enterprises enter the Network Society.* Proceedings of the Twenty second Annual International Conference on Information Systems, New Orleans, US.

Skogseid, Ingjerd, and Antony V. Seaton. 1998. *D3.1 Booktownnet - book town status and user needs analysis*: Stiftinga Vestlandsforsking, VF-rapport 19/98.

Smith, Keith. 1997. Economic infrastructures and innovation systems. in *Systems of innovations. Technologies, institutions and organisations*, ed. I. Edquist. London: Pinter.

Walsham, G. 1995. The emergence of interpretivism in is research. *Information Systems Research.* 6:4: 376-394.

Chapter 15

Mobile Commerce as a Solution to the Global Digital Divide: Selected Cases of E-Development

Nikhilesh Dholakia and Nir Kshetri

1. Introduction

In terms of accessing, delivering, and exchanging information in digital forms, a substantial gap has developed between rich and poor nations. Mobile telecommunications networks have been touted as 'leapfrogging alternatives' that may allow the technologically disadvantaged segments of the world to close or at least narrow the 'digital divide' that separates them from the information rich. Thus, according to the International Labour Organization (ILO 2001):

> Acceleration of development can occur through the leapfrogging potentials inherent in the technologies, where leapfrogging is defined as the ability to bypass earlier investments in the time or cost of development. Leapfrogging has first of all a technological foundation: through wireless applications, developing countries can bypass more costly and time-consuming investments in fixed-wire telecom infrastructures.

During the introductory phase, mobile phones diffused rapidly in high-income countries and widened the digital divide between them and developing countries (UNDP 2001). In recent years, mobile communications are experiencing higher growth rates in low-income countries. For instance, during 1995-2001, mobile subscribers in Africa registered a cumulative average growth rate (CAGR) of 82.1 per cent compared to 47.8 per cent for the world. As a result, Africa's share in the world mobile market increased from 0.7 per cent in 1995 to 2.5 per cent in 2001 (ITU 2002). During the same period Asia's share in the world mobile market increased from 25 per cent to 36 per cent (ITU 2002). More importantly, a large proportion of the newly added mobile phones in developing countries are getting into the hands of relatively poor people (Economist 1999).

Drawing from macro-level data as well as two case studies, this chapter presents a meta-model of which mobile telecom business models may 'work' in various development settings. In our view a 'mobile e-Development' (or MED) model 'works' when it creates the projected socio-economic changes – the sought-for 'development' impact. It also generates political-economic payoffs for the development agencies and firms that sponsor and implement the model. In other words, successful MED models yield dividends for target populations as well as policy sponsors.

This chapter is organized as follows. The following section discusses briefly the research questions addressed and the methodology employed. Then we outline the MED model. This is followed by an analysis of several current and possible uses of mobile phones and the impact of environmental factors on the degree and types of mobile phone uses. Then, we relate the MED model to the existing theories on innovation diffusion and elucidate some mechanisms whereby mobile diffusion can be accelerated in developing countries. Next, we provide two cases to illustrate how contextual factors can shape the diffusion pattern of mobile phones. Finally some conclusions are provided.

Research Questions and Methodology

This chapter is guided by the following three research questions:

1. What are the benefits that mobile phones currently or potentially offer to the users in developing countries?
2. What factors influence the diffusion of mobile phones in general and their types of uses in particular?
3. What mechanisms are available for influencing and accelerating the diffusion pattern of mobile phones?

In broad terms, this chapter employs interpretative epistemology and multiple case studies to construct theory about the role of mobile commerce in economic development (Montealegre 1999; Orlikowski and Baroudi 1991; Yin 1989).

2. The Proposed MED Model

Figure 1 outlines our Mobile e-Development (MED) Model. The essence of our model is that the ability and willingness to use mobile phones and their benefits are influenced by a number of forces in the environment. These include political, cultural, and economic forces. The success of a firm's mobile commerce efforts is, thus, a function of its ability to identify and align with the mechanisms that spur mobile telecommunications adoption and usage. Policies that fail to consider the impact of the contextual factors, on the other hand, will not be very effective in bridging the existing digital divide.

3. Elements of the MED Model

3.1 Benefits of Mobile Communications

First, one of the important uses of mobile phones in developing countries has been in *information search* activities.

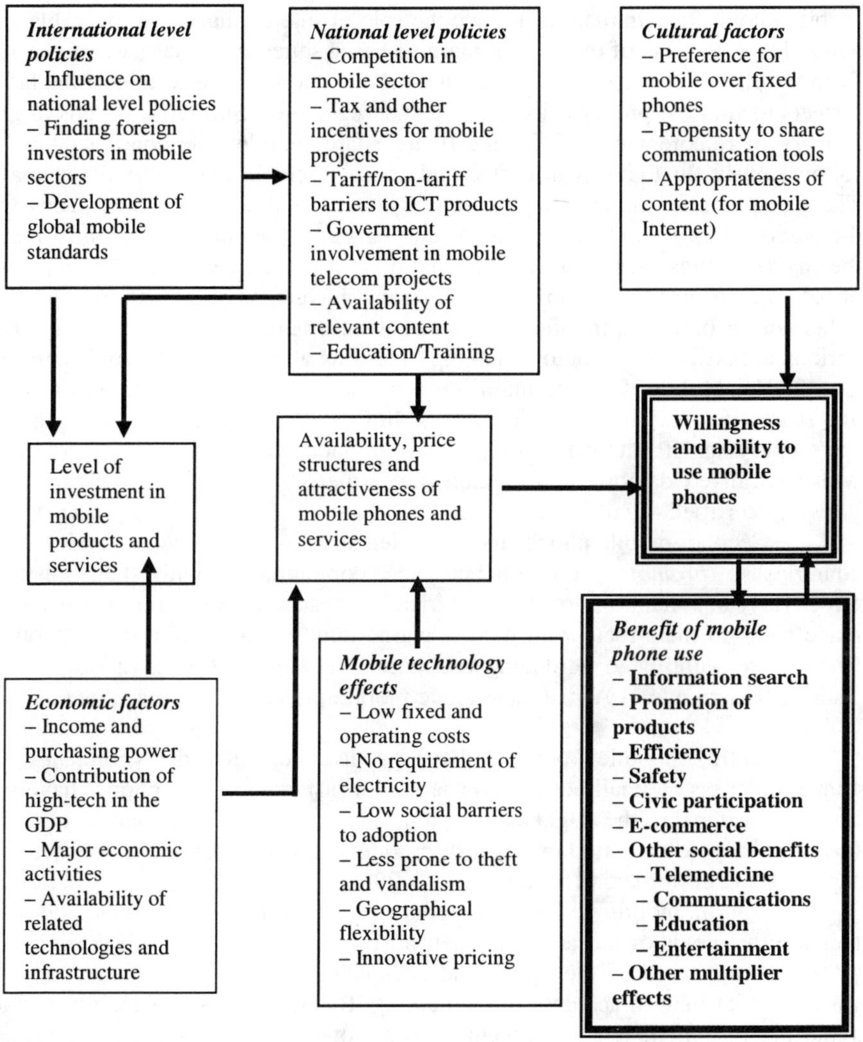

Figure 15.1 Mobile e-Development (MED) Model

Farmers and small business owners are utilizing the information gathered via mobile phones to eliminate or reduce the role of intermediaries in the value chain and to lower the risk of their profit margins being squeezed by larger firms or firms from developed countries.[1] For example, mobile phones have enabled Bangladeshi farmers to find the proper prices of rice and vegetables. Similarly, groups of small farmers in remote areas of Côte d'Ivoire share mobile telephones so they can follow hourly fluctuations in coffee and cocoa prices in the international market. Thanks to mobile phones, they can now choose the time to sell their crops when the world prices are in their favour. A few years ago, the only way to find out about the market trends was to go to the capital city and the deal making was largely based on oft-unreliable information from buyers (Lopez 2000). Similarly, fishermen in India use mobile phones to get information about the price of fish at various accessible ports before making decisions about where to land their catch (Rai 2001). Mobile data communication methods are enabling farmers to obtain and share information beyond just prices. In Costa Rica, small farmers in the field are employing HP handheld computers, equipped with simple icons, to interact with centralized databases that guide the farmers through the complex steps of growing 'certified organic' coffee beans.[2]

Second, mobile phones have enabled small business owners in developing countries to *promote* their products and communicate with their customers effectively. In Johannesburg, South Africa, for instance, one can see many home-made signs in the streets with mobile phone numbers that offer services ranging from house painting to gardening (Economist 1999). As Lopez (2000) observes 'huge billboard ads in Africa have made mobile phones as popular there as Coca-Cola.'

Third, mobile phones have contributed to the *efficiency* and competitiveness of small business owners. For instance, mobile phones have made taxis in Kampala, the Ugandan capital, more efficient. Similarly, tradesmen travelling on bicycles in Jamaica use mobile phones to communicate with their suppliers and customers (The World Bank 2000b).

Fourth, mobile phones have reduced the cost of doing business and helped increase the yields of farmers and small business owners by providing *safety*. ITU (1999) documents how the driver and occupants of a van laden with readymade garments that met an accident in Chittagong, Bangladesh used a mobile phone to avoid the risk of their consignments being looted. Similarly, in Lubumbashi the Democratic Republic of Congo, mobile phones given by maize farmers to their security guards have been effective deterrents against robbery and increased the farm yields significantly (Lopez 2000). In addition to business safety, mobile phones are also providing social safety. Lopez (2000) reports the opinion of a Venezuelan parent:

> My daughter never goes out at night without her mobile. I can call her every hour or less to see if she's OK.

Fifth, mobile phones have been used in e-government and *civic participation* as well. During the 2000 elections in Senegal, for instance, FM radio reporters used mobile phones to improve their coverage (Lopez 2000). Villagers in Uganda fire questions at Yoweri Museveni, the Ugandan president, via an FM station that the villagers contact with their mobile phones (Sebunya 2001).

Sixth, mobile sets in developing countries are being used for *e-commerce activities*, increasing the convenience of shopping at home. For instance, mobile phones are more popular than fixed lines connected to the Internet for buying and selling stocks online in some Chinese cities (Ebusinessforum.com 2000).

Seventh, mobile phones are delivering and have the potential to deliver a number of other *social benefits*. They enable families and friends to *communicate* with each other, improve *education*, and extend medical benefits to rural and remote areas through distance learning and *telemedicine* (Hammond 2001). For example, rural Bangladeshis use mobile phones to call their family members staying abroad or in other parts of the country, call doctors or the police for emergencies, etc. (Schwartz 2001). Also mobile *data networks* are being used for such purposes. In Uganda, despite limited bandwidth, GSM telecommunications are being used to provide Internet access and email connectivity (Ernberg 1998). Mobile phones can also be used for *entertainment* activities; however, such applications are more prevalent in developed countries such as Japan.

In addition, mobile phones are creating employment and producing a number of *multiplier effects* by triggering new economic activities. The GrameenPhone case provided later in this chapter illustrates such activities.

The benefits discussed above can be realized in developing countries only when mobile phones are easily *available at reasonable prices* and potential adopters are *willing* to use them. A number of contextual factors influence the *availability of and willingness to use* mobile phones.

3.2 Cultural Factors Affecting Mobile Technology Use

First, cultural factors influence the level of *preference for mobile phones over fixed phones*. Asians and those from Newly Industrialized Economies (NIEs) exhibit a greater preference for mobile phones than their counterparts in Europe or America. As an m-commerce analyst observes, people in Asia are more 'comfortable with a lot of different, small electronic devices and appear to be more comfortable with wireless phones' (Wilson 2001).

Second, cultural factors influence the *propensity to share mobile phones* in the community. In some African countries, for example, although a mobile phone belongs to a person, it is regarded as a device for the community, because of a culture of sharing of tools (Lopez 2000). If the people in these countries were as individualistic as those in Western countries, at the current level of penetration rates the social benefits of mobile phones would be much lower. In these countries, the children of the owners of mobile phones often run to neighbours to tell them that a relative living abroad will be calling back in a few minutes. As indicated in the GrameenPhone case in this chapter, in Bangladesh, 70 people on the average use a single mobile phone.

Third, cultural values determine *appropriateness of the contents* in mobile Internet. The sites most favoured by I-mode users in Japan, for example, deal with such trivialities as downloadable Pokemon characters or call melodies that 'may not cut ice elsewhere' (Ebusinessforum.com 2001).

3.3 National Level Policies

Availability and price structure of mobile phone are at least as much political issues as they are economic ones. First, *opening of mobile market for competition* can boost the growth rate of mobile adoption. The experience of developing countries such as Sri Lanka that have opened their mobile markets indicates that competition among operators leads to lower prices (UNDP 2001). India, for instance, opened its telecom market for competition and is experiencing a rapid growth in mobile penetration rate (Rai 2001). Governments' willingness to open the market for competition and invest in mobile sector, in turn, is influenced partly by their perception of the appropriateness and usefulness of mobile phones for different sections of the society. Many governments still view mobile phones as luxury items appropriate only for business executives and rich people; and this has become a major obstacle in bringing mobile communications to the least developed areas (Lopez 2000). As illustrated in the GrameenPhone case later in this chapter, the project of providing mobile phones to rural Bangladeshis was not well received initially by the development agencies and telecommunications companies.

Governments can also help accelerate the diffusion of mobile phones in an economy *by providing tax and other incentives* for mobile phone projects and by *reducing tariff and non-tariff barriers* to Information and Communication Technology (ICT) products.

In addition, government involvement in *mobile telecom projects* and making *relevant contents available* can boost mobile diffusion. Lack of suitable portals and specialized sites in developing countries is hampering the development of mobile Internet in these countries. Finally, governments can influence the diffusion of mobile phones by providing appropriate *education and training*.

3.4 International level policies

International organizations can influence the global diffusion of ICT in general (e.g., see Montealegre 1999) and mobile phones in particular in various ways. First, they can influence *national level policies* on competition, tax incentives, and tariff/non-tariff barriers. For instance, many developing countries have eliminated or reduced customs duties on telecom and switching equipment to comply with the Information Technology Agreements (ITA) of the WTO (Bhatnagar 1999).

Second, international agencies are helping developing countries find *foreign partners for mobile telecom projects*. For instance, WorldTel is an investment venture launched by the ITU and organized according to business principles. WorldTel was set up to help businesses identify and execute profitable telecom investment opportunities in developing countries. Leading handset makers and service providers such as AT&T, Cable and Wireless, NEC and Nokia have expressed interest in WorldTel (Garcia and Gorenflo 2001).

Third, ITU is also working to develop a *single global standard for mobile communications*. The economies of scale achievable with a single global standard would drive down the price of terminals and services to the user, boosting the penetration of mobile phones in developing countries (ITU 2000).

3.5 Economic factors

First, *income and purchasing power* determine the level of investment in mobile sector as well as the economic sacrifice potential adopters can make to acquire mobile phones.

Second, the *contribution of high technology in the gross domestic product* (GDP) of countries determines the extent to which mobile sets are available or imported in developing countries. High technology contributes a relatively high proportion of GDP in some developing countries such as China, Malaysia and Thailand and mobile sets are likely to be cheaper and easily available in these countries. Many developing countries do not produce mobile sets domestically. Tariff and non-tariff barriers often make mobile phones expensive and unavailable in such countries.

Third, the types of uses of mobile phones depend upon the *economic activities* in the country. Mobile phones in developing countries, for instance, are being used in such activities as buying and selling stocks online, protecting maize farms from robbery, and tracking world prices of agricultural products.

Fourth, *availability of related technologies and infrastructure* plays an important role in the diffusion of mobile phones. For example, the operation of mobile phone is same as fixed phones and mobile networks can be connected to fixed networks. So, potential adopters are not required to learn new skills. Moreover, formation of a critical mass of cellular phones is not necessary if there are already a large number of fixed phone users.

3.6 Mobile Technology Effect

Several characteristics of mobile technology make it attractive for potential adopters in developing countries (Figure 14.1). For instance, fixed and operating costs of mobile phones are lower than those of fixed phones; they are geographically flexible and do not require electricity to operate; and innovative mobile pricing mechanisms are emerging.

3.7 Summary of the MED model

The relationship between the various elements of the MED model can be summarized as follows:

- The willingness and ability of potential adopters to use mobile phones depend upon the *availability, price structure* and *attractiveness* of mobile phones as well as other *cultural factors*.

- These in turn, are influenced directly or indirectly by *economic factors*, *national* and *international level policies*, and the *characteristics of mobile technology*.
- Taking cultural and economic factors and the characteristics of mobile technology as endogenous factors, the available *mechanisms to influence* the diffusion patterns of mobile phones are via *national* and *international level policies*.

4. Conceptual Foundations

The model presented in Figure 14.1 and discussed in the preceding sections is grounded in the observable and reported trends in mobile telecommunications in the developing world. While the model appears to have face validity, it needs strengthening in conceptual terms. In particular, the following issues arise:

- How does the proposed MED model relate to theories of technology diffusion and technology-based development?
- What are the specific mechanisms available to accelerate the process of development using mobile telecommunications?

4.1 MED model in relation to existing theories

Several characteristics of a technology influence its diffusion pattern: relative advantage, compatibility, complexity, observability, and trialability (Rogers 1983). Rogers (1995: 245-6) suggests that cellular phones have an 'almost ideal set of perceived attributes' with respect to these classic dimensions. He argues that:

- Rapidly falling costs and the potential to save time boost the *relative advantage* of mobile technologies
- Ability to connect to existing telephone network boosts the *compatibility* of mobile devices and networks
- With a method of operation same as the "regular" phone, mobile phones offer *low complexity*
- Status-conferral to potential buyers enhances the *observability* of mobile phones
- Possibility to borrow a friend's cellular phone increases the *trialability* of such devices.

Such factors drove the rapid rate of cellular phone adoption in the United States. Although the evaluation of mobile phones by potential adopters in developing countries may differ slightly from the adopters of the U.S,[3] the characteristics listed in 'Mobile technology effect' (Figure 14.1) are likely to make them more attractive than fixed phones. Several factors lead to *high relative advantage* and *lower complexity*. The fixed and operating costs are lower than the fixed p[1,2,3,...]hones (see GrameenPhone case) and, unlike computer-based Internet; mobile phones do not require electricity to operate and sophisticated skills to use. Some mobile service providers make handsets available at zero or nominal cost when the subscribers sign a contract, leading to favourable assessment of mobile phones on the *trialability* dimension. Norms of neighbourly sharing in developing countries also boost *trialability*.

The influence of national institutions on the diffusion of modern technologies by legal and non-legal means such as new laws, investment incentives, technology transfer, and other supply-push and demand-pull forces is well documented in the literature (e.g., King et al 1994; Montealegre 1999; Van de Ven et al 1999). With the help of numerous case histories, Van de Ven et al (1999) demonstrates that institutionalized environment plays an important role in the diffusion of new technologies. For instance, Singapore has been able to develop itself as an ICT hub of Asia by providing attractive infrastructure, skilled workers, and a stable labour environment that attracted a large number of ICT firms (Kraemer et al. 1992; Wong 1998). Strong university-industry linkages, likewise, have driven technology diffusion in Israel (Porter and Stern 2001). Similarly, privatization, competition, and trade policies have stimulated technology diffusion in Southeast Asia (Shultz and Pecotich 1997). In the case of Scandinavian countries Dalum et al. (1988) document how public regulation and support to integrate new technology, skills, and existing social needs led to the rapid diffusion of mobile technology (Dalum et al 1988).

The optimum role of national institutions in influencing the diffusion of a technology, however, may depend upon the type of the technology as well as the level of economic development. As the GrameenPhone case in this chapter indicates, institutions in Bangladesh are helping to accelerate the diffusion of mobile phones by *providing loans and training to the retailers,* among other means. Such training reduces the gap between the prevailing and required knowledge about mobile phone usage and thus helps potential adopters (of mobile technology) as well as mobile retail businesses to move from one to the next stage of the technology adoption model (TAM).

Past studies have also found that national governments oppose ideas, products, or technologies that are against their *political goals*. Rogers (1966, p.58) reports that in Vietnam it took three years to accept tilapia fish as a local diet after U.S. technical assistance workers introduced this fish. To oppose American influence, the communists fed tilapia to sick persons and spread a rumour that the fish caused sickness. Similarly, given their respective income levels, Internet diffusion is relatively slow in two authoritarian regimes of Asia – Malaysia and Singapore – because of the incompatibility of the Internet with the policies of the regimes (Kshetri 2001). Political factors, similarly, seem to play an important role in the diffusion of digital signatures in Asian countries (Kshetri and Dholakia 2001). In the case of mobile phones, governmental perceptions of mobile phones as luxury items have hindered mobile projects, including the GrameenPhone project in its initial stages.

International agencies' involvement in diverse projects aimed at enhancing economic and social well-being of the people in developing countries has been widely documented. Examples include projects in areas such as irrigation (e.g., Willems 1998, Wright and Liao 1999), agriculture (e.g., Giorgio 1998) and health care (e.g., Lucas 1998). Diffusion of ICTs in developing countries can fulfil the *goals of various institutional players* in the 'international relation game' in various ways. These include allowing developing countries to 'leapfrog' over many stages of industrialization (McGray 1999), increasing the overall utility of the network thereby benefiting users from developed as well as developing countries (Gore 1996), and providing opportunities for interaction, learning, socialization and values exchange which could promote world peace and social justice (Fink 1997; Mansell and When 1998). Realizing such potential of ICTs, international agencies are showing an increasing level of involvement in the diffusion of ICTs in developing countries. For example, technical expertise provided by the United Nations Development Program (UNDP) played an important role in the initial phase of Peru's Internet adoption (Montealegre 1999). As shown in the GrameenPhone case in this chapter, international agencies are playing an important role in the diffusion of mobile phones in Bangladesh by providing loans and equity for the mobile projects, finding foreign partners, etc.

Diffusion researchers have also studied the impact of socio-cultural factors on the diffusion of innovations. For instance, Rothwell and Wissema (1986) point out that one of the important reasons why technologies diffused relatively slower in Ancient Greece, despite its expertise in technology and mathematics, was the easy availability of cheap slave labour. Klonglan and Coward (1970) hypothesise that *sociological variables* play more important role in the *symbolic adoption phase* (adoption of the idea component of the innovation) whereas *economic variables* play more important roles in the *use adoption phase* (adoption of the actual product). Rogers (1995) argues that cellular phones led to 'status-conferral' on potential buyers (p. 246) in the U.S., resulting in favourable attitudes towards symbolic adoption. The previous section indicates that economic activities influence actual uses of the mobile phones (use adoption) for such activities as e-commerce, promotion, information search, safety, etc. Past studies have also found that *cultural factors* influence the way an *innovation is integrated* in existing ways of lives (Harris 1940). As the discussion of the elements of MED model in the previous section indicates, cultural factors have influenced the types of mobile phone uses. For instance, Japanese mobile phones are used for Samurai Romanesque, a massive multi-player online role-playing game.

Past studies have also found that 'market and infrastructure factors that control the availability of the innovation to potential adopters' (Brown et al 1976, p.100) influence the diffusion pattern. Manufacturers of new technological products such as mobile phones are likely to give priority to large distributors (Gatignon and Robertson 1985), often located in developed countries. Compounded by other unfavourable environmental factors including 'physical and social barriers' (Gatignon and Robertson 1985), perceived risk of ventures is likely to be higher in developing countries than in developed countries. Multinational companies are thus likely to delay their entry to developing markets.

4.2 Mechanisms for Accelerating Development via the MED Model

The challenge for policy makers involved in bridging the digital divide is to break the trickle-down 'hierarchical pattern' (Gatignon and Robertson 1985, p. 858) of technology diffusion, which favours developed countries. It is important to understand the 'hierarchical pattern' in the case of mobile phones and to identify opportunities for leapfrogging.

International institutions and national governments can play important roles in breaking the hierarchical pattern. The problem of supply constraint can be attacked if International institutions influence multinational companies to channel their investment in the mobile sectors of developing countries. Such investments can be further accelerated if national governments put investor-friendly policies in place such as opening markets for competition and providing tax and other incentives for mobile projects. Merely opening the markets may not be enough to overcome these barriers. Governments in developing countries may also need to launch visible mega-projects or provide additional incentives to encourage investments in mobile telecommunications. In addition, reducing the existing tariff and non-tariff barriers to mobile ICT products is likely to have positive impact on mobile diffusion. Developing locally relevant applications and content can boost the perceived relative advantage of mobile phones and mobile Internet, further increasing mobile diffusion.

Finally companies involved in mobile businesses should consider the normally adverse 'hierarchical pattern' as a business opportunity to exploit. There are over four billion potential customers not yet connected to any telecom network. What is really needed is imagination to serve this huge market profitably.

5. Cases

5.1 GrameenPhone Bangladesh

The number of subscribers of GrameenPhone, a mobile telecom company in Bangladesh, increased from 368,000 in June 2001 (GrameenPhone.com 2001b) to 500,000 in early 2002 (GrameenPhone.com 2002). GrameenPhone has become the fastest growing and the largest mobile phone firm in South Asia. Thanks to the rapid expansion of GrameenPhone subscriber base, cell phone users in Bangladesh outnumber the fixed-line telephone subscribers.[4] The case of GrameenPhone (GP) Company shows that the trickle-down 'hierarchical pattern' of technology diffusion can be overcome effectively if proper policies are put in place at various levels.

The success story of GP can be explained with the help of the MED model proposed in the previous section of this chapter. The MED model indicates that national and international level policies influence the level of investment and hence the availability and price structure of mobile phones. The Bangladeshi government liberalized the telecom sector in 1995 and decided to auction cell phone operation licenses to private firms (Cohen 2001) (*national level policy*).

Grameen Telecom was awarded license to access 300 kilometres of fibre route along the railway lines between Dhaka and Chittagong, to which it can connect its radio base stations (UNCTAD 1997). Three foreign telecom companies – Telenor of Norway, Marubeni of Japan and Gonophone of the U.S. – were attracted to collaborate with Grameen Telecom because of its possession of this license and GrameenPhone was formed as a joint venture.

As explained in the previous section, *national level policies* are not always favourable for the diffusion of a new technology. In case of the GP, when Iqbal Quadir[5] was knitting together his project of providing mobile phones to rural Bangladeshis, his idea was not well received by development agencies and telecommunications companies (Boyle 1998). Like in many developing countries, Bangladeshi policy makers viewed mobile phones as the communication tools of rich business people. Quadir was, however, successful in linking up his idea with Grameen Bank that was established by Mohammed Yunus to loan small amounts without collateral to the Bangladeshis who were 'unbankable' for other financial institutions (Chowdhury 2001).

International agencies also played a crucial role in accelerating the diffusion of mobile phones in Bangladesh (*international level policies*). Of the total $125 million initial funding of GrameenPhone, $60 million was loaned from four international agencies – International Finance Corporation (IFC), Asian Development Bank (ADB), Commonwealth Development Corporation in Britain and Norwegian Agency for Development and Co-operation. In addition to a loan of $16.7 million, Asian Development Bank (ADB) provided an equity investment of $1.6 million (Wescott 2001). Similarly, IFC provided a $16.67 million loan and an equity investment of $1.57 million towards the company's expansion (World Bank 2001).

The MED model also argues that *providing appropriate education* and training to potential adopters can accelerate mobile adoption. In the case of GrameenPhone, one of the criteria for selecting a village-phone operator is that at least one member of the family knows English letters and numbers (Quadir 2000). For those interested in becoming operators but lacking such knowledge, GrameenPhone provides training.

Mobile technology effect shown in the MED model has played an important role in the diffusion of mobile phones in Bangladesh. The fixed as well as variable costs of operating mobile phone services in Bangladesh are lower than those of landline phones. For example, the fixed cost to install each mobile phone for GrameenPhone came out to be $735 (Quadir 2000), which compares very favourably with International Telecommunication Union's estimate of $1,300 to add one landline phone for a poor economy like Bangladesh. According to Iqbal Quadir, founder of GrameenPhone, the rural phone system, using mobile phones, is three times more profitable than urban phone systems in Bangladesh (WRI 2000). In fact, the GrameenPhone system used in rural Bangladesh delivers overall better quality than landline phones at a much lower rate. A reporter of *On- The New World of Communication* expresses her experience:

> Two years ago [in 1999], my hotel in Dhaka, the capital of Bangladesh, were not able to connect me to Madras in South India because of which I could not wish my child a happy birthday. 'Sorry ma'am, international lines are down,' was the reply. But a few hours later, in a small village 35 miles from Dhaka, Hasina, the village 'telephone lady' connected me on her mobile phone at half the rate.[6]

Innovations such as *prepaid pricing* are also driving the rapid penetration of mobile phones in Bangladesh. GrameenPhone is making its EASY pre-paid mobile phones available from many sales centres and authorised sales outlets located around the country (Grameenphone.com 2001).

The propensity to share communications tools *(cultural factor)* is another factor influencing the diffusion pattern of mobile phones. Collectivist eastern culture of Bangladesh emphasises the welfare of a community rather than an individual. The propensity to share is also driven by economic reasons in developing countries like Bangladesh. Research indicates that each phone serves an average of nearly 70 customers in Bangladesh (Businessweek.com 2001).

This case also illustrates how mobile phones can bring multiplier effects as well as social change in developing countries. Cohen (2001), Quadir (2000) and Wescott (2001) provide several examples of such effects of mobile phones in Bangladesh.

- One woman who wanted to raise chickens could not undertake the project earlier because she was afraid that if the chicken developed disease she would not be able to call a veterinarian on time.
- Another woman reported that she was able save her child, who was running a dangerous high fever by calling the doctor in time.
- A farmer said that he was planning to cultivate bananas on a larger scale because mobile phones would enable him to obtain the market price in good time to make correct selling decisions.
- Immigrant workers throughout the world with roots in Bangladeshi villages can now call home to find out how their families are doing and if the money they send home is indeed reaching its destination.
- Studies have found that with increased in income and participation in family decision-making, women have become socially empowered in Bangladesh. Because villagers have to travel to the phone ladies' homes to make or receive calls, their homes have become an important place in the village. Moreover, unlike in other public places, women can go to the Village Phone Office even unescorted by a male relative.

5.2 GWCom China

Whereas the GrameenPhone case provides an insight into the factors influencing the diffusion of mobile phones in general, this case focuses on more advanced uses of mobile phones. Unlike GrameenPhone, which has at least some component of philanthropy, GWCom runs entirely on a commercial basis.

GWCom is a mobile wireless applications services provider. It launched its wireless portal byair.com[7] in 1998 to provide timely information and e-commerce capabilities such as stock trading and banking to users with mobile phone or wireless palmtop devices in the U.S. and Greater China. The company provides its networks as well as handheld device (netset) to individual investors.

By March 2000, byair.com had over 6,000 subscribers with the number of stocks traded as high as 3,500 daily and number of page views 250,000. By early 2002, it delivered services to over 250,000 mobile users as well as larger number of users of Information on Demand (IOD) and messaging services. GWCom users mostly use the two-way paging capability for trading stock electronically and such transaction-type services have turned out to be the 'killer application' (TDAP 2002).

GWCom's growth trajectory has been influenced by a number of factors. First, thanks to factors such as heavy investment in and reengineering of Chinese telecom sector; huge foreign investment inflow in Chinese mobile telecom sector and the Chinese government's promotion of mobile phones as 'people's phone' (*national level policy*), China has become the largest mobile market in the Asia-Pacific region (Kshetri and Cheung 2002).

Second, the Chinese government granted license (*national level policy*) to the company to operate in the radio-frequency spectrum allocated for mobile-data transmission.

Third, it has found domestic and foreign partners to finance its growth as well as to provide relevant content. New World Infrastructure invested US$49 million in GWCom in 2000.[8] GWCom has partnered with over 30 Internet content providers and e-commerce portals both in the U.S. and Greater China and connected with more than 20 securities trading firms. Moreover, China's entry in the World Trade Organisation (WTO) has made conditions more favourable for finding foreign partners in its business *(international level policy)*. As a source indicates, GWCom is in the 'most lucrative segment of China telecom/Internet market and best positioned to benefit China's entry of WTO.[9]

Fourth, the company's pricing structure made stock investment on its paging network more attractive than on the fixed network (a *mobile technology effect*). Because of low PC penetration and relatively higher Internet access fees, the only way for a large proportion of Chinese to trade stock is to read newspapers or magazines and then pick up a phone.[10] These factors have made GWCom's web portal more attractive (Ebusinessforum.com 2000). GWCom describes its network product, PLANET, as a 'high-capacity and low cost cellular packet data network that is optimised for serving wireless palm computers and PDAs.[11] The users pay a monthly service charge of only about US$5-10. With the increasing demand, GWCom has decided to specialise in the mobile wireless data network infrastructure and outsourced the equipment manufacturing to Ericsson and some Chinese vendors. This is likely to result in further reduction in the price.

As indicated in the MED model, major economic activities (*economic factors*) influence the types of mobile phone uses. China's stock market is growing very fast[12] and the stock exchange companies are located in Shanghai and Shenzhen. GW Trade selected these two cities for the initial trial. Wireless users have been using GWCom's application platforms to conduct online trading since 1998 in Shanghai[13] and from 1999 in Shenzhen. In March 2000, 3,000 investors in Shanghai, and 100 in Shenzhen, were trading stocks over the paging networks managed by GWCom. The average daily volume of 3,000 Shanghai users in early-2000 was $3.6 million, about 30 times as much as the average trading volume on stockstar.com, the largest and most popular Web-based stock trading company.

This case provides additional evidence to support the view that *economic factors* influence the types of uses of mobile technology. In developing countries like China, cheaper, easy-to-rollout, mass-market network using non-voice technologies like paging have the potential to offer a cheap and reliable way of transmitting data that could be a viable alternative to the mobile phone. In other parts of the world however, big players do not follow the paging route (Holland 2000). The GWCom case also provides some evidence of the leapfrogging potential of mobile technologies. For instance, the world's first electronic stock trading over the wireless network took place on the GWCom network in 1998 in Shanghai.

6. Discussion and Implications

This chapter suggests that although economic factors do matter, they explain only a small portion of the variation in the diffusion patterns of mobile phones. Characteristics of mobile phones such as zero requirement of electricity and complete geographical flexibility make these a more appropriate technology for developing countries. Moreover, the experience of Bangladesh indicates that the per unit cost of installing a mobile network is just about half of that of a fixed network. Mobile technology is, thus, a better technology at a cheaper price – a perfect technology for developing countries. Recent innovations in pricing such as prepaid pricing (thus eliminating credit checks, billing, etc.) have made mobile phones more attractive, opening possibilities for faster diffusion of mobile phones.

The GrameenPhone case indicates that the potential benefits of mobile phones for rural populations can be realized if proper policies at various levels are combined with innovative ideas and entrepreneurial culture. The case also shows that, for technologies such as mobile phones, national and international level initiatives may help overcome the conventional trickle-down 'hierarchical pattern' of diffusion. The causes of rapid diffusion of mobile phone in Bangladesh identified in the GrameenPhone case, however, may not be 'detachable, isolable, homogeneous, independently operative, and hence susceptible of being added to or subtracted from the causal complex' (MacIver 1964, p.94). Put differently, they cannot be 'individually analyzed and assessed' (Fischer 1970, p.179). Hence, a developing economy may have to implement the strategy in its own form, taking into account the characteristics of mobile technology as well as the prevailing local conditions. The MED model can provide guidance in this regard.

The discussion and cases indicate that the locus of mobile diffusion in developing countries is likely to be different from that in the developed countries in several ways. For instance, two-way pagers are popular in China whereas other developed countries are not following this route of mobile technology development. Moreover, in developed countries mobile phones are substituting the fixed phone. The skills needed to operate a mobile phone and a fixed phone are the same. Since mobile networks are 'compatible' with fixed networks, mobile service providers are able to create a critical mass immediately. These conditions do not exist in many developing countries.

The GrameenPhone case indicates that there is in fact 'market' for mobile phones even in the poorest countries. As rapid technological advancements make mobile phones increasingly accessible and affordable, the only missing variables in the digital divide equation are appropriate policies on the part of governments and imaginative marketing strategies of mobile set manufacturers and service providers. As indicated in the previous section, mobile phones in developing countries have the potential to benefit all players in the 'international relations game' and hence represent the right technology for international agencies to focus on. The GWCom case indicates that, apart from directly influencing factors such as providing loans and assistance, international agencies such as the WTO can also indirectly influence mobile diffusion by making the market more competitive.

The GrameenPhone case also indicates that manufacturers and service providers have a serious lack of understanding of the unique needs of potential adopters in developing countries. For example, although GrameenPhone provides training to those who are interested in the business, the requirement to learn English in order to qualify as an operator, may reduce a person's willingness to become one. Given that there are already about 400,000 subscribers and the number is growing at an exponential rate, providing mobile telecom products and services in the local language would help accelerate mobile diffusion and at the same time boost the revenues of manufacturers and service providers.

Notes

1 Most farmers from developing countries are commodity producers that come low down in the supply chain. Since e-commerce has shifted power from sellers to buyers, corporate buyers from developed countries are likely to squeeze the profit margins of farmers from developing countries (see Economist.com 2000).

2 See http://www.hp.com/e-inclusion/en/project/cats.html

3 For instance, potential adopters of mobile phones in developing countries may not have prior experience of using 'regular' phones.

4 In 2002, there were over 650,000 mobile phone users in Bangladesh compared to 590,000 fixed-line users (GrameenPhone.com 2002).

5 Iqbal Quadir founded GrameenPhone in collaboration with Grameen Bank of Bangladesh and Telenor AS of Norway.

6 See 'Micro-steps to mega-changes' *On- The New World of Communication, February 2001,* http://on.magazine.se/pdf/1_2001/Portrait.On_1_2001.pdf

7 GWcom restructured the corporation in April 2002, dividing the business into two companies. The short messaging service (SMS) business has been renamed to byair Corporation which encompasses the mobile media services. The network business is GWcomPlanet Corporation.

8 See http://www.gwcom.com/html/news0303.htm

9 See http://www.chinatelecomconference.com/china-dc/bio/bio13.html

10 See http://www.gwcom.com.cn/gwcom_news-m17.htm

11 See http://www.chinatelecomconference.com/china-dc/bio/bio13.html

12 See http://www.gwcom.com.cn/gwcom_news-m17.htm

13 The world's first electronic stock trading over the wireless network took place on byair.com in Shanghai in 1998 (See http://www.mobic.com/news/2000/01/gwcom_receives_capital_investmen.htm)

References

Bhatnagar, Pradip (1999) 'Telecom Reforms in Developing Countries and the Outlook for Electronic Commerce,' *Journal of World Trade* 33(4): pp.143-158.

Boyle, David (1998), 'A Mobile Phone is a Cow,' *New Statesman*, July 31, p. 33.

Brown, Lawrence, Edward Malecki and Aron Spector (1976), 'Adopter Categories in a Spatial Context: Alternative Explanations for an Empirical Regularity,' *Rural Sociology* 41, pp. 99-118.

Businessweek.com (2001), 'Providing Rural Phone Services Profitably in Poor Countries,' http://adsections.businessweek.com/digital/profit.htm

Chowdhury, Afsan (2001), 'Local Heroes,' *New Internationalist*, March, pp. 22-23.

Cohen, Nevin (2001), What Works: Grameen Telecom's Village Phones, World Resources Institute, http://www.digitaldividend.org/pdf/grameen.pdf.

Dalum, B., J. Fagerberg and U. Jorgensen (1988) 'Small Open Economies in the World Market for Electronics: The Case of the Nordic Countries,' In Small Countries Facing the Technological Revolution, ed. B.-A. Lundvall and C. Freeman. pp. 113-38. London: Pinter Publishers.

Ebusinessforum.com (2000a), *GW Trade: Serving a High-tech Niche in China*, March 23rd, http://www.ebusinessforum.com.

Ebusinessforum.com (2000b) 'Africa and the Internet: An Unrealised Opportunity,' 6 May 2000, http://www.ebusinessforum.com

Ebusinessforum.com (2001) 'Business Asia: How Mobile Technology and the Internet Come Together,' 15 February.

Economist (1999), *Survey: Telecommunications*, October 9th.

Economist.com (2000), 'Falling through the Net,' September 23.

Ernberg, J. (1998), 'Universal Access for Rural Development: From Action to Strategies,' IRST International Conference on Rural Telecommunication, November 30 to Dec 2, Washington DC.

Fink, Robert A (1997) 'Look What else the Internet can Do', *Medical Economics* 74(5): pp. 197-201.

Fischer, David Hackett (1970), *Historians' Fallacies: Toward a Logic of Historical Thought*: New York: Harper & Row.

Garcia, D. L. and Gorenflo, N. R. (2001), 'Rural Networking Cooperatives: Lessons for International Development and Aid Strategies,' http://www.fao.org/docrep/x0295e/x0295e21.htm.

Gatignon, Hubert and Thomas S Robertson (1985) 'A Propositional Inventory for New Diffusion Research,' *Journal of Consumer Research* 11, pp. 849-867.

Giorgio, Emmanuelle Moors de (1998) 'The rural finance revolution,' *African Business*; (December), pp. 33-34.

Gore, Al (1996), 'Bringing Information to the World: The Global Information Infrastructure,' *Harvard Journal of Law and Technology* 1 (winter).

Grameenphone.com (2001a), GP Pre-Paid phones available now, http://www.grameenphone.com/

Grameenphone.com (2001b) GP Largest Operator in South Asia, http://www.grameenphone.com/news/new.htm

Grameenphone.com (2002) 500,000 subscribers and counting, http://www.grameenphone.com/

Hammond, Allen L. (2001), 'Digitally Empowered Development,' *Foreign Affairs, 80, 2,* pp.96-106.

Harris, S. The White Knife Shoshani of Nevada. In Ralph Linton (Ed.) *Acculturation in Seven American Indian Tribes,* New York, Appleton-Century Company Incorporated, 1940, pp. 39-116.

Holland, Lorien (2000), 'Turning a New Pager,' *Far Eastern Economic Review,* 163 (8), February 24, p. 44.

ILO (2001), *World Employment Report 2001: Life at Work in the Information Economy,* http://www.ilo.org/public/english/support/publ/wer/overview.htm.

ITU (1999), 'The "Mobilization" of Bangladesh: The introduction of cellular phones has dramatically changed the lives of businesses and individuals,' *World Telecommunication Day 1999*, Geneva: International Telecommunications Union.

ITU (2000) *The ITU Takes Mobile into the Third Millennium* http://www.itu.int/plweb-cgi/fastweb?getdoc+view1+www+44474+18++standard.

ITU (2002), ICT - Free Statistics Home Page, http://www.itu.int/ITU-D/ict/statistics/at_glance/cellular01.pdf

King, J.L., Gurbaxani, V., Kraemer, K.L., McFarlan, F.W., Raman, K.S., and Yap, C.S. (1994), 'Institutional Factors in Information Technology Innovation,' *Information System Research*, 5(2), pp. 139-169.

Klonglan, Gerald E. and E. Walter Coward (1970), 'The Concept of Symbolic Adoption: A Suggested Interpretation', *Rural Sociology*, 35 (1), pp. 77-83.

Kraemer, Kenneth L., Gurbaxani, Vijay and King, John Leslie (1992) 'Economic Development, Government Policy, and the Diffusion of Computing in Asia-Pacific Countries', *Public Administration Review*, 52 (2), pp.146-56.

Kshetri, Nir (2001), 'The Dynamics of Government Regulation and E-Commerce Development: A Comparison of Malaysia and Singapore,' *Proceedings of the 23rd Annual Conference of Pacific Telecommunications Council*, January 14-18, Honolulu, HI.

Kshetri, Nir and Maggie Kei Cheung (2002), 'What Factors are Driving China's Mobile Diffusion?,' Electronic Markets, 12(1), pp. 22-26.

Kshetri, Nir and Nikhilesh Dholakia (2001) 'Impact of Cultural and Political Factors on the Adoption of Digital Signatures in Asia,' *Proceedings of the Americas' Conference on Information System*, Boston, Massachusetts, August 3-5.

Lopez, Asbel (2000),'The South Goes Mobile,' *UNESCO Courier*, July/August http://www.unesco.org/courier/2000_07/uk/connex.htm.

Lucas, Adetokunbo (1998) 'WHO at country level,' *The Lancet*, Mar 7th, pp.743-747.

MacIver, R.M. (1964), *Social Causation*, rev. ed. New York.

Mansell, Robin and When, Uta (1998) *Knowledge Societies: Information Technology for Sustainable Development,* New York: Oxford University Press.

McGrey, Douglas (1999), 'The Silicon Archipelago,' *Daedalus*, 128 (2), pp.147-176.

Montealegre, Ramiro (1999), 'A Temporal Model of Institutional Intervention for Information Technology Adoption in Less-Developed Countries,' *Journal of Management Information Systems*, 16(1), pp.207-232.

Orlikowski, W.J. And J.J. Baroudi (1991), 'Studying Information Technology in Organizations: Research Approaches and Assumptions,' *Information Systems Research*, 2(2), pp. 1-28.

Porter, Michael E and Stern, Scott (2001) 'Innovation: Location matters,' *Sloan Management Review*, 42(4): pp.28-36.

Quadir, Iqbal Z. (2000), 'Connecting Bangladeshi Villages,' http://www.devmedia.org/documents/ACF1055.htm

Rai, Saritha (2001), 'In Rural India, a Passage to Wirelessness,' *New York Times*, August 4, pp. C1-C3.

Rogers, E M. (1966) *Diffusions of Innovations*, New York: Free Press.

Rogers, E.M. (1983) *The Diffusion of Innovations*, 3rd edn. New York: Free Press.

Rogers, E.M. (1995) *The Diffusion of Innovations*, 4th edn. New York: Free Press.

Rothwell, Roy and Hans Wissema (1986), 'Technology, Culture and Public Policy,' *Technovation*, 4, pp.91-115.

Schwartz, Ephraim (2001), ' "Telephone Ladies" Turn into Entrepreneurs; and will Silicon Valley Change its Dress Code,' *InfoWorld*, February 4, p. 59.

Sebunya, Crespo (2001), 'Mobile Phone Use Has Improved Public Discourse', July 10, http://allafrica.com/stories/200107100343.html

Shultz, Clifford J II and Anthony Pecotich (1997) 'Marketing and Development in the Transition Economies of Southeast Asia: Policy Explication, Assessment, and Implications,' *Journal of Public Policy & Marketing*; 16 (1), pp. 55-68.

Stout, Kristie Lu (2001) 'China Mobile Has Eyes Only for 2.5G', CNN.Com, 5 June.

TDAP (2002), 'China's New Regulatory Environment Spurs UNICOM's Subscriber Growth' Interview with Wang Jianzhou, Executive Vice President of China Unicom, *TelecommunicationsDevelopment,Asia-Pacific,* http://www.tdap.co.uk/uk/archive/interviews/inter(unicom_0012).html.

The World Bank (2000a) *World Development Report: Entering the 21st Century,* http://www.worldbank.org/wdr/2000/fullreport.html

The World Bank (2000b), The Role of Science and Technology in Small and Medium Sized Enterprise Development, http://www.worldbank.org/html/fpd/technet/gk-smes.htm

Tsuchiyama, Ray (1999), 'The Cellular Industry in China: Politics, Rewards, and Risks,' *Telecommunications Review*, 2nd quarter.

UNCTAD (1997) Telecommunications, Business Facilitation and Trade Efficiency, Expert Meeting on Telecommunications, Business Facilitation and Trade Efficiency Geneva, 8 - 10 September 1997 http://www.unctad.org/en/special/c3em3p2.htm

UNDP (2001), *Human Development Report 2000*, United Nations Development Program, New York, 2001 http://www.undp.org/hdr2001/completenew.pdf

Van de Ven, Andrew, Douglas Polley, Raghu Garud and Sankaran Venkataraman (1999), The Innovations Journey, New York: Oxford University Press.

Wescott, Clay (2001), E-Government: Enabling Asia-Pacific Governments and Citizens to do Public Business Differently, Workshop on Governance and ICT, 14 June Bangkok,Thailand, http://www.worldbank.org/html/extdr/offrep/eap/eapprem/govpaperwescott.pdf

Willems, Peter (1998) 'UN team up with the Taliban to end opium production,' *Middle East*, (April) 11-12.

Wilson, Drew (2001) 'Is Asia ready for M-Commerce?' *Electronic News*, Jan 15, 47 (3), 30.

Wong, P. K. (1998) 'Leveraging the global information revolution for economic development: Singapore's evolving information industry strategy' *Information Systems Research*, 9(4): pp.323-341.

World Bank (2001) 'Linking Rural Bangladesh Through Cellular Phones IFC invests in Grameenphone,' http://wbln1018.worldbank.org/sar/sa.nsf/2991b676f98842f0852567d7005d2cba/71044b08a15612588525686d0060040b?OpenDocument

Wright, Daniel and Liao, Darlene M (1999) 'The other side of China's prosperity,' *The China Business Review*, 26 (5), pp.22-24.Yin, R. (1989), *Case Study Research: Design and Methods*, Newbury, California: Sage Publications.

Chapter 16

ICT Networking in Vietnam: The Limitations of an Information Needs Assessment

Grant Boyle

1. Introduction

Since the mid-1990s there has been considerable discussion in development circles over the potential of new ICTs to facilitate access to information and opportunity in developing countries. The United Nations Development Program (UNDP) says for example:

> The ultimate objective is a knowledge and information society – one with the ability, capacity and skills to generate and capture new knowledge and to effectively access, absorb and use information, data and knowledge with the support of ICTs. (UNDP, 2000:1)

In addition to opportunities, there is also discussion of dangers. The *G-8 Digital Opportunities Task Force* discusses the necessity of overcoming the 'digital divide', where the divide is defined as:

> unequal possibilities to access and contribute to information, knowledge and networks, as well as to benefit from the development enhancing capabilities of ICT. (Crowder and Michiels, 2001:4)

In reflecting on my participation in an ICT project in Vietnam, I argue here that programmes to deploy ICT infrastructures may underestimate the complexity of social change involved in such deployments. What I am concerned with is the degree to which complex social development goals become seen as technical problems when ICTs are a project focus. Although there is a range of approaches among those involved in ICT transfers, the dominant discourse in recent years has been one of marked technological determinism (Heeks, 1999), as demonstrated by the above quotations.

The case in question is a university capacity-building programme, which linked five Vietnamese research institutes collaborating on poverty reduction in

Vietnam through an Internet-based network. As a participant in this programme, I was part of a team that had high expectations for what the Internet could accomplish in this setting. The significant organizational change, however, underlying the computer deployment was highlighted for this writer in a study undertaken to identify the substantive 'information needs' of one partner institution. It became apparent in trying to assess those needs, that many vital information processes among the recipients could not be met with computers and Internet connections. The information attainable through computer databases and e-mail correspondence seemed less locally relevant than the 'information' constituted in the personal relations of the research group. The organisational culture of the institution, and specifically the role of authority relations in the Vietnamese context, diverged considerably from implied culture of outward information seeking and information sharing of the envisioned network.

This paper describes the story of carrying out the information needs assessment and consolidates various aspects of re-evaluation that took place after conducting the assessment. A key assumption behind the assessment was that the network should meet the needs of the recipients and that those recipients should develop new incentives to use the network. This appears to be an increasingly common approach to ICTs in development. For example, Madon remarks:

> Connecting countries is just the beginning and, though expensive, perhaps the easiest part. Individuals, organisations, even countries must have the incentives and capabilities to use information effectively. Especially for the poor and vulnerable, strengthening their capacity to receive and use knowledge will require special effort, and knowledge that comes from the outside will need to be adapted to fit local contexts and needs. (2000, p. 86)

While the exploration of information needs and incentives is probably the best step forward, there are questions about what this means at a project level. Surely, for example, there is a vast array of processes regarding incentives and capabilities for information-use that already exist in developing countries. Are we referring to *new* incentives and capabilities? Which ones? What processes of change (in social relations, organizational norms, forms of production, educational styles etc.) are implied in such calls to action and how *directly and explicitly* are those processes of change dealt with or discussed in policy discourses and ICT programs? Does the idea of 'information needs' adequately capture what we are trying to get at? Akrich (1992: p.222) suggests that

> ...technical objects and people are brought into being in a process of reciprocal definition, in which objects are defined by their subjects and subjects by their objects.

Here, I aim to deal primarily with the latter component of this interaction: the definition of subject by object. There has been a considerable amount written on the problems of adopting a narrow view of technology itself in the context of information technology transfers to developing countries, where technologies, as objects, are seen by their subjects (planners and designers) as discrete, 'value-free', a-cultural instruments (Avgerou and Walsham, 2000; Bhatnagar and Odedra, 1992). Here, I am primarily concerned with the reciprocal side of that discussion concerning how those instruments reflexively generate a new 'subject' or new way of looking at the world, and ultimately how ICTs impact the way we see development goals such as cooperation, communication, learning, research and so on. What is the adequacy of labels like 'information exchange' or 'information absorption' for such processes? Below I describe the limitations of an 'information needs assessment' as conceived by a Canadian planner in Vietnam seeking to identify the relevance of an ICT network and aims to highlight the social and organisational basis of the information needs of Localized Poverty Reduction in Vietnam (LPRV) partners.

Certainly there are political-economic and ideological undercurrents that impact the way we understand the role of information technologies in socio-economic development. Valdes (1987) and Avgerou (2000), for example, discuss the influence of western modernity in forging the way technologies are understood and deployed in developing countries. It would seem that any discussion of information technology transfer necessarily implicates larger issues, which pervade many North-South discussions. Although these concerns are related to the discussion below, my approach is to consider the specific aspects of concept and design at a programme level and the lessons that flow from my involvement in a particular project. However, it is useful to begin with a rough sketch of dominant and critical understanding of information in disciplinary discourses in order to carve a larger context for a discussion of information needs.

2. Information in Society

The treatment of information (and knowledge) as an independent and essential aspect of development is not unlike the treatment of information in many contemporary theories of social change. Anthony Oettinger, for example, argues:

> ...every society is an information society and every organization an information organization, just as every organism is an information organism.

Information is necessary to 'organize and run everything from a cell to General Motors or the Pentagon.' (cf., Robins and Webster, 1987. p. 97) And Castells (1996) describes a new information technology-based economic paradigm in a 'network society', centred around micro-electronic information technologies, where 'information is raw material' and 'technologies act on information.'[1] According to Hobart and Schiffman:

> Today's scientists, engineers, and technicians, not to mention social scientists, scholars, and bureaucrats of all stripes, seek, and find information everywhere. From the movement of subatomic quarks to the evolution of the entire cosmos, many natural systems are understood as governed by the information they receive and process. Social systems too, in what some pundits tout as the postindustrial

> age, are seen as structured by information, rather than say, production. Information is now commonly depicted as the general principle of organized phenomena. (1998, p. 3)

This type of emphasis on information in social relations is often attributed to the work of Shannon and Weaver (communications theory), and Wiener (cybernetics) in the middle 1950s (Roszak, 1986; Boland, 1987). In the case of Shannon and Weaver, information was understood as a transmittable message in communications engineering. As for Wiener's cybernetics, information was seen as 'messages' or 'feedback' in systems, where both natural and social systems rely on feedback to be self-regulating:

> Information is a name for the content of which is exchanged with the outer world as we adjust to it, and make our adjustments felt upon it. The process of receiving and of using information is the process of our adjusting to the contingencies of the outer environment, and of our living effectively within that environment. (Wiener, 1950, p. 19)

Despite the resonance of such theories, there has been difficulty in operationlizing such ideas in specific terms since the beginning. In a critique on cybernetics, for example, Jonas (1953) emphasises 'purpose' in social relations rather than 'information' as in Wiener's theory. He says that action is not based necessarily on received information or feedback per se, but rather on the contingents of human need and interest.

> According to cybernetics, society is a communications network for the transmitting, exchanging, and pooling of information, and it is this that holds it together. No emptier notion of society has ever been propounded. Nothing is said on what the information is about, and why it should be relevant to have it...Any theory of man's sociability, however, crude or distorted, that takes into account his being a creature of need and desire, and that looks for the vital concerns which bring men together, is more to the point. (*ibid*, p. 191)

Similarly, Marvin contends that

> information cannot be said to exist at all unless it has meaning, and meaning is established in social relationships with culture and value. (Marvin, 1987)

> Our own ethnocentric and historically provincial notion of information has narrowed our analysis of it to forms of expression and transaction in which it becomes a self-contained series of autonomous products without context....There are communities where oral communications systems have been in place for centuries, but which count for little in any world that measures the value of information by the range and speed of its travels and the number of its packages. (*ibid*, p. 57)

Moving into the international development realm, critical examinations of the role of information as a developmental resource have taken a similar route.

Menou says, for example, that proving information is an essential resource may not be 'solvable in general terms.' As a developmental resource, 'it seems almost impossible to identify general benefits and their related indicators, as the concept, nature, and goals of development may differ from one person to another, from one time to another, and from one situation to another.' (1993, p.37) It is important to note, then, that the theoretical importance of information in western thoeries of society does not necessarily translate into the importance of information in specific social contexts and development projects. Although this may be a straightforward argument, a considerable number of ICT projects and policy positions likely, adopt an understading of information that has its origins in theories like cybernetics or network society. There is a risk that ICT deployments are based more on an ideology of information rather than the objectives and needs of the specific recipients involved.

3. Case Background

The 'Localized Poverty Reduction in Vietnam' (LPRV) programme is a development co-operation project that brings together five Vietnamese universities and two Canadian universities. The goal is to help implement policy reforms in Vietnam aimed at making social planning and public policy- making more decentralized and integrative. Specifically, the programme aims to build domestic university capacity in participatory public planning methods at five designated Centres for Poverty Reduction (CPRs) in Vietnam, by undertaking a series of development projects in local communes and integrating lessons learnt into scholarship and practice. The programme can be seen in the larger context of the decentralisation and institutional reform, which has been taking place in Vietnam since that country began restructuring in 1986 under the 'Doi Moi' process.[2]

The deployment of information technologies to the five CPRs (each having approximately 12 researchers and students) has been viewed in LPRV by Vietnamese and Canadian planners as a key component of the overall capacity-building programme. Primarily, the technology was intended to service research and community planning efforts, as well as to solidify the cohesion of the project, provide lasting opportunities for institutional networking in Vietnam, and lay the infrastructure for enhanced information resource access at the universities. Specific technologies included:

- PCs (two at each CPR) with Internet connections.
- Internet and e-mail software.
- Electronic libraries of community planning and poverty reduction literature from international sources.
- Computer and software training.

Although no specific levels of use were specified at the time of deployment, expectations for the technology were high. It was hoped that communication between university partners would be 'effective, deep, and regular', and emerging programme outcomes and research materials would be shared and accessed using e-mail, programme websites, electronic libraries and the Web. As one Canadian planner reflected:

> We assumed that there was a paucity of information available to our partners and that two steps: 1. supplying that information and 2. creating channels and opportunities for dialogue would result in a true functioning network of collaborating researchers. (Verlaan, 2001)

As the deployment entered its third year, these aspirations appeared not to be forthcoming. Although the tools were used occasionally for administrative purposes, use of the Internet for programme research or collaboration was minimal. Over a two-month period in the summer of 2000, I worked with one institute, the Dalat CPR, as a participant observer in an exploratory study focused on raising local awareness of the network and gaining insights into why it was used at considerably lower levels than was originally hoped for. A major part of the study was the information needs assessment.[3] Before exploring the details of the case, I will sketch a rough background of social relations in Vietnam to highlight the nature of organisational change called for in the network.

4. Organizational Change Explored

This section explores one slice of the larger potential discussion of the socio-cultural environment in Vietnam by looking at the impact of *micro-level* authority relations in Vietnamese society and how such relations influence incentives to adopt technologies for research and collaboration in LPRV. What I would like to suggest is that the legacy of micro level, superior-subordinate organizational linkages in Vietnam is a key factor to be considered in explaining low levels of use of the network for collaboration and research. While descriptions of national cultures and socio-cultural structures and behaviours always risk criticisms of stereotyping, denial of cross-cultural differences is equally inappropriate and the analyses provided below do represent components of real, albeit varying, influence within Vietnam's socio-cultural environment.

4.1 Patron-Client Organizational Structures in Southeast Asia

According to Scott (1977) the traditional pattern of interaction in political organizations in Southeast Asia is superior-subordinate exchange relationships, characterized by reciprocal and personal ties between people or groups who control unequal resources. According to Scott,

> The basic pattern is an informal cluster consisting of a power figure who is in a position to give security, inducements, or both, and his personal followers who, in return for such benefits, contribute their loyalty and personal assistance to the

> patron's designs. Such vertical patterns of patron-client linkages represent an important structural principle of Southeast Asian politics. (*ibid*, p. 124)

The reciprocal bond that constitutes the basis for patron-client structures, is characterized by *an imbalance in exchange* between the two partners, (where the client is unable to reciprocate in full and is thus bound to the patron), by a *face-to-face* relationship, (continued reciprocity establishes trust and affection among the pair), and by a diffuse or *whole-person* relationship, (covering a wide range of potential personal exchanges). According to Scott, the vitality of patron-client structures in traditional and contemporary Southeast Asian societies is a result of the persistence of inequalities in control of wealth, status, and power; the relative absence of firm, impersonal guarantees of security or status, and the inability of kinship units to facilitate personal security or advancement.

4.2 The Confucian State

Neher (1987) suggests that deference to authority has been a central characteristic of Vietnamese political philosophy:

> Historically, Vietnamese attitudes and beliefs were determined by Confucian philosophy, which pervaded Vietnam for centuries. Confucianism stressed principles of government under which political authority was centralized, with the emperor at the top and a mandarin bureaucracy administering the state according to its whims.
>
> The centralized mandarin state was crucial for building an extensive network of dikes for irrigation, for preserving national independence, especially against constant intervention of the Chinese, and for guarding against peasant revolts. To carry out these goals, the state had the capacity to mobilize fully the entire society.
>
> Two important values emerged from the traditional Confucianist state. First, traditional Vietnamese culture rested in the notions of duties of the lower to the higher: the ruled to the ruler, the son to the father, and the pupil to the teacher. Second, the individual did not view himself as an independent and isolated person, for he did not distinguish himself from his position in society. Obligations to superiors were the cement of the Confucian order. These obligations were translated into deferential and unquestioning behavior toward those in authority. (*ibid*, p. 144)

4.3 Family Relationships as Models of Social Organization

Drawing primarily on Vietnamese folklore, Jamieson (1995) identifies the hierarchical structure of the family as a defining archetype for greater social relations in pre-colonial Vietnam.[4]

> Family relationships were models of social organization. Both child-rearing practices and formal education emphasized learning to behave properly toward other family members. First and foremost, children were taught filial piety (*hieu*), to obey and respect and honor their parents. Children were made to feel keenly

> that they owed parents a moral debt (*on*) so immense as to be unpayable...The parent child relationship was at the very core of Vietnamese culture, dominating everything else. (*ibid*, p. 16)

Unlike most Western children, children growing up in traditional Vietnamese families learned dependence and nurturance, not independence. They learned the importance of hierarchy, not equality. They learned the rewards of submission to those in senior status, not assertiveness. The paradigmatic example for extending this basic family model to society was *de*. One was suppose to behave toward those senior to one, or of higher rank, or older, as if they were older brothers.

Younger brothers were supposed to be self-denying and docile in their relationships with older brothers. Yet in Vietnamese folk tales younger brothers prosper despite their meekness. They triumph precisely because they are true to the prescribed role behavior appropriate to the situation. They were supposed to be meek and compliant to older brothers, as toward parents, despite all provocation. In submitting even to unreasonable demands from an older brother, they were earning merit. Never does a younger brother triumph because of boldness, cleverness or assertiveness. The ideal role model provided by school and family and folklore is one of compliance with wishes of superordinate figures in a social hierarchy: child to parent, younger brother to older brother, and wife to husband. (*ibid*, p. 17)

4.4 Communist Neo-Traditionalism

Superior-subordinate relations in Vietnam can also be explained within the context of the single-party communist state and the legacy of the communist regime. Although he does not deal with Vietnam directly, Walder's (1986) discussion of 'communist neo-traditionalism' in Chinese factories, as a form of vertical and clientelistic relations unique to communist societies, likely has relevance for the character of micro-level authority relations in Vietnam. He argues a form of authority relations unique to centrally planned regimes, and consequential of non-market-based employment relations and the role of the state in the activities and structure of the workplace.

According to Walder, communist neo-traditionalism manifests in two main institutional features. The first is 'organized dependence' or the extent to which, and the ways in which, workers are dependent- economically on their enterprises, politically on the party and management, and personally on supervisors.

> In communist economies workers are highly dependent on their enterprises, but in a different way. Despite the many nonwage benefits that may come with employment in some industrial sectors in market economies, the employment relation there is primarily a labor market relationship: a specific contractual exchange of efforts and skills for money and other compensation. In a communist economy, employment in the state enterprise is not primarily a market relationship. It is a position that establishes the worker's social identity and rights to specific distributions of welfare and entitlements provided by the state.

> Moreover, the enterprise exercises authority not only over one highly specialized role, but over the whole person: the state factory is a branch of government and, through the factory's party branch, exerts a measure of the state's political rule over the worker as citizen.(*ibid*, p. 16)

The second feature is the 'institutional culture' of the factory: the patterns of association between superior and subordinate, the patterns of association among workers, and the strategies employed by workers to advance their interests.

> The central feature of this institutional culture is a network of patron-client relations that links party organization and shop management to a minority of loyal workers on the shop floor...Yet this personal dimension is not the significant feature of these ties. Party-clientelism is created 'from above'; it is an institutionally prescribed clientelist network that has both formal and informal, impersonal and personal aspects.This mixed character of party-clientelism is distinctively neo-traditional. It represents a mixture of ideological commitments and impersonal loyalties demanded by the Leninist party and the role expectations of modern industrial organization with the personal loyalties characteristic of traditional authority and patrimonialism. It is, therefore, distinct from traditional patron-client ties, built upon personal loyalties, and it is also distinct from cliques and factions that exist separately from formal organizational roles.' (*ibid*, p. 25)
> '...[These] pervasive ties comprise a network that is officially sponsored and is part of the prescribed role structure of the organization. These clientelist ties are a central institution through which authority is exercised; they are not an incidental or supplemental aspect of official institutions. (*ibid,* p.165)

There are a number of overlapping perspectives that can be drawn on to show that micro-level vertical ties are a notable feature of social structures in Vietnam and likely have a particular resonance in Vietnamese organizations of various types. It is important to note that although we can likely make such a general claim, the historical production of those relations is obviously complex, and not adequately described simply as a high degree of hierarchy per se. Instead, authority relations appear to be a mix of factors based on economic, state-led and pre-colonial historical dimensions.

In the context of the academic institutions involved in the LPRV program it is difficult to demonstrate explicitly how these various dimensions of authority relations manifest in the organizational behaviour of those groups. Although it is beyond the scope of this paper to make a historical analysis of educational institutions in Vietnam or the production of certain authority relations in the context of the CPRs, the institutes certainly exhibit characteristics of the features outlined by the above authors, including, for example, the dominant roles of CPR directors, the resilience of formal and hierarchical practices in activities in LPRV and the existence of institutional associations to the Communist Party in Hanoi. For my purposes, the above authors provide an adequate basis for presuming potentially strong and complex vertical ties among LPRV groups in Vietnam. I will now review some observations made while working on network issues at the Dalat CPR.

4.5 Method and Observations in Vietnam

The central objective of the Dalat study was to identify the substantive 'information needs' of the researchers at the CPR in order to identify key issues for collaboration with other institutes and develop criteria for collecting appropriate content for websites and other library resources. The main technique was a workshop (developed co-operatively in the field), where CPR members were invited to brainstorm pertinent research questions or 'information needs' pertaining to their work in the CPR. They then identified, evaluated and ranked the possible 'sources of information', which could be consulted to help fulfil those information needs. Sources were evaluated on the basis of accessibility, language, and quality, and then ranked for overall utility.[5]

It was hoped that this workshop would facilitate more active use of the network. The assumption was that if CPR members were to collaborate with counterparts throughout the country, then identifying specific information needs and matching incentives could help to induce the desired collaboration. In addition, identifying and ranking sources would help to prioritize and clarify possible action and spur activity.

Through undertaking the field study, a number of larger questions arose concerning the propensity of the CPR actors to participate in the processes of collaboration and independent research envisioned for the network. (In addition to the workshop, participant observations over the two-month stay, as well as interviews with people in Dalat and other program partners were employed) Observations concerning the nature of social change can be cast in two related areas: inward focus and individual volition.

Inward Focus As an organization, the Dalat CPR appeared to be quite inwardly focused in regard to its academic work. Outside information resources did not seem to play a great role in the institute's activities, which tended to centre more on meetings and fieldwork, than on say, article writing. Most of the information held in CPR databases and library collections was data that had been collected on local communes. Far fewer resources could be found that dealt with experiences, case studies, theories, or models of poverty reduction or community planning in different parts of Vietnam or Asia. This, of course, is partly due to the early stage of information resource development at the CPR. In preparing for the workshop, however, one CPR member, raising skepticism over the relevance of the proposed approach of the workshop, suggested that 'case studies from other parts of Vietnam were not interesting to the CPR members'.

During the workshop the pre-planned notion of brainstorming information needs or pertinent research questions did not prompt the robust, group brainstorming hoped for, but instead elicited primarily the input of the director and accompanying re-iterations from other senior people in the room. In light of expectations, participants, did not appear to have a set of pertinent research questions. A senior CPR member suggested that in addition to the readily solvable problems of cost and training, the main barrier to Internet use in Vietnam was that 'people did not understand their own information needs'.

A local focus is clearly reflected in attitudes towards collaboration with LPRV partners in other parts of Vietnam. Significantly, in the workshop, *other CPRs* (the LPRV partners with whom Internet collaboration was to take place) were ranked a low 9th out of 10 as an 'information source'. According to participants, this low ranking was due to 'distance' and 'lack of relationship'.[6] Similarly, the issue of 'relationships' emerged again when the *accessibility* of information sources was contemplated. Participants pointed out that the accessibility of *local government*, for example, would depend on 'who you were and who you knew in the government.' In sum, then, the CPR appeared to be quite locally focused without much practice in external activities or engagements.

Individual Volition In terms of activities such as e-mail discussion groups or other information exchange activities, the propensity of people to participate in such a role is questionable in that people did not appear to have the sanctioned or felt agency to express ideas openly in professional settings. The workshop, for example, is best characterized by a sense of hesitancy to discuss ideas.

Although breaking into groups was an effective way to include more CPR members in the discussion, the more junior participants seemed to take the role of a scribe rather than a collaborator. In one case, one junior participant refrained from voicing her ideas for project development, which I knew to exist from previous conversations. Similarly, students did not attempt to share their ideas openly when prompted.

In debriefing after the workshop, one CPR member, commenting on the low level of participation, suggested that people did not have 'the confidence to raise their ideas'. And when questioned further, suggested that people were afraid to leave their 'area of study', and added that 'people could get in trouble ten years ago just for speaking English.' In an interview with one Vietnamese network development worker in Hanoi, it was suggested that feedback in official or formal settings was uncommon and 'gossip in the street' was the most significant channel for communicating opinions in Vietnam. Similarly, one foreign development worker stressed that the people with whom he worked were, in his eyes, 'very afraid to make mistakes'. It would appear that people in the CPR were hesitant to take independent action or openly express opinions in such settings as the workshop.

The process of undertaking such a workshop highlighted the complexity of the network aspiration as a social innovation, and called into question the previous expectations concerning what activities would or could be accommodated by the deployment of ICTs. While the 'under-use' of the network could be explained by the lack of local efficient Internet service delivery, low computing and English-language skill levels, as well as by the relatively early stage of LPRV programme development, what emerged as a point of equal or greater concern, in light of original expectations, were the not-so-obvious (or readily identifiable) social issues involved. The incentives of CPR members to adopt Internet technology as it was applied in that organisational context became the larger question.

5. Questions Concerning 'Information Needs'

It appears that many of the information needs of the CPR did not necessary fall in the scope of the envisioned computer network. The term 'information need,' as revealed in the findings of the study, is really within the domain of something greater, pertaining to the unique incentives of actors in a certain social context. If indeed, the goal of our work is to stimulate new incentives for new forms of human association in that context, then to label those phenomena as 'information needs' could give the impression that those incentives are readily discernible, collectible or malleable objects that can be treated effectively as inputs for the network. On the other hand, it could be argued that people do not really have information needs. Instead, they choose to engage in solving a felt problem or in answering a question pertinent to their personal environment. There is a real risk that complementary, non ICT, or culturally different forms of relevant social processes could be excluded in ICT project planning.

Although the LPRV has looked at a number of ways beyond the Internet to foster organizational collaboration and enhance learning, (through the designation of information officers at each CPR for example), network development has followed a fairly technologically determinist path and there has been a tendency to gravitate toward 'high-tech' technologies in network discussions. Where the allocation of resources toward enhanced web interfaces has been entertained, for example, the translation of existing printed materials may be a more productive allocation of resources in meeting information needs. This becomes an issue of how to integrate the ICT deployment with the larger purpose it was intended to serve, within a larger socio-cultural environment. This is a common challenge for information systems in development, (Menou, 1993) and for organisational information systems generally (Boland and Hirschheim, 1987).

The important background question is one of ends, rather than means. And it is here where more of the discussion belongs: over different aspirations and ends (and subsequent evaluation indicators) in a particular context, rather a fixed construction of ends as 'use of technology' per se or the process of 'meeting information needs.' This investigation demonstrated that a universal conception of such processes does not adequately address the diversity of historical, organisational, or programme experience that comes to uniquely shape those processes. Where technology is an icon of progress, there is a risk that novel and tangible tools can neutralize that discussion before it takes place.

In fact, when ICTs are introduced in development, the inclination is often to describe socio-cultural issues, such as authority relations, as nebulous and intractable barriers to that end. What is neglected in such an analysis is a necessary discussion over what greater collaboration or greater independent research means in a given context. This is not to say that the socio-cultural circumstances within such settings as LPRV are static or that such an aspiration as the LPRV network is not a worthwhile or appropriate pursuit. It is important, however, to clarify these issues if we intend to seek out balanced and attainable goals and accurate understandings of why we reach or miss those goals. In this regard, a conception-reality framework such as the one developed by Bhatnagar and Heeks (1999) could be useful.[7]

6. Conclusion

Although there is much discussion about how ICTs can foster access to information and opportunity in development contexts, there are many questions, which have arisen from the practical experience of working toward such an aspiration in the LPRV. What requires more vigorous questioning are the expectations and assumptions embedded in current efforts to deploy access to ICTs. When concepts are put into action, the issue becomes more complex than of providing access to the technology. One important question that needs to be addressed at a design level is: *Why would people choose to 'access' that technology and how does the technology fit within a larger set of objectives?* It is here where we are drawn into a necessary discussion concerning the diversity of human experience and purpose among the specific actors involved and the divergence or convergence between the intentions of the intended users and the intentions of those designing and deploying the technology.

Such questions are particularly important in a climate where the general importance of information in society is widely accepted at an abstract level, but rarely articulated in specific terms. Ascribing to the universal and instrumental importance of information can help build consensus in projects and mobilize resources, but it can also undermine the complexity inherent in such projects, and ultimately the effectiveness of the technologies themselves.

Acknowledgements

The author acknowledges the contribution to the project described here by the Canadian International Development Agency, under its Localized Poverty Reduction in Vietnam programme. The views expressed here are the author's own, but he would also acknowledge the special assistance provided in writing this paper from Dr. Michael Leaf and Mr. Vincent Verlaan at the Centre for Human Settlements, University of British Columbia, and from Dr. Nguyen Tuan Tai, University of Dalat.

Appendix 1 Information Needs Assessment Workshop

Introduction and Plan

The Dalat CPR and I developed the Information Needs Assessment Workshop in the summer of 2000. The purpose of the workshop was to help bridge the gap between the organizational information needs of CPR members and current efforts to deploy information and information technologies in LPRV through network development activities.

The workshop involved:

1. identifying a current organizational goal,
2. generating questions (or information needs) related to that goal,
3. identifying potential information sources,
4. and evaluating sources on the basis of accessibility, language and quality.

The overall aim was to make information resource development in LPRV (network development) valuable and useful for CPR members and to raise awareness and to encourage use of the resources as they were deployed. The methods themselves are best seen as experimental and in the spirit of learn-by-doing. The workshop was completed in two separate sessions.

Session 1: Information Needs Assessment

Planned Activities: At the start, an organizational goal was to be established. Time would be spent both in small groups and the larger group discussing and generating research or planning questions related to that goal.
Planned Outputs: At the end of this session, the CPR would be left with a series of current and important research and planning questions. This exercise was to have a number of benefits or uses:

- To help clarify current questions and challenges facing the CPR.
- To identify opportunities where the CPR could work collaboratively with other CPRs.
- To give UBC faculty and staff direction in helping select information resources that would be useful to the CPR. (library contributions and websites)
- To provide content for personalizing Internet training.

Session 2: Information Source Evaluation and Strategy

Planned Activities: Once a series of questions were identified, participants would then turn to brainstorming possible sources or services outside of the CPR, which could be consulted to help meet or answer those questions. Once all possible sources were listed, they would be grouped and evaluated on criteria of language, accessibility, and quality. Sources would then be given an overall ranking.
Planned Outputs: At the end of this session the CPR would have a more clear understanding of what information resources were potentially valuable and what challenges existed in bringing those outside sources into the research and planning activities of the CPR. This exercise was to have a number of benefits or uses:

- To identify different opportunities for outside consultation and lay the groundwork for future action in this respect.
- To generate greater and explicit awareness over new and existing opportunities for outward collaboration and consultation.
- To give UBC faculty and staff direction in providing information sources that were considered valuable and helpful to the CPR members.
- To provide a forum for dialogue between Canadian and Vietnamese partners over existing and anticipated information processes for the CPR.

Theoretical Background of Workshop

The method was an adaptation of *Guidelines for Developing an Information Strategy* (the JISC Information Strategy Steering Group/Coopers and Lybrand, 1999) This is a methodology aimed at strategizing the use of information for academic institutions. The essence of the Information Strategy is to promote a bottom-up approach to optimizing the use and management of information and information technology. Guidelines for developing such a strategy were assembled by the authors on the basis of consultation with universities in the UK and meant to assist academic institutions in responding effectively to opportunities presented by new information technologies. The strategy is intended to help mitigate the following risks:

- fragmentation within the academic community,
- failure to develop student-centred learning,
- ill-conceived, wasteful investments in technology,
- technological investment without necessary changes in working practices, attitudes and behaviour.

The strategy itself is thought of as a 'set of attitudes,' rather than a report, in which:

- any information that should be available for sharing is well defined and appropriately accessible,
- the quality of information is fit for its purpose,
- all staff know and exercise their responsibilities toward information,
- there is a mechanism by which priorities are clearly identified and then acted upon.

The central method for developing such a strategy is categorizing the information needs of the institution through the identification of 'information groups' that correspond to the functions and processes of the university (eg. course-preparation, institutional planning). The joint identification, evaluation, and discussion over such information groups is supposed to foster the new attitudes in the organization. According to the authors:

> The process itself, designed to produce a set of attitudes, will be a learning process which evolves and changes over time: it will be iterative, which means that the production of an Information Strategy is not a once-and-for-all task but will need updating. In various ways, which we discuss, the process will need to involve all those concerned with information; thus the derivation of the Information Strategy will also put in place the means by which it is to be implemented. (1999, p. 34)

Although the JISC method is intended for the internal use of information in large academic organizations, it was felt that the overall premise could be adapted toward the goal of helping establish new processes in the CPR for outside networking. In the same spirit of an iterative and bottom-up approach to optimizing internal 'information groups' in the model, it was felt that identifying and discussing existing external 'information groups' or 'information sources' at the CPR could help to shift attitudes towards a more optimal use of technologies and help to better steer the deployment of technology.

Findings

Session 1: Information Needs Assessment

Session One was co-faciliated by myself and translator, Pham The Thuong and attended by six faculty members and several students. The organizational goal agreed upon by the participants was 'to design commune projects' (development projects in local communities). In the case of the Dalat CPR there were three associate communes, which I will call x, y, and z communes. The CPR members responsible for work in each commune reviewed existing knowledge of the community and then agreed upon the best possible project to explore:

Commune:	**Project:**
x	Agricultural Diversification
y	Micro-Credit
z	Micro-Credit

The next step was to identify the *information needs* regarding project design and planning. We started by brainstorming general thoughts as a group and then divided into groups of two to conduct interviews. Each individual was paired with someone who was responsible for a different aspect of the project design. Participants were encouraged to develop a picture of what was already known, and then, produce a list of questions or unknowns. After reconvening and discussing the results with the larger group, we were left with the following questions or *information needs*. (The micro-credit project teams y and z grouped their results together.)

Commune	Information Needs
x	Agricultural Diversification 1. What kind of crop should be selected? 2. What kind of livestock should we raise? 3. Do we invest in each household? How much?
y and z	Micro-Credit 1. What techniques are available for teaching local people to use a loan? 2. How can we make a micro-credit project sustainable? 3. What are example project designs used elsewhere?

Session 2: Information Source Evaluation and Strategy

Session two was co-facilitated by myself and translator, Pham The Thuong and attended by the same six faculty members as the first but this time without the students due to availability. In the second workshop *we brainstormed all the possible sources of information that could help the CPR answer the questions generated in the first workshop.* Participants were encouraged to list as many sources as possible, both Vietnamese and other:

- *Local Government*
- *Department of Agriculture*
- *Local Commune Officials*
- *World Bank*
- *Other CPRs (Particularly HCMC, which is interested in Micro-credit)*
- *HCMC Labour Association*
- *World University Service of Canada Interns*
- *Business Schools in Canada*
- *Business Schools in Dalat*
- *International NGOs: Oxfam, ENDA, UNDP*
- *Internet*
- *E-mail List and newsgroups on Micro-credit*
- *Websites on Micro-credit*
- *CPR Library Collections*
- *UBC Library*
- *LPRV Partners*
- *Laval Library*
- *Local State Bank*
- *Vietnamese Farmer Association*
- *Women's Association*

We then categorized the sources into workable groups and arranged those groups against the criteria of access, quality, and language in a matrix and rated each source using a basic three-point scale, which reflected how well or how poorly the source met the three different criteria and then ranked each source for overall utility. (1= well and 3=not well.) We then discussed the responses and possible courses of action.

Information Source Grouping	Access	Quality	Language	Overall Ranking
Local Government (Agriculture Department)	2 (depends)	2	1	4
Local Labour Unions, Farmers and Women's Groups	1 (depends)	3	1	7
Local University Library	1	3 (worsening)	1	10
Vietnamese LPRV Partner Universities (Other CPRs)	3 (improving)	2	1	9
International Institutions and NGOs	2	1	3	3
Canadian Universities and Libraries	3	1	3	2
State Bank	2	2	1	8
Dalat CPR Book Library	1	2 (improving)	3	1
Visiting Students	1	1	2	6
Internet Searches	2	2	2	5

Appendix 2 ICT Management Guide for LPRV[8]

		Managment Component			
Development Goal Hierarchy	ICT Dimensions	Current Where are we now?	Concept Design Where do we want to be?	Implementation What action to take?	Evaluation Where are we after time?
Access to Internet technology.	Technical Functionality System proficiency?	(No computers, but telephone links)	(Two computers with proficient Internet connections at each institute)	(Buy and install systems and software)	(Systems in place, connections slow)
Above, plus access to select information resources.	Information Content Appropriate content?	(No local or foreign content available online at institutes)	(Database of information resources accessible in English and Vietnamese)	(Elicit information needs of users. Retrieve, organize resources. Translate where necessary)	(Web based database in place., Deficiency of Vietnamese language materials)
Above, plus skills for computer maintenance and use.	Staffing and Skills Technical support, operation skills	(Few possess required computer skills. Some are familiar with e-mail.)	(Members can perform internet and database searches and communicate on e-mail.)	(Conduct training. Hire or train maintainance staff.)	(Skills have improved. Many still cannot perform basic computer manipulations.)

Above, plus integration of system into management structures.	Management Management of new work processes?	(No management structures for collaboration/ networking)	(A central facilitates collaboration. Protocols and guidelines in place.)	(Hire or second staff. Find local champion to lead.)	(No central node in Vietnam yet. Some guidelines for cooperation, new info. officers)
Above, plus integration of system into larger organizational work processes.	Work Processes Organizational functions enhanced or afforded by system?	(Collaboration between institutions and use of foreign information resources is low.)	(Members make independent searches and collaborate with distant partners electronically.)	(Identify local goals and flesh out qualitative descriptions of desired processes.)	(Minimal research collaboration, limited searching. Used for administration purposes.)
Above, plus development of new incentives for activities and behaviours.	Objectives and Values Social and organizational incentives of recipients?	(Locally focused, vertically oriented organizations.)	(Confident and cooperative users, with incentives to reach out to other groups)	(Participatory and negotiated approach to above implementation activities.)	(Increasing capacity but lack of confidence, and inward focus.)

Notes

1 Castells has added, however: ... 'what is characteristic of the network society is not the critical role of knowledge and information, because knowledge and information were central in all societies. Thus, we should abandon the notion of 'Information Society', which I have myself used sometimes, as unspecific and misleading.' (2000, p. 10)

2 Doi Moi involves 'a comprehensive renovation of the whole country based on three fundamentals: shifting from a highly centralized planned economy based chiefly on public ownership...to a multi-sector economy...; democratizing social life with the aim of developing the rule of law; implementing an open door policy and promoting (international) cooperation.' (LPRV, 1997)

3 See Appendix 1.

4 Jamieson qualifies his account of pre-colonial Vietnam as 'oversimplified, somewhat idealized and selective.' (1995, p. 15)

5 See Appendix 1.

6 It should also be pointed out, however, that foreign *information sources* (*International Institutions, Canadian Universities*) were rated highly, showing that the CPR did have an interest in outside sources, at least as expressed within my study. When asked why, people said that the quality of information was very high for these sources, especially compared to the quality of information at the general campus library in Dalat, which was considered very poor. The CPR library was ranked most highly due to its quality and close vicinity.

7 See Appendix 2 for an adapted LPRV model.

8 Based on (Bhatnagar and Heeks, 1999).

References

Akrich, M. (1992) The de-scription of technical objects. In *Shaping Technology/Building Society*, Bijker WE, Law J (eds.). MIT Press, Cambridge, Massachusetts; 1992. pp. 205-224.

Avgerou, C. (2000) Recognising alternative rationalities in the deployment of information systems. *The Electronic Journal on Information Systems in Developing Countries,*3. http://www.is.cityu.edu.hk/ejisdc/ejisdc.htm (January 2001).

Avgerou, C. and Walsham, G. (2000) *Information Technology in Context: Studies from the Perspective of Developing Countries*. Ashgate, Burlington, Vermont.

Bhatnagar, S.C, and Heeks, R. (1999) Understanding success and failure in information age reform. In *Reinventing Government in the Information Age,* Heeks, R. (ed.) Routledge, London; pp. 49-74.

Bhatnagar,S.C, and Odedra, M. (1992) *Social Implications of Computer in Developing Countries*. McGraw-Hill, New Delhi.

Boland, R.J. (1987) The in-formation of information systems. In *Critical Issues in Information Systems Research,* Boland, R.J. Hirschheim, R.A. (eds.), John Wiley & Sons, Chichester; pp. 363-380.

Boland, R.J, and Hirschheim, R.A. (1987) *Critical Issues in Information Systems Research.* John Wiley and Sons Ltd, Chichester, UK.

Castells, M. (1996) *The Rise of Network Society.* Blackwell, Cambridge.

Castells, M. (2000) Materials for an exploratory theory of the network society. *British Journal of Sociology,* 51, pp. 5-23.

Crowder, L.V, and Michiels, S. (2001) *Discovering the 'Magic Box': Local Appropriation of Information and Communications Technologies (ICTs).* Sustainable Development Department, Food and Agriculture Organisation, Rome. http://www.fao.org/sd/2001/KN0602a2_en.htm (July 2001).

Heeks, R. (1999) *Information and Communication Technologies, Poverty and Development.* Development Informatics Working Paper Series No. 5; Institute for Development Policy and Management, Manchester.

Hobart, M.E. and Schiffman, Z.S. (1998) *Information Ages: Literacy, Numeracy, and the Computer Revolution.* The Johns Hopkins University Press, London.

Jamieson, N. (1995) *Understanding Vietnam.* University of California Press, Berkeley, California.

JISC Information Strategies Steering Group and Coopers & Lybrand. (1999) *Guidelines for Developing an Information Strategy. Retrieved* May 10, 2000 from the World Wide Web: http://www.jisc.ac.uk/pub/infstrat/

Jonas, H. (1953) A critique of cybernetics. *Social Research*, 20, pp. 173-192.

LPRV (1997) *LPRV Proposal*.http://www.chs.ubc.ca/lprv/overviewF.html (January, 2001).

Madon, S. 2000.The internet and socio-economic development: exploring the interaction. *Information Technology and People*, 13 (2), pp. 85-102.

Marvin, C. (1987) Information and history. In *The Ideology of the Information Age,* in Slack J.D, Fejes F, (eds.), Ablex, New Jersey; pp. 40-62.

Menou, M.J. (1993) *Measuring the Impact of Information on Development.* International Development Research Centre, Ottawa.

Neher, C.D, (1987) *Politics in Southeast Asia.* Schenkman Books, Cambridge, Massachusetts.

Robins, K. and Webster, F. 1987. Information as capital: a critique of Daniel Bell. In *The Ideology of the Information Age,* Slack JD, Fejes F, (eds.). Ablex, New Jersey; pp. 95-117.

Roszak, T. (1986) *The Cult of Information*. Pantheon, New York.

Scott, J.C. (1977) Patron-client politics and political change in Southeast Asia. In *Friends, Followers and Factions*, Schmidt SW, Gausti L, Lande C, Scott JC (eds.). University of California Press, Berkeley, California; pp. 122-145.

Shannon, C. and Weaver, W. (1964)*The Mathematical Theory of Communication.* The University of Illinois Press, Urbana.

UNDP. (2000) *New Levers for Development and Prosperity.* UNDP, New York. http://www.undp.org/dpa/choices/2000/june/p8-9.htm (August 2001).

Valdes I. (1987) Third world countries and conflicting ideologies of the information age. In *The Ideology of the Information Age,* Slack JD, Fejes F, (eds.). Ablex, New Jersey; pp. 200-220.

Verlaan, V. (2001) *Personal Correspondence.*

Wiener, N. (1950) *The Human Use of Human Beings.* Sphere Books, London.

Chapter 17

Strategic and Institutional Response to the Digital Challenge: A Perspective on how Global IT Trends are Expressed in Developing Countries

Abiodun O. Bada

1. Introduction

In this study, we examine the relationship between global IT and organizational change initiatives in banking and IT and organizational change initiatives within the Nigerian banking system.[1] It is generally argued that the globalization process is more advanced in wholesale banking than in the retail sector because retail banking is more local in nature and is expected to be much more closer to customer needs and preferences (O'Brien, 1992). Yet, to completely isolate retail banking from global trends will be misleading. Frazer and Vittas (1982) identified the substantial level of similarities between consumer financial needs and the ease with which new financial technology can be transferred across many different countries as reasons why the retail-banking sector cannot be isolated. Similarly, Reinicke (1995) discussed the ease with which foreign banks are able to penetrate local markets after deregulation as constituting a major aspect of the globalization trend within retail banking. In addition, O'Brien (1992) identified the increasing ownership of local banks by foreigners, the increasing formation of alliances and mergers between banks of different national origins, and the important role that the new information and communications technology is playing in banking activities, as important global tendencies in retail banking.

Implicit in these discussions is an increasing interconnection of economic activities[2] in the environment of retail banks. As banks are now able to enter alliances and increase presence in foreign territories, the discussion about retail banking can increasingly be carried out from within the globalization discourse. Consequently, a study of the impact of globalization on banking institutions in developing countries (DCs) becomes more important in view of some of the arguments about the possible homogenizing effect such environments portend. According to Aldrich (1979):

> A homogenous environment rewards the development of standardized ways of relating to the domain population, and may lead to the development of an undifferentiated set of products and services (pg. 66).

Clearly influenced by some of these concerns, studies in IS are beginning to examine the nature of this relationship between global IT-based initiatives and developments in DCs organizations (Bada, 2000a and b; Walsham, 2000).

The Nigerian economy was deregulated – with the introduction of the Structural Adjustment Program (SAP) – towards the end of the 1980s and different sectors of the economy – including banking – were liberalized with a view to promoting competition and efficiency. In the face of wider regulatory, competitive and technological changes Nigerian banks have, over the past few years, been investing extensively in IT and adopting global IT-based practices. The body of our review focuses mainly on some of these major trends that have been observed in the transformation of the retail-banking sector.

The general research question addressed in this study is: what are the consequences of changes within the international banking system – within the contemporary discourse of an increasing integration of financial service in a developing country context like Nigeria? In particular, we examine how global practices are articulated through the reformation of the Nigerian banking system. We hope a study such as this one will contribute to our understanding of the relationship between global IT-based developments and initiatives within a developing country context.

2. Data sources

Data to support the description of changes in banking from the global perspective comes from secondary sources, mainly a literature review of existing body of knowledge on the subject. Data to support the description of changes within the Nigerian banking industry comes from both primary and secondary sources. Secondary data sources were mainly government publications, newspaper articles and reports from professional bodies such as the Chartered Institute of Bankers of Nigeria (CIBN). Valuable insight was also gained from research studies available on the impact of deregulation and liberalization on the performance of the industry. Primary data sources include bank managers and directors, bank operators and IT personnel, management consultants, professional bodies, regulatory agencies and IT vendors in Nigeria. In all, twenty-six (26) interviews were conducted between March 1997 and September 2000. In the next section, we will briefly discuss the theoretical perspectives adopted in the study. Then, we will discuss IT-based developments within the international banking context before going on to study IT and organizational change in Nigerian banks.

3. Theoretical Perspectives: Institutional and Strategic Views

In this section, we set out the theoretical frameworks for this study. As the research intends to study how Nigerian banks are responding to global pressures of liberalization and IT-based change, an organization-environment interaction perspective to the study of change (Goodman, 1982) was identified as appropriate.[3] To assist our understanding, this study appeals primarily to two theories – strategic management and institutional perspectives. Such perspectives, we hope, will give insights into some of the issues that arise in the study of IT-based organizational change in Nigerian banks, within the contemporary globalization discourse.

3.1 Strategic Management

One possible definition of strategic management could be the management of the process of strategic decision-making,[4] including decisions on how organizations should respond to changes in their environment (Talbot, 1994). A common goal of the strategic management school is to study and identify an organization's strategic position in relation to its environment. According to Johnson and Scholes (1989), strategic management is concerned with the scope of an organization's activities, which includes defining the boundaries of the organization and the kinds of businesses and products to be involved in. Strategic decisions also involve matching the activities of the organization to the needs of a constantly changing environment, where the focus is to identify opportunities and threats engendered by such environmental change and how the organization should cope with them. Aldrich and Pfeffer (1976), suggest three possible ways by which strategic decisions are made about the environment.

The first is autonomy where decision-makers have freedom in choosing how to deal with the environment. According to the authors, there exist more than one choice in deciding which segment of the environment the organization wants to operate from and there are free entries and free exits into these environmental segments. Second, organizational decision-makers can choose to manipulate the environment by creating markets for their products and joining forces with others to regulate the environment. Examples given in this respect are mergers, advertising and sales promotions to influence customers' purchasing habits. Third, choices about the environment are functions of how it is perceived, interpreted and evaluated. This can be used to explain diversity between organizations, based on the assumption that environments are acted upon by organizational actors depending on their perceptions, interpretation and evaluation of the importance of environmental conditions (Hall, 1991).

Organizational-environment interaction therefore, is a rational process of identifying and analysing the organization's relation to its environment and devising long-term plans to cope with this. According to Oliver (1997a), in strategic management organizations make economically rational choices that are influenced by the economic context of the firm. In other words, decision-making in strategic management is deliberate and oriented towards economic or efficiency goals.

However, this approach to managing has been challenged with the argument that the socio-cultural, political and historical contexts within which decisions are made also influence the nature of such decisions made (Oliver, 1997a). Decision-making and organizational behavior are not just based on efficiency considerations but also on legitimacy considerations where organizations compulsively conform to some taken-for-granted assumptions and widely held beliefs and expectations about the appropriate ways of doing things within the organization and its environment. This is the argument of the new institutional theory (DiMaggio and Powell, 1991).

3.2 Institutional Theory

In recent times, the debate about the relationship between organizations and the environment has been taken up and extended by the institutional theory, which posits that the environment of organizations should not just be seen in economic or strategic terms; but rather, as consisting of socially prescribed and accepted ways of behaving (Scott and Meyer, 1991). This entails a re-conceptualization of the environment[5] of organizations from the technical-rational perspective to a focus on the social and cultural features of the environment.

These features of the environment are the systems of belief – socially constructed and widely shared - about what the purpose(s) of an organization or an organizational sector are, and what constitutes appropriate ways of conducting the business of such sector (Powell and DiMaggio, 1991). A major argument of the institutional theory is that these systems of belief could also involve technical procedures or requirements of how to organize. However, after a certain level acceptance, these procedures become 'infused with values beyond the technical requirements of the tasks at hand' (Selznick, 1957).[6] In other words, they become institutionalized (Scott and Meyer, 1991). By becoming institutionalized, these procedures become taken-for-granted and unquestioned as the appropriate way of doing things. Consequently, these procedures take on a rule-like structure as organizations are expected to adhere to them for survival and to achieve legitimacy[7] (Scott and Meyer, 1991).

For a study of IT and organizational change, this means that the ability of the organization to change depends – to a considerable extent – on environmental prescriptions (rational concepts of work) about the appropriate ways of organizing within the organizational field or institutional context. Subsequently, organizations do not just change for efficiency reasons but primarily to achieve legitimacy through conformity. However, a number of studies employing institutional arguments have come up with contrary results to the institutional arguments of conformity and homogenization.

Scheid-Cook (1992) examined the response of mental health organizations to a new policy program and concluded that the responses of these mental health organizations were highly variable to a common institutional demand. The study by Orru et al (1991) applying institutional arguments to the study of businesses in three East Asian countries concluded that while firms in each of these countries were highly subjected to local institutional traits, they were also highly successful business enterprises. This led the authors to suggest that both institutional and technical-rational pressures can both co-exist in organizations and that institutional pressures do not necessary imply a neglect of efficiency factors.

In light of these criticisms and increasing empirical evidence that suggests that both institutional and strategic factors can, and do operate alongside each other, an increasing number of studies now regard them as complementary and combine them into single frameworks (Oliver, 1991; 1997 a and b; Dacin, 1997; Hung and Whittington, 1997). Therefore, in this study we adopt a combination of both theories as such combination would lead to a better understanding of the various developments in Nigeria *vis-à-vis* the increasing use of IT. These two theories highlight the strategic choice of organizations on one hand and the quasi-deterministic power of the environment on the other. In the next section, we will briefly examine the global context of banking with a view to highlighting salient features of this context and to provide a useful setting from which to examine developments within the Nigerian sector.

4. Technology and Organizational Change in Banking: an International Perspective

In the 1980s, it became commonplace to speak of changes in the environment of banks particularly changes in banking regulations, competitive behaviour and banking technology. The environment of banking organizations changed dramatically with new structures to existing banks and a much broader scope of financial services/products that were developed. Entirely new forms of banks were developed as well as a proliferation of non-financial service organizations competing with banks in their traditional domain. In addition to all these, customer expectations of banks also changed quite significantly. The body of our review focuses mainly on several of these major trends that have been observed in the transformation of the banking industry.

4.1 Changes in the Environment of Banks

According to Carrington et. al., (1997) the international banking scene, in contemporary times, is characterized by an increased level of competition due to regulatory, structural and technological changes. This led to the transformation of an industry better known for its cautious, internally-focused and transaction-oriented culture to that of a dynamic, customer-focused and sales-oriented approach (Shemwell and Yavas, 1998). It represented an exit from an organizing principle based on caution, conservatism and tradition to that of an aggressive and more open industry. To sustain this new image, banking responded accordingly with a set of new rules and procedures, which saw banks expanded to incorporate new procedures into their structures. Consequently, banks adopted retailing concepts and strategic planning (Essinger, 1993) as well as marketing strategies (Combs and Graham-Bourne, 1995; Sargeant and Asif, 1998). In addition, banks increasingly redesigned their business processes and invested in Business Process Reengineering (BPR) projects in order to operate more efficiently and refocus their operations (Maull and Childe, 1994; Willcocks and Currie, 1997; Newman et. al., 1998).

In this competitive environment, the use of technologies by banks became taken-for-granted as essential, not only to the profitability of banks, but ultimately to their survival (Essinger, 1993:p. 13). Gandy and Chapman (1996) suggested that the huge amount of resources that banks invested in IT was a testament to this taken-for-granted attitude to IT. According to the authors, IT spend in UK and U.S. banks, for instance, were consistently high in the 1990s. In 1994, the total IT spend of UK banks was $5.9 billion while in the USA IT spend was estimated at $16.3 billion in 1994 and expected to rise to 19.8 billion by 1997 (Gandy and Chapman, 1996). A similar study suggests that the banking industry became the biggest user of IT of all industries by the late 1990s (The Economist, April 1999). Thus, the banking industry became replete with a number of technology-based products and services such as phone banking, Internet banking and electronic purse to complement others already in use such as ATMs and MICR (Essinger, 1993; Gosling, 1996, Dannenberg and Kellner, 1998).

4.2 New Delivery Mechanisms: Less Focus on Bank Branches

Changes in delivery mechanism involved the use of IT to provide direct delivery of services to customers, which in turn led to a reduction in the number of branches in operation. Traditionally, the bank branch had been the main avenue for interacting with customers. Bank branches usually formed the major component of a bank's strategy and banks competed on the basis of the number of branches they had. A high presence in a particular area meant that a bank would have a better advantage of attracting customers (and their deposits) than its competitors. Banks therefore tended to have a vast network of branches to maintain their competitive edge and to provide convenience for customers. This organizing principle however changed with the continued introduction of technology into banking.

Given the increasing use of IT and the development of new technology-based banking products and services, there is less focus on branch banking as the main source of delivering services to customers. The US-based Banking Administration Institute (BAI) in a 1996 study predicted that the proportion of transactions conducted by branches in the USA would fall from 40 percent in 1993 to below 20 percent by the turn of the Century. Similarly in the United Kingdom, major UK banks reduced the number of branches in their networks considerably.[8]

4.3 New Technology-based Products and Services

With the increasing emphasis on e-commerce, banks are also moving the delivery of services and interaction with customers to the Internet. Electronic or Internet banking has become a common feature of modern day banking as the Internet is becoming increasingly pervasive in countries such as the U.S. and U.K. (Bener, 2000), Malaysia (Suganthi et. al., 2001) and Saudi Arabia (Jasimuddin, 2001). Therefore, the urge for banks to provide more services through the Internet has become ever more important. Banks now offer services ranging from general information-type services such as providing customers with information about the bank, to other more interactive services like personal account management, online loan application via the Internet (Dannenberg and Kellner, 1998). In addition to having Web banks that complement traditional outlets, there are newer forms of 'virtual' or 'pure Web banks' which are independent entities that depend entirely on the Internet as their main communication and distribution channel.

The electronic purse or smart card is another example of new technology-based products in banking. It is designed as an alternative to carrying cash and it involves storing money values in a microchip embedded in the card, to the value that is available in the holder's account (Gosling, 1996; Awad, 2002). The popularity of this innovation has been more in countries where social circumstances such as high levels of crime and the risk of carrying cash have made it popular (Gosling, 1996). In the UK, the system was tried out with the Mondex card, but with less success. This led Essinger (1993) to raise the concern about the lack of proper investigations into whether customers actually want technology-related payment methods. Other studies also point to the lack of fit between technology-related products and the socio-cultural environment of their introduction (Gosling, 1996); failure to conduct proper studies into what customers want (Bebbington et al, 1991) and the fact that some technology-based products may actually be solutions looking for problems to solve (Carrington et. al, 1997).

These various studies point to one major argument: that technology is driving applications within the industry (see for instance Essinger, 1993): 'Within the [financial service] industry the technology has usually come first, and then the application has been designed to fit with the technology' (p. 19). With regard to the use of ATMs by banks, Essinger (1993) also argued that any modern bank wishing to compete effectively must offer customers more services through ATMs. It follows therefore, from an institutional point of view, that the use of ATMs and technology in general, has become taken-for-granted within the banking industry.

In the next section, we will examine some of the IT-based changes that have taken place within the Nigerian banking sector with a view to highlighting how some of the developments on the international scene are taking place and what the implications are for the Nigerian context. This description of the local context of banking will serve as background to providing an analysis of the relationship between the global context and the Nigerian scene.

5. IT and Organizational Change in Nigerian Banks

The introduction of the Structural Adjustment Program (SAP) in 1986 began the process of deregulating the Nigerian economy and led to the liberalization of the banking industry. Liberalization of the banking industry started with the relaxation of entry procedures in the financial service sector, which saw the number of banks more than doubled from 42 in 1986 to 117 by the end of 1995. Another major financial sector reform is the 'decompartmentalization' of the industry with the introduction of the 'Universal Banking' scheme. Through this scheme, government hoped to encourage a level playing field within the industry by allowing merchant banks to operate in the domestic retail market. Thus, the lifting of the ban further increased the level of competition as some merchant banks have since seized this opportunity and moved into the sector,[9] while others plan to join in the immediate future.[10]

An increasing number of technology-based banking products such as smart cards, home and Internet banking have been introduced into the sector.[11] New generation banks such as All States Trust Bank and Diamond bank pioneered the introduction of card-based payment systems with cards such as the 'ESCA' and 'Diamond' cards respectively. The ESCA card was the first to be launched in the country in December 1995 with the aim of reducing dependence on cash and its attendant problems. Some of the problems relate to the depreciation of the local currency (Naira) and the huge amounts carried around – even for the most basic transactions. Carrying these huge sums of money around is a major security risk for both customers and banks and specifically for banks it represents a huge cost in terms of handling cash.[12] Customers who travel around the country to transact business need only to carry the charged card with them as they can withdraw money from the card at any of the banks' branches. These products have received wide acceptance due to some of the problems related to handling cash and especially those related to security and risks of carrying large sums of money around. Old generation banks like UBA have also followed suit with UBA's Easy Card and First bank with its First Bank Value card.

Another related development within the industry is the consortium of 26 banks established to operate a multi-bank smart card payment scheme with a view to further reducing the dependence on cash. This joint effort runs in parallel with individual schemes already underway in some banks and it is intended to help banks achieve the critical mass that is needed in order to change people's orientation from cash transactions. In addition to providing a cashless wallet within the banking system, the scheme is also expected to facilitate and improve inter and intra-bank communication as well as developing an all-industry standard in smart card implementation.[13]

The financial distress within the industry,[14] in addition to other problems, led to an increasing focus on finding better and more efficient ways of providing services to customers and winning back their confidence. Nigerian banks have invested a substantial amount of resources on IT in order to improve their services. In a survey of banking institutions in Nigeria, Woherem (2000) found that the average annual IT budget of banks increased from 126 million Naira in 1997 to 265 million Naira[15] in 1998. Banks are investing directly in IT,[16] and with the assistance of IT and Management consultants, are also introducing IT-related change programs such as Business Process Reengineering (BPR). A number of old generation banks embarked upon major reengineering initiatives[17] with a view to improving operations and redesigning their branch processes for efficiency.[18] In addition, banks have increasingly focused on developing the requisite manpower to sustain these changes and encourage further development of the industry.[19]

6. Analysis: Conformity or Variation; Efficiency or Legitimacy?

To what extent have changes within the Nigerian banking system been influenced by institutional or strategic considerations? Relating the developments in Nigeria to the wider banking context, clearly there are similarities and differences between the Nigerian banking industry and the global banking context. As in to the global context, the Nigerian banking industry too, after liberalization, was decompartmentalized as the number of operating banks in the industry increased dramatically and the level of competition increased further with the increasing presence of foreign banks. In addition, the increased level of competition was accompanied by aggressive marketing techniques:

> There is an increased focus on marketing and the manager has got to learn new marketing skills. This is because we previously played down the role of marketing as the customers always come to us; we did not have to look for them. But now, you have to search for customers. Therefore, you need the marketing skills to look for them and the relationship skills to keep them.
>
> (Branch Manager of an 'Old' generation bank)

In addition, the new banks brought in new dimensions of technology-based service delivery and products. The older banks, in the face of heavy competition and dwindling resources, sought new and better ways to serve their customers, which led to an increase in the use of technology. This description of the national environment of banks in Nigeria suggests an increased level of investment in IT since liberalization:

> The basis of competing within the industry has since changed from just a focus on people and process to a more technology-based approach. Every bank in Nigeria today now knows that to survive the turbulence of the environment they have got to be able to provide on-line, real-time banking for their customers.
>
> (CEO of an old generation bank)

An increasing number of banks are computerizing their operations and in addition, are linking branches in a Wide Area Network (WAN) to offer customers a unified banking system, whereby customers can go into any branch and transact business. In addition, there is an increase in the number and quality of financial services and products on offer. Products such as cheque guarantee cards and other plastic based payment systems, aimed to reduce the dependence on cash and its attendant problems, have been highly welcomed in the country. Seminars, local training schemes and overseas training were identified as means through which banks have been developing their staff to meet the challenges of the industry and to forge closer ties with their customers. These various developments are being encouraged or supported by both local and international IT and management consultants.

From an institutional point of view, these developments could be regarded as a form of re-institutionalization (Jepperson, 1991) of the Nigerian banking system. Influenced by changes at the global level, the industry is now organized on new sets of principles based on service quality, timely and accurate information, increased co-operation and technology input. To sustain this new image, the industry has responded accordingly with a set of new rules and procedures that have seen banking in Nigeria incorporate new global procedures and practices into their structures. Banks in Nigeria now have vibrant marketing and advertising departments charged solely with the responsibility of building and sustaining relationships with customers. There is an increased investment in IT – leading to the introduction of the unified banking platform in most banks, new technology-based payment systems as well as an improved focus on manpower development to sustain these various initiatives.

However, despite the incorporation of global practices, major differences still exist in the acceptance level of some of these practices within the Nigerian context. Although new technology-based products such as phone banking, smart cards and ATMs are increasingly being implemented in the country, their level of acceptance varies. While smart cards are increasingly being implemented, ATMs have been tried with very little success. Similarly, the use of cash is institutionalized within the payment systems in the country. Despite the increasing use of plastic mode of payments, the Nigerian economy is still predominantly cash-based:

> The Nigerian economic environment is purely a cash system. It is not uncommon to see customers coming into the bank wanting to withdraw 1 (one) million Naira in cash; perhaps to buy a car and the car dealer wanted cash. The customer has no choice but to collect the money and lock it in his car. This is very much unlike what we have in other economies whereby a withdrawal of such magnitude would generate some controversy.
>
> (Senior Manager of a 'new' generation bank)

Due to successive governments poor fiscal control policies and the neglect of local manufacturing base, Nigeria has over the years been plagued with a high rate of inflation which has consequently led to a decline in the value of the local currency. This has therefore made it imperative for people to carry huge sums of money around in order to carry out even the most basic of transactions. Therefore, the high rate of inflation and the small currency denominations have made ATMs a less attractive option for banks. In the words of an IT Director in a new generation bank:

> Given the importance and popularity of ATMs in the banking world, we discussed the idea of installing ATMs in all our branches nationwide but we had to shelve the original plan of installing outside ATMs given the security fears in the country and the problem of vandalism. So we decided that instead of having outside ATMs perhaps we should install them inside the banking halls for quick service to customers who do not really need to see a teller. But even this plan had to be reconsidered given the state of our economy and the inflationary pressures on our economy. In addition to this, the highest currency denomination in Nigeria is 50 Naira which, coupled with the inflation, makes it unworthy to install ATMs. [20]

Additionally, the heavy reliance on cash, coupled with poor telecommunications infrastructure, still makes branch banking quite popular within the country. According to a manager interviewed:

> Our branching policy has always been informed by the exigencies of the business. Some of our customers require that we are close to them and we had no choice but to comply; because to remain competitive you need to be close to the customer. This is because of the difficulty of travelling several miles to transact business. Given transportation problems and traffic situation, plus the added risk of carrying huge sums of money all over the place, you really need to be close to them. So the issue of proximity to customer is an important one for us.

In the advanced economies technology is replacing the need for geographic presence, whereas in Nigeria, proximity to customers is still very much a part of the business strategy of banks. Unlike in the USA and UK for instance, Nigerian banks are opening more branches to be closer to their customers.[21] This shows the importance of the local environment in shaping the type of changes taking place in the industry and the argument that organizational forms are not equally adapted to all environments (Aldrich, 1979:17).

7. Discussion

In discussing the interplay of global practices and local initiatives, we suggest that the implementation of global IT-based practices within the Nigerian banking system takes place under the influence of both strategic considerations and institutional influences. Further, we argue that institutional influences of conformity and legitimacy are supported by strategic and efficiency considerations where the strategic needs of the local context and the economic realities of the Nigerian context determine the willingness of banks to conform, as well as their ability to resist institutional influences.

Strategic considerations informed the decision not to invest in ATMs; where the economic situation in the country, exemplified by the high rate of inflation and the small denominations of the national currency increased banks' capacity to resist conforming to the taken-for-granted attitude to ATM use in banks. Another important consideration is the decision by banks to establish increased branch network in Nigeria. This decision is influenced by economic or business needs where bank customers demand closer proximity to their banks because of the attendant problems of transportation, telecommunications and inflation. Therefore, the perception of branch banking in Nigeria, different from the wider practice of closing branches, further boosted banks' ability to resist conforming to this practice.

Similarly, economic considerations, borne out by the high rate of inflation, the need to carry huge sums of cash and the associated risk of carrying the cash around, influenced the increasing emphasis on plastic modes of payments within the country. Banks' ability to create markets and demands for their products, through aggressive marketing and the creation of the SmartCard joint venture by 26 banks, bolstered their willingness to conform to this global practice within banking. Finally, the credibility crisis suffered by banks, coupled with the consequent need to win back customer-confidence and finding better ways to serve customers, increased banks' willingness to conform. This led banks to invest heavily in 'state-of-the-art technologies' and to introduce BPR projects as they found its promise of 'quantum leap improvements' rather appealing.

Strategic considerations such as banks' ability to create markets and demands for their products, management's perception of the importance of branch networks and new technology and their ability to resist certain practices taken for granted within the wider context of banking influenced their willingness to conform. This suggests a dynamic relationship between global (institutional) imperatives and strategic requirements of local context. In implementing global IT-based practices, Nigerian banks were found to comply with taken-for-granted procedures within the wider context of banking and equally, they were able to resist conforming to these rules and procedures. This willingness to conform and ability to resist conforming to global pressures were influenced by strategic or efficiency considerations. Similar to Orru et. al., (1991), this study also confirmed that both strategic and institutional pressures combine to influence organizational actions.

At the level of practice, this study further highlights the importance of contextualizing technology-related banking products and services. This however is not an exclusive problem of developing countries (DCs) alone as studies such as Bebbington et. al (1991) and Gosling (1996) have indicated that similar problems exist in developed countries as well. The context of IT implementation in DCs though, is much different than in developed countries given the lack of resources and infrastructural and technological capabilities, which these countries have to contend with. It follows therefore, that the use of IT needs to be adapted to the priorities and contextual characteristics of the local context (Madon, 1992).

8. Conclusion

In conclusion, this study has highlighted why it may not be possible for organizations in DCs wishing to be active players in the digital age to just conform to taken-for-granted assumptions within the wider global context. A taken-for-granted assumption about the use of technology in banks could mean a focus only on technology as the appropriate strategy on which to compete. It could lead to banking services becoming detached from the needs of bank customers and the wider context in which banks operate. A taken-for-granted view of IT implementation may sometimes lead to a mechanistic transfer of technology and technology-based products and services from developed to developing countries – which may not be ideal in the local context. Such products and services may make a bank or industry look global and modern but may not meet the needs of the local consumer and local strategic needs. Therefore, local organizational response to the digital challenge needs to conform to global institutional demands and be sensitive to local economic realities in order to make any meaningful impact.

Notes

1 Our focus is on retail or commercial banks. These banks are commonly referred to as 'old generation banks' for banks that were in operation before liberalization and 'new generation banks' for those that started business after liberalization.
2 Aptly referred to as 'a networked, deeply interdependent global economy' (Castells, 1996: 67).
3 The organization-environment interaction perspective focuses on the importance of the environment in the welfare of organizations and its central message is that organizations affect and are affected in varying degrees by the environment within which they operate (Goodman, 1982).
4 Strategic decisions entail committing substantial amount of resources, setting precedents and taking crucial actions which affect the long-term health and survival of the organization (Mintzberg et. al, 1976). In addition, such decisions usually have implications for the entire organization and its customers.
5 The institutional school argue that environments, in contemporary times, do not just involve the immediate environment of organizations, but that organizations are also involved in non-local and vertically structured relationships (Scott and Meyer, 1991).
6 Quoted in DiMaggio and Powell (1991).
7 Legitimacy is explained as an evaluation method which places emphasis on meeting societal expectations, and which may be at odds with the internal efficiency needs of the organization (DiMaggio and Powell, 1991).
8 In 2000, Barclays, Lloyds TSB and NatWest - announced the closure of 172, 400 and 60 branches respectively See, 'MPs join battle to save branches' (The Guardian, April 1 2000).
9 See, 'Industrial, Fidelity, Fountain get CBN nod, convert to commercial banking' (Vanguard, May 31, 1999).
10 See, 'NIMBL may dump merchant banking' (The Guardian, April 26, 1999); See also, 'Indo-Nigerian Merchant Bank set for U-banking' (This Day, August 15, 2001).
11 See, 'Banks parade new products and strategies to keep afloat' (The Guardian July 5, 1998).
12 On a normal day, it is not uncommon for bank branches to handle and process cash of up to 40 million Naira and above.
13 See, 'VALUECARD: How 26 banks changed the face of money mart' (Vanguard, June 21, 1999).
14 For more discussions on this, see Bada (2000aandb), Lewis and Stein (1997) and Utomi (1996).
15 110 Naira = U.S. $1 (January, 2002).
16 See, 'NCR clinches 140 million Naira IT orders' (The Guardian March 10, 1999).
17 See, 'Bank restructures, lays-off 900 workers' (The Guardian, June 6, 2000).
18 See, 'Re-engineering in banking sub-sector propels investment in stocks' (Vanguard, March 16 1999).
19 See, 'Banks prepare workers for millennial challenge' (The Guardian, February 24, 1999). See also, 'Afribank tests 7,000 graduates for jobs' (The Guardian, June 29, 1999).

20 Government recently introduced higher denominations of 100, 200 and 500 Naira, which banks hope would ease some of the problems associated with the use of ATMs.

21 See, 'Bank to open 20 new branches' (The Guardian, April 2, 1999).

References

Aldrich, H. (1979). Organizations and Environments. New Jersey, Prentice-Hall, Inc.

Aldrich, H., and Pfeffer, J (1976). 'Environments of Organizations.' Annual Review of Sociology **2** (Palo Alto, California: Annual Review).

Awad, E. M. (2002). Electronic Commerce: From Vision to Fulfillment. New Jersey, Prentice-Hall, Inc.

Bada, A. (2000a) 'Institutional intervention in the adoption of computer-based information systems (CBIS): the case of the Nigerian banking industry'. In Information Technology in Context: Studies from the perspectives of developing countries. C. Avgerou and G. Walsham (Eds). Aldershot, Ashgate Publishing Ltd: pp. 168-181.

Bada, A. (2000b) 'Actually existing globalization': A case study of IT and organizational change within the Nigerian banking system. International Federation for Information Processing *(IFIP - Working Group 9.4) conference on Information Flows, Local Improvisations and Work Practices, Cape Town, South Africa.*

[BAI] Banking Administration Institute (1996). The Information Superhighway and Retail Banking.

Bebbington, L., Cronin, B., and Davenport, E (1991). 'Consumer Attitudes to Information Technology in Banking.' International Journal of Information Management 11: pp. 220-237.

Bener, A. (2000). Risk Perception, Trust and Credibility: A Case in Internet Banking, PhD Thesis. London School of Economics, University of London.

Carrington, M., Langguth, P., and Steiner, T (1997). The Banking Revolution: Salvation or Slaughter? London, FT Pitman Publishing.

Castells, M. (1996). The Rise of the Networked Society. Cambridge, Massachusetts, Blackwell Publishers.

Combs, H. W., and Graham-Bourne, S (1995). 'Preparing Retail Banking for a Competitive Environment.' Review of Business 17(1 (Fall)): pp. 3-6.

Dacin, M. T. (1997). 'Isomorphism in Context: The Power and Prescriptions of Institutional Norms.' Academy of Management Journal 40(1): pp. 46-81.

Dannenberg, M., and Kellner, D., (1998). 'The bank of tomorrow with today's technology' International Journal of Bank Marketing 16(2): pp. 90-97.

DiMaggio, P. J., and Powell, W.W. (1991). The Iron Cage Revisited: Institutional Isomorphism and Collective Rationality in Organizational Fields. The New Institutionalism in Organizational Analysis. W. W. Powell, and DiMaggio, P.J. London, University of Chicago Press: pp. 63-82.

Essinger, J. (1993). Managing Technology in Financial Institutions. London, FT/Pitman.

Frazer, P., and Vittas, D. (1982). The Retail Banking Revolution: An International Perspective. London, Michael Lafferty Publications.

Gandy, A. and Champman, C (1996). The Electronic Bank: Banking and IT in Partnership, Chartered Institute of Bankers.

Goodman, P. (1982). Change in Organizations: New perspectives on theory, research, and practice. San Francisco, Jossey - Bass Publishers.

Gosling, P., [Ed.] (1996). Financial Services in the Digital Age: The Future of Banking, Finance and Insurance. Work in the Digital Age. London, Bowerdean Publishing.

Hall, R. (1991). Organizations: Structures, processes and outcomes. London, Sage.

Hung, S., and Whittington, R (1997). 'Strategies and Institutions: A pluralistic account of strategies in the Taiwanese Computer Industry.' Organization Studies 18(4): pp. 551-575.

Jasimuddin, S.M. (2001). 'Saudi Arabian Banks on the Web' Journal of Internet Banking and Commerce. 6(1) pp. 10-15.

Jepperson, R. (1991). Institutions, Institutional Effects, and Institutionalism. The New Institutionalism in Organizational Analysis. Powell, W., and DiMaggio, P. (Eds) Chicago, University of Chicago Press: pp. 143 - 163.

Johnson, G., and Scholes, K (1989). Exploring Corporate Strategy: Text and Cases. New York, Prentice Hall.

Lewis, P., and Stein, H (1997). 'Shifting Fortunes: The political economy of financial liberalization in Nigeria.' World Development 25(1): pp. 5-22.

Madon, S. (1992). The impact of computer-based information systems on rural development: A case study in India, PhD Thesis. Imperial College, University of London.

Maull, R., and Childe, S., (1994). 'Business process re-engineering: an example from the banking sector.' International Journal of Service Industry Management 5(3): pp. 26-34.

Newman, K., Cowling, A, and Leigh, S (1998). 'Case Study: service quality, business process re-engineering and human resources: a case in point?' International Journal of Bank Marketing_16(6): pp. 225-242.

O'Brien (1992). Globalization: The End of Geography. Boston, Bankers Publishing Company.

Oliver, C. (1991). 'Strategic responses to institutional processes.' Academy of Management Review 16(1): pp. 145-179.

Oliver, C. (1997a). 'Sustainable Competitive Advantage: Combining Institutional and Resource-Based View.' Strategic Management Journal 18(9): pp. 697-713.

Oliver, C. (1997b). 'The influence of institutional and task environment relationships on organizational performance: The Canadian construction industry.' Journal of Management Studies 34(1): pp. 99-124.

Orru, M., Biggart, N.W., and Hamilton, G (1991). Organizational Isomorphism in East Asia. The New Institutionalism in Organizational Analysis. W. W. Powell, and DiMaggio, P.J. (Eds) London, University of Chicago Press: pp. 361-389.

Powell, W. W., and DiMaggio, P.J., Ed. (1991). The New Institutionalism in Organizational Analysis. Chicago, University of Chicago Press.

Reinicke, W. H. (1995). Banking, Politics and Global Finance: American Commercial Banks and Regulatory Change, 1980-1990. Aldershot, Edward Elgar Publishing Ltd.

Sargeant, A., and Asif, S. (1998). 'The strategic application of internal marketing – an investigation of UK banking' International Journal of Bank Marketing 16(2): pp. 66-79.

Scheid-Cook, T. L. (1992). 'Organizational Enactments and Conformity to Environmental Prescriptions.' Human Relations 45(6): pp. 537-555.

Scott, R., and Meyer, J (1991). The Organization of Societal Sectors: Propositions and Early Evidence. The New Institutionalism in Organizational Analysis. W. Powell, and DiMaggio, P. (Eds) London, University of Chicago Press.

Selznick, P. (1957). Leadership in Administration. Row, Peterson, Evanston, III.

Shemwell, D.J. and Yavas, U. (1998). 'Seven best practices for creating a sales culture: transitioning from an internally-focused, transaction-oriented culture to a customer-focused, sales-oriented culture' International Journal of Bank Marketing 16(7): pp. 293-98.

Suganthi, M., Balachandher, K and Balachandran, B (2001). 'Internet Banking Patronage: An Empirical Investigation of Malaysia' Journal of Internet Banking and Commerce. 6(1) pp. 1-9.

Talbot, C., (1994) Developing strategic managers for UK public services: a competing values and competences approach. PhD Thesis. London School of Economics.

Utomi, P. (1996). 'Institutions and the evolution of competition in the Nigerian banking industry.' Lagos Business School Management Review 1(2): pp. 71-82.

Walsham, G. (2000). IT, Globalization and Cultural Diversity. In Information Technology in Context: Studies from the perspective of developing countries. Chrisanthi Avgerou and Geoff Walsham (Eds), Aldershot, Ashgate Publishing Ltd: pp. 291-303.

Willcocks, L. P., and Currie, W (1997). Does Radical Reengineering Really Work? Emerging Issues in Strategic Projects. Managing IT as a Stratgeic Resource. L. Willcocks, Feeney, D., and Islei, G. London, Mc-Graw-Hill Companies: pp. 238-273.

Woherem, E. E. (2000). Information Technology in the Nigerian Banking Industry. Ibadan, Spectrum Books Limited.

PART IV
ICT DEVELOPMENT AND GLOBAL SOFTWARE OUTSOURCING

Chapter 18

Mapping the Micro-Foundations of Informational Development: Linking Software Processes, Products and Industries to Global Trends

Kyle Eischen

1. Introduction

In 1949, at the very beginning of the current information technology revolution, John von Neumann stated,

> Science, as well as technology, will in the near and farther future increasingly turn from problems of intensity, substance, and energy, to problems of structure, organization, information, and control. [1]

Mapping the impact of this transformation – from a technology of substance to one of information – is central to understanding the social and economic impact of information technologies and industries. However, such mapping is a difficult process, requiring a general analysis that is subtle and flexible enough to incorporate the diverse experiences, histories and realities that a global, informational environment produces. Fortunately, there is rich theoretical analysis of the nature of this new environment. These are mirrored by equally important detailed case studies of regions, industries, policies and strategies. What is missing is a mechanism to bring the two streams together, to incorporate specific issues of structure, organization, information and control within broader global trends.

The central premise here is that bridging the gap between the theoretical and operational streams requires an understanding of production in an information economy. Such an understanding clarifies question around the nature of information, its transformation into power and profit, and the distinctions between industrial and information economies. It is exactly these questions that are crucial to understanding the possibilities for economic and social development through information technologies and industries.

The argument proceeds through three distinct levels, moving from the micro and specific towards the macro and general. First, the production structure of software is detailed, opening the 'black box' of one of the quintessential informational industries of the coming decades. This lays the basic foundation for a broader consideration of the social nature and impact of software-centered industrialization. Finally, the anticipation of software industry structures by general 'information' and 'network' society theories opens the possibility of developing an 'ideal type' of informational production. This ideal-typology is then applied to two distinct information regions examples in Andhra Pradesh, India and Iceland.

2. The Micro-foundations of Informational Development and the 'Black Box' of Software

The technical and production structures of information industries remain opaque, especially as contrasted with well-defined industrial models. Yet, clarifying informational practices helps answer simple questions — what is information, how is it produced, is this production structure significantly unique — that are essential to both evaluating the impact of industries like software and locating their evolution within broader global economic patterns.

Specific studies do offer detailed mappings of software (Cusumano 1991, Schware 1992, Langlois and Mowery 1996, Heeks 1999, Malecki and Oinas 1999, O'Riain 1999, Parthasarathy 1999, Hoch et al 2000). However, the analysis often only covers partial or case specific aspects of software, limiting the development of more general patterns or helping define the unique 'informational' processes, products and organization of the software industry. Macro-level 'information economy' theories detail the institutional and geographic structures that structure information industries on regional (Saxenian 1994 and 1999, Storper 1997) and global (Gordon 1994, Borrus 1993) levels through new organizational forms (Bartlett and Ghoshal 1994, Benveniste 1994) and mechanisms (Castells 1996, Held et al 1999), but remain difficult to operationalize and evaluate in terms of the simple questions above or locate in specific industries, policies and regions.

Both approaches benefit from defining the technical and production structures of information technologies at the micro-level. Defining the practices that underpin informational development is essential to understanding an information-driven environment in concrete terms with defined and predictable outcomes. Following Rosenberg, 'this is because the specific characteristics of certain technologies have ramifications for economic phenomena that cannot be understood without a close examination of these characteristics (p. vii).' It is exactly these characteristics that are missing or simply assumed in much of the analysis above, and without whom a detailed understanding of von Neumann's transformation remains difficult.

Moving inside the 'black box' of software, it is possible to consider the 'micro-foundations of economic dynamics (Dosi 1984: 1)' that link technical change with the macroeconomic and social forces that structure a globalized, informational environment. Focusing on micro-level practices – and their embeddedness in norms, organizations and practices that translate information into power and profit – opens a path to a more rigorous and systematic understanding of how global trends and micro-processes are interconnected, how software is simultaneously technical and social, and how 'informational development' compares with industrial models.

The extensive literature that considers Fordism and Taylorism indicative of essential social relationships, production processes and organizational structures in the twentieth century (Doray 1988, Giordano 1992, Waring 1991) establishes a pattern for linking 'shop-floor' and larger macroeconomic and social trends. Debates on the transformation of this structure, linked specifically to 'Japanese-style' production systems (Womack et al 1991, Jurgens et al 1993, Sheldrake 1996), indicate how micro-level changes in the organization of production impact upon broader industry and social patterns. Similar arguments have already been made for information technologies as a 'new mode of industrialization'. Henderson considers that 'semiconductors are not only the heart of microelectronics and information industries generally, but that semiconductor companies themselves constitute a production and organizational form that is a paradigm example for the global option in practice'(1989:p.4). Angel (1994) continues this line of reasoning by stating that semiconductor firms are optimized for innovation, which in turn shapes the organizational and geographic structure of the industry. This 'structuring for innovation' is embedded in the linking of flexibility and innovation on the factory floor, shaping formal and informal learning and information exchange.

However, while interesting analytically and methodologically, such analysis is far more similar to considerations of industrial practices than to the informational structures of software. There is no real clarification of what comprises innovation, knowledge or information, and how such practices structure an 'informational mode of development' (Castells 1989). Opening the 'black box' of software, however, provides exactly such definitions and links them to broader social practices and organizational structures that shape software's evolution and social impact.

3. 'Engineering' New Social Architectures: Software as an Informational Practice

The practice of producing software is often defined as software engineering, which (though not exactly accurate) is a helpful starting point to distinguish software's unique production practice. The term 'Engineering' originated in 1720 and is defined as

> **1**: the activities or function of an engineer **2a** : the application of science and mathematics by which the properties of matter and the sources of energy in nature are made useful to people in structures, machines, products, systems, and processes **b**: the design and manufacture of complex products <software

engineering> **3** : calculated manipulation or direction (as of behavior) <social engineering>.
(*Source*: Merriam-Webster New Collegiate Dictionary 2000).

This suggests that software development, like all engineering, is a scientific, rational activity with a quantifiable process. It states that software is manufactured as well as designed, suggesting that software like other engineering practices is amenable to industrial processes and organization – maximized for efficiency by a distinct division of labor, with defined inputs and outputs, managed by an effective rule-bound structure. However, even if accurate, there is a very significant difference between engineering and software development. Engineering is the *application of science and mathematics by which the properties of matter and the sources of energy in nature are made useful*. Software engineering, in contrast, *applies science and mathematics to social phenomenon, translating them into digital, algorithmic forms that are in turn made useful to society*.

The partial weakness of current analysis is the failure to recognize and unpack this process of domain-knowledge transformation at the micro-level. Software development is the process of converting social knowledge and practices into digital form, so that they can be manipulated, disseminated and controlled within a coded binary architecture. Software's intrinsic link to social resources is its essential characteristic, defining its uniqueness, its social impact through products and industry structures, and the inherent limits on its rationalization.

4. The Technical and Informational Structures of Software Production[2]

4.1 The Technical Patterns of Software: Algorithmic, Digitalized Information

The simplest definition of information technology is one word: algorithm. All information technologies essentially define a logical, binary algebraic function that produces consistent outcomes for specific processes, which is then codified either in software or hardware formats. Overall, the technical patterns of information technologies are summarized as:

- The expansion of binary logics and architectures to new knowledge-domains, giving rise to mathematically derived, digital mediums of information exchange.
- The accelerating exploration and discovery of natural and social algorithms that can be translated to binary forms and architectures.
- A constant miniaturization of processing power.
- The pervasive interconnectedness and interoperability of all technology systems (as digitally and algorithmically defined), increasingly wireless and embedded in both organic and inorganic models.
- The increasing dominance of software over hardware as the optimal solution for understanding, developing and implementing digital, algorithmic processes.

The extension of basic digitalized, algorithmic technical patterns throughout society have placed information technologies as a basic medium for the production, manipulation and dissemination of information. The push for flexible, general 'information machines' throughout the development of computing has increasingly involved and been more easily achieved through software, which has become the central method for digitalizing information and implementing algorithmic-based processes.

4.2 The Informational Patterns of Software: Process, Rationalization and Domain-knowledge

Software development involves specific micro-foundational patterns that underlie the evolution of meso and macro-level patterns of software products and industries. The technical aspects of software are not sufficient to understand this process. While the algorithmic digital patterns of software are constant, the technical patterns are built upon socially derived perceptions and understandings, not fixed universal, physical laws. Detailing the production of software places information, as opposed to technology, at the center of the analysis.

The software development process, the human-aspect of producing code, comprises high-level design, low-level design, coding, unit test, system test, beta test (most recently), and final deployment (Jalote 1997). Development is structured, with aspects of automation and engineering, but is fundamentally a 'labor-intensive, intellectually complex, and costly activity in which good management and communication count for much more than technology' (Fenton et al 1994). This structures software processes between

1. the need for skilled labor, and
2. the flows of communication throughout the production process.

The skilled design and quality aspects of the process invariably require contingent decision-making and tacit knowledge that is generally learned 'by doing'. Productivity revolves around labor, with skilled, experienced programmers in high demand to meet increasingly complex application demands. Software development is most effective when each of the development stages is combined within a single individual. As software development increases in size and complexity, from individual to team to firm, the communications transaction costs increase significantly, often resulting in poor quality, missed shipping dates and cost-overruns (Brooks 1995).

Increasing product complexity, low quality and weak productivity growth framed by a skilled-labor and highly interactive process pushes for rationalizing software development. Yet, software development has continually resisted the creation of a repeatable, quantifiable and improvable process. A series of 'magic bullets' – ranging from new development methodologies to new programming languages – have been presented over the last thirty years.[3] All have promised to rationalize or 'industrialize' software development. None have succeeded (Brooks 1987, Gibbs 1994).

So, what prevents software rationalizations? Why don't industrial patterns – 'software manufacturing', 'software engineering', and 'software factories' – predominate in the industry?[4] The simple reason is communication (McBreen 2002). The process of software development, and building basic requirements, is a process of tacit knowledge communication both within the process itself and its translation function (Armour 2002). Translating knowledge from one context to another, like translating any language, involves not just basic rules of grammar and syntax, but also issues of meaning and intent that are contextual and subjective. Programming does have rules of syntax and semantics, but like all languages both the structure and the meaning vary over time and space, even between programmers within a project. The lack of fixed physical laws defining software leaves no direct method to quantify processes and products against a universal standard of quality and efficiency. This informational, communicative aspect of software development inherently limits its rationalization, and thus its engineerability and industrialization.

Software is fundamentally an exercise in translating existing algorithms, in nature or social practices, into digital form. Like other forms of intellectual work, software development is a skilled process that invariably requires contingent decision-making and tacit knowledge. Rationalizing the process involves rigorous definitions of knowledge-domains and the rationalization of the design process. Domain-knowledge, however, is generally tacit, uncodified, dynamic, and often not even explicit to knowledge-holders or participants. Even where knowledge is assumed to be rigorously and fully mathematically defined, there remains the strong possibility of randomness or incompleteness in the algorithms themselves (Norretranders 1998: chapter 3). It should not be surprising that rationalizing the modeling of such processes is exceedingly difficult, and that such efforts are often incomplete, impractical or unsatisfactory.

Overview of Software Development Characteristics

- A process that is organized around the definition, generation, manipulation and transmission of information into socially and economically applicable forms.
- Production tends toward craft-like (or creative or research-like), non-rationalized, tacit knowledge-based systems.
- Skilled human resources, from multiple domains of knowledge, will be the central resource, with a weakly defined division of labor.
- Extensive production structures and growth will take precedence, regardless of the organizational model (proprietary or open-source).
- Increasingly value-added will be greater in the design or mapping the algorithmic aspects of a process than in its actual implementation, manufacture or replication.

4.3 The Impact of Software Development Practice upon Products and Industries

The unique aspects of software development are tightly coupled with the structure and impacts of software product and industry characteristics. The algorithms and domain-knowledge translations, as well as software processes themselves, directly impact upon social and economic interactions through software products and industry structures.

4.3.1 Products The uniqueness of software is not limited to the production process, but extends to products produced through the transformation of information and domain-knowledge. Discussions around software generally fail to grasp the specific nature and interconnection of production and the products produced. Software development produces products that are both

- embedded with information and social assumptions, and
- a challenge to industrial-based social and economic frameworks.

First, the complex processes modeled and the informational, human-centric aspects of production inherently limit software products. Common examples of this, from the Y2K problem to noted software system failures at NASA, clearly demonstrate the limits of software to offer robust (five 'nines' reliability) products (Ullman 1999), even reliable software frames interactions within the assumptions built into the product. A trivial example is the need to go to the 'Start' menu in Windows to shut down a computer. A more important example, given the two billion illiterate individuals in the world, is the assumption that interactions with digital technologies should be text based (and in Roman characters) (Dertouzos 2001).

Second, software can be viewed as congealed social knowledge, but it is unclear if this constitutes innovation or mere documentation. In an industrial model, the traditional answer has revolved directly around the value-added in production (what raw materials become what product). The informational base of software products shifts the debate to a question of control of intellectual property. However, this creates the potential for patenting the 'intellectual commons' of humanity simply through translation to software code (Lessig 1999). The ramifications of such new intellectual property frameworks are not trivial. While software value-added lies in mapping algorithmic forms, recovery of development costs requires control of distribution and replication. 'When access requires reproduction, the right to control reproduction is the right to control access, even to an individual copy already distributed (Davis 2001),' and access in the case of software is access to knowledge and information.

Software also tends toward monopoly around standards, suggesting that patents are not necessarily temporary or limited by legal frameworks. For normal competitive conditions, intellectual property rights are essential to maintaining innovation (Shapiro and Varian 1999), but the establishment of legal software product monopolies may create *de facto* standards upon which the architecture of the informational economy and society rest. Arguably, current legal (the Microsoft or DeCSS trial), social (open-source licensing, patenting of business processes), political (privacy and security issues) conflicts revolve around the fundamental characteristics of software products.

Overview of Software Product Characteristics

- Products have both functional and expressive qualities that increasingly blur and extend existing legal codes and norms based on industrial models of intellectual property.
- Central debates will focus on balancing privacy, intellectual property, public and private goods, and speech concerns around software products.
- Products reflect and are embedded with social knowledge and assumptions.
- Products will be the central source of competition, particularly around *de facto* market standards designed to control innovation and product cycles.
- Competition and legal debates will center on whether the translation and codification of existing processes into digital or algorithmic forms constitutes innovation or mere replication of existing knowledge.
- The nature of competition will tend to produce dominant monopoly products that structure the pace and direction of multiple industries.
- Products will inherently contain flaws derived from their non-rational production, the complexity of processes being mapped, and the assumptions built into their design.

4.3.2 Industry The evolution of the software industry, while on the surface similar to other global industrial or manufacturing patterns, is structured by the unique production and product patterns resulting in very different organizational forms than non-informational industries.

The dominant pattern in the industries evolution has been extensive growth through new sources of skilled-labor. The full utilization of the existing software labor pool within regions and nations, particularly the United States, has pushed spatial and firm reorganization (Hoch et al 2000). However, software is not a footloose industry, but tends to locate in specific regions. Agglomeration is not simply a function of access to sufficient quantities of labor, but is coupled with the communication, design and tacit aspects of the development process. Globalization has occurred, but within the demand of vertically integrated production. This has promoted the agglomeration of production in specific regions within specific firms, with global migration flows fueling production growth. Where production has been globalized, full development of specific products tend to be established in new regions, either as new divisions of firms or as 'outsourced' services to foreign companies. Simultaneously, these patterns have been reinforced by the domain-knowledge structure of both process and products, which pulls production to regions with specific industry, social or economic domain-knowledge. The geographic diversity of this knowledge, often linked to specific culture and institutional patterns, constantly pulls software development into new regions.

Fundamentally, software firm and industry patterns revolve around the need to access, transform and distribute information, resulting in tendencies towards monopoly (both temporary and permanent), vertical integration and regional agglomeration. The industry evolution and globalization directly reflect the demands of its informational practice and products, which are supported through a global network of regional centers of innovation, sustained by global skilled-labor markets, and clustered around globally distributed products within very specific knowledge domains.

Overview of Software Industry Characteristics

- Flexible networked organizational forms, are able to efficiently and rapidly manage the flows of information and 'knowledge workers' will predominate.
- The place and context specific nature of domain-knowledge insures that regions and culture will remain significant in software development.
- Organizations will locate in regional environments that both produce knowledge and stimulate its transformation into congealed marketable forms.
- Regional centers (either independent or within a global firm) will be responsible for the full development cycle of individual products.
- Regions will be globally networked through flows of individuals.
- Labor markets will increasingly be globally defined, though product markets will be fragmented.
- Firms will tend to be vertically integrated and dominant in specific knowledge domains.
- Monopolies will tend to occur, both through the establishment of standards and the drive of firms to control innovation and product cycles.

5. The Importance of 'Informational Practice': Linking Software's Micro-foundations with Information Theories

Opening software details the technical and production practices at the heart of software products and industry structures. It clarifies both why information is valuable and how information is transformed into value through software. Supporting this informational practice are organizational forms that revolve around accessing, managing, translating and distributing information. The source of innovation is centered on products and not processes, where access to unique sources of knowledge and human resources combined with market dominance are central to long-term competitive advantage. These patterns are played out on both globally (as firms seek global labor and product markets), and regionally (agglomerating production and gaining access to unique domain-knowledge).

Table 18.1 Patterns Operating in an Informational Environment

General Patterns	Aspects
Institutional Mechanisms, Norms and Flows Structuring the Informational Environment	• Migration • Investment • Innovation networks • National and regional policy • Private-public partnerships • Entrepreneurial firms-global firm linkages
Informational Production: Processes, Products and Industries Patterns	• Tacit, innovation-driven and informational processes • Products embedded and defined by social-knowledge • Global markets and regional, networked production for industries
Local Processes and Structures Interacting with the Informational Environment	• Regional economic and social networks • Unique local knowledge/information • Regional governance institutions and capacity • Unique social capital • Unique cultural practices • Regional educational and scientific institutions

These micro-foundational patterns help link micro-level (shop floor) processes to broader organizational and institutional trends in the global environment. (See Table 18.1.) The well-theorized institutional mechanisms, norms and flows that structure a global, information economy are clearly visible in software. Global migration, investment and innovation networks, national and regional software strategies supported by public-private partnerships and entrepreneurial-global firm linkages are all well documented for software. Mapping the tacit, domain-knowledge, informational practice of software moves beyond describing such patterns to explaining how and why they exist. Software product innovation is defined by access to unique local domain-knowledge and skills supported by regional economic and social networks, operating in global markets. Regional governance institutions and capacities structure this interaction, building upon local social capital, cultural practices, and educational and scientific institutions.

Software's informational aspects also detail why software is not manufacturing, and why high-technology industry models are limited in explaining its expansion and development. The lack of a defined, rational production process and a constant demand for skilled labor has directed the industry's globalization, but strategically focused such expansion on the management and control of information and knowledge in people and products.

5.1 The Increasing Impact of Software in the Global Environment

Bridging the micro and macro aspects of software is central to understanding a key industry of the coming decades. By 1995, software packages and services had exceeded the value of hardware produced (BSA 1999), with a global market of $470 billion (OECD 1998a) in 1998 expected to grow to exceed $1.7 trillion by 2008 (BSA 1999). Direct global employment was estimated at 2 million in 1998 (OECD 1998a), with just over 40 per cent of these located in the US. If indirect employment (i.e. professionals working outside of the industry) is included, total US employment rises to 2.8 million individuals (BSA 1999). If US patterns hold true, total global employment could reach as high as six million. In 1998, the US software industry was second to motor vehicles and motor vehicle equipment manufacturers in terms of value added. Software was anticipated to become the leading 'manufacturing' sector in 2000, being second only to health-care as the largest overall US industry (BSA 1999).

Equally important, software's impact extends far outside the industry through the increasing extensivity of software processes and products. Multiple industries, organizations and institutions increasingly embody the processes and challenges of software development. The recent mapping of the human genome is excellent example. Celera's success in completing the DNA outline prior to the government-led Human Genome Project rests on the proprietary algorithms developed by the firm, in the form of software run on a series of supercomputers, to determine the exact sequencing of identified individual gene segments ('Monsters in a Box', *Wired* December 2000). Rather than patenting the individual gene discoveries, as was possible, Celera chose to distribute these results freely via the Internet ('Area 22', *Wired* August 2000). Widespread access to the genes was thought to promote the use of Celera's real competitive advantage, the proprietary algorithms for analyzing gene sequences and the accompanying sequence database. In other words, Celera is not a biological research lab, but a firm that converts biological knowledge into binary forms that can be manipulated and analyzed. Its expertise is in performing this analysis more rapidly and cost effectively then competitors, within a constant pattern of new innovation that gives it a series of temporary monopolies. Its ultimate goal, however, is to establish the dominant standard for gene information that will enable it to control the pace and direction of competition with the industry.

The ramifications of these trends are that software patterns are increasingly prevalent in other industries not through replication, but reflection as software processes and products increasingly influence these industries. The increasing embeddedness of software products in new sectors of the economy exposes these industries to the unique patterns of software development as well as the overall industry strategic, locational and labor patterns.

6. Moving towards an Ideal-Typology of 'Informational Production'

Software is an example of a unique information industry and practice reflecting patterns anticipated by existing information society and economy theories. The resonance between software's informational practice and higher-level theories opens up a possibility of defining an 'ideal type' of production in an information society. Developing an ideal-type guides analysis towards more rigorous definitions of both specific and general processes structuring information production and distribution in the global environment.

Constructing an ideal type involves abstracting from reality to build a pattern through which accurate 'terminology, classification and hypotheses' (Weber 1968:19-21) can be developed. Such definition and precision is exactly what is missing from current analysis. Defining information or informational industries and processes remains difficult and subjective at best. The analysis of software demonstrates the practical importance of clarifying the informational, qualitative and social aspects of new information-based technologies. Moving toward an ideal-typology is an attempt to generalize the analysis and elaborate on key concepts within theories of globalization and the information society. An informational production typology should be one aspect explaining linkages between local culture, social and economic formations and broader global patterns focused on information, network organizational forms, innovation and flows.

Building on the analysis of software, an initial ideal-type of production in an informational environment can be briefly and initially outlined as containing:

6.1 Informational Production or Shop-floor Processes

- A process that is organized around the definition, generation, manipulation and transmission of information into socially and economically applicable forms.
- The primary source of information will be domain-knowledge.
- A tacit, subjective and interpretive design practice, difficult to rationalize.
- The division of labor will be weakly defined, with skilled-human labor being the central constraint on productivity and growth.

6.2 Product and Competitive Patterns

- Value-added will be greater in the design, that is in the ability to define and model a process, than in its actual implementation, manufacture or replication.
- Products will have both functional and expressive qualities.
- Market competition will focus on products and not process.
- The knowledge embedded in products will institutionalize social norms, and result in limitations derived from their non-rational production, the complexity of processes being mapped, and the social assumptions.

6.3 Organizational Patterns:

- Monopolies will tend to occur, both through the establishment of standards and the drive of firms to control innovation, product cycles and distribution.
- Firms will tend to be vertically integrated and dominant in specific knowledge domains, but globally networked to efficiently manage information flows and information or knowledge workers.
- Regional sources of knowledge, especially culture, will play a significant role.
- Economic growth and development will center on the development, control, management and location of domain-knowledge.
- Flows of individuals will tend to predominate, as carriers of tacit knowledge and skill, with labor markets increasingly global.

6.4 Applying the Typology: Iceland and Andhra Pradesh [5]

Does this ideal-typology of informational production have value? Table 18.2 shows a preliminary working through of two regional examples in Iceland and Andhra Pradesh.

Table 18.2 Global Patterns, Informational Production and Regional Factors in Iceland and Andhra Pradesh

General Patterns	General Aspects	Aspects in Iceland	Aspects in Andhra Pradesh
Institutional Mechanisms, Norms and Flows Structuring the Informational Environment	– Immigration – Investment – Innovation networks – National and Regional Policy – Private-public partnerships – Entrepreneurial firms-Global Firm linkages	– Skilled immigrant networks – Ties to US venture capital – National development initiatives – DeCode-dovernement partnership – DeCode-Global pharmacy firm links	– Skilled global immigrant networks – Ties to US venture capital – FDI by leading IT firms – National & regional development initiatives – Regional government-Satyam Partnership – Global firm outsourcing linkages to local firms

Informational Production: Processes, Products and Industries Patterns	– Tacit, innovation-driven and informational processes – Products embedded and defined by social-knowledge – Global markets and regional, networked production for industries	– 'Bioprospecting' for unique genetic patterns using skilled researchers, software and hardware – Development of new drugs derived from Iceland's unique culture and regional industry characteristics – Global biotechnology industry linked with local firms and institutions to access and market local genetic information	– Development of software using skilled researchers, engineers and firms – Use of AP exposure to foreign cultures – Global software industry linked with local firms and institutions to access and market local labor
Local Processes and Structures Interacting with the Informational Environment	– Regional economic and social networks – Unique local knowledge/ information – Regional governance institutions and capacity – Unique social capital – Unique cultural practices – Regional educational and scientific institutions	– Population homogeneity – Widespread and in-depth geneology practice – Centralized state-controlled medical records covering most of the 20th century – Tissue samples of the national population through state-controlled medical system – Returning immigrant researchers and doctors	– Regional Telugu identity – Weak existing industrial structure – IT used for better governance and regional development – Regional political party – Extensive immigrant networks in software firms globally – Over production of skilled SW labor and English-language university education

Source: Eischen 2000b, Eischen 2001a and Eischen 2001b.

On a first take, the two regions are quite distinct, and it seems counterintuitive to include them in a comparative analysis. However, the typology opens a means to understand how both regions interact with and respond to broader trends in the global environment, filtering such interactions through unique regional social, historical and political factors.

Both regions have historically been marginalized from the global economy, but are rapidly emerging as important nodes within global networks of informational production. While emerging in two distinct industries, biotechnology and software, the overall patterns linking these new industries to the global economy are similar. Both industries benefited from extensive immigrant networks to the US, skilled software professionals in the case of Andhra Pradesh and leading biomedical professionals in the case of Iceland. Such networks bridged unique knowledge of local resources, policies and initiatives with global venture and foreign investment. Distinct public-private partnerships, specifically Satyam in Andhra Pradesh and deCode in Iceland, have been crucial to establishing the specific informational industry in both regions. Such partnerships have also taken the form of linkages between local entrepreneurial and global firms to participate in global networks of innovation and production.

Both biotechnology and software follow similar patterns of informational industries. Both are tacit, innovation-driven, informational processes with products derived from and embedded with specific social-knowledge and characteristics. They both are intimately linked into global markets for services and products that are structured through specific regional networks of production, both being nodes in overall global networks. Both regions provide unique and in many senses central resources to their global industries. Andhra Pradesh supplies a large share of the software professionals for the global industry, most importantly an estimated 25 per cent of all H1-B visa holders in the US alone. Iceland provides a genetically pure population that is forms an ideal database for genetic research. Comparative advantage of each region is thus based on local social factors and not natural endowments.

It is on the local level that the two regions diverge dramatically. Most significantly, the issue of scale and development are central. Andhra Pradesh has a population of roughly 80 million people, with an average per capita income of approximately $400/year and an illiteracy rate of 50 per cent. In contrast, Iceland has roughly 280,000 people with a per capita income of $31,000/year and almost full literacy. Politically, Iceland is an independent nation, while Andhra Pradesh works within the Indian national context. Socially and culturally, the differences are equally distinct, particularly around the cultural and religious homogeneity of Iceland contrasted with the diversity and richness of Andhra Pradesh's social structure.

The differences, however, should not be overlooked or underemphasized. The potential of the typology is that is helps define both biotechnology and software as informational industries, integrally linked to broader global patterns and networks through similar production patterns. The structure and shape of the connections are filtered through the basic social and economic environments of the distinct regions. The interactions with the global environment, and importantly the development of informational production, will raise similar strategic and policy issues for both regions, but the response of each region –which will structure the impact of such interaction in the long term – is and will be shaped by regional social resources, demands and developments. The typology – while allowing for comparison by signaling the underlying informational patterns of biotechnology and software – still retains the unique regional features and connections to global networks operating in both industries. It thus allows for contrasting individual industry and regional factors within an overall framework of an informational economy.

Analysis of globalization and the information society (Castells 1996, Gordon 1994, Held et al 1999, Amin 1994, Drucker 1993, Shapiro and Varian 1999) has already established similar macro-level patterns for innovation and knowledge, global flows, network organizational forms, and new social structures. Clearly, the typology is preliminary, particularly needing a deeper mapping of the regulation and institutional aspects of production. However, the typologies purpose is to help sharpen analysis that can link well-established theories of governance and power in the informational society with on the ground developments, without losing the richness and subtlety of micro-level and regional differences in the process. The ideal-type of information production serves as a general tool to clarify why information is valuable, and how it is structured and valorized in the global economy on a micro-level.

7. Coda: Towards and Understanding of Informational Development

Detailed analysis of informational production helps understand exactly how and why informational economies are different. As the detailed analysis of software demonstrates, the informational patterns involved in the development of new technology industries signals specific organizational, institutional and environmental incentives and requirements. These factors in turn both reflect and impact specific strategies and policy initiatives at the firm and regional level. In this sense, software as an industry may have a far greater impact as an engine of social transformation than as an engine of economic growth. This helps explain many of the apparent contradictions and trends visible in informational industries like software that cannot be adequately explained through existing models of economic development.

Given the well-documented expansion of the global software industry to new regions, the patterns embedded in the production process will also continue to emerge in new regions. Clearly, while the emergence of these patterns creates similar incentive structures, opportunities and challenges for firms and governments, the long-term impact is not predetermined. The establishment of industries like software may present a similar set of issues for each region, but the emergence of the industry and its structure will be filtered through local capacities, resources and demands. In other words, information economies raise similar social issues that each existing and new region will filter and address through local histories, cultures and institutions. This is exactly what information or globalization theories would anticipate.

The purpose of moving toward an ideal-typology of informational production is twofold:

1) To help rigorously define informational industries, and
2) understand the general social and economic impacts of informational development.

In the first case, the production, product and industry patterns visible in software are also present in other 'informational' industries. This helps explain why informational industries tend to converge as well as emerge in similar regions. In the case of Iceland and Andhra Pradesh, it is not surprising that the initial establishment of a specific industry has evolved into new but linked informational sectors, with Iceland moving into software development and Andhra Pradesh moving into biotechnology. Similar global patterns of immigration, investment and innovation support both industries, and arguably even require inputs from both sectors to be successful sustained. Such global patterns are supported by specific organizational and institutional structures on the firm and regional level that establish the basic knowledge and processes of informational production.

In the second instance, similarities across informational sectors signal the general social and economic impacts of informational development. Simply, informational industries share similar ties to the global environment and similar production structures on the regional level. This explains why diverse regions as well as diverse industries generate similar issues surrounding, to name just a few, monopoly, privacy, education, employment, immigration, social and economic equity and intellectual property. This similarity has very specific consequences for policy and strategy. Most positively, it provides a very distinct roadmap for economic development linked to informational industries, with similar institutional and organizational transformations and advantages providing a general platform for competitive advantage in the global economy. More negatively, it suggests that the social and economic problems linked to informational development, as witnessed in some of the more advanced regional economies like Silicon Valley, are not linked to a particular information industry or political environment. The challenge for governments and firms is that specific industry constraints as well as broader general implications must and should be addressed to develop sustainable growth trends.

The diversity of regional capacities and resources guarantees a diversity of solutions to both specific industry issues and more general issues derived from informational production. This, arguably, is the hidden challenge as well as opportunity for informational development. While global trends and information industries promote similar constraints and incentives, they simultaneously encourage diversity and allow space for innovative regional policy and social solutions. The diversity of such responses requires careful and detailed analysis, which then can be located within broader global trends. Lessons learned in one sector or environment have potential significance for strategy and policy for even seemingly distinct experiences in other regions. The relative cohesion of experience derived from informational production provides a means to not only understand the general impact of new technologies and industries, but to actively develop policies and actions that institutionalize and frame such patterns within local needs and values.

Acknowledgement

I would like to thank Lisa Nishioka and Del Cielo at CGIRS, and the UC Institute for Global Conflict and Cooperation for administrative and financial support that made this work possible. I have also benefited greatly from insightful comments by anonymous reviewers as well as dynamic discussions with participants of the IFIP 9.4 conference. As usual, however, all errors and statements are solely attributable to the author.

Notes

1 From Rhodes (1999).
2 A more detailed version of this section can be found in Eischen (2000a) and Eischen (2002).
3 Structured design and programming have been attempted. Process models like the Waterfall (Pressman 1997), Spiral (Boehm, 1998), Software Life-Cycle (Davis 1997), personal process model (Ferguson et al 1997) and open source (Raymond 1999) have been implemented. New programming languages such as C++ that are based in object-oriented programming have been used to maximize software reuse and maintenance. Software metrics have been created that attempt to quantify and map the software process based on TQM principles (Grady, 1994). Cost and quality models such as COCOMO (Legg, 1997) and the Capability Maturity Model (Herbsleb et al 1997) have also been developed.
4 Though some analysis still seems to suggest that it has or will be. See Cusumano (1991), Baetjer (1998) and Poppendieck (2001).
5 For a more detailed overview of both Andhra Pradesh and Iceland, see: Eischen 2000b, Eischen (2001a) and Eischen (2001b).

References

Amin, Ash, Editor (1994) *Post-Fordism: A Reader*, Cambridge, USA: Blackwell.

Angel, David P. (1994) *Restructuring for Innovation: the Remaking of the U.S. Semiconductor Industry*, New York: Guilford.

Armour, Phillip G. (2002) 'The Spiritual Life of Projects: the Human Factor in Software Development is the Ingredient that Ultimately Gives a Project Team its Soul' *Communications of the ACM*, vol. 45, no.1, January.

Baetjer, Howard (1998) *Software as Capital: an Economic Perspective on Software Engineering*, Los Alamitos, CA: IEEE Computer Society.

Bartlett, Christopher and Sumantra Ghoshal (1994) *Beyond the M-Form: Toward a Managerial Theory of the Firm*, Carnegie Bosch Institute for Applied Studies in International Management, Working Paper 94-6.

Benveniste, Guy (1994) *The Twenty-First Century Organization: Analyzing Current Trends – Imagining the Future*, San Francisco: Jossey-Bass Publishers.

Boehm, Barry W. (1988) 'A Spiral Model of Software Development and Enhancement', *Computer*, May.

Borrus, Michael (1993) *The Regional Architecture of Global Electronics: Trajectories, Linkages and Access to Technology*, Berkeley, California: Berkeley Roundtable on the International Economy, University of California, Berkeley.

Brooks, Frederick P. (1987) 'No Silver Bullet: Essence and Accidents of Software Engineering', *Computer Magazine*, April.

Brooks, Frederick P. (1995) *The Mythical Man-month: Essays on Software Engineering*, Reading, Massachusetts: Addison-Wesley.

Business Software Alliance [BSA] (1999) *Forecasting a Robust Future: An Economic Study of the U.S. Software Industry*, June, *http://www.bsa.org/*

Castells, Manuel (1989) *The Informational City: Information Technology, Economic Restructuring, and the Urban-regional Process*, Oxford: Blackwell.

Castells, Manuel (1996) *The Information Age: The Rise of the Network Society*, Cambridge, Massachusetts: Blackwell Publishers.

Cusumano, Michael A. (1991) *Japan's Software Factories: A Challenge to U.S. Management*, New York: Oxford University Press.

Davis, Alan M. (1997) 'Software Life Cycle Models', in *Software Engineering Project Management*, Richard Thayer, Editor, Los Alamitos, California: IEEE Computer Society.

Davis, Randall (2001) 'The Digital Dilemma' *Communications of the ACM*, February Vol.44, No.2.

Dertouzos, Michael L. (2001) *The Unfinished Revolution: Human-centered Computers and What They Can Do for Us*, New York: HarperCollins.

Doray, Bernard (1988) *From Taylorism to Fordism: a Rational Madness*, London: Free Association Books.

Dosi, Giovanni (1984) *Technical Change and Industrial Transformation*, New York: St. Martin's Press.

Drucker, Peter Ferdinand (1993) *Post-Capitalist Society*, New York: HarperBusiness.

Eischen, Kyle (2000a) *Information Technology: History, Practice and Implications for Development*, Working Paper 2000-4, Center for Global, International and Regional Studies, University of California, Santa Cruz, www2.ucsc.edu/cgirs

Eischen, Kyle (2000b) *National Legacies, Software Technology Clusters and Institutional Innovation: The Dichotomy of Regional Development in Andhra Pradesh, India*, Presented at the Association of Collegiate Schools of Planning Annual Conference, November 2-5, Atlanta, Georgia.

Eischen, Kyle (2001a) *The Micro-Foundations of E-commerce: Informational-focused Development in Andhra Pradesh, India*, Prepared for the OECD Development Centre *E-Commerce for Development: Reviewing Experiences, Comparing New Ideas* conference, Bologna, Italy: (4 - 5 May).

Eischen, Kyle (2001b) 'Commercializing Iceland: Biotechnology, Culture, and Global-Local Linkages in the Information Society', Working Paper 2001-2, Center for Global, International and Regional Studies, University of California, Santa Cruz, www2.ucsc.edu/cgirs

Eischen, Kyle (2002) *'Engineering' Social Architectures: The Social Nature and Impact of Software*, Working Paper 2002–1, Center for Global, International and Regional Studies, University of California, Santa Cruz, www2.ucsc.edu/cgirs

Fenton, Norman, Shari Lawrence Pfleeger and Robert Glass (1994) 'Science and Substance: A Challenge to Software Engineers', *IEEE Software*, Volume 11, Number 4, July.

Ferguson, Pat, Watts Humphrey, Soheil Khajenoori, Susan Macke and Annette Matvya (1997) 'Results of Applying the Personal Software Process', *Computer*, May.

Gibbs, Wayt (1994) 'Software's Chronic Crisis', *Scientific American*, Volume 271, Number 3, September.

Giordano, Lorraine (1992) *Beyond Taylorism: Computerization and the New Industrial Relations*, New York: St. Martin's Press.

Gordon, Richard (1994) 'State, Milieu, Network: Systems of Innovation in Silicon Valley', Santa Cruz, CA: Working Paper 94-4, Center for the Study of Global Transformations, University of California, Santa Cruz.

Heeks, Richard (1999) *Software Strategies in Developing Countries*, Institute for Development Policy and Management, University of Manchester, Working Paper #6, June, http://www.man.ac.uk/idpm

Held, David, Anthony McGrew, David Goldblatt and Jonathan Perraton (1999) *Global Transformations: Politics, Economics and Culture*, Stanford, California: Stanford University Press.

Henderson, Jeffrey (1989) *The Globalisation of High-Technology Production: Society, Space, and Semiconductors in the Restructuring of the Modern World*, New York: Routledge.

Herbsleb, James, David Zubrow, Dennis Goldenson, Will Hayes and others (1997) 'Software Quality and the Capability Maturity Model', *Communications of the ACM*, Volume 40, Number 6, June.

Hoch, Detlev J, Cyriac R. Roeding, Gert Purkert and Sandro K. Lindner (2000) *Secrets of Software Success*, Boston: Harvard Business School Press.

Jalote, Pankaj (1997) *An Integrated Approach to Software Engineering*, New York: Springer

Jurgens, Ulrich, Thomas Malsch and Knuth Dohse (1993) *Breaking from Taylorism: Changing Forms of Work in the Automobile Industry*, London: Cambridge University Press.

Langlois, Richard N. and David C. Mowery (1996) 'The Federal Government Role in the Development of the U.S. Software Industry', in *The International Computer Software Industry: A Comparative Study of Industry Evolution and Structure*, Edited by David C. Mowery, Oxford University Press, New York.

Legg, Deanna B. (1997) 'Synopsis of COCOMO', in *Software Engineering Project Management*, Richard Thayer, Editor, Los Alamitos, California: IEEE Computer Society.

Lessig, Lawrence (1999) *Code: and Other Laws of Cyberspace*, New York: Basic Books.

Malecki, Edward and Paivi Oinas, Editors (1999) *Making Connections: Technological Learning and Regional Economic Change*, Brookfield USA: Ashgate.

McBreen, Peter (2002) *Software Craftsmanship: the New Imperative*, New York: Addison-Wesley.

Norretranders, Tor (1998) *The User Illusion: Cutting Consciousness Down to Size*, New York: Viking.

OECD (1998a) *The Software Sector: A Statistical Profile for Selected OECD Countries*, Committee for Information, Computer and Communications Policy, January, *http://www.oecd.org*

O'Riain, Sean (1999) 'The Flexible Developmental State: Globalization, Information Technology and the 'Celtic Tiger', Presented at the *Global Networks, Innovation and Regional Development: The Informational Region as Development Strategy* conference, November 11-13, UC Santa Cruz, http://www2.ucsc.edu/cgirs/globalnet

Parthasarathy, Balaji (1999) 'Institutional Embeddedness and Regional Industrialization: The State and the Indian Computer Software Industry', Presented at the *Global Networks, Innovation and Regional Development: The Informational Region as Development Strategy* conference, November 11-13th, UC Santa Cruz, http://www2.ucsc.edu/cgirs/globalnet

Poppendieck, Mary (2001) 'Lean Programming,' *Software Development*, May.

Pressman, Roger S. (1997) 'Software Engineering', in *Software Engineering: A Practitioner's Approach*, M. Dorman and R.H. Thayer, Editors, New York: McGraw-Hill.

Raymond, Eric (1999) *The Cathedral and the Bazaar: Musings on Linux and Open Source By an Accidental Revolutionary*, Sebastopol, California: O'Reilly.

Rhodes, Richard, Editor (1999) *Visions of Technology: A Century of Vital Debate About Machines, Systems and the Human World*, New York: Simon & Schuster.

Rosenberg, Nathan (1982) *Inside the Black Box: Technology and Economics*, New York: Cambridge University Press.

Saxenian, AnnaLee (1994) *Regional Advantage: Culture and Competition in Silicon Valley and Route* 128, Cambridge, Massachusetts: Harvard University Press.

Saxenian, AnnaLee (1999) *Silicon Valley's New Immigrant Entrepreneurs*, Public Policy Institute of California.

Schware, Robert (1992) 'Software Industry Entry Strategies for Developing Countries: a 'Walking on Two Legs' Proposition,' *World Development*, vol 20, no 2, Feb: 143.

Shapiro, Carl and Hal R. Varian (1999) *Information Rules: A Strategic Guide to the Network Economy*, Boston, Massachusetts: Harvard Business School Press.

Sheldrake, John (1996) *Management Theory: from Taylorism to Japanization*, Boston: International Thomson Business Press.

Storper, Michael (1997) *The Regional World: Territorial Development in a Global Economy*, Los Angeles: Graduate School of Architecture and Urban Planning, University of California, Los Angeles.

Ullman, Ellen (1999) 'The Myth of Order', *Wired*, Version 7.04, April, *http://www.wired.com*

Waring, Stephen P. (1991) *Taylorism Transformed: Scientific Management Theory since* 1945, Chapel Hill: University of North Carolina Press.

Weber, Max (1968) *Economy and Society; An Outline of Interpretive Sociology*, New York: Bedminster Press Brooks.

Wired (Various), www.wired.com

Womack, James P., Daniel T. Jones and Daniel Roos (1991) *The Machine that Changed the World*, New York: Harper Perennial.

Chapter 19

Risky Business: A Case Study on Information Systems Development in Nigeria

Anja Mursu, H. Abimbola Soriyan, Mikko Korpela

1. Introduction

The role of information technology (IT) in socio-economic development, and human development, in developing countries has been emphasized in the literature (Odedra-Straub 1996; Waema 1996). In all societies technology (any technology) has always been subjected to change (Andah 1992) and information technology is considered to narrow the gap between industrialized countries and developing countries. Still, the introduced IT applications have not been successfully applied, for example in Africa, thus inadequately fulfilling the desired outcomes (Odedra-Straub 1996, Avgerou and Land 1992). Appropriate and sustainable software packages and organizational information systems must therefore be developed locally, even if a foreign package can be used as a starting point for adaptation (cf. Heeks 1999). 'All major IT projects must have local content and involvement for sustainability' (a notion made in the Made-in-Nigeria software exhibition in Lagos 2001). In that sense, the question of IT introduction is not about the 'transfer of technology' alone, but adopting and applying the technology appropriately to the extent that its adoption produces the expected socio-economic effect.

Information System Development (ISD) is an essential part of the diffusion and implementation of IT. There is not much empirical evidence on whether ISD is very similar or widely different in industrialized and developing countries, since very little empirical research has been conducted in the field of ISD in developing countries. In this paper we present a Finnish-Nigerian joint project, named INDEHELA-Methods. The main interest of the project is to study ISD work practices and methods in Nigeria, and the kind of risks and constraints software companies face in their business. The main emphasis of this paper is to introduce one case (of several cases) as an example of systems development work in Nigeria, and problems faced by the company. We compare the case to a picture of a 'typical software company in Nigeria' based on the results we have obtained from a survey of software industry in Nigeria. We also relate the case to a risk study we conducted concerning most important risk factors in software development in Nigeria.

The structure of the paper is as follows. The research objectives, settings and the research context of the INDEHELA-Methods project are described in the first section, as well as some basic definitions. Also the results of the survey of software industry and risk study are briefly presented as a part of the context description. The following section introduces the theoretical research framework used in case studies. The case is then described as an example of systems development project in Nigeria. We particularly want to clarify the differences in systems development work, compared to more industrialized countries – most differences seem to be in a socio-economic context. The paper ends with a discussion of the case in light of the survey results, an evaluation of the software industry in Nigeria and conclusions.

2. Research Objectives, Settings and Context of INDEHELA-Method project

The research project – INDEHELA-Methods (Methods for Informatics Development for Health in Africa) – is a joint project by the Department of Computer Science and Engineering of the Obafemi Awolowo University (OAU), Nigeria, and the Computing Centre of the University of Kuopio, Finland. The main objectives of the project are, firstly, to produce empirical information and an understanding of the practice and problems of ISD in Nigeria, and secondly, to provide improved methods, techniques and practices for IS developers in Nigeria, based on the empirical results as well as literature. One objective is also to contribute to the education of IS at universities. Healthcare is used as the main field of application in practical experiments when testing the improved practices in the development of health informatics at OAU teaching hospital.

By information system (IS) we mean a social system, which is facilitated by modern technology (Land 1994). It means an information technology (IT) – for example, a software product – *in use* (Korpela et al. 2000a). Accordingly, software engineering (SE) deals with the *technical construction* of software products and information systems development (ISD) deals with how to *serve organizational purposes* by means of software products. ISD is a change process which is driven by certain more or less clear objectives. It includes phases such as analysis, design, programming, implementation, and maintenance, as well as some support activities like project management and quality assurance (Mathiassen 1998). It can be assumed that SE is more similar across countries, while ISD deals with social issues and thus varies more according to the socio-economic and political setting in question (Mursu et al. 2000).

The main units of analysis and research questions of the project deal with an entire service chain of activities around ISD in Nigeria, including university education, IS development in software companies, and IS use in customer organizations who provide services to citizens and communities. Communities should be the ultimate beneficiaries of IT. In this paper we concentrate on the research questions dealing with *methods, techniques and practices used in ISD work* and the *most common risk factors in software projects*. To answer these questions we have conducted empirical research in several parts. We started with an interview study focusing narrowly on *risk factors* in software development projects (Mursu *et al.*, 1999). We then enlarged the scope to cover ISD in a wider sense. An overall view can be achieved through *interview surveys* among a representative sample of the software companies. The overall view is supplemented by descriptive *in-depth case studies* of a few companies and projects. The overall research design has been reported in more detail elsewhere (Korpela et al. 2000b, Soriyan et al. 2001).

The research is taking place in Nigeria, which is the most populous developing country in Sub-Saharan Africa (SSA). There were more than 200 registered companies offering computer-related services in 1988 (UNIDO 1989) and more than 500 in 1994 (Alabi 1994). By the turn of the century, the number of companies is by extrapolation at least 1000, maybe even 1500. However, most of them concentrate on areas such as hardware sales, training courses and others. We estimate that probably no more than 20 per cent of the companies, i.e. 150-200, develop their own software or provide information systems services. We are interested in the companies providing information systems services by developing their own software or by customizing foreign produced software to local needs.

3. The Industry Profile Based on Survey

Based on our survey study (sample size of 103), we have got a picture of 'the typical Nigerian software company'. The sampling principle was to get as many software companies as possible, retaining geographical spread to give the study a national outlook. The Computer Association of Nigeria (CoAN) and the chartered Computer Professionals (CPN) provided the initial working list of software companies and their addresses. (Soriyan et al. 2002)

Most of the software companies (56 per cent) are located in the Lagos state, which is the commercial centre of Nigeria. The rest in our sample (44 per cent) are quite evenly distributed among 13 other states (37 states altogether), mostly in the southern part of Nigeria. Only 3 per cent of the companies are located in the Federal Capital Territory, Abuja. (Soriyan et al. 2002)

The companies are mostly Nigerian owned (89 per cent), since foreign investors are not encouraged to establish any business in the country due to the instability of economic and political system – 62 per cent were established in the 1990s, 20 per cent in the 1980s (after 1985 increasing along with the use of the PC) and 7 per cent in the year 2000 or after. (Soriyan et al. 2002)

Most of the companies (78 per cent) have less than 15 employees (92 per cent less than 50), 1 per cent have more than 100 employees. The average educational background is a bachelor's degree or equivalent. The average age of a typical IT professional is within the age bracket of 30-39 years and with an average work experience of 1-5 years. (Soriyan et al. 2002)

Typical customer companies are medium-size (51-250 employees) or large enterprises; there were not many small-size or very large enterprises. The main customer branches (Figure 19.1) are in the private sector services (wholesale and retail trade, transportation, financial services, IT and other business services) or public sector services (healthcare, education or administration), industry (mining, oil, construction, electricity, gas, water supply.) and manufacturing (food, textiles, machinery, equipment, etc,). The average number of customer companies per a software company is 36, every fourth company has at least one customer outside of Nigeria. (Soriyan et al. 2002)

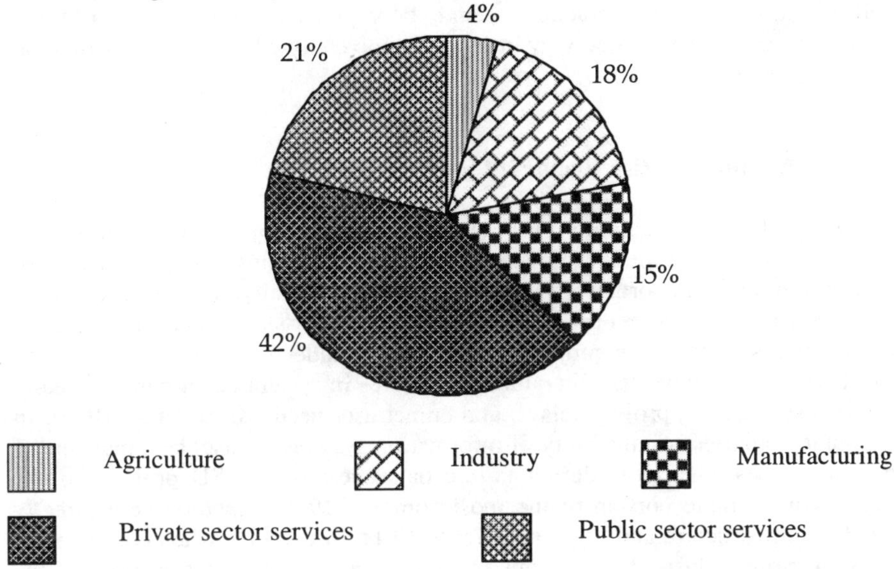

Figure 19.1 Customers' main business activities

Regarding the products, the majority of the companies install imported applications or customize self-made applications. 45 per cent of services are based on imported packages, 29 per cent on locally developed packages, and the rest on tailoring. However, companies usually provide more than one type of service, for example a company can offer both imported packages and tailoring from scratch. (Soriyan et al. 2002)

The software companies mostly use fourth generation programming languages or application generators (51 per cent) with in-house developed analysis and design methods (54 per cent) or formal object-oriented methodologies (28 per cent). Concerning the platform of the customer, 33 per cent use client-server system with graphic interface, 26 per cent stand-alone PCs, only 13 per cent have web-based system. (Soriyan et al. 2002)

Typically projects last less than a year, involving less than six people. A typical organization for a project is a formally established implementation team of IT professionals with an internal supervisory board. Usually the project leader comes from the software company, being a senior manager or IT person. Projects are structured to specific phases (44 per cent), or they are flexible because of a prototyping approach. All in all, the main business of software development seems to lie in small-scale projects at the moment. (Soriyan et al. 2002)

In the questionnaire, the possible problem areas in companies' systems development work practices were also asked to be stated. The most problematic areas seem to be in risk management, database design, testing, and project planning and management. But when seen in light of problems that the companies point to in ISD ducation, their work practices seem to be in pretty good order. According to respondents, there seems to be very little in the university education that is in good shape. (Soriyan et al. 2002)

4. The Most Common Risk Factors of Software Projects

In the study of the most common risk factors in software projects in Nigeria we got responses from 39 IT experts from eleven software companies in Lagos. We asked to name ten most important risk factors each and finally to rank the whole combined list of risk factors in order of importance. By risk we mean a product of uncertainty associated with projects and the magnitude of potential loss due to project failure. In the western literature the failures in system development usually refer to cost overruns, project delays, and unmet user needs (Barki et al. 1993). In developing countries sustainability of information systems (in use) becomes one of the major issues when considering failure or success of an ISD project. In our study, a considerable portion of the most common 19 risk factors were directly related to infrastructure and economy (Table 19.1). In contrast, when compared to results in more industrialized countries, our results lacked risks related to the business strategy level. The other factors were very similar to those collected in other risk studies conducted in industrialized countries (see Keil et al. 1998, Mursu et al. 1999b). The results of the Delphi study on risk factors in software projects will be published separately (e.g. Mursu 2002).

In the case studies of INDEHELA-Methods projects one objective is to understand how these risks and constraints affect ISD work activities in local software companies. Before presenting one case as an example, the following section describes the methodological framework used in case studies.

Table 19.1 The most common risk factors in software development in Nigeria

1.	Misunderstanding requirements
2.	Lack of effective development process/methodology
3.	Lack of required knowledge/skills in the project personnel
4.	Lack of skilled personnel
5.	Under funding of development
6.	Importing of foreign packages
7.	Lack of 'people skills' in project leadership
8.	Unclear/misunderstood scope/objectives
9.	Changing scope/objectives

10	Energy supply
11.	Artificial deadlines
12.	Inadequate user training
13.	Choosing the wrong development strategy
14.	Lack of top management commitment to the project
15.	Failure to gain user commitment
16.	IT awareness in the country
17.	Huge capital requirements
18.	Erratic and unreliable communication network
19.	Trying out new development method / technology during important project

5. Methodological Framework for Case Studies

The research framework used in the case studies is based on Activity Theory (see Korpela et al. 2000 a; 2001 a; 2001 b). Figure 19.2 presents basic elements of the model of a work activity, called as central activity. In short, a collective work activity (e.g., information systems development) consists of the actions of a number of individual *actors* (managers, analysts, programmers), whose job it is to transform a shared *object* of work (a problem in some activity in a user organization) into a joint *outcome* (information system for that activity in a user organization). The actors influence the transformation process through material and nonmaterial *means of work* (methods, techniques, IT skills and knowledge, etc.). The actions of the individual actors, which do not necessarily take place simultaneously and in the same place, are linked together by *means of coordination and communication* (division of labour, rules, standards, meetings, project plan, documentation) into the *collective actor* (project team). The overall way of carrying out an activity can be characterized as the *mode of operation* (e.g., hierarchical, team-oriented, collaborative, phased).

The core of ISD activity can be seen as a temporary activity between two departments, companies or other organizations. In Figure 19.3, ellipses illustrate different activities, ISD being in the centre. The starting point or object of the ISD activity is the solving of a problem in the users' work process, or the possible need for better facilities. For example, the ISD activity could be between a software company and a bank that has problems in its human resource management. The outcome is the development of a human resource management system for the bank and its personnel management concerns.

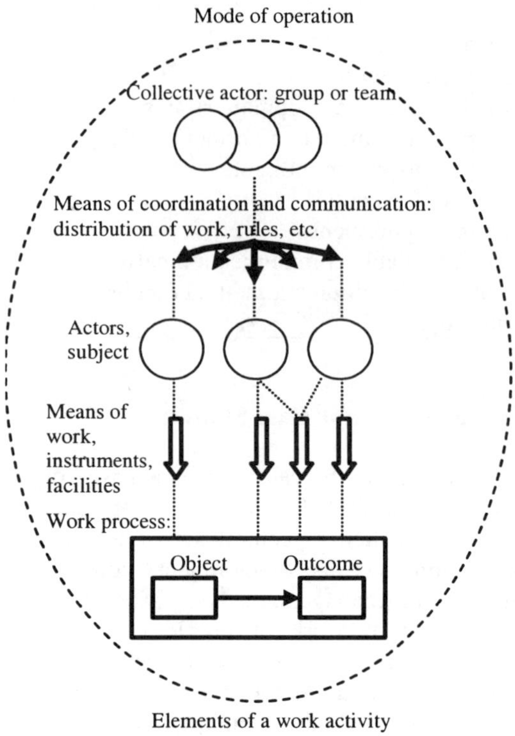

Figure 19.2 The elements of a collective work activity (Korpela et al. 2000a)

Likewise, an analysis includes *supporting activities* which 'produce' the means, objects, actors and rules, required in the central activity. These supporting activities can be inside or outside of the company. For example in case of ISD, the producers are universities, vendors, government (with legislation etc.) and also management activity or other activities inside the company. We can therefore talk about the *network of activities*.

This framework was used as a guideline to direct the interviews. In the following section we briefly present one case as an example of the main elements of ISD activity in Nigeria by using the presented framework as a method for analysis (c.f. Mursu 2002).

6. A Case of ISD as an Activity in a Small Locally-Owned Software Company

Gamma Corporation was established in 1988 for IT training, software development and engineering. The company now has 35–40 employees altogether in Lagos and Abuja (the new capital city). The organization is hierarchical, divided into software solutions, training and consultancy units, as illustrated in Figure 19.4. Besides the IT experts, there are secretaries, some drivers and security men. We interviewed the executive director of software solutions, and two analysts.

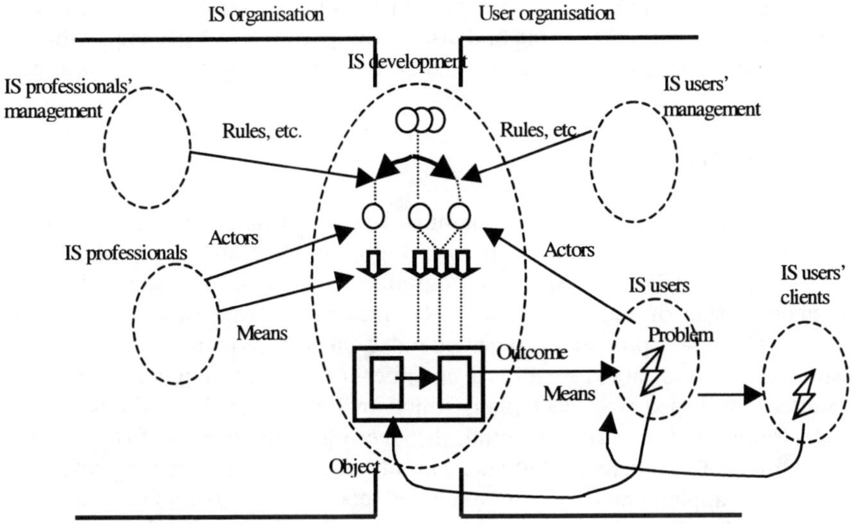

Figure 19.3 The composition of IS development as an activity (Korpela et al. 2001a)

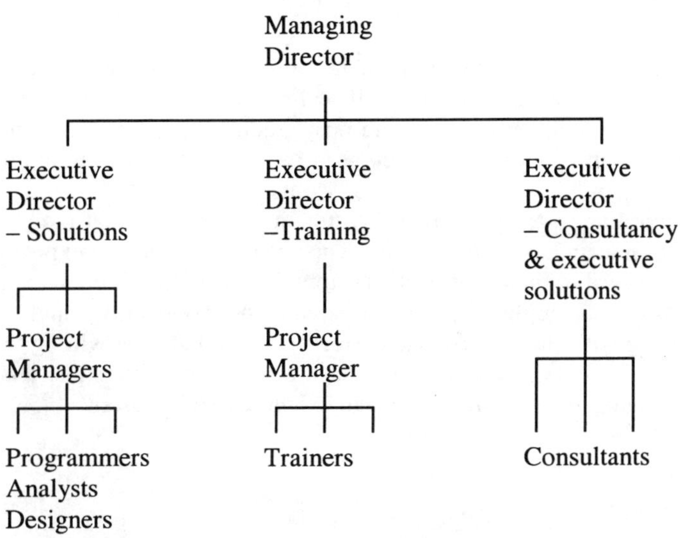

Figure 19.4 The organizational structure of the company

6.1 Object

The customer in the case was a bank. The bank was in the process of re-engineering its business processes (BPR). One of the aspects to be renewed was human resource management (HRM), for which the company Gamma was chosen as a provider. The bank had an old system for HRM, which was developed in-house some years earlier. Gamma had also developed an HRM package, which had been customized to a number of organizations. The project was commissioned in mid-1998.

6.2 Collective Actor

After the contract was signed by Gamma and the bank, they created a project organization. It was consisted of the steering committee and the implementation team (Figure 19.5). The steering committee consisted of heads of relevant departments, head of audit and head of IT-department (who was a woman) from the bank. Gamma's project manager attended steering committee meetings as a consultant; he was not formally a member of the committee. The steering committee confirmed a project plan, which included a project schedule, all the tasks, activities and resources. Overall, the steering committee had two main tasks: to solve financial problems and to take care of human resources in the project.

The implementation team included people from both Gamma and the bank. From the bank there was a team leader (one of the senior users), users, bank's own IT-people and the audit representative. From Gamma there were analysts and programmers.

6.3 Actors

At Gamma, three to five technical persons were involved in the project at various times (two of them were women). All technical staff had at least a Bachelor's degree in Computer Science, some had post-graduate degrees. Since the company is also a training institution, they made use of the opportunity to train their staff on relevant courses in-house, and occasionally outside.

According to the executive director, it is important that the people in the implementation team have '*right skills*'. This means that Gamma expect users to be experts with regard to their work. The customers expect that Gamma be the experts in technology and application. Both should be cooperative and capable of communicating with each other. The customers should also be willing to learn new technologies. These expectations however are not always met. The team leader's role is very crucial and his attitude sets an example to other users.

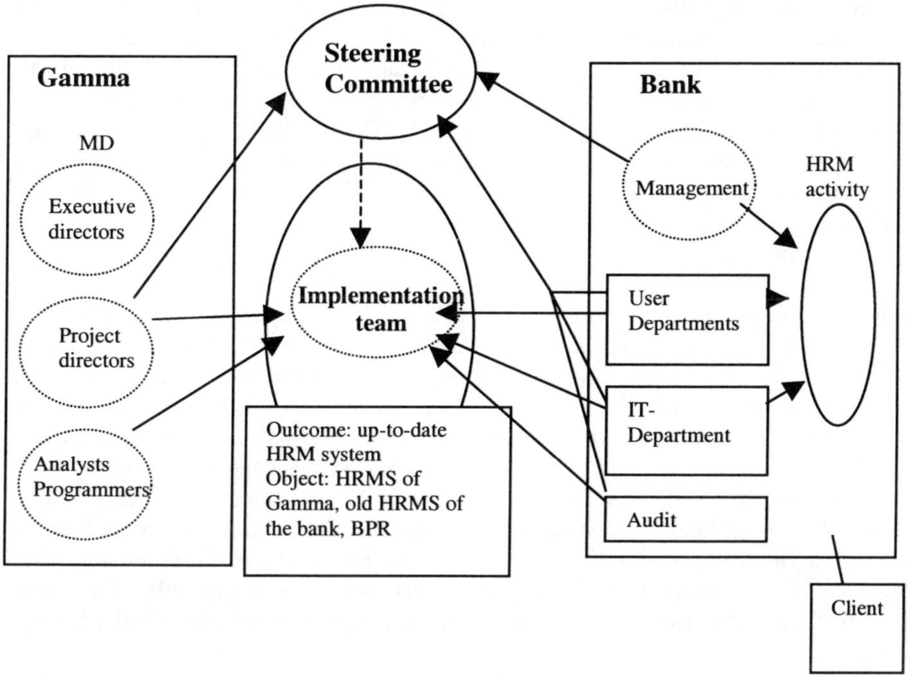

Figure 19.5 Project organization of HRMS project

6.4 Work process

Usually projects begin with a requirement analysis, but in this case, the requirements were initially based on the old system, although mid-stream, unexpected new set of requirements were given as a result of the on-going BPR. The development and customization of the HRMS was like a rapid prototyping done module by module. They started by converting their own system to the client's environment. The IT professionals in the bank were helpful as they knew the functionality of HRM and understood computerization work quite well. The modules went through two test phases. First there was a quality assurance test in terms of documentation, screen design and error messages, done by Gamma. Then the users tested the modules. In that phase there emerged new requirements for some of the modules. After adjustments, the modules were moved into the production environment and the implementation was begun. The most demanding aspect in the implementation was to get the old data into the new system, because of the lack of compatibility between the old system and new system. Data in electronic form was transferred using scripts. But the computer crashed midstream, and some of the data was lost since there was no backup. Thus they had to 'fill the gaps' in the system manually, and that was slow.

During the first interview at the end of 1999 although the system was in use, the users were still in the process of getting the data into the system.

Additionally, since the BPR was still on-going, there was one module under construction. The situation has not changed much within the year. The second interview was done in the end of 2000, and the system was still in the implementation phase because of the new requirements. The process had taken longer than was initially expected. Accordingly, Gamma had conducted only crash training course to the key staff that were involved in entering data into the environment.

6.5 Means of Work

The technology used by Gamma is Oracle, Unix and Java with Windows workstations. Medium and small customers use SysBase and Microsoft databases because of the cost factor. Software development is based on high-level tools like Oracle Designer, Visual Basic and JBuilder. Standards for screens, security, on-line help, documentation and reports are more heavily used when they are developing from scratch. In customizing an existing package however, the tools guide the work. Database design is considered very crucial; and very strong standards exist in that area. With regard to project management methods there is not much rigidity - '*a few guys who come together and get things going*'. For technical documentation there are specialists who are responsible. The bank specified standards for the interface, security, integrity (company standards) and on-line help.

6.6 Means of Coordination and Communication

Communication and coordination in the project happened through meetings. The project plan was the main document driving the process. The communication and coordination within activities and the means of networking between activities are presented in figure 19.6.

The steering committee had meetings once a month, sometimes every two weeks. In their meetings they checked the project situation against the project plan. The project team leader was the official link between the steering committee and implementation team. The consultant, who was the project leader in Gamma, was a link between the steering committee and Gamma.

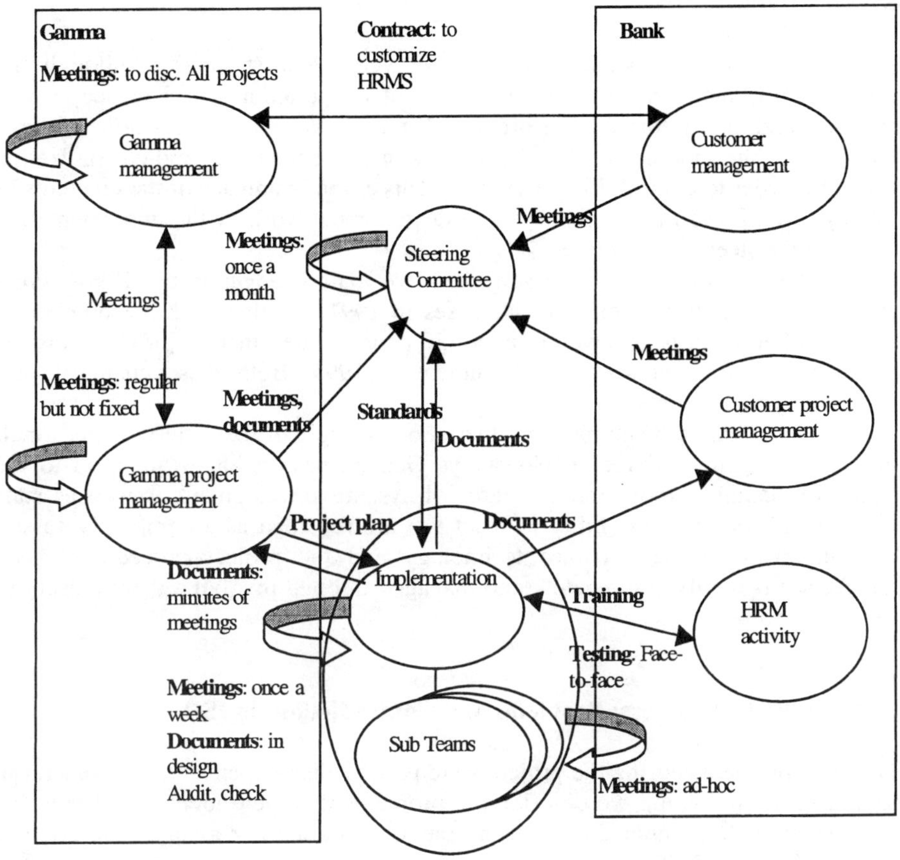

Figure 19.6 The means of networking *between* activities, and the means of coordination and communication *within* activities

The implementation team met formally about once a week. In the event of a critical situation there might be sub-meetings, only for the people concerned. Besides meetings, design and programming documentation distributed information among the group.

The implementation team also met with users in testing and training situations. Usually a person who had developed a module took care of the training since he/she knew the situation. Only in special training did Gamma use its training unit.

There were some checking points, '*crucial points*', when the audit representative came and audited the whole process in terms of requirements, security and so on. Still, in this case the auditing was not very formal.

6.7 Mode of Operation

The project was so organized as to have very clear structure. Although the operation was hierarchical, there was a lot of cooperation. The key people met regularly and also informally in order to keep things going. The whole package was divided into modules so that the process of implementation and customization would be easier to control. Figure 19.7 presents a brief summary of the elements of the key activities of information systems development work by the implementation team and the steering committee.

Historically, Gamma experienced two main changes in the 1990s. First, there was a shift from Cobol to databases in 1991. By that time the number of personnel had risen from seven to about 30 people. The other major shift was the movement to a client server environment in 1995. Both these changes were triggered by their clients.

In summary, Gamma is a rather good example of the locally-owned small software company in Nigeria. Nowadays Gamma pays a lot of attention to the high-level technical tools and standards of systems development as well as staff training. Flexibility and ability to react fast are regarded as a competitive asset, both in terms of the software technology and the project procedures. User satisfaction is highly appreciated, and managed through involving them closely in the projects.

7. Why a Risky Business: Problems and Contradictions in ISD

The chief problems during the project were partl project-dependent, part general in nature. In the following we describe the problems that were identified during the discussions with the company by using the same framework as in the description above (c.f. Mursu 2002).

Problems arising in the area of human research management were related to the functioning within an old system that was not geared to new requirements. The existing HRM system first developed by Gamma was then converted to client's environment and customized to their initial needs. Thus the requirement analysis was based on the old system, even though the bank was at that time in the process of business re-engineering. The bank was too eager to install a new system before a proper requirement analysis was done. This gave rise to extra work during the process, since many modules had to be re-developed, and the final solutions of some modules were still under construction for a long time. The old system being used as a basis for requirement analysis appeared to be a mistake. The initial schedule was unrealistic and all the dead lines were passed.

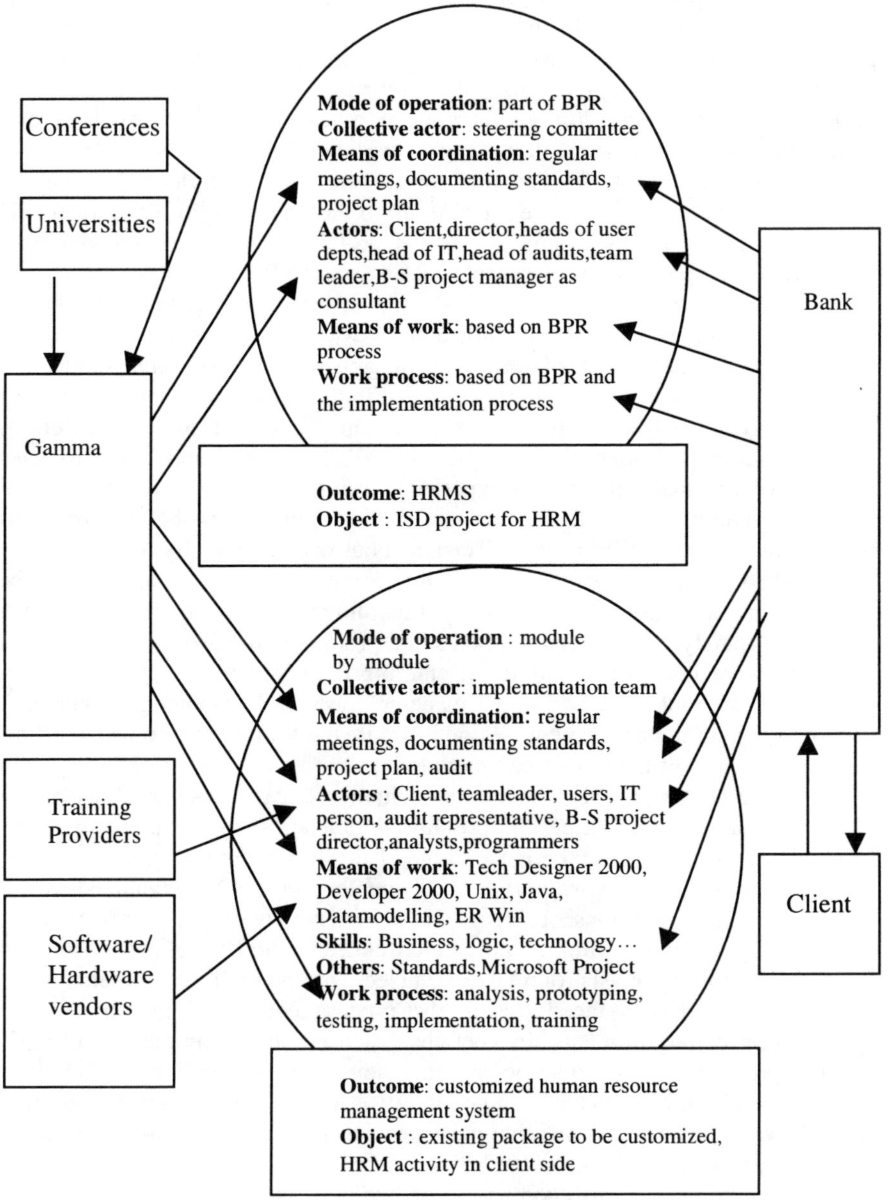

Figure 19.7 The elements of activity of the implementation team and the steering committee

The project organization (*collective actor*) was a normal procedure for Gamma, with a steering committee and an implementation team, both headed by the customer. Normally the role of the steering committee is strong, but in this case the executive manager evaluated it as weak. This could be partly due to the on-going BPR process in the bank and its management, and partly, the experienced management could not recognize the embedded changes caused by a new information system. In addition, there were other stakeholders involved in the BPR, who affected the decision making of the client's management. One of them was the external consultant. The situation therefore was not clear. Also the users lacked the experience to analyze their needs in the beginning of the process. This led to new requirements arising during the project. Gamma wanted to keep the client happy and get a good reference, so it chose to be flexible.

With respect to *actors*, analysts and programmers at Gamma, the main problems lay in their insufficient skills and knowledge. According to the executive director, this is due to lack of formal training in new methods and trends and in basic skills like database planning and logical thinking needed when designing and analysing object activities. It takes the company time to train people for these important tasks. Although Gamma was (and is) very careful about who to send to meet customers, the users lack of experience in information technology can easily lead to attitude problems. But in the case of this bank, the problems were caused more by the inexperienced users indecision about what they really wanted.

Problems concerning the *work process* were much the same as has been discussed in analysing the problems regarding the object, focusing on the requirement analysis. New requirements had prolonged the process, and plans and deadlines were not met. In addition, entering data into the system encountered problems- with integrity and also a machine crashed, thus causing impatience on the part of client's management. Added to this, the training phase had not started properly, because of the unfinished modules.

The *means of work* concerning technology, standards and skills were not too problematic in this case. The possible deficiencies of domain knowledge in Gamma was offset by the experience of the IT department in the bank.

The *means of coordination and communication* were organized as usual, and there were no obvious problems. However, the steering committee was not strong enough in maintaining coordination, related to the BPR process as a whole. The *mode of operation* was routinely organized ,with no obvious problems.

The problems faced during the process concerned mainly the under specification of requirements, inexperience of users and their management. This far, the problems in information systems development could be faced by any country. Similar problems can also be identified in more industrialized countries as well. However, we can assume that these problems are at a little more serious level in Nigeria, than it is in say Finland. For a start, the requirement analysis is much more formal in most Finnish companies. In addition, users in Finland are nowadays much more familiar with computers than they were a few years ago. They now know better what to expect from computers. In a country like Nigeria, managers don't necessarily understand the difference between software and hardware: 'why should I pay so much for software, is it not enough if I buy a computer?' Our interviewee emphasized especially the difficulty in assessing the time needed for a job and agreeing with the client on that. He also emphasized deficits in personal and human relation areas that can put the whole project at risk. But these kinds of problems may be encountered in Finland as well.

However, to see the real contextual characteristics and problems of systems development in Nigeria, we have to extend our perspective to a more societal and economical level. The problems mentioned above can arise due to social reasons as well; the history of software development in Nigeria is still quite recent, so the society and the environment are not at the level needed to support software business. Several other studies in the literature (e.g. Waema 1996, Heeks 1999) emphasise problems in the socio-economic context of developing countries, related to information systems development and implementation.

The most visible problems that affect the business directly are *poor energy supply*, and *erratic and unreliable communication network*. Companies must put in a lot of effort to guarantee steady electricity supply; they need generators and stand-by generators. The shortage forces them to buy fuel from the black market, which is very expensive. Unreliable communication networks block quick access and makes organizing activities difficult.

The *lack of resources for IT investments* is a problem faced by many organizations. It is mainly the big companies that can afford to invest in software applications, for example banks, insurance companies and oil companies. Smaller companies have to struggle to survive and they do not have enough resources for IT investments. Thus software business in Nigeria is dependent on the big and/or international companies at the moment. In addition, it is difficult to find new customers, since data regarding the domestic market is insufficient. The *absence of an official IT policy* by the government (so far) has not helped in the development of a local software industry. The IT investments are incidental and the contracts are often based on relationships: '*man knows man*' is a Nigerian saying that influences business arrangements (c.f. Bada 2000). In addition, corrupt managers or officials, or employees inclined to misuse company property, may resist new systems and even sabotage the development process.

Competition is hard because of *import of foreign packages*. This is of course true of all countries in the 'globalized' world, but in Nigeria particularly it is difficult to compete with well-known foreign companies. Firstly, it is difficult to find people who know the latest technological trends since these are not taught at universities. The latest technology and books are also sometimes difficult to access, even for a software company, and they are expensive. In addition, even though the first computers to Nigeria came in 1960s, the history of indigenous software development is short. Like the executive director of Gamma said '*we have no tradition in computer business*'. There have been cases where business ethics could have been better; the vendors followed the principle of 'sell and run' (c.f. Korpela 1994). Thus many potential customers still prefer foreign rather than local software. Registered associations such as Computer Professions of Nigeria (CPN). and CoAN (Computer Association of Nigeria) are promoting the reputation of local software vendors. But as our interviewee said '*Rome was not built in a day*'.

The social climate around the company does matter as the *political and economic tradition* gives root to enterprise. The launch of Structural Adjustment Program (SAP) in the 1980s influenced the beginning of computerization in Nigeria (e.g. Okuwoga 1990), even though the program itself was not a success (Falola 1999). According to the software company, neither a dictatorship nor a democracy has directly affected the business. But in general the *environment* does have its impact with regard to overall security, openness, possibility of riots or conflicts, general atmosphere, bureaucratic systems and so on. For example, the more close to government the partner is, the more difficult and bureaucratic the activity.

8. Discussion

Comparing the results of the survey of '*the typical software company in Nigeria*' and the three cases that we studied, we find that they match, the only difference being that at Gamma the project teams were headed by the customer. That is how Gamma ensured user commitment and participation. Compared to this, the other companies surveyed were somewhat different; one big foreign-owned and one mixed ownership company making its own packaged product. The main differences between the companies are size, user relationships and informality of activities. The environmental and contextual problems are the same for the other companies as well, perhaps less for the foreign owned company. Some had problems also with illegal duplicates and software piracy, which is a familiar feature in other developing countries also (e.g. Heeks 1999). In general, all the companies are well established and professionally ambitious.

In the study of risks in software development, the most common risk factors in Nigeria was largely related to infrastructure and economy directly. In the case of Gamma, the executive director we interviewed admitted that these infrastructural and economical factors are very crucial in their everyday business. The problems of interrupted electric supply and poor networks are faced every day and companies have to buy alternative sources of power, which also break down easily. The requirements of capital, poor IT awareness in the country and foreign competition have to be considered in their business strategy. In order to face foreign competition, their strengths lie in local support services, understanding local requirements better, being able to customize, providing implementation support and being flexible.

Comparing the other risk factors to Gamma, the common problems were the changing requirements, artificial deadlines and inadequate user training. The changing requirements and prolonged process refer to results that indicate a lower level of alignment between software development and business development in Nigeria. In addition, the software solutions have not been that critical to business solutions to the same extent as in industrial countries. The executive director in the interview also emphasized the lack of required skills, knowledge and experience in the project personnel and staff. He also admitted to the lack of effective development methodology to keep a project on track and the relationship problems in the project group in general. These risks refer to project management activity and echo the growing awareness of the importance of putting proper project management practices in place in Nigeria, and the risk associated with failing to do so (Keil et al. 1998).

In summary, when comparing the results of the survey studies to the Gamma case, we can assume that the case is a representative example of the ISD project in Nigerian software companies. On the other hand, we must consider that the companies selected for the study are probably more 'advanced' than software companies in Nigeria on average, since they are members of the Computer Association of Nigeria and known to have some software development activities. Systems development practice in the smallest and most recently established software companies are thus probably not quite as professional, formal and efficient. However, given the socio-economic problems, the risk factors in general are familiar to all companies and in many other developing countries as well (see e.g. Heeks 1996).

When we consider the differences of ISD between Nigeria and more industrialized countries, like the US or Finland, the differences are not based on technology or software engineering. The risks of software projects are quite similar. In Nigeria, software companies are, however, struggling with many socio-economic and infrastructural constraints, which make it difficult to run a business. *Our results do not bring in new issues concerning the contextual problems in developing countries.* On the contrary, the results support what has been reported in other studies. But they do indicate that *software companies in Nigeria are capable of providing the kind of software and information systems the organizations in Nigeria require.* At the moment, the big customers seem to be providing the local software industry in Nigeria an opportunity to work and participate in the socio-economic development of the country.

In order to promote this, and hopefully also human development in the long run, IT applications should be *appropriate* (c.g. Avgerou and Land 1992) and *sustainable* (Mursu et al. 1999). Technology itself is not a solution in itself, it must have *ethical and socio-economic justification*, and its development must be based on *user participation* (Korpela et al. 2000b, Mursu et al. 2000). A new Nigerian IT policy (summer 2001) gives hope to the reach of a comprehensive development with the help of information technology.

But in order to work for development, software companies must realise that they are not living on an island. However effective and 'modern' they are, technological 'innovation' is not an isolated instance (Castells 1996). Castells (1996, p.37) writes that

> it (technological innovation) reflects a given state of knowledge, a particular institutional and industrial environment, a certain availability of skills to define a technical problem and to solve it, and economic mentality to make such application cost-efficient, and a network of producers and users who can communicate their experiences cumulatively, learning by using and by doing.

He is talking about a '*milieux*' of exchange of ideas, problems and solutions based on experience of past. Maybe Castells refers more to 'Silicon-

Valley' types of environments, but this idea is also relevant in more 'modest' environments, such as the growing software industry in Nigeria. The software industry in Nigeria is in its infancy, so it requires nurturing and meeting challenges to work for development rather than for quick profit.

The software industry in Nigeria cannot be separated from 'global' or foreign markets, since these markets pressure the companies to improve their functioning and methods. Software business and software export is big business in some developing countries, for example, India (Heeks 1999). Heeks sees five strategic positions for software companies in developing countries, as presented in Figure 19.8.

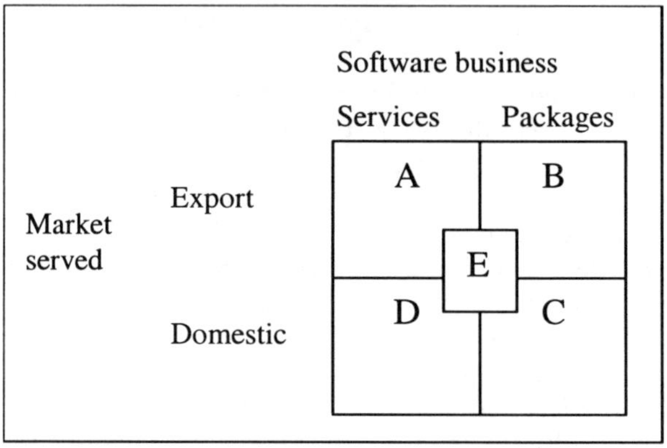

Figure 19.8 Strategic positioning for developing country software enterprises (Heeks 1999)

Many of the successful first-movers, like India, are in position A (Heeks 1999). In our survey there were no software companies providing export services or packages as their major business. According to Heeks (1999), position C is a difficult choice. It means competing with imported packages – legal or pirated. The vast majority of software companies in developing countries are in position D, as was the case in Nigeria. In Nigeria some multinational IT companies also provide services, in collaboration with local partners, which points to a sizeable domestic market in the country. However, most position-D companies in developing countries remain so, because the domestic market is not sizeable or demanding. Being at position D is more a survival strategy than a development strategy, but at least it is a starting point, and if the companies in position D are best at providing solutions for domestic needs, it is something to start with.

The domestic market could also provide opportunities with specialized niche markets, in position E, like sectoral niches, application niches, or linguistic niches (Heeks 1999). In our study we met companies focusing, for example on banking, industry, or health administration applications for hospitals (Mursu 2002). We can summarize that in Nigeria the diversity of software companies in the domestic market is already notable, thus signalling a belief in software companies to the presence software business in the country, despite the constraints.

We agree with Akpan (2000) that strategies for harnessing IT for development should include some actions by the government, for example, implement concrete popular development strategies, create an enabling environment to facilitate the production of a local communication infrastructure, software and hardware and moreover, to invest in education.

A very interesting question for further research would be as to how managers control the work in unstable environments and mitigate the risk of a failure in information systems development projects. Risk management methodologies (e.g. Keil et al. 1998) seem to get a new emphasis in developing countries, these methodologies need to be applied first. However, results imply that *project management* has an extremely critical role for successful ISD process, and this should be emphasized rather than technical details.

9. Conclusion

In this paper we presented our objectives and analytical framework for studying information systems development as a work practice in a given socio-economic context, Nigeria. As far as we know, systems development as a work practice has not been studied previously in any African country. The activity-theoretical research framework that we applied in case studies proved to be practical and focused attention to relevant issues. The method provided a theoretically founded framework for the empirical study.

We also presented one case study as an example of an information systems development project in a typical Nigerian software company. We introduced the problems faced in the project and compared the case with the results of the survey where we collected risk factors in software development in Nigerian software companies and with another survey aiming to create a picture of 'the typical Nigerian software company'. The comparison indicates that these two ways of collecting information of systems development work in Nigeria support each other. Having several research methods helped to obtain quite a comprehensive picture of the issue.

The results indicate that the software industry in Nigeria is not very different when we are speaking about technology or software engineering. The differences can be found from the socio-economic environment and its problems, which are common to any other developing country. But technically and methodologically speaking, software companies are capable of providing the kind of software and information systems the organizations in Nigeria require, provided the customer can afford the services. Nevertheless, the software development management should pay more attention to project management and risk management methodologies. The results also indicate how important it is to take the societal level into consideration when analysing, for example, activities in companies. We argue that researchers should always identify their specific research scope and context on a societal level also to allow other researchers to assess the peculiarity or wider applicability of the study.

Acknowledgements

This research was funded by the Academy of Finland through the INDEHELA-Methods project. The first version of the paper was presented in the 24 Information Systems Research Seminar in Scandinavia (IRIS), in Norway, August 2001. We like to thank the people in our working group for their valuable comments to improve this paper.

References

Akpan P.I. (2000), Africa and the new ICTs: Implications for Development, in the proceedings of IFIP WG 9.4 conference '*Information Flows, Local Improvisations and Work Practices*', South Africa.

Alabi G.A. (1994), *Case Study Effectiveness of Informatics Policy Instruments in Africa: Nigeria*, IDRC.

Andah B.W. (1992), *Nigeria's Indigenous Technology*, Ibadan University Press, Ibadan, Nigeria.

Avgerou C. and Land F. (1992), Examining the appropriateness of information technology, in: Bhatnagar, Odedra, eds., *Social Implications of Computers in Developing Countries*, Tata McGraw-Hill, New Delhi, pp. 26-41.

Bada A.O. (2000), 'Actually existing globalisation': A case study of IT and organizational change in a Nigerian bank, in: proceedings of the IFIP WG 9.4 conference, *Information Flows, Local Improvisations and Work Practices*, Cape Town, May 2000.

Barki H., Rivard S., Talbot J. (1993), Toward an Assessment of Software Development Risk, *Journal of Management Information System*, 10:2, pp. 203-225.

Falola T. (1999), *The history of Nigeria*, London: Greenwood Press.

Heeks R. (1996), Building Software Industry in Africa, *Information Technology in Developing Countries*, A Newsletter of IFIP Working Group 9.4 and Commonwealth Network for Information Technology, 6:4, pp. 5-7.

Heeks R. (1999), Software strategies in developing countries, *Communications of the ACM* 42:6, pp.15-20.

Keil M., Cule P., Lyytinen K. and Schmidt R. (1998), A Framework for Identifying Software Project Risks, *Communication of the ACM* 41:11, pp.76-83.

Korpela M., Mursu A. and Soriyan H.A. (2001 a), Information systems development as an activity, *Computer Supported Cooperative Work, Special Issue on Activity Theory and Design*, 11:1-2, pp.111-128.

Korpela M., Mursu A. and Soriyan H.A. (2001b), Two times four integrative levels of analysis: A framework and a case, in Russo, Fitzgerald, DeGross eds, *Realigning Research and Practice in Information Systems Development: The Social and Organisational Perspective*. Boston, Massachusetts: Kluwer Academic, pp. 367-377.

Korpela M, Soriyan H.A. and Olufokunbi K.C. (2000a), Activity analysis as a method for information systems development: General introduction and experiments from Nigeria and Finland, *Scandinavian Journal of Information Systems* 12:1, pp.191-210.

Korpela M., Soriyan H.A., Olufokunbi K.C. and Mursu A. (2000b), Made-in-Nigeria systems development methodologies: An action research project in the health sector, *in*: Avgerou, Walsham, eds, *Information Technology in Context: Implementing Systems in the Developing World*, Ashgate, Aldershot, pp.134-152.

Mursu A. (2002), *Information Systems Development in Developing Countries – Risk Management and Sustainability Analysis in Nigerian Software Companies*, University of Jyväskylä: Jyväskylä University Printing House.

Mursu A., Lyytinen K., Soriyan H.A., Korpela M. (submitted), Identifying Software Project Risks in Nigeria: An International Comparative Study, submitted.

Mursu A., Soriyan H.A., Olufokunbi K.C. and Korpela M. (1999), From software risks to sustainable information systems: Setting the stage for a Delphi study in Nigeria, *Journal of Global Information Technology Management* 2:3, pp.57-71.

Mursu A., Soriyan H.A., Olufokunbi K.C. and Korpela M. (1999b), Toward a Successful ISD in Developing Countries: First Results from a Nigerian Risk Study Using the Delphi Method, *in*: Käkölä, ed., Proceedings of the 22nd Information Systems Research Seminar in Scandinavia (IRIS 22): *Enterprise Architectures for Virtual Organizations*, Jyväskylä University Printing House, Jyväskylä, Finland, August 7-10, Volume 2, pp. 397-414.

Mursu A., Soriyan H.A., Olufokunbi K. and Korpela M. (2000), Information systems development in a developing country: Theoretical analysis of special requirements in Nigeria and Africa, in: Sprague RH Jr, ed., *Proceedings of the 33rd Annual Hawaii International Conference on System Sciences*, Hawaii, USA, January 4-7, IEEE Computer Society, Los Alamitos, p. 185 (full text on CD-ROM).

Odedra-Straub M. (1996), Introduction, in: Odedra-Straub ed., *Global Information Technology and Socio-Economic Development*, Nashua: Ivy League.

Okuwoga O. (1990), Impact of Information Technology on Nigeria's Socio-Economic Development, in: Bhatnagar, Bjørn-Andersen (eds.), *Information Technology in Developing Countries*, North-Holland: Elsevier Science Publishers B.W. pp. 101-148.

Soriyan H.A., Korpela M., Mursu A. (2002), Information Systems Development in Nigerian Software Companies: The Industry Profile, *Proceedings of the WG9.4 conference*, Bangalore, India.

Soriyan H.A., Mursu A.S., Akinde A.D. and Korpela M. (2001), Information Systems Development in Nigerian Software Companies: Research Methodology and Assessment from the Healthcare Sector's Perspective, *Electronic Journal on Information Systems in Developing Countries*, 5:4.

UNIDO (1989), *Computers for Industrial Management in Africa: The case of Nigeria*, Prepared by Michal A. and Nwachuku. United Nations Industrial Development Organization, B.89-57624, PPD.126, 29 p.

Waema T.M. (1996), Implementation of information technology projects and economic development: Issues, problems and strategies, in: Odedra-Straub M., ed. *Global Information Technology and Socio-Economic Development*, Nashua: Ivy League, pp. 106-115.

Walsham G. (2000), Globalization and IT: Agenda for research, *in*: Baskerville R., Stage J. and DeGross J.I., eds., *Organizational and Social Perspectives on Information Technology*', Boston: Kluwer Academic pp. 195-210.

Chapter 20

Nurturing a Software Industry in Kerala

N. Dayasindhu, Pradeep G.

1. Introduction

India has established its presence as a global center for the software services industry. 185 of the Fortune 500 firms source software from India. The exports of software from India have been growing at a CAGR of over 60% to touch US$ 6.2 billion for 2000-2001. The biggest chunk of India's software exports in 2001, about US$ 1.6 billion,[1] originates from the southern Indian state of Karnataka (state capital: Bangalore). The other southern states; Tamil Nadu (state capital: Chennai) accounted for about US$ 0.7 billion,[2] and Andhra Pradesh (state capital: Hyderabad) about US$ 0.4 billion[3] of India's exports in 2000-2001. Kerala (state capital: Thiruvananthapuram) another southern Indian state that does not boast of a metropolis like Karnataka, Tamil Nadu or Andhra Pradesh has registered software exports of about US$ 32 million in 2000-2001.[4] The challenge of nurturing a software industry in Kerala is the agenda of this paper.

2. Research Questions

The two questions that have motivated this research are

- Why has Kerala been a slow starter in the software industry?
- How can a vibrant software industry be nurtured in Kerala?

An attempt is made to answer these questions by understanding the social, economic, and cultural factors that have contributed to the success of the Silicon Valley in information technology, and India (in particular Bangalore) in software services. These factors will be used to unravel the challenges in nurturing a software industry in the Kerala context.

3. Silicon Valley, India and Bangalore: The Success Stories

Silicon Valley continues to be the hotbed of the information technology industry in the world. There have been numerous attempts to replicate the Silicon Valley model in various other locations in the USA and other parts of the world without much success. History has shown that Frederick Terman (the father of Silicon Valley) was not successful in replicating the model even in other locations like New Jersey and Texas in the USA (Leslie and Kargon 1996). Though it is next to impossible to provide a roadmap for building a Silicon Valley model, it is worthwhile to keep in mind the factors, and their networks that lie at the heart of the Silicon Valley model. The following discussion draws upon from *Regional Advantage Culture and Competition in Silicon Valley and Route 128* by AnnaLee Saxenian (1994).

3.1 Universities

Silicon Valley is endowed with USA's top research universities, Stanford, and University of California at Berkeley. These places attract the best talent the world over, many of whom end up staying in the area infusing it with innovation. Stanford is the pioneer in establishing relationships between research institutions, entrepreneurs and firms. The Stanford Research Institute (SRI) was established to conduct government-supported research, and to assist technology firms in securing government contracts. Stanford opened its engineering classrooms to local firms through its Honors Cooperative Program in which employees could enroll in graduate courses. Stanford also promoted the creation of the Stanford Industrial Park, one of the first in the USA that reinforced the emerging pattern of cooperation between the university and electronics firms in the area for a symbiotic prosperity of both (Leslie and Kargon 1996). Community colleges like San Jose State University contract with local firms to teach their employees while firms provide consultants to the colleges to help develop curricula.

3.2 Industry

Kenney and von Burg (2000) see the new firm formation process in the Silicon Valley as a critical factor that has nurtured a world-class information technology industry. Silicon Valley is an amalgam of two separate ecologies. The first consists of the existing firms, and institutions that not only produce their expected outputs, but also generate innovations that can be exploited commercially outside these existing firms and institutions. The second consists of venture capitalists and start up firms that are often sold to larger firms or grow into large firms. The open culture in Silicon Valley assists in the dissemination of technical information through informal networks. Furthermore, high labor mobility, and the role of 'mentor' venture capitalists enhance personal and professional relations to create a tighter network. The creation and maintenance of informal networks is an important feature of the Silicon Valley model that gets a critical mass of firms and service providers. This critical mass builds relationships and networks of inter-dependence and trust. A sophisticated service infrastructure exists and allows firms to focus on their chosen competence, rather than dissipate their energies across a broad range of peripheral or supporting activities.

3.3 High Labor Mobility

Most professionals in the Silicon Valley believe that it is like one large company. Loyalties tend to be more to advancing technologies or the region than to any individual company. Opportunity for mobility is not only seen as a fixation with technology on the part of engineers and entrepreneurs, but also the lure of greater financial gain either through higher salaries and/or through stock options.

3.4 Culture

Given the high job mobility, high wages, and high investment returns in the Silicon Valley network, people face comparatively little return-adjusted risk in becoming entrepreneurs. Failure is treated like a stepping-stone and is quickly forgotten. In Silicon Valley, most of the money made out of the technology industry has been ploughed back either via people starting their own firms or via angel investors (Florida and Kenney 2000). There is an openness in Silicon Valley, a flow of people and ideas and collaboration between universities, local industry and venture capital. Silicon Valley is very tightly integrated with people who can move back and forth between academia, industry and venture capital.

3.5 Role of the State

The impetus for the early growth of the semiconductor industry came almost exclusively from the military since there were virtually no other customers when they were initially developed. By 1960, Silicon Valley had become the center of an aerospace complex rooted in microwave electronics technology for reconnaissance, communications and countermeasures (Leslie 2000). The most striking fact is the truly international character and enormous diversity of nationalities in the high-tech community. This is a result of the liberal labor laws in the USA that allow for foreign skilled labor and allow labor mobility. Skilled immigrants account for at least one-third of the engineering workforce in many of the region's technology firms, and are increasingly visible as entrepreneurs and investors (Saxenian 1999). Cohen and Fields (2000) argue that the openness of the labor market to foreigners is one of Silicon Valley's most valuable assets. Silicon Valley's premier ranking as the world's innovation and commercialization center could not be sustained without the steady influx of educated and motivated high-level technical/entrepreneurial talent. Laws in USA have encouraged entrepreneurship and California's tax structure has historically treated capital gains more generously than income. Patent laws in the USA ensure protection for intellectual property.

3.6 Stock Market

The dream of making it rich just through stock options alone is necessarily a huge temptation for employees, engineers and entrepreneurs. Silicon Valley firms are legendary for creating millionaires based on the fact that employees usually own shares. It is a common enough fact in the region that even secretaries, receptionists and janitors have earned millions through stock options (Bronson 1999). This inevitably brings more people to the area seeking employment with high-tech firms and motivates would-be-entrepreneurs to start their own firms.

To summarize, the Silicon Valley model is characterized by the rich social and professional networks in the region that in turn support Silicon Valley's decentralized industrial structure. AnnaLee Saxenian sums up the Silicon Valley Model best in a keynote address at a conference in Sweden on *What We Can Learn From The Silicon Valley: American and Swedish Experiences*.

> What matters in this network system are relationships. The rich social, technical and productive relationships in the region foster entrepreneurship, experimentation, and collective learning. As a result, the region's social, technical and productive infrastructure is as critical to the successes of local firms as their own individual activities.

The factors discussed above and the networks that determine the Silicon Valley model are that which nurture information technology innovation. However, the focus of the Indian software industry that predominantly caters to global clients is innovation in providing software services. There is a set of unique factors that has been instrumental in making India a global software services center. Krishna, Ojha, and Barrett (1998) have identified four factors that have nurtured and made Indian software industry competitive in the global software services domain.

People

Software development is a creative activity where the value addition stages in its production process cannot be significantly automated. The rate of technology change in this industry makes it imperative for software professionals to frequently acquire new expertise. This makes skilled professionals an essential resource, which fits in well with the Indian value system that has natural disdain for physical labor and high regard for intellectual work. Professionals are attracted to this industry by the high salaries offered (compared to other industries in India), rapid career progress and opportunities for immigration to developed countries like the USA. This social context provides the Indian software industry with the best available skilled labor.

Technology

Rapid technology change characterizes this industry, and success depends on constant renewal of skills rather than on one-time investments. This facilitates the success of small technocrat entrepreneurs. With the liberalization of the Indian economy in the early 1990s, the software industry has been able to access the latest technology that has not only assisted in developing skills in these technologies but also for shifting client work to offshore centers in India.

Organization

Software development requires flexible organization structures with professional management. The traditional Indian family owned firms are hierarchical and the superior subordinate relation has been paternalistic. However, software firms are less hierarchical, less formal and less paternalistic than firms in other Indian industries. The organization structure of software firms has made it easy for them to adapt easily to changing market needs and manage globally dispersed teams. The reduced formality in the software firms is conducive to the Indian penchant of attending to personal work during office hours and a looser definition of time. In short, a flat, flexible and professionally managed organization that is the norm in the software industry best suits the nature of work in the Indian social context.

Communication

Since software development is a collaborative activity, it is characterized by a high degree of communication both within and between firms. With advances in telecommunication technology and liberalization of the Indian economy it is possible for Indian firms to execute projects that are extended over time and space. The familiarity with English, the dominant language of the global software industry is another advantage for Indian firms. More than the English language, Indians are familiar with the cultures of the major markets of the USA and Europe. This familiarity is a result of the availability of liberal education and the fact that a number of senior professionals have either studied and/or worked in the USA or Europe.

Among the regions in India that have a software industry, Bangalore stands out as one location that is most successful. Bangalore's software expertise has been acknowledged globally and UNESCO has ranked Bangalore among the top five global locations for software. Lateef (1997) has identified factors that have helped Bangalore achieve this preeminent position. Bangalore is home to India's best science and technology research university, the Indian Institute of Science. It is also home to a number of Government owned organizations. Notable among them are Bharat Electronics Limited, Indian Telephone Industry, Hindustan Aeronautics Limited, National Aerospace Laboratories and Indian Space Research Organization. The Government owned organizations provide a concentration of electronics and aerospace industries that are a storehouse of technically skilled human resources. The Government owned organizations and the defense establishments have employed professionals from all over India making Bangalore a cosmopolitan melting pot. The salubrious climate and the cosmopolitan culture of Bangalore still attract professionals from all over India. Nearly all of Karnataka's software exports of about US$ 1.6 billion (out of India's US$ 6.2 billion) for 2000-2001 come from Bangalore.

The factors for the Indian context will alone be directly applicable to Kerala. The factors for Silicon Valley and Bangalore are stylized and are difficult to replicate. However, the presence or absence of these factors in Kerala's economic, social and cultural context will definitely play an important role in nurturing a vibrant software industry.

4. Industry Clusters and National Systems of Innovation: The Conceptual Foundation

The success of Silicon Valley can be understood by invoking the industry cluster concept. Though this concept is useful at a generic level, the specific stylized factors in Silicon Valley and Bangalore (discussed in the previous sections) are determinants of successes of these regions. Typically, constituents of an industry cluster are suppliers, producers, customers, labor markets and training institutions, financial intermediaries, professional and industry associations, university departments and schools, regulatory institutions and bodies of law, and the government. The clusters can be a subset of the industry formed by only some constituents of the industry characterized by a persistent relationship over a period of time (Maskell and Malmberg 1995).

Important factors that sustain industry clusters are external economies, environment of innovation, co-operative competition, inter firm rivalry, and path dependence (Bergman and Feser 1999). The industrial location theory based on Weber, and the Marshallian theory explains external economies. The industrial location theory states that the cost savings that occur as a result of spatial concentration are a major cause for creating industry clusters. The cost savings usually result from increased market power, availability and use of specialized facilities, shared infrastructure, reduced risk for budding entrepreneurs and knowledge transfer. Marshallian theory states that external economies are the cost savings resulting from the size and growth of output of the industry. These are the economic consequence of spatial proximity between the constituents of the industry. More important than the static external economies (like cost savings) are the dynamic external economies associated with knowledge transfer, innovation and specialization. The focus on knowledge related externality is predominant in advanced technology industries (Krugman 1997). An environment of innovation helps to spur industrial growth by creating new products and opening new markets. Innovation and productivity are dynamic social processes that evolve best when intense relationships, both economic and technological, exist between the various constituents of the industry cluster. Co-operative competition is the notion that drives most competing firms to find ways to work together even as they compete with each other in the product markets. Vertical co-operation refers to co-operation between constituents across the value chain while horizontal co-operation refers to co-operation in lobbying, foreign market research; export promotion, specialized infrastructure investments and other areas. The levels and forms of co-operative competition depend on trust, experience and relationships prevailing among the constituents of the industry. Rivalry is an important feature of industry clusters since the constituents not only compete for markets but also for labor and capital. Path dependence refers to the phenomena where certain initial choices by a constituent or a few constituents of an industry, even when inefficient, assumes a dominant lead over other alternatives and becomes self-reinforcing (Krugman 1993). This often leads to a comparative advantage to the industry, and happens due to the external economies of scale. The basic building blocks for industry clusters (especially in a knowledge intensive industry) seem to be embeddedness and knowledge transfer. Dayasindhu (2002) gives a detailed explanation of the model and its application to the Indian software industry.

In the context of organizations involving in economic transactions with several other organizations, the sociological concept of embeddedness articulated by Granovetter (1985) becomes an important determinant of competitiveness. Embeddedness refers to the fact that economic behavior is affected by the industry constituents' dyadic (pair-wise) social relations and the structure of the overall network of social relations. Embeddedness is an ongoing process continuously shaped by the relations between the different constituents. It not only shapes the agents but is also shaped by them. (Jones et. al. 1997) Embeddedness emphasizes on the role of social relations and structures of these relations in generating trust and discouraging opportunism. There is a preference for transacting with constituents of known reputation (known from social relations) than others. The importance of embeddedness is that the role of other constituents, trust and experience not discussed by Transaction Cost Economics are recognized and addressed. Embeddedness leads to the formation of social mechanisms like restricted access (a limit on the number of members), macroculture (shared values and norms among constituents), collective sanctions (punishment meted out by constituents on erring partners) and reputation (the skills and reliability of the constituents) that coordinates and safeguards relations and enhances knowledge transfer (Jones et. al. 1997). Grant and Baden-Fuller (2000) state that clusters result when the knowledge domains and product domains of the different organizations are incongruent and collaboration increases the efficiency of knowledge utilization. Industry clusters offer risk-spreading benefits when there is an uncertainty over future knowledge needs. The central feature of an industry cluster seems to be the social infrastructure and social relations that is prevalent in it. Silicon Valley is probably the best example of an industry cluster in the information technology industry (Saxenian, 1994). Though Bangalore has some elements that make a successful cluster, it is not yet a cluster (Dayasindhu, 2002).

Powell (1987) argues that changing industry environment, limits of hierarchies, importance of speed and information and generalized reciprocity have a role in sustaining industry clusters (especially in technology intensive industries). Change has forced a shift towards flexible forms of production to serve more specialized markets. The change in industry environment is not conducive for hierarchies, arguably the most popular form of governance in the last half century. This is because of the serious mismatch between the typical predictable, formal, risk averse, and slow response of hierarchies to the changing environment. Increasingly the knowledge required by constituents of an industry cluster to survive is located outside its boundaries and most of this knowledge is tacit. This brings out the importance of speed and information in creating a web of relationships among the constituents to share a large tacit pool of knowledge in a short time frame. Generalized reciprocity is the social dimension where transactions occur not by discrete exchanges or administrative fiat but through relations based on trust and reputation between the constituents.

The concept of flexible specialization (Piore and Sabel 1990) is a key feature of the constituents of an industry cluster. It is rooted in both the economic and sociological approach. Flexible specialization is the production of a variety of products in small volumes for specialized markets, using general-purpose machinery, and skilled or adaptable labor. It is a modern form of craft production. Flexible refers to the nature of production systems where general-purpose machinery is used to produce a variety of products and specialization refers to the fragmented nature of product markets requiring more variety and innovation. This leads organizations to vertically disintegrate since economies of scale makes it difficult to remain flexible, and usually results in an industry cluster characterized by a number of specialized organizations with a complex web of relationships among them. Flexible specialization results in the formation of industry clusters that maintain an optimal balance between competition and co-operation among constituent organizations.

Storper (1997) argues that industry clusters need to be understood more in terms of the relationships and knowledge sharing among the constituents. The dynamic technologically innovative industry clusters are a result of interactions between technologies, organizations and territories that produce a path dependent process of industry cluster creation. Economic reflexivity is the ability of the constituents to shape the course of the cluster evolution by taking a critical distance from their actions, and results from changes in production, information processing, communication and other factors. There is also the possibility for groups of constituents in a cluster to shape the course of economic evolution by reflecting about the functioning of their environments in a way that is not limited by existing parameters. The industry clusters are a preferred structure when both internal economies as well as external economies of scale and scope are high.

Porter (1998) posits that competitiveness (that contributes to industry leadership) is achieved in three ways viz. increasing the productivity of organizations, driving the direction and pace of innovation and stimulating growth of new organizations and institutions. Industry clusters allow each constituent to benefit as if it had greater scale and as if it had joined with others formally without sacrificing its flexibility. Productivity, innovation and growth of new organizations are enhanced by better access to labor and suppliers, access to specialized information, complementarities, access to institutions and public goods, motivation to perform better as a result of peer pressure and measurement of performance since the cluster constituents often share common resources. Industry clusters evolve, that is they are born, grow and can decay (Porter 1998). Industry clusters usually emerge from historical circumstances or unusual, sophisticated local demand and prior existence of supplier industries, related industries or industry clusters. New clusters may also arise from one or a few innovative organizations that stimulate the growth of others. Sometimes a chance event can create some advantages that foster the creation of an industry cluster. Once a cluster begins to form, a self-reinforcing cycle promotes its growth facilitated by supportive institutions and policy. A growing cluster signals opportunity, and attracts the best talent. Research, infrastructure, resources and innovation, emergence of new constituents, socio-economic milieu and government policies foster the growth of clusters. The decay of clusters is usually brought about by technological discontinuities, shift in customer needs, deteriorating relations among constituents, degeneration of institutions, groupthink, and non-supportive government policies that annihilates a position of leadership. A diagrammatic representation of the cluster concept is shown in Figure 20.1. The characteristics of industry clusters are useful to keep in mind as the conceptual foundation when specific factors for nurturing a software industry in Kerala are discussed.

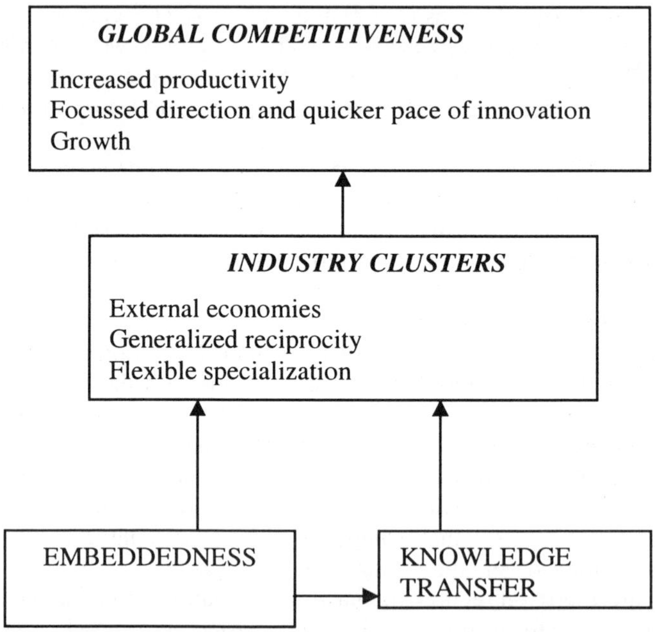

Figure 20.1 The Industry Cluster Concept

Another concept closely related to industry clusters is the national systems of innovation. A set of organizations that individually, and more important jointly contribute to the development and diffusion of new technologies providing a framework for policy making to influence the innovation process is a national system of innovation. (Metcalfe 1995 and Lundvall 1988). The interconnection among organizations is a critical factor that creates, stores and transfers technical knowledge that defines new technologies. The nationality aspect is rooted in the shared vision, culture and policies; in short the institutional frameworks that condition the innovation environment. The national system of innovation involves different organizations; Government, Government laboratories, universities, private firms, and others working in collaboration. Although there is a formal division of labor among the different organizations constituting the national system of innovation, informal networks are the important routes for transferring the more tacit technical knowledge. It usually reflects a predominance of co-ordination by non-market means due to the economic peculiarities of information. When the national system of innovation is organized well, it is a powerful engine for progress as is evident in the case of Japan (Freeman 1987).

The central concern of the national system of innovation is the innovation process that operates under a set of institutions within which technological capabilities are accumulated. The evolutionary approach of economic change is useful in understanding the dynamics of the national system of innovation. Evolution means a cumulative and path dependent change where the focus is on adapting rather than optimizing. From the national system of innovation viewpoint, change is interpreted as the emergence of novel forms of technology configurations under a certain set of institutions and the development of these configurations through a sequence of innovations (Metcalfe 1995).

The national systems of innovation are not easily transferable but are country specific, and rooted in skills, capabilities, and knowledge that are accumulated over a period of time (Archibugi and Michie 1995). Though the national systems of innovation are not transferable, the process of creating these systems can at least provide a road map for other countries in a similar context on how to attempt developing national systems of innovation. In this context it is interesting to study the software industry in Kerala using the factors that have made Silicon Valley and Bangalore successful.

5. Methodology

Case study research is used to unravel the factors that play a role in nurturing a software industry in Kerala since it is best suited to understand the complex social, economic, and cultural phenomena. The underlying philosophical assumption that powered the case study methodology in this research is the interpretive approach. Interpretive studies attempt to understand phenomena through the meanings that people assign to them (Walsham 1993). The case study research is best suited to the empirical inquiry that investigates contemporary phenomena within the real life context. The characteristic of a case study is that it strives towards a holistic understanding of the phenomena under research (Yin 1994). This research is based on semi-structured interviews and published material to collect information.

Sixteen interviews were conducted on a representative sample of stakeholders in the software industry in Kerala. The breakup of the interviewees: Four chief executives or senior management of software firms in Kerala, two senior officials in the Government of Kerala who coordinate the information technology initiatives, two academicians associated with the information technology initiatives in Kerala, two journalists who are keen observers of the information technology initiatives in Kerala, four middle or junior management executives of software firms in Kerala and two middle or junior management executives who are educated in Kerala and are working in software firms outside Kerala.

6. Kerala: Can it become a Success Story?

Kerala has the distinction of having the highest literacy rate of 90.92 per cent[5] among all Indian states. A study on *How Are The States Doing* by the Rajiv Gandhi Institute for Contemporary Studies for the Confederation of Indian Industry (CII) states that Kerala has an overall composite rank of three, compared to the 12 of Andhra Pradesh, ten of Karnataka, and six of Tamil Nadu. For investment attractiveness, Kerala is ranked five ahead of Andhra Pradesh's eight, Karnataka's ten and, Tamil Nadu's six (Debroy, Bhandari and Banik 2000).

Kerala seems to have an ideal set of physical infrastructure that is conducive for nurturing a software industry. India's largest software technology park, Technopark, promoted by the Government of Kerala is located in Thiruvananthapuram and has been functional since 1994. Two more software technology parks are to be set up in the cities of Ernakulam and Kozhikode in a few years time. The cost of office space in the cities of Kerala is about half of that in Bangalore.[6] Kerala will be connected by a fiber optic back bone and Ernakulam is the landing point of two submarine cables South East Asia - Middle East - Western Europe - 3 (SEA-ME-WE-3) and South Africa Far East (SAFE) in the Indian subcontinent. The SAFE link has a capacity of 7.3 million simultaneous telephone calls, 1.5 million high-speed data channels (64Kbps equivalent) and 12000 8Mbps digital video channels is expected to be operational in a year.[7] This leads to a cost advantage of about US$ 0.1 million per annum to firms located in Kerala compared to Bangalore. The human resources for the software industry in Technopark are drawn from the pool of around 7500 engineers who graduate every year in Kerala.[8] In fact, the density of science and technology professionals is highest in Kerala compared to other Indian states. The existing attrition rate in the software industry in Kerala is about five per cent,[9] about one fourth of the rate prevalent in places like Bangalore. From the discussion on Silicon Valley, India and Bangalore it is evident that physical and communication infrastructure seem to be the 'hygiene factors' while the social infrastructure are the 'motivational factors' for nurturing a software industry. It is interesting to note in this context that in 1994-1995 (when Technopark became functional) Kerala's neighbor, Tamil Nadu had software exports of only about US$ 8 million[10] and Andhra Pradesh, about US$ 5 million.[11] As stated earlier, Tamil Nadu exported about US$ 0.7 billion, and Andhra Pradesh US$ 0.4 billion during 2000-2001 compared to Kerala's US$ 32 million for the same period. A detailed discussion on the factors that have contributed to Kerala's slow start in the software industry, and those factors that are critical to nurture a software industry in Kerala follows.

6.1 Universities and Institutions

Kerala is home to two leading engineering colleges in India, the Regional Engineering College at Kozhikode and the Thiruvananthapuram Engineering College. There are a number of good science and humanities colleges spread throughout the state. The school system in Kerala is amongst the best in India. The largest facility of the Indian Space Research Organization, the Vikram Sarabhai Space Centre (VSSC) is located in Thiruvananthapuram. There are no close links between VSSC and the software firms in Kerala apart from the fact that senior executives in some software firms in Kerala have begun their careers in VSSC. Another institution that has supplied senior management to the software industry in Kerala is the State Government owned Keltron, that designs and manufacturers electronic products and systems. Like VSSC, Keltron too does not have any close links with the software firms in Kerala.

The Indian Institute of Information and Management-Kerala (IIITM-K) was set up in 2000 in the Technopark campus in Thiruvanthapuram. IIITM-K is expected to become Kerala's internationally reputed center for research and teaching excellence in information technology. Apart from providing the software industry a trained pool of graduates, IITM-K will be the nodal center to formulate relevant information technology syllabus for other universities in Kerala. IIITM-K also plans to promote the use of information technology facilitated education throughout India.

At present the trend among the graduates of the engineering colleges in Kerala is to seek employment in the software firms in cities like Bangalore and Chennai. One engineer, who after graduating from an engineering college in Kerala joined a software company in Bangalore feels,

> For engineers from Karnataka the choice is between working in Bangalore or the USA and similarly for those from Tamil Nadu the choice is between Chennai and the USA. However, for engineers from Kerala the choice is between Bangalore, Chennai, and the USA. It is not any location in Kerala. If one does not have a valid personal reason, it is considered a failure if you remain to work in Kerala.

It remains to be seen if the graduates from IIITM-K would prefer to work in Kerala or will follow the path taken by their friends in the engineering colleges of Kerala. This is different from the scenario in Kerala's neighboring states. Karnataka's capital Bangalore is the home of the prestigious Indian Institute of Science, a world-renowned research university. As stated earlier, Bangalore is also home to many Indian electronics and aerospace laboratories. Karnataka was also among the first few Indian states to allow the private sector in higher education that resulted in a steady flow of engineers to work in the software industry. Tamil Nadu's capital Chennai has the prestigious Indian Institute of Technology. Like Karnataka, Tamil Nadu too is dotted with private engineering colleges whose graduates find employment in the state's software industry. Universities and Government owned organizations are just one half of the support for a software industry, the other half being the presence of an industrial hinterland in the state.

6.2 Industry and Stock Market

Kerala is traditionally known for its agro based, and plantation industry. Most of this industry operates out of the port city of Ernakulam. Kerala has not had a large industrial hinterland in spite of its high rank among Indian states for investment attractiveness. One of the main reasons for this phenomenon is a perception of entrepreneurs (both Indian and foreign) that Kerala is home to a strong labor movement that is entrepreneur unfriendly. This perception seems to have rubbed off to the software sector too. The big Indian software firms seem to be still in a dilemma on what to believe; the reality of a good infrastructure for software industry or the deep-rooted perceptions of investor unfriendly labor. As one chief executive of a software company in Thiruvananthapuram summarizes,

> The hard facts are favorable for firms to set shop in Kerala but the soft facts are not.

Neither Indian firms nor the multinationals have thought of Kerala as a serious investment destination in the past due to the perception of Kerala as a private capital unfriendly state. Among the south Indian states, Tamil Nadu has well-diversified industrial hinterland. This presence of a vibrant industrial hinterland made it easier for Tamil Nadu to attract investments in the software industry. There is also another perception that people in Kerala look down on private enterprise. But the case with information technology and software seems to be different. All the political parties in Kerala recognize these sectors as an ideal opportunity for employment and growth. One senior academician notes,

> The Technopark in Thiruvananthapuram was outside the purview of political influence from its genesis.

The political parties in Kerala seem to agree that the software industry is 'socially less hazardous' than the other industry sectors and must be encouraged. This is a result of the flat organization and absence of a 'blue collar/white collar divide' in software firms.

Most of the industrial activity in Kerala is controlled by the public sector. There have not been many private firms that started in Kerala that have tapped the stock markets. This phenomenon seems to be changing with the advent of the software industry. Most software firms in Kerala have been funded with personal capital of the entrepreneurs or through the subsidiary route. One company has recently obtained venture funding and there is a possibility of more firms taking the venture capital route. At present, employee stock options are not a prevalent practice amongst these firms. The junior software professionals believe that stock option schemes will attract more skilled labor from within and outside Kerala, and is also likely to prevent some of the migration to Bangalore, Chennai and the USA. The absence of a large industrial hinterland in Kerala has resulted in increased labor mobility and poor social infrastructure.

6.3 Labor Mobility and Culture

Kerala has witnessed a number of social revolutions in the last century against the then prevalent feudal system. The quest for self-respect also heralded the rise of a strong trade union culture in Kerala. The historical oppression of the feudal class made the Keralite (native of Kerala) suspicious of entrepreneurs, and industry in the mid 20th century. Though there has always been an emphasis on higher education in Kerala, most of the graduates from colleges preferred Government jobs for the stability and security they afforded. Since the opportunities for educated professionals were limited in private industry in Kerala, there has been a migration of Keralites to other metropolitan cities in India in the last 50 years. Most of these Keralites have been employed in the private sector in India and abroad. In fact the Keralites are among the largest diaspora of the software industry in other centers like Bangalore, Chennai and the USA.

A significant portion of the employees in the software industry in Kerala consists of Keralites with only a token presence of employees from other Indian states. This is surprising since the physical infrastructure in places like Thiruvananthapuram and Ernakulam is better than that of metropolitan cities like Bangalore and Chennai. The junior software professionals interviewed perceive that there are better career opportunities in centers like Bangalore. They cited personal reasons for staying back in Kerala. One young executive said,

> It is a boring life here in Thiruvananthapuram. I get e-mails from my classmates in Bangalore and Chennai, and envy the fun they have. Most of their work is comparable to what I do here though some of them are in the big name firms, and work in challenging high technology areas.

The middle and senior management seem to relish the quality of life in Kerala. Real estate costs are cheaper than most other metropolitan cities in India. The quality of physical infrastructure namely water, electricity and transport is excellent. There are good quality schools, colleges and hospitals in Thiruvananthapuram and Ernakulam. However, these may not be comparable to the best available in Bangalore and Chennai. Though there are plenty of locations to holiday in Kerala, its cities lack a vibrant social infrastructure. As a senior official with the Government of Kerala put it,

> The software industry is a urban metropolitan phenomenon and traditionally the Indian states with big metros have done well in this industry.

The software professionals have very few locations to unwind in a city like Thiruvananthapuram. This is especially glaring for those who have moved from a place like Bangalore. One chief executive of a software company in Thiruvananthapuram said,

> All the social infrastructure can and will come up only when there is a critical mass of software professionals in a location. This has not happened to any place in

Kerala yet. The professionals will miss a cosmopolitan lifestyle and facilities of a big city in Kerala.

This critical mass of software professionals or firms can be got in place only with the effort of the Government of Kerala.

6.4 Role of the State Government of Kerala

Kerala's Information Technology Policy of 1998 states that information technology specific infrastructure will be given top priority. The policy also states that the Government of Kerala will be sensitive to the needs of the information technology industry and provide special incentives for this industry. While most of the objectives of this policy have been met, it is time for the Government of Kerala to get more focused to nurture a software industry. The Information Technology (IT)/Information Technology Enabled Services (ITES) Policy[12] released in November 2001 encompasses a comprehensive package of incentives and policies for IT products, Software and Information Technology Enabled Services (ITES) industry. The IT/ITES industry policy seeks to

- Build a custom regulatory/labor framework for IT/ITES Industry
- Provide an enabling framework for attracting private sector investment in the IT industry, and IT infrastructure creation and IT education in particular
- Leverage Kerala's communication infrastructure as a unique competitive strength
- Provide the best enabling conditions for accelerated growth of ITES industry spurring employment generation
- Articulate and implement an HRD strategy that meets IT and ITES industry needs
- Encourage home grown IT industry/companies
- Bring in accountability in implementing the IT/ITES industry policy
- Recognize the holistic role of IT in transforming the socio-economic fabric of Kerala.

Information technology enabled services and Internet data centers seem to be thrust areas since the required data communication bandwidth will be available after the submarine cables get activated and feed into the fiber optic backbone that will traverse the entire state.

The Government of Kerala plans to utilize the communications infrastructure to provide the residents of Kerala with a range of services on line. The Government of Kerala plans to establish Internet kiosks in every village to enable the residents to transact on a pay per transaction with the Government online. This model of E-Governance is likely to be successful in Kerala since there is an already a culture of devolution of powers in the Government's functioning in Kerala. The E-Governance activity could contribute to developing a local level enterprise software market in Kerala. At present, the software firms in Kerala complain that the local market for software services is miniscule.

The software industry in Kerala feels that the Government of Kerala should make a strong pitch to highlight the excellent physical infrastructure and the cost advantages of operating in Kerala in a big way. Kerala has missed out on a high spokesperson to attract investment in the IT sector. The absence of someone like Chandra Babu Naidu, the Chief Minister of Andhra Pradesh or a senior industry spokesperson to market Kerala has been missed. In fact, the first time that a President of NASSCOM (National Association of Software and Service Firms, the nodal association of software firms in India) visited Technopark was as late as 2000. As one senior software industry executive explains,

> Icons are needed to market Kerala to potential investors. The excellent infrastructure that exists needs to be projected to the world. At the moment someone in the Government needs to take up this role.

The Government of Kerala has not marketed Kerala to software professionals as a great place to work and relax. In fact one chief executive of a software company in Thiruvananthapuram has a plan to start a tourist resort cum software development center that will attract software professionals from not only India but also from other countries. He feels that a cosmopolitan mix of different people is required to establish a vibrant software industry, and it may be worthwhile for the Government of Kerala to work on this idea.

The Government of Kerala has not yet built a relationship with the software industry. This can be done after the Government is clear about the role that it envisages for the software industry. The prevalent perception about Kerala as an industry unfriendly state needs to be addressed to attract investments. The education system needs to be tuned to the requirements of the software industry with the help of IIITM-K. More colleges need to started, and if necessary in the private sector. Last but not the least, the Government of Kerala also needs to motivate the big diaspora of non-resident Keralites to help build a software industry.

7. Conclusion

The case on Kerala has once again brought out the significance that a region not only needs to understand the factors that nurture a software industry but also develop a unique model of its own. This model needs to be firmly rooted in the social, economic, and cultural environment of the region. Applying a Silicon Valley model without recognizing the difference in the social, economic, and cultural environment will be difficult. The implications of this study on the research questions are discussed.

Why has Kerala been a slow starter in the software industry?

Reasons for sluggish growth of Kerala's software industry have been the

- Absence of educational and research centers of excellence in technology and information technology
- Weak relationships between the research institutions, software industry and the Government
- Preference of engineering graduates to work outside the state
- Perception as an industry unfriendly state
- Absence of a large industrial hinterland
- Absence of a large cosmopolitan city
- Lack of social infrastructure
- Poor marketing efforts to attract investments in the software industry.

How can a vibrant software industry be nurtured in Kerala?

Providing a set of initiatives that can guarantee nurturing a software industry is difficult. However, the following issues need to be addressed when implementing the initiatives in Kerala

- Defining the role of IIITM-K, the university system, institutions like VSSC and the Government
- Fostering relationships between research institutions, software industry and the Government
- Creating a larger domestic market within the state for software
- Developing the social infrastructure for software professionals to make the state an interesting place to live and work
- Focused marketing efforts to address the perception that the state is industry unfriendly
- Setting target growth rates for the software industry based on availability of human, physical and social infrastructure
- Identifying domains (like information technology enabled services) that will provide the initial momentum to jump-start the software industry.

Although it is possible, it is still a challenge for Kerala to nurture a software industry. At this point in time, it seems prudent for Kerala to concentrate on preparing the soil that will nurture a software industry.

Notes

1 Karnataka Tops in Software Exports, Times of India, April 22, 2001.
2 TN Registers Software Exports of Rs. 3116 crore, The DQ Week, June 30, 2001.

3 Bangalore Leads in Software Exports, Deccan Herald, June 16, 2001.
4 Senior official in the Government of Kerala.
5 Provisional Population Totals: India, Census of India 2001, Paper 1 of 2001.
6 Industry and Technopark estimate.
7 SAFE Submarine IT Cable 'Lands' in Cochin, The Hindu, February 12, 2001.
8 Technopark estimate.
9 Industry and Technopark estimates.
10 Industrial Economist, http://www.indeconomist.com/south_1504_software.html.
11 Surging South, India Today, May 29, 2000.
12 Kerala's IT/ITES Industry Policy, http://www.technopark.org/itpolicy.html.

References

Archibugi D. and Michie J., Technology and Innovation: An Introduction, Cambridge Journal of Economics, 19:1, 1995, pp. 1-4.

Bergman E. M. and Feser E. J., Industrial and Regional Clusters: Concepts and Comparative Applications, Regional Research Institute, West Virginia University, 1999.

Bronson P., The Nudist On The Late Shift, Random House, New York, 1999.

Dayasindhu N., Embeddedness, Knowledge Transfer, Industry Clusters and Global Competitiveness: A Case Study of the Indian Software Industry, Technovation, in print, 2002.

Debroy B., Bhandari L., and Banik N., How are the States Doing, Rajiv Gandhi Institute for Contemporary Studies for CII, 2000.

Freeman C., Technology Policy and Economic Performance: Lessons from Japan, Pinter, London, 1987.

Granovetter M., Economic Action and Social Structure: The Problem of Embeddedness, American Journal of Sociology 91:3, 1985, pp. 481-510.

Grant R. M. and Baden-Fuller C., Knowledge and Economic Organizations: An Application to the Analysis of Interfirm Collaboration, Knowledge Creation: A Source of Value, von Krogh, Georg et. al. (editors), Macmillan Press, London, 2000, pp. 113-150.

Jones C., Hesterly William S. and Borgatti Stephen P., A General Theory of Network Governance: Exchange Conditions and Social Mechanism, Academy of Management Review 22:4, 1997, pp. 911-945.

Kenny M. and von Burg. U., Institutions and Economies: Creating Silicon Valley, Understanding Silicon Valley, Kenney M. (editor), Stanford University Press, Stanford, 2000, pp. 218-240.

Kenny M. and Florida R., Venture Capital and Silicon Valley: Fueling New Firm Formation, Understanding Silicon Valley, Kenney M. (editor), Stanford University Press, Stanford, 2000, pp. 98-123.

Krishna S., Ojha A. K. and Barrett M., Competitive Advantage in the Software industry: An Analysis of the Indian Experience, IFIP WG9.4, Bangkok, 1998.

Krugman P., Geography and Trade, MIT Press, Cambridge Massachusetts, 1993.

Krugman P., Pop Internationalism, MIT Press, Cambridge Massachusetts, 1997.

Lateef A., Linking up the Global Economy: A Case of the Bangalore Software Industry, International Institute for Labour Studies, ILO, 1997.

Leslie S. W., The Biggest 'Angel' of Them All: The Military and the Making of Silicon Valley, Understanding Silicon Valley, Kenney M. (editor), Stanford University Press, Stanford, 2000, pp. 48-67.

Leslie S. W. and Kargon R. H., Selling Silicon Valley: Fredrick Terman's Model for Regional Advantage, Business History Review, Number 70: Winter 1996, pp. 435-472.

Lundvall B. A., 'Innovation as an Interactive Process: From User-Producer Interaction to the National System of Innovation', in Dosi G. et. al. (Eds.), Technical Change and Economic Theory, Pinter, London, 1988, pp. 349-369.

Maskell P. and Malmberg A., Localized Learning and Industrial Competitiveness, Regional Studies Association European Conference on Regional Futures, 1995.

Metcalfe J. S., Technology Systems and Technology Policy in an Evolutionary Framework, Cambridge Journal of Economics, 19:1, 1995, pp. 25-46.

Piore M. J. and Sabel C. F. (contributor), The Second Industrial Divide: Possibilities for Prosperity, Basic Books, New York, 1990.

Porter M. E., Clusters and the New Economics of Competition, Harvard Business Review, November-December 1998, pp.77-90.

Powell W. W., Hybrid Organizational Arrangements: New Form or Transitional Arrangements California Management Review, Fall 1987, pp. 76-88.

Saxenian A., Regional Advantage Culture and Competition in Silicon Valley and Route 128, Harvard University Press, Cambridge Massachusetts, 1994.

Saxenian A., Silicon Valley's New Immigrant Entrepreneurs, Public Policy Institute of California, San Francisco, 1999.

Storper M., The Regional World: Territorial Development in a Global Economy, Guilford Press, New York, 1997.

Walsham, G., Interpreting Information Systems in Organizations, Wiley, Chichester, 1993.

Yin R., Case Study Research: Design and Methods, 2nd edn, Sage Publications, Newbury Park, 1994.

Chapter 21

The Globalization of Software Outsourcing to Dozens of Nations: A Preliminary Analysis of the Emergence of 3rd and 4th Tier Software Exporting Nations

Erran Carmel

1. Introduction

There has been tremendous excitement around the globalization of software development – in what the business press calls *offshore outsourcing*. Dozens of nations have launched their own *software export industries*. For many nations this is the first time that they are able to compete successfully in the knowledge-based, high technology world marketplaces.

An important taxonomy of a national software export industry is that of *products versus services*. Only a small minority of software firms around the world successfully do both products and services (Hoch, et al 1999). The broader global market is that of services in which the client firm contracts for development of a specific project to a software services firm. The services category is generally more appropriate for developing nations with an abundance of human resources and entry-level skills and relatively little experience in the more complex product category. Services entail lower risk for the individual firm because services do not require an up-front investment in product development. However, the upside potential is smaller since services do not scale; instead revenue is a multiplier of people's hours. The somewhat narrower and more competitive market is for software products. Software product development requires greater investment upfront. It also requires experience in innovative activity and market knowledge, which few in developing nations have.

This chapter presents tiers of software exporting nations. Specifically the third and fourth tier nations are defined and discussed here for the first time. Next, the chapter defines ten success factors in national software export industries and discusses these factors in light of data from nations in tiers one through four. This chapter draws from and extends the article by Heeks and Nicholson (2002). Heeks and Nicholson take a similar approach in classifying nations into tiers, but do not go beyond the second tier. Similarly, Heeks and Nicholson define success factors in national software export industries, though the approach in this chapter differs.

2. The Classification of Software Exporting Nations into Multiple tiers

It is useful to create *tiers* in order to examine firms, industries, and nations because we can then:

- build an analytical frame that can be used to understand a phenomenon.
- compare nations based on their classification in tiers
- inspect the tiers as a surrogate for a maturity model.

Tiers one and two are described in full in Heeks and Nicholson (2002) and are therefore described in brevity here. Both tiers one and two can be viewed, at the moment, as widely accepted categorizations. Note, though, that these first two tiers were developed by country groupings rather than more rigorous definitional boundaries.

3. Traditional Software Exporting Nations

The traditional software exporting nations are the advanced industrialized economies. Until quite recently close to 100 percent of tradeable software products and services came from G7 nations. In particular the USA (with Microsoft and IBM) has dominated world markets (Carmel 1997). Japan, Great Britain, Germany, France, Canada have all had successful software (and computer hardware) industries over many decades. Italy, by comparison, has never had a strong software sector for an economy of its size.

Several other advanced industrialized economies may be classified in this tier. The Netherlands, Sweden and Finland, in particular, have strong software sectors. Other nations' industries have also had moderate success: Australia, Spain, Belgium and the other Nordic countries.

3.1 Tier One Nations

The 1990s saw the celebrated cases, the 3 'I's: Israel, India, and Ireland. Each of these nations has established itself in very different forms as a global software powerhouse. India in offshore programming, Israel as an incubator of software products, and Ireland in programming services and localization services.

3.2 Tier Two Nations

Like the classification of tier one, this tier is defined by three particular cases – those of China, Russia, and the Philippines. Each of these nations already has a significant software export industry, in the $100 million to $200 million range. Note that the size of this export industry is far smaller than any of the tier one nations and closer to the size of the export sector of some of the tier three nations. The key difference is the potential for considerable growth due to the three nations' large domestic workforce pool and other favorable conditions. All three have the potential to grow quickly in the coming years.

3.3 Tier Three Nations

These nations are defined as having significant software export industries ($20-$50 million range) and a small *cluster* of successful organizations. As is the case for nations from tier one and two these organizations may be subsidiaries of MNCs or home-grown, independent software firms. Nations in this tier include: Costa Rica, Mexico, Romania, Bulgaria,[1] Brazil, Pakistan.[2]

3.4 Tier Four Nations

These national software export industries are still in infant stages, though some may have reached $20 million. The fourth tier is defined by one or both conditions present:

- Some national attention and policy (by the government) has focused on the software exporting sector
- A significant number of firms have been exporting software for at least several years.

It is not possible to enumerate all of these nations in this chapter. A partial list includes: Cuba, Jordan, Egypt, Bangladesh, Vietnam, and El Salvador.

3.5 Non-competing Nations

Finally, many nations have *few to no* software-exporting firms to speak of. Perhaps half of the world's countries, most quite small, are in this category.

4. The Success Factors for Tier Three and Tier Four

Heeks and Nicholson (2002) propose a five-factor model for analyzing the success of national software export sectors that is derived from the success of the tier one nations. The success factors delineated and discussed here draw from and extend their work. Note that a detailed analysis of each of the nations of tier three and tier four is beyond the scope of this chapter.

4.1 Demand

Demand is defined as the degree of reliance on domestic and/or foreign demand for the industry's products and services (in order to bootstrap or propel the industry). Most tier three and tier four nations have little domestic demand. Furthermore, demand is not sophisticated vis-à-vis global customers—in other words, local demand is not as exacting as foreign clients. Most tier three and tier four nations' markets are too small and underdeveloped. Some exceptions are noteworthy. Brazil and Pakistan, tier three nations, grew their export sectors from firms focused initially on satisfying domestic demand. The cases of Mexico (tier three) and South Africa (tier four) point to the opposite – when domestic demand is too strong, it inhibits growth of a national export sector even when other success factors are present.

4.2 National Vision

National Vision refers to the government's role in setting the foundation (in infrastructure, education, etc.), facilitating, funding, encouraging, and successfully politicking the success of the industry. The government may play a key role as it did in Costa Rica, a tier three nation. In Costa Rica the government set a national vision (Digital Opportunity Initiative, 2001) and successfully lobbied for a massive investment by US-based Intel to open a plant in San Jose. This was a milestone that spurred the domestic IT industry in general, and software specifically. In Jordan, a tier four nation, King Abdullah was personally involved in the 1999 national plans for the software industry. In Cuba, a tier four nation, the national vision is led by a senior politician, Vice Minister Melchior Gil. In Romania, the government spurred the industry considerably when on July 1, 2001; it eliminated income tax for the employees of software firms.

4.3 Human Capital

Human Capital for the software sector encompasses the collective abilities of the software professionals. These abilities stem from a multi-generational tradition of science and engineering that emanates from strong universities and polytechnics. Related factors are the managerial skills taught in business as well as the English-language abilities (stemming from primary and secondary education). Competitive human capital, perhaps more than other factor in this list, emerges only after many years of national investment.

While domestic human capital is vital, some nations have attempted to bypass the need for homegrown human capital. Barbados in the Caribbean was the base of a (briefly) successful IT services firm that imported software professionals (mostly from India) to work on projects for large US customers. Similarly, in 2002, in Panama, in former US-Army bases, a new technology park is emerging that is planning to emulate this model by importing hundreds of software professional from outside Panama. Time will tell if this is a sustainable model.

4.4 Wages

There is fierce competition in wages between national software industries. Sawhney and Ariav (2002) place offshore software outsourcing in the context of global technology arbitrage, where:

> Global technology arbitrage: Sourcing labor and capital where it is cheapest and selling to where it is most profitable. National borders do not matter.

For example, variations on Table 21.1 have appeared frequently in recent years in the US business press. The relatively high wages are less important for two of the tier one nations, Ireland and Israel. However, in recent years, wages in India were bid up and India is no longer the lowest cost nation in software. Instead, US and European firms are examining on working with China, Vietnam, and others, where wages are low. There is little that nations can do to compete in this cycle in which foreign investment and interest quickly shift to low wage nations. Perhaps Romania's policy of doing away with income tax for software professionals is a necessary competitive act in such a global marketplace.

Table 21.1 Wages for software professionals. Annual, starting, in US$

USA	**63000**
Japan	**44000**
Indonesia	**12200**
Russia	**7500**
China	**5000**
Philippines	**6500-10000**
India	**5000-8000**
Pakistan	**3600-6100**

Source: Field 2002, using Aberdeen data; Forbes.com; Author's data.

4.5 Global, Regional, Geographic, Cultural, and Linguistic Linkages

The national diasporas of tier one nations played a critical role in market access. These are the highly talented scientists and engineers who left their home countries in what is termed 'brain-drain' and, sometimes many years later, returned, or invested in, or encouraged acquisition from their home country. Furthermore, the English language capabilities of the Indians, the Irish, and to a slightly lesser extent, the Israelis, have facilitated the linkages to the US and to the UK. While the diasporas have been critical for tier one nations and are playing a supporting role for tier two nations, they are unlikely to play a dominant role in tier three and tier four nations. Instead other types of linkages have emerged.

We see interesting permutations on these new linkages in tier three and tier four nations. Their industries are generally not global actors and somewhat less focused on the US market. For example, Pakistan mines its cultural ties to the wealthy Gulf nations by exporting services to that region. Mexico advertises itself as a 'near-shore' destination for offshore outsourcing. One of the clusters of Mexico's software industry is in Monterrey, an hour's drive from the US border. South Africa has the potential to capitalize on same time-zone advantages with EU nations. Similarly, some Caribbean islands emphasize the time-zone proximity, which facilitates communication with customers in the US East Coast. The Chinese have capitalized on their closer linguistic and cultural ties with the Japanese to become a destination for offshore work, thus bypassing the English-language 'monopoly' that international software development has, until recently, mandated. The Costa Ricans work with other Spanish-speaking customers in Latin America.

4.6 Technological infrastructure

Technological infrastructure refers to the sophistication and reliability of communication technology. Software firms require both telephone and broadband data communication connections. The case of India, a tier one nation, is instructive: Beginning in the 1980s India bypassed the unreliable terrestrial infrastructure by using satellite technology to communicate between top software firms and clients abroad. Today cell phones bypass the local telephone system for voice communication. In addition, all Indian firms operate in buildings and technology parks with alternative power generation to compensate for unreliable public sources. Regardless of the tier, many firms operate out of so-called technology parks in which the construction and support for data communication infrastructure (and power) is taken care of. The Philippines, a tier two nation, is sprinkled with such parks that advertise high connectivity. Tier three and tier four nations recognize these needs and have built, or are building, such technology parks.

4.7 Software Industry Clusters

This refers to the degree to which the firms compete with one another to spur innovation; are geographically proximate so as to benefit from common infrastructure and specialized services; and have fostered a healthy range of medium-sized firms of more than 100 employees.[3] Most tier three and tier four nations have software industries that are naturally clustered around the large metropolitan business areas: in Pakistan in Lahore, in Costa Rica around San Jose, etc. Both Romania and Bulgaria (both tier three nations) have a healthy range of medium sized firms (10 in Romania according to Mroczkowski et al, 2002).

4.8 Industry Collaboration, Vision, and Specialization

This factor is discussed at two levels: first, and more important, specialization or coherence of the national industry and second, the degree to which the industry is able to pool some resources into a national association or consortia that serve to promote the nation's industry aboard and provide services back to its member firms.

Beginning with the first item, Heeks and Nicholson (2002) argue that the national industry success is driven by the coherence of the industry (and to some extent the government's) vision and strategy in defining the industry's focus. None of the many national software-exporting industries can successfully compete simultaneously on all fronts. For example, Ireland chose to diversify into software services projects and into niche market products, while Israel has developed products in existing and new market niches. Now that there are dozens of national industries competing, differentiation is even more critical.

Second, is the industry's ability to collaborate behind a strong national association is seen as important. The prominence of the industry association in India, NASSCOM, is recognized by many to have helped the *branding* (in the marketing sense) of the Indian industry. Similarly, the inability of the Russians (until recently) or the Mexicans, to build strong associations may have inhibited their success.

An example of the recognized need for national branding is a recent promotion by a Philippines IT agency (Department of Trade and Industry, 2001) which advocates doing business with the Philippines by stating: 'Me, the Filipino: Think American, feel Spanish, act Asian; Strong English language capability; Value education highly; Naturally hospitable, naturally caring; Peaceful; Patient temperament.'

The industry can collaborate beneficially in other ways: Several firms can pool their resources to market their services abroad. This strategy has been conducted with some success by firms in at least three clusters: St. Petersburg, Russia (called Fort Ross); Novosibirsk, Russia (called SibIT); and Bulgaria. We will likely see more of these consortia in tier three and tier four nations.

4.9 Finance

Software firms require outside financing to grow. Tier one nations have now mastered the art of multiple rounds of financing and equity offerings. Tier two nations such as Russia and tier three nations such as Bulgaria have significant foreign direct investment in many of their local software firms. In other words, many local, home-grown firms are partially or fully owned from abroad. As the global software industry continues its maturation it will be increasingly difficult – without financing – for a tier four nation to advance to become a tier three nation.

4.10 International Benchmark

This factor addresses the following problem: purchasing software from a distant, exotic foreign supplier is a risky proposition. The Indian industry understood this predicament early on and embraced the international quality standard of the US-based Software Engineering Institute called the Capability Maturity Model. Now that Indian firms have acquired the highest international quality standards and practice these standards with greater success than do most US organizations, India is seen as a safe (or even desirable) destination in this regard. Other nations have quickly followed suit: Russia, a tier two nation, in 2002 had one CMM5 firm (the Motorola subsidiary) and 2 CMM4 organizations. Pakistan's (a tier three nation) industry has been on a quality initiative since 1999. In Bangladesh, a tier four nation, Grameen Software was the first in that nation to receive the ISO9001 certification.

5. Concluding Remarks

The national industries in the fourth tier – most of which are in developing nations – are faced with a difficult challenge: namely, how do they move their national software export industries beyond that of a 'Cottage Industry' in which most of the firms are small, managerial processes are informal, marketing is immature, and the firms are selling commodity skills in programming (e.g., experience with platform X or programming language Y) with no national specialization and differentiation. Certainly, following some of the prescriptive success factors discussed in this chapter will help move these national industries forward.

Now that multiple tiers have been identified and the success factors are understood, can we say that that the model is deterministic and nations will tend to move *up* the tiers?[4] This is unlikely. The tiers will likely remain fairly stable for some years to come, during which time, most the nations on the list will see their national software export industries *grow* rather than move up the tiers.

Notes

1 Hoffman, T (2002).
2 Several other nations may qualify for Tier 3, such as Malaysia.
3 It is assumed that most tier three and tier four nations cannot produce large software firms, by world standards, because of the small domestic labor markets and the absence of a managerial tradition of large-scale firms.
4 Heeks and Nicholson (2002) present a concluding model that also predicts a maturity. In their model national software industries progress from IT-enabled services (e.g., call centers) to services and on to products. With some partial exceptions this has not been the case in most of the nations of all 4 tiers discussed here.

References

Carmel, E. American hegemony in packaged software trade and the 'culture of software.' *The Information Society,* 13(1), 1997, pp. 125-142.

Digital Opportunity Initiative, Creating *a Development Dynamic, Final Report of the Digital Opportunity Initiative*, July 2001. http://www.opt-init.org/

Field, T. The man in the middle, *CIO magazine*. April 1, 2002.

Forbes Magazine, Can India retain its reign as outsourcing king? *Forbes.com* February 28, 2001.

Heeks, R. and Nicholson, B. (2002). Software export success factors and strategies in developing and transitional economies. *University of Manchester, Institute for Development Policy and Management*, Paper Number 20020-12.

Hoch, D.J., Lindner, S., Roeding, C., Purkert, G. *Secrets of Software Success: Management Insights from 100 Software Firms around the World.* Harvard Business School Publishing, 1999.

Hoffman, T. Bulgaria: The next offshore frontier, *Computerworld*, May 20, 2002, http://www.computerworld.com/softwaretopics/software/appdev/story/0,10801,71292,00.html.

Mroczkowski, T. Carmel, E. Saleh, N. *Opportunities and Barriers to Integrating Central Europe into the Transatlantic Information Economy.* American University, Kogod School of Business, Washington D.C., March 2002.

Sawhney, M. and Ariav, G. 2002. Global Technology Arbitrage, class notes at Northwestern University and Tel Aviv University.